PSEUDO-DIONYSIUS
AND
THE METAPHYSICS OF AQUINAS

STUDIEN UND TEXTE
ZUR GEISTESGESCHICHTE
DES MITTELALTERS

HERAUSGEGEBEN VON

Dr. ALBERT ZIMMERMANN

PROFESSOR AN DER UNIVERSITÄT KÖLN

BAND XXXII

PSEUDO-DIONYSIUS
AND
THE METAPHYSICS OF AQUINAS

PSEUDO-DIONYSIUS
AND
THE METAPHYSICS OF AQUINAS

BY

FRAN O'ROURKE

E.J. BRILL
LEIDEN • NEW YORK • KÖLN
1992

Published with financial support from The National University of Ireland and The Faculty of Arts, University College Dublin.

The paper in this book meets the guidelines for permanence and durability of the Committee on Production Guidelines for Book Longevity of the Council on Library Resources.

BR
65
.D66
O76
1992

Library of Congress Cataloging-in-Publication Data

O'Rourke, Fran.
   Pseudo-Dionysius and the metaphysics of Aquinas / by Fran O'Rourke.
      p.   cm. — (Studien und Texte zur Geistesgeschichte des Mittelalters. ISSN 0169-8125 ; Bd. 32)
   Revision of thesis (Ph. D.)—Hoger Instituut voor Wijsbegeerte, Leuven.
   Includes bibliographical references and index.
   ISBN 9004094660 (alk. paper)
   1. Pseudo-Dionysius, the Areopagite—Influence.   2. Thomas, Aquinas, Saint, 1225?-1274.   3. Metaphysics—History.   I. Title. II. Series.
BR65.D66076   1992
186'.4—dc20
                                                                                92-13959
                                                                                CIP

ISSN   0169-8125
ISBN   90 04 09466 0

PRINTED IN THE NETHERLANDS

For my Mother

CONTENTS

ABBREVIATIONS

Pseudo-Dionysius

DN	Divine Names
CH	Celestial Hierarchy
Ep.	Letters
MT	Mystical Theology
PG	Patrologia Graeca

St Thomas Aquinas

Comp. Theol.	Compendium Theologiae
De Reg. Princip.	De Regimine Principum
De Spirit. Creat.	Quaestio disputata de spiritualibus creaturis
De Subst. Separ.	De substantiis separatis
In Boeth. de Trin.	In librum Boethii de Trinitate expositio
In de Causis	In librum de causis expositio
In DN	In librum Dionysii de divinis nominibus expositio
In Metaph.	In duodecim libros Metaphysicorum Aristotelis expositio
In Peri. Herm.	In libros Peri Hermeneias Aristotelis expositio
In Physic.	In octo libros Physicorum Aristotelis expositio
In Poster. Anal.	In libros Posteriorum Analyticorum Aristotelis expositio
In Sent.	Scriptum super Sententiis magistri Petri Lombardi
ST	Summa Theologiae

PREFACE

The sun, Aquinas remarks in his Commentary on the *Divine Names*, is itself too powerful to look at, and is best viewed as it is reflected upon the mountain peaks or fills the clouds with light. The Holy Mountain of Athos was resplendent in the first light of dawn and the clouds were filled with ochre rays from the sun which was not yet visible. The small caïque had left the pier below the Monastery of Megiste Lavra while it was still dark and made its way slowly southwards along the coast. Out of the shelter of the isthmus the craft was hit by the fury of a sudden storm, and thrown from crest to trough by wave after wave which crashed with fury from the west. One recalled the fate of Xerxes' fleet as it sailed around this same promontory. Relieved to dock in the nearest harbour, we made our way up the steep and rocky—but altogether safe—path to the Monastery of Saint Dionysius, which was perched like a fortress some hundreds of feet above the ocean.

The reading at mealtime in the *Trapezaria* an hour later held no special significance at first, but on hearing the words Ἅγιος Διονύσιος, ὁ Ἀπόστολος Παῦλος, Ἅγνωστος Θεός, even the name of Πρόκλος, I was seized with excitement and curiosity—a frisson more overwhelming than the fear of the early morning. A friendly monk explained that the reading concerned the life of an ancient bishop of Athens who had been a disciple of St Paul; he was a sacred writer, renowned for his treatises on contemplation and the life of monks. The text explained that a writer of the fifth century had relied greatly upon these writings but lacked the grace to acknowledge his debt. Today the feast of this holy man was being celebrated.

But surely, I exclaimed, no one still believed that this writer was the disciple of St Paul! Had not modern research, with all its means of historical critique, shown beyond doubt that these writings belonged to a later writer who had indeed relied upon the work of Proclus. My question offended; 'Man of little faith!' I was guilty of blasphemy—whether by irreverence or disbelief I was unsure—but judged that courtesy to my host called for silence. I nodded in agreement that science is no measure in matters of belief. Reason must bow before the testimony of faith and tradition. Indeed, if proof were needed, I was told, were not some bones of Saint Dionysius, including his skull and a portion of a finger, still preserved in another monastery on Athos, to be venerated on that very day?

I examined the lectionary as soon as I could.[1] The page was opened at October 3rd! Had I lost track of the days, thinking it was October 16th? I recalled the difference between the calendars of East and West. At the ceremony in the afternoon the monks intoned the life and encomium of Dionysius, relating among other things his presence with the apostles at the dormition of the Blessed Virgin.[2] Listening to the monks chant the solemn hymns in praise of Dionysius, my appreciation of his work was transformed. The myth still survived in this remote haven of fervour and devotion, palpably attested to by the scent of incense and the glow of oil-lamps before the icons of this holy man. It survived, not as a myth, but as a history of love and veneration. For how many centuries had these hymns been sung in unbroken tradition? Dionysius assumed for me at that moment a new significance and actuality. I had a forceful appreciation of the significance of Dionysius for Aquinas, who was profoundly influenced by his writings and personality. Like the monks of Athos, whose veneration of Dionysius now seemed so strange, so Aquinas had also experienced the draw of the ancient writer. I saw that, regardless of its authorship, the *Corpus Dionysiacum* was still a living tradition, with a power for truth and inspiration. Despite the falsehood of their apostolic authority, the works of Dionysius have a timeless message and a quiet power to draw those who read them closer to the divine secrets of the universe.

One of the many questions which I do not touch upon in the present study is the identity of the Pseudo-Dionysius. My interest is directed exclusively toward the philosophic vision of his writings and their influence upon Aquinas. Aquinas' interest in Dionysius is itself many-sided, extensive and profound. He refers to the *Corpus Dionysiacum* in his elucidation of many theological doctrines; his speculations both on evil and aesthetic beauty are largely derived from Dionysius. Most of the literature on Dionysius and Aquinas deals with the question of knowledge and language about God. Few deal with the global influence of Dionysius on the metaphysics of Aquinas: this influence, however, extends to such central questions as the very nature of existence, the hierarchy of beings, the nature of God and the theory of creation. It is my aim to show that, in the encounter of Aquinas with Dionysius, there emerges an integral and comprehensive vision of existence, a

---

[1] Ὁ Μέγας Συναξαριστής τῆς Ὀρθοδόξου Ἐκκλησίας, I, Athens, 1981, pp. 62-109.
[2] This is printed in *PG* IV, 577-84: Βίος καὶ ἐγκώμιον τοῦ Ἁγίου Διονυσίου Ἀρειοπαγίτου. Ἐκ τῶν μηναίων τῆς ἐν Ἑλλάδι Ἐκκλησίας, μηνὸς ὀκτωβρίου τῇ γ΄.

vision embracing the finite and the infinite, depicting the universe in its procession from, and return to, the Absolute, and according to each grade of reality, including man, its place in the hierarchy of being.

Part I of this book also begins with the question of knowledge about God. In Chapter 1 we examine the value attached by Dionysius to philosophy in the discovery of the divine and establish that, within the horizon of revelation, he grants an autonomous role to philosophical reflection. This is based upon the relation of causality: God both reveals and conceals himself in creation; on this dual status of creatures is grounded the renowned distinction of positive and negative theology. Primacy is accorded to the negative path, since God is the transcendent Good beyond all reality. In Chapter 2 we study Aquinas' appraisal of this doctrine. Granting primacy likewise to negative knowledge, he refines Dionysius' apophatic doctrine by grounding it in the positive value of existence, which is capable of unfolding the reality of God, who—precisely as Being itself—is beyond the range of human thought.

Part II examines the nature and transcendence of God. For Dionysius, God is supreme goodness beyond Being and Non-Being. We study this doctrine in Chapter 3, and consider in particular his understanding of 'non-being'. In Chapter 4 we examine Aquinas' reaction to this, together with his arguments for the primacy of Being. Part III, 'Transcendent Causality and Existence', begins by examining Dionysius' influence on Aquinas in two doctrines: the immediacy and universality of God's causation (Chapter 5), and the primacy of existence as the first perfection of creation (Chapter 6). Aquinas' notions of *esse commune*, *virtus essendi*, and *esse intensivum* are considered at some length. All of these doctrines, which show the inspiration of Dionysius, are unified more profoundly in Aquinas' theory of God as subsistent and absolute Being. This is examined in Chapter 7, at which point we are in a position to review more adequately Aquinas' perspective on Being and 'non-being'.

Part IV deals with creation as the cyclic diffusion of the Good in Pseudo-Dionysius and St Thomas. Chapter 8 outlines Dionysius' vision of creation as a cyclic process, and in Chapter 9 we observe the importance of this motif as an inspiration for Aquinas' universal vision. Specific questions concerning creation are considered: the freedom of creation and the diffusion of goodness, the emanation and return of creatures, the relation of God to creation, and the hierarchic order and harmony of the universe of beings. In each of these aspects I seek to illustrate both the central influence of Dionysius and the originality of Aquinas' vision. An underlying motif, which provides a background to our enquiry, is the point at which the two writers diverge, namely, the primacy accorded by each, respectively to the Good or to Being as the highest principle of reality.

The present work is a revised version of a doctoral dissertation, submitted to the Hoger Instituut voor Wijsbegeerte, Leuven, under the guidance of Professor Gérard Verbeke, who generously placed at my disposal his profound and extensive knowledge of classical and medieval philosophy. To him I express my warmest gratitude for his keen interest, constant support and encouragement. It is a privilege and pleasure to record my deep personal gratitude to Most Reverend Desmond Connell, Archbishop of Dublin, former Head of the Department of Metaphysics, University College, Dublin, for his many kindnesses while I was a member of his Department. Invited to be external member of the examination jury, he read my dissertation with the closest possible attention and subsequently made many valuable suggestions. I record my sincere thanks to Professor Urbain Dhondt, President of the Hoger Instituut voor Wijsbegeerte, for his kind attention in many ways. I thank his successor, Professor Carlos Steel, both for his expert advice during the early stages of my research and for his valuable comments as examiner.

Portions of my dissertation were developed and expanded into article form for the journal *Dionysius* (1991), and the volume *The Relationship between Neoplatonism and Christianity* (Dublin, 1992). I am grateful to the editors of these publications for permission to incorporate this material. I wish to thank Dr Deirdre Carabine, Dr John Chisholm, Dr Colm Connellan, Dr Gerald Hanratty and Dr Brendan Purcell, of University College Dublin, for their instructive comments. I record my grateful appreciation to Dr Koen Verrycken and Professor Andrew Smith for help with the printing of the Greek passages. My thanks are due in a special way to Professor Werner Beierwaltes, who showed keen interest in my work and facilitated me in many ways during the academic year 1984–85 which I spent at the Ludwig-Maximilians-Universität, Munich.

The opportunity of spending several years in Leuven was due to scholarships from the Katholieke Universiteit te Leuven and the Belgian Ministerie van Nederlandse Cultuur. I express my sincere thanks to these institutions. I am grateful to University College Dublin for sabbatical leave to complete this study. My stay in Munich was partly financed by the Deutscher Akademischer Austauschdienst. For financial support towards publication, I gratefully acknowledge grants from the National University of Ireland and the Faculty of Arts, University College Dublin. I express my appreciation to Professor Albert Zimmermann, who accepted the work for the present series. My thanks to Brunswick Press, Dublin, who prepared the text for press.

The dedication of this book, finally, is a very inadequate attempt to return the least repayable debt of all.

PART ONE

KNOWLEDGE OF GOD

CHAPTER ONE

KNOWLEDGE OF GOD IN PSEUDO-DIONYSIUS

REASON AND REVELATION

We begin our enquiry into the metaphysics of the Pseudo-Dionysius and Aquinas with the primary question of metaphysical knowledge, more specifically, knowledge of the metaphysical absolute. It is in this significant area that we first discover in Aquinas the deep-running presence of Dionysius' Neoplatonism. Aquinas appropriates from Dionysius the entire method of his natural philosophy of God, of knowing and not-knowing, while yet transforming and transfiguring, however subtly, certain elements in accordance with his own theory of knowledge and being. These modifications will emerge as we consider Aquinas' reaction and the measure of his indebtedness to the Pseudo-Areopagite.

Dionysius is keenly aware from the start of the humble value of his endeavour, yet the dutiful dignity of his task, to search out with the aid of reason and share with his fellow humans a deeper knowledge of God. Thus we may have, he believes, what he himself has called a *divine philosophy*, i.e. a 'reflection on the intelligible divine things'.[1] And while its fruits are meagre in view of the unfathomed mystery of the divine, or indeed even in comparison with the merits of mystical experience, it is incumbent upon us to exercise diligently whatever power has been given us to know God. This twofold aspect of the

---

[1] 3, 3, 93. References to Dionysius' *Divine Names* and to Aquinas' *In Librum Beati Dionysii De Divinis Nominibus* are distinguished by using Arabic numerals for chapter and paragraph of Dionysius' work, and Roman numerals for chapter and *lectio* of Aquinas' Commentary. When given, the third number (Arabic) refers to the paragraph of the author's text in the Marietti edition. Thus, for example, '4, 2, 108', refers to the second paragraph of Chapter 4, *Divine Names*, as printed in paragraph 108 of Pera's edition, and 'IV, ii, 295' to Aquinas' commentary on this passage (see Pera's edition, pp. 95–6). It is therefore normally not necessary to give the title of these works when referring to them in footnotes. References to other works of Dionysius are according to the Migne edition.

philosopher's vocation, the humility of his enquiry into the nature of
God and the duty to seek him in the measure given to us, is an express
command of God:

> The splendid arrangement of divine laws commands it. We are told not to
> busy ourselves with what is beyond us, since they are beyond what we deserve
> and are unattainable. But the law tells us to learn everything granted to us
> and to share these treasures generously with others.[2]

Dionysius begins his treatise the *Divine Names*, therefore, with a
grandiloquent avowal of humility, professing his utter inability to speak
of the divine nature. The truth of things divine, he tells Timothy, is not
presented 'with persuasive words of human wisdom', but by giving
witness to the inspiring power of the Spirit. Through this inspiration
we become united to the ineffable and unknowable in a union more
perfect than that of reason or intellect.[3] He will not dare, therefore, to
speak or conceive of the divinity, hidden and transcendent, in any way
other than has been divinely revealed in Scripture. To God alone
pertains a true knowledge of himself, transcending Being (ὑπερούσιον)[4]
and surpassing reason and intellect; it is more properly an 'un-knowing'
(ἀγνωσία), when compared with human cognition. For our part, we
may aspire to the splendour of the divine mystery only in so far as the
ray of divine wisdom is imparted to us.[5]

   We are wholly reliant on God, therefore, for all knowledge of himself.
In his love for us, however, says Dionysius, the absolute and divine
Good reveals himself, measuring out the divine truth according to the
capacity of each spirit (κατὰ τὴν ἀναλογίαν ἑκάστου τῶν νόων), and
separating from the finite that which in its infinity must remain
unapproachable.[6] Dionysius provides an incisive insight into the
participation both of being and knowledge:

---

   [2] 3, 3, 93. Luibheid's translation, p. 71. When not otherwise stated, translations from
Dionysius are mine. Luibheid's excellent translation does not always convey the full
metaphysical sense which I wish to emphasise. Occasionally, in citing Luibheid, I have
made minor changes to suit the context. While the aim of Jones' version has its merit,
its neologistic language cannot be easily quoted outside its context. Rolt's translation,
while faithful, is somewhat archaic and stylised. That published by the Editors of the
Shrine of Wisdom is for the most part admirable for its accuracy and elegance. (A
blatant omission is a major portion of *DN*, 7.) The translations by John Parker, who
still accepted the authenticity of the works are generally very acceptable. For translations
into other languages, those of Stiglmayr, de Gandillac, Scazzoso and Turolla can be
recommended.
   [3] 1, 1, 1.
   [4] 'Being' is occasionally written in upper case in order to signify universal being, or
being as the primary perfection of reality.
   [5] 1, 1, 4.
   [6] 1, 1, 6.

The Good is not absolutely incommunicable to everything. By itself it generously reveals a firm, transcendent ray, granting enlightenments proportionate to each being, and thereby draws sacred minds upward to its permitted contemplation, to participation and to the state of becoming like it.[7]

We may observe how careful Dionysius is to situate the sure knowledge which we can have of God within a reverence and obedience to his unutterable mystery. While our response to God's self-relevation should be one of holy veneration, listening with 'pious ears',[8] and honouring with humble silence those things which remain unfathomed and unspoken—the mystery of divinity beyond thought and Being[9] — we must also be heedful to the rays of illumination as they are imparted to us, and allow ourselves to be guided by the light of revelation and so behold the radiance of the divine. In this spirit of piety and obedience we best praise and celebrate the principle of all light as it has revealed itself in Scripture.[10] Scripture affords, therefore, a secure guide: 'a most beautiful standard of truth'; it offers a 'divine wisdom' to which philosophy must concord.[11]

In Scripture, God has revealed himself as Cause, Principle, Being and Life of all things.[12] We notice how Dionysius first introduces on the authority of revelation itself even the positive knowledge we may have of God in relation to reality. This he undoubtedly does in his original spirit of piety and humility concerning the things of God. He will, of course, further develop the argumentation on philosophic grounds, specifically along Neoplatonist lines; but this occurs within the initial security of what is first laid open in revelation.[13]

Dionysius explicitly recognises indeed two distinct approaches within the tradition of theology itself: the one silent and mystical, the other open and manifest; the former mode is symbolic and presupposes a mystic initiation, the latter is philosophic and demonstrative. Dionysius notes, however, that the two traditions intertwine: the ineffable with the manifest.[14] Some truths about God, he states elsewhere, are unfolded 'according to true reason' ($\tau\tilde{\omega}$ $\dot{\alpha}\lambda\eta\theta\epsilon\tilde{\iota}$ $\lambda\dot{o}\gamma\omega$), others 'in a manner beyond our rational power as mysteries according to divine

---

[7] 1, 2, 10; Luibheid, p. 50.
[8] 1, 8, 29.
[9] 1, 3, 11.
[10] 1, 3, 11.
[11] 2, 2, 36.
[12] 1, 3, 12.
[13] See René Roques, Introduction, *La hiérarchie céleste*, p. xxv: 'En réalité, si la plupart des attributs expliqués sont bibliques, ils sont aussi bien philosophiques; et, en tout cas, la manière dont ils sont systématiquement expliqués est plus philosophique que biblique.'
[14] *Ep.* 9, 1105D.

transmission.'[15] And he summarises his attitude to the relation between both: 'The human mind has a capacity to think, through which it looks on conceptual things, but also a unity which transcends the nature of the mind, through which it is joined to things beyond itself.'[16] Through this union we receive that 'foolish wisdom' which has neither reason nor intelligence but is their cause and in which are hidden 'all the treasures of wisdom and knowledge'.[17]

There is in Dionysius, therefore, the assumption of an autonomous activity of natural reason concerning God, although this is itself the object of divine revelation and operates moreover within the horizon of divinely established truth. The 'philosophic' content of divine revelation may be summed up: God reveals himself 'supra-ontologically as the supra-original principle of all principles', as Life of the living, Being ($o\dot{v}\sigma\acute{\iota}a$) of all that is, the principle and cause of all life and being, which through its goodness brings beings into existence ($\varepsilon\tilde{\iota}v\alpha\iota$) and maintains them.[18] Now, the aim of Dionysius is to demonstrate and celebrate those things which pertain to God in so far as possible through the natural powers of human cognition. The difficulty is that 'knowledge' as such is only of 'being': 'That which is beyond all being also transcends all knowledge.'[19] This problem he himself clearly confronts: 'It is necessary to enquire how we know God, since he cannot be known either through thought or sense, nor is he at all any of the things which are.'[20]

It is reasonable to expect that if we are to discover anything about God, our discovery should take as its point of departure that which is the proper realm of our cognitive encounter, namely beings. Dionysius does not begin with a reflection on the things of experience and conclude God's existence from their ontological insufficiency. There is no evidence of any attempt on his part to disclose God's existence through the medium of reality as given. However, we may well assume that the total dependence of creation is from the start an implicit element of his 'divine philosophy' ($\theta\varepsilon\acute{\iota}a$ $\varphi\iota\lambda o\sigma o\varphi\acute{\iota}a$). He is not preoccupied with the question how we know that God exists, but more precisely how we can know the nature of God. This may be concluded from the manner in which he poses the question 'How do we know God?'

---

[15] 2, 7, 54.
[16] 7, 1, 302; Luibheid, p. 106.
[17] Col. 2:3; See 7, 1, 302.
[18] 1, 3, 12.
[19] 1, 4, 19.
[20] 7, 3, 320.

CAUSALITY AND THE KNOWLEDGE OF GOD

The radical relation of causality already pervades Dionysius' thought on the relation of God and the world and provides, furthermore, the key to our knowledge of the transcendent. Dionysius may respond therefore in a passage which is one of the most significant in the entire treatise:

> It may be true to say that we know God, not from his own nature—for this is unknown and transcends all reason and intellect—but that from the order of beings, which, having been established through him (ἐξ αὐτοῦ προβεβλημένης, literally, 'projected out of') bears certain images and similarities of his divine exemplars, we ascend with method and order, in so far as possible according to our capacity, to him who is beyond all things, both by removing all things from him and affirming them superlatively, and through the causality of all things.[21]

Dionysius, therefore, attributes a real value to the knowledge afforded by the beings of the finite world concerning their cause. He explicitly states it as evidence of human reason itself: 'The creation (κοσμουργία) of the visible universe manifests the invisible things of God, as Paul has said, and also true reason.'[22] Elsewhere Dionysius quotes from St Paul with emphatic approval that 'The invisible things of God are clearly seen from the creation of the world, being *understood* (νοούμενα) from the things that are made.'[23] Thus, although there is in no sense a demonstration of God's existence, there is the unmistaken presupposition of its demonstrability. It never crossed Dionysius' mind that it was necessary to establish the existence of the absolute Good. The problem is rather what we can discover in its regard. What is clear in the present context is the real epistemological and methodological value attributed by Dionysius to the relationship of cause and effect, and in particular as it holds between creator and creature:

> For all divine things, even those which are revealed to us, are known only through their participations; that which they themselves are according to their own principle and foundation is beyond mind, and transcends all being and knowledge.[24]

Granting the value of causality as opening up the way to transcendent reality, we may nevertheless ask how, according to the noetic of Dionysius, we may proceed in our discovery of God. Dionysius gives certain clear indications. All knowledge, he states, has the power of

---

[21] 7, 3, 321.
[22] *Ep.* 9, 1108B.
[23] Rom. 1: 20; See 4, 4, 124.
[24] 2, 7, 55.

unifying the knower with that which is known.[25] The most perfect
knowledge is that which binds us to God. Dionysius conveys this
through the symbolism of the circular movement of the soul, while
conveying the less perfect through the images of spiral and straight
movement. In its 'circular motion' the soul turns inward from the
multiplicity of external things in simple and unitive contemplation.
Having become fully recollected and unified within itself, it is united
with those powers (δυνάμεσι) which are themselves completely unified;
guided by these it is led to the Beautiful and the Good which enlightens
it intellectually (νοερῶς).[26]

It could be argued that the expression 'unified powers' should be
interpreted, not in the psychological sense of Corderius[27] as the unity
of the soul with its own faculties, or in the 'theological sense' of
Aquinas as signifying unity with angels,[28] but in a metaphysical sense
as the knowledge of the *creative powers* or exemplary Ideas which, in
the Platonist language of Dionysius, are the medium of God's creative
causality and which are amenable to our reflection as perfections evident
in the world. It seems more reasonable that we should first perceive
these created perfections in their intellectual purity, then retrace their
variety and multiplicity to a single and absolute cause.[29] As a medium
of discovery from the finite realm to the absolute Good, these concepts
of divine perfection exercise an indispensable role. This coincides with
other texts of Dionysius; it is the meaning of the celebrated text already
cited, that from the order of all things we unfold 'certain images and
similarities of the divine exemplars'; from these we 'ascend' (ἄνειμεν)
to the universal cause of all.[30]

More significant is Dionysius' statement that, in naming God
affirmatively, 'we are thinking of none other than the powers (δυνάμεις)

---

[25] 7, 4, 327.

[26] 4, 9, 148. See Werner Beierwaltes, *Proklos*, pp. 208–9.

[27] *Patrologia Graeca* III, 741–2. This is followed by de Gandillac, *Oeuvres complètes du Pseudo-Denys*, p. 102.

[28] 4, vii, 376; See also Joseph Stiglmayr, *Des heiligen Dionysius Areopagita angebliche Schriften über 'Göttliche Namen'*, p. 69; also C. E. Rolt, *Dionysius the Areopagite. The Divine Names and The Mystical Theology*, p. 99.

[29] The psychological interpretation renders the phrase superfluous. It would merely repeat what has already been stated, namely, that the soul has become unified in itself, and provides no explanation how the soul proceeds from itself to the absolute. A metaphysical interpretation allows a gradual passage from the soul, led through its contemplation of exemplars, towards God. Aquinas' interpretation that the soul is united to angels is even more venturesome than the reading which we propose. Moreover, Dionysius characterises in a division of its own the movement of knowledge which relies on revelation. Our suggested interpretation follows a midway line between the 'psychological', which appears unnecessary, and the 'theological' which is here unwarranted.

[30] 7, 3, 321.

which flow forth to us from . . . the transcendent mystery beyond Being . . . producing Being (οὐσιοποιούς), bearing life or granting wisdom.'[31] The very sense of Dionysius' exposition appears to be that we can know these powers: the gifts of God are unfolded through their participations. In naming God as 'Being', 'Wisdom', etc., we know him by way of his creative perfections. The importance of exemplars is again enforced by the following passage from the *Mystical Theology*: 'That which is most divine and sublime in the visible and intelligible universe are the fundamental (foundational) reasons (ὑποθετικοὶ λόγοι) of the things which are immediately beneath him who transcends all. Through these is revealed his presence which is beyond thought.'[32] Here I follow V. Lossky,[33] according to whom the ὑποθετικοὶ λόγοι refer to the divine ideas or exemplars—in Dionysius' words 'the creative reasons of things which pre-subsist as a unity in God.'[34]

We will have further opportunity to consider the role of these creative perfections. Here is signalled their epistemological significance in the discovery to God. There is, however, a more elementary step in Dionysius' noetic, namely the passage from the sensible to the intellectual, which, of its own power, provides the principle of the passage from the finite to the infinite. This principle is expressed by Dionysius in his tenth letter: 'Visible things are in truth clear images of the invisible.'[35] We may indeed apply to the realities of the created universe the words of Dionysius:

> Let us not think that the visible appearances of signs were fashioned for their own sake; they are a veil for that knowledge which is forbidden and concealed to the multitude, lest the most holy realities be easily grasped by the profane but may be unveiled only by the noble lovers of the holy.[36]

The key word to Dionysius' discovery of God's causality in the world is προβάλλειν. Dionysius uses it in two closely related significations to convey the same fundamental reality from distinct viewpoints, namely both the veiling and the unveiling or unfolding of God through creation. On the one hand, 'the creation of the visible universe is a veil before the invisible things of God (προβέβληται, literally, is placed before).'[37] But, on the other hand, it is 'from the order of all things' that we know God, as 'projected' or 'established' by him (ὡς ἐξ αὐτοῦ

---

[31] 2, 7, 56.
[32] *MT* I, 3, 1000D-1001A.
[33] Vladimir Lossky, 'La théologie négative de Denys l'Aréopagite', 218.
[34] 5, 8, 282.
[35] *Ep.* 10, 1117A: ἀληθῶς ἐμφανεῖς εἴκονες εἰσι τὰ ὁρατὰ τῶν ἀοράτων.
[36] *Ep.* 9, 1105C.
[37] *Ep.* 9, 1108B.

προβεβλημένης).[38] The world of finite beings revealed in our experience was created by God and may, therefore, be taken as a symbol of the divine. The spiritual is cloaked in the sensible, the supra-ontological with that which has being. In creation God has established throughout the universe multiple images of his infinite perfection, fashioning a tapestry (ποικιλία) of separate symbols to unfold his simplicity, covering in form and shape what is formless and without shape.[39]

We can gather from Dionysius a cogent and complete theory of the relation between cause and effect and of its epistemological value, bearing in particular on the relation of finite beings to their transcendent cause:

> It is not strange that ascending from obscure images to the cause of all, we should with supramundane vision contemplate all things, even those which are opposites, in the simple unity of the universal cause. For it is the principle of all principles, from which are Being itself and all things, whatsoever their mode of being.[40]

Allied to the validity of causal inference there is also in Dionysius a sophisticated theory of analogy founded upon the individual and limited participation of effects in the power of their cause. Although we may ascend from finite effects to an infinite cause, 'we see no life or being which exactly resembles the cause which in complete transcendence is beyond all things.'[41] There is no perfect likeness between cause and effect, since effects possess the images of the cause only according to their capacity.[42]

Dionysius grants, however, that there is a veritable relation between the creature and its infinite origin, bearing both on their similarity and distinction. There is a certain likeness, although this is incommensurable with the fullness of its cause. He may reason therefore:

> The same things are both similar and dissimilar to God: they are similar in the measure that they imitate the inimitable; dissimilar because as effects they are inferior to their cause, in an infinite and incomparable measure removed from him.[43]

This perspective provides a real ground for the relation between cause and effect, since it recognises the ambivalent value of the effect as revealing and concealing its cause. In the measure that beings resemble their Cause, the more infinitely are they transcended by it. The finite is

---

[38] 7, 3, 321.
[39] 1, 4, 15.
[40] 5, 7, 273–4.
[41] 2, 7, 56.
[42] 2, 8, 58.
[43] 9, 7, 376.

sufficient to unfold the existence of the absolute cause but is infinitely inadequate to reveal it such as it is, since God himself is 'in the manner of no being; the cause of all being, is yet himself non-being since he is beyond all being.'[44]

The visible world has for Dionysius, therefore, a twofold character. The realities of the world at once reveal and conceal the divine. They are an image of God, yet shroud his true nature; they are a help and a hindrance. As images established by God, they reflect something of his creative nature and providential goodness; but since they are but images they also limit their disclosure to their own measure. Yet this limited world of experience is the only ground from which we may proceed, according to an appropriate method, to a natural knowledge of God. This method must be, therefore, at once to attribute all perfections to God, since they reveal and affirm him as their source, and to deny or remove them, as unable to unfold him as he is. By this we further imply that God is transcendent to them all and so contains them pre-eminently within his unbounded perfection.

As their cause, God is both intimately immanent to all things, yet eminently transcendent. Dionysius summarises the mystery inherent in all search for the divine:

> God is known in all things and apart from all things; and God is known through knowledge and through unknowing; on the one hand he is reached by intuition, reason, understanding, apprehension, perception, opinion, appearance, name and by all other means and yet on the other hand, he cannot be conceived, spoken or named; and he is not anything among beings nor is he known from any being. He is all things in all and nothing in any; he is known from all things by all men, yet is not known from anything by anyone.[45]

The Absolute Good, therefore, Dionysius states, is celebrated by theologians 'both as nameless and as having all names' (ὡς ἀνώνυμον . . . καὶ ἐκ παντὸς ὀνόματος). [46] On the one hand, 'it is the cause of all beings, but is itself none of these as supra-ontologically transcending them all.'[47] It is, therefore, 'best celebrated by the removal of all things',[48] i.e. by denying of it every attribute taken from finite beings. On the other hand, Dionysius is compelled by the evidence that only through its effects can the cause be known:

---

[44] 1, 1, 7.
[45] 7, 3, 322.
[46] 1, 6, 25.
[47] 1, 5, 23.
[48] Ibid.

> Since as the very subsistence of Goodness, by its very Being it is the cause
> of all beings, we should praise the beneficent providence of the divine
> principle from all of its effects; for it is the centre of all things, and because
> of it all things are. It is before all, and in it all things subsist; through its
> Being all things are produced and have their existence.[49]

Dionysius draws on Scripture to support both approaches of signification.
In Genesis, for example, God rebukes the question 'What is Thy
name?', leading the enquirer away from every name by saying 'It is
wonderful' (ἐστι θαυμαστόν). Is not this the most wonderful name,
asks Dionysius: 'the Nameless', which is beyond all names? As 'many-
named', God reveals himself as Being ('Εγώ εἰμι ὁ ὤν), as Life, Light,
and Truth. And the 'wise in God' (θεόσοφοι) praise him with many
names drawn from the whole created universe: 'such as Good, Beautiful,
Wise, Beloved ... as Being, Giver of Life, Wisdom, Intellect, Word,
Knower, as preeminently possessing all the treasures of knowledge ...
surpassing all things in greatness, yet present in a gentle breeze.'[50] In
the following paragraphs we will consider from a philosophical point
of view Dionysius' analysis of the affirmative and negative knowledge
of God. We examine firstly the more profound metaphysical ground of
the distinction between the two, and subsequently how the distinction
unfolds to human reflection.

We have seen that according to Dionysius, God is known through
the attribution and negation or withdrawal of all things. Metaphysically,
this is possible because of their status as creatures, both revealing and
veiling the chiaroscuro of the divine. It appears, however, that for
Dionysius the tension between positive and negative theology is
grounded more originally in the very nature of God himself, in that
distinction which, according to Dionysius, tradition has made between
'divine unions' (ἑνώσεις) and 'divine distinctions' (διακρίσεις). [51] The
'divine unions' are the 'hidden and unrevealed foundations of a super-
ineffable and eminently unknowable identity'.[52] This is the supra-
ontological self-subsistence of the divine nature in itself, the divine
silence[53] which dwells in that 'darkness which is a superabundance of
light'.[54] (Dionysius follows here the words of Psalm 17, 121, that God

---

[49] 1, 5, 24.

[50] 1, 6, 25.

[51] Vladimir Lossky, "La notion des 'analogies' chez Denys le pseudo-aréopagite", 282:
'On ne peut pas réduire une voie à l'autre; leur opposition a un caractère réel qui se
fonde sur la distinction entre les ἑνώσεις et les διακρίσεις divines, entre la Substance
(ὕπαρξις) inconnaissable et les processions (πρόοδοι) révélateurs de Dieu.'

[52] 2, 4, 39.

[53] 4, 2, 104.

[54] MT 1, 1, 1000A.

'made darkness his secret dwelling place'.[55]) From its own primordial unity, it does not unfold outwardly in any way.

The 'divine distinctions', on the other hand, are 'the generous processions (πρόοδοι) and revelations (ἐκφάνσεις) of the divine nature'.[56] The very first procession, on which we need not dwell, is of course the distinction, within the most secret depths of the divine nature itself, of the persons within the Trinity. Of first significance for us is that 'distinction' whereby God communicates himself through a generous effusion of goodness in a manifold profusion of outward perfections. The 'divine distinction' is the 'generous emanation of the absolute divine unity which, superabundant with goodness, overflows into a multiplicity.'[57] Dionysius insists, nevertheless, that all participations or perfections which are shared, those imparting Being, Life, and Wisdom and the other gifts of the Good, which is the cause of all, are united in a manner consonant with the divine distinction.[58] In brief, the Good, according to Dionysius, remains 'united even in its distinction, overflows in its unity and multiplies without departing from the One'.[59]

From the doctrine of the Pseudo-Areopagite as just outlined, we may understand how what appear as contradictory predications may be proposed concerning the absolute Good, i.e. that he can be known both from all things and from none. Considered fundamentally in his divine union he is unapproachable; yet through his creative distinctions he reveals himself in and through the multiplicity of the created universe, especially in the participated perfections. Creatures, in particular the sublime and spiritual, are 'emissaries of the divine silence', as lights which shine in witness to him who is hidden and inaccessible.[60] As cause he remains, nonetheless, free from all finitude of Being, and his nature transcends the limitations which mark our manner of conceiving beings. This is well expressed by Dionysius in his *Mystical Theology*:

> It is necessary to attribute all the positive attributes of beings to him, as the cause of all; yet it is more proper to deny them since he transcends them all. But one may not think that these negations are in contradiction with the affirmations, but that God infinitely precedes all deprivation, as beyond all attribution and negation.[61]

---

[55] *MT* 1, 2, 1000A.
[56] 2, 4, 40.
[57] 2, 5, 49.
[58] 2, 5, 49.
[59] 2, 11, 72.
[60] 4, 2, 104.
[61] *MT* 1, 2, 1000B.

POSITIVE AND NEGATIVE NAMES OF GOD

It is customary to present the Areopagite's approach to God as simply taking a twofold path, the affirmative and the negative, respectively καταφατική and ἀποφατική.[62] However, although Dionysius himself sometimes uses the words κατάφασις/καταφάσκω and ἀπόφασις/ἀποφάσκω, only on one occasion does he use the terms καταφατικὴ θεολογία and θεολογία ἀποφατική. More frequent is the word-couple θέσις : ἀφαίρεσις; this expresses more concretely and graphically the attribution and removal of humanly conceived qualities as they are pronounced in relation to the Absolute.[63] Dionysius uses both terminologies synonymously, interchanging them occasionally.[64]

By the affirmative method, reason progressively applies to God as their cause and super-eminent exemplar the intelligible attributes discovered in created beings. As the cause of all things, God must possess the perfections which he imparts, a necessity which bears, needless to say, not upon God but upon creatures. Since creation is entirely a work of goodness, God is in the first place called Good; from the first participation in creation he is named as 'Being'; as cause of wise and living creatures we call him Life and Wisdom. This project of naming God positively, according to the perfections through which he is revealed in creation, is undertaken by Dionysius in his treatise the *Divine Names*. Here he praises God through his participations, with the names of 'Good', 'Beauty', 'Love', 'Being', 'Wisdom', 'Power', 'Peace', 'Perfect', 'One', etc. These perfections, which we discover partially in human experience, exist—more properly 'subsist'—in God in a radically distinct manner. He is their 'superplenitude': he is Goodness unbounded, Being, Life, Wisdom, and Power themselves, all such perfections distilled within a unique fullness and simplicity.[65]

In taking the path of affirmation we begin, according to Dionysius, by referring to God first those perfections which appear primary or most universal, and then by descending through the intermediary ones, until finally we attribute to him those which are particular and remote. This is because we appropriately begin with that which is akin to the transcendent, upon which the subsequent affirmations depend.[66] We first attribute to God that which is most worthy, since as Dionysius

---

[62] E.g. Frederick Copleston, *A History of Philosophy*, Vol. 2, p. 93.
[63] 2, 4, 42.
[64] *MT* 3, 1033C.
[65] 5, 2, 257; 6, 3, 296; 7, 1, 298.
[66] *MT* 2, 1025B.

comments, it is more proper to affirm that he is Life and Goodness than that he is air and stone.[67]

Now, in proposing the negative way, Dionysius argues on the other hand that we praise that which transcends Being in a manner proper to the transcendent itself, by removing from it every concept derived from finite being. In this approach the movement of reflection follows the inverse order to that of affirmative theology. We begin by negating of God those attributes which are most inferior and therefore least worthy: 'Is it not truer to say that he is not drunken or angry than that he does not speak or think?'[68] By the negative path, the soul first withdraws from the things that are akin to itself, and ascending gradually from these most distant attributes, continually denies ever more and more noble qualities; finally we remove even the most sublime as, strictly considered, being unworthy of God. We purify thus our knowledge of God as transcendent, and submit to him in an 'unknowing' (ἀγνωσία) which is freed of all concepts drawn from creatures.[69] Dionysius compares this process of purification to the act of the sculptor 'who from the unshaped mass fashions a statue by taking away all the impediments which stand in the way of a clear vision of the hidden image, and simply by this removal reveals the hidden beauty.'[70]

Each of these ways is necessary; they are mutually complementary and reciprocally sustaining. They present a dialectic of reflection and utterance, which is grounded in experience and purified through a tension between the concept and the reality which is intended: the infinite unity beyond every division of human thought. This distinction of method is illustrated in Dionysius' own works: the *Divine Names* commences with a consideration of the Good and proceeds downwards with a positive reflection on Being, Life, Wisdom, and so forth. *Mystical Theology* rises beyond sense perception, and abandoning the activity of reason, denies all intellectual knowledge of the transcendent divinity.

The inverse symmetry of the two ways, moreover, is significant. The affirmative mirrors the creative profusion of God, unfolding his generosity in a continuous cascade of perfections from the most noble to the most lowly, the multiple and humble perfections being contained virtually within the sublime and unified. On the other hand, the negative path recharts the ascent of finite beings, which seek through a native and creaturely impulse to return to their original presence within their

---

[67] *MT* 3, 1033C.
[68] *MT* 3, 1033D.
[69] *MT* 2, 1025BC; *MT* 3, 1033C; See *DN* 13, 3, 452.
[70] *MT* 2, 1025AB. See Plotinus, *Enneads*, I, 6, 9.

single source. More specifically, it reflects the movement of human thought from diversity to simplicity, from participation to presence, from limitation to transcendence, from the manifold towards unity, from sense to an all-surpassing silence, as it retraces upwards the great chain of being, discovering the reasons of things in ever more universal principles until it is resolved in a source which embraces and transcends the categories of finite understanding.

PRIORITY OF NEGATION

While Dionysius gives to the way of positive affirmation a real value, it is nevertheless evident that he attaches even greater significance to the path of negative knowledge. Concluding the *Divine Names*, which among his writings materially indicates a greater reliance on the principle of attribution, Dionysius states that 'no thing, which either exists or is known in the manner of being, can reveal the mystery, beyond intellect and reason, of the transcendent divinity which is supra-ontologically beyond all things.'[71] The complete endeavour of positive attribution is thus strikingly evaluated:

> Not even the name of Goodness do we attribute to it as being appropriate; but with a desire to think and speak of its ineffable nature, we consecrate to it the most sacred of names. Here we are in agreement with theologians; but since we leave the truth of the matter far behind, they also have chosen the ascent through negation.[72]

The priority of the negative way is particularly clear in the brief but intense treatise *Mystical Theology*. God is better praised through the removal, rather than by the attribution of humanly conceived perfections. Since God is totally transcendent, 'negations concerning divine things are true, but affirmations are unsuitable ... We may celebrate the divine realities with true negations.'[73]

Dionysius notes that the divine tradition has on the one hand named God as 'substantial Word and Spirit' (so proclaiming his divine rationality and wisdom), as real and authentic Being (the true cause of existence for all beings), and as Light and Life. Such designations, however, do not reflect a true resemblance of the divine principle since it is beyond all Being and Life. No light can represent it; every word

---

[71] 13, 3, 452.
[72] 13, 3, 452.
[73] *CH* 2, 3, 141A. See 2, 5, 145A.

and spirit is incomparably removed from any resemblance to it.[74] This same tradition, however, also extols the transcendent in a supra-mundane manner as the invisible and infinite, using terms which signify, not that which it is, but what it is not. Dionysius professes:

I believe that this is more proper to its nature, since, as the secret and holy tradition itself suggests, we are right in saying it does not exist in the manner of any being, and that we cannot know its super-essential infinity which is both inconceivable and unspeakable.[75]

Dionysius sums up the relation between the positive and negative paths, the priority of, and his preference for the latter: 'It is necessary to affirm of him all the positive attributes of beings, since he is cause of all; more properly, however, they should be denied of him, since he transcends them all.'[76] God is, therefore, 'celebrated most fittingly by the removal of all beings,'[77] i.e. of all attributes drawn from finite things. We must be careful, of course, to understand the proper meaning of 'removal' as employed by Dionysius. Scarcely does the term connote absolute privation.[78] More than once does he emphasise that the use of the negative in the privative prefix signifies not a defect but rather a superabundance.[79] Moreover, in the majority of cases, the word ἀφαίρεσις is used together with ὑπεροχή, pointing to the transcendence of the Absolute (τῆς ὑπεροχικῆς ἐστιν ἀφαιρέσεως).[80] Negation as such, therefore, is of value for Dionysius only because it is interior to the affirmation of a transcendence. Through negation a concept is purified of all finite connotation and, in a union of affirmation and negation, its content is intensified towards infinity. R. Roques sums up the dialectic of positive and negative theology, and their resolution in transcendent affirmation:

Il faut que la négation ait pénétré au coeur même de l'affirmation pour que l'affirmation vaille. Et c'est dans cette affirmation transcendante et purifiée que la négation elle-même se justifie. Par là, la théologie négative se présente comme une théologie éminente (ὑπεροχικῶς), comme la vraie théologie de la Transcendance.[81]

Negative theology is profoundly significant and mysteriously meaningful, therefore, precisely as the avowal of a superabundant transcendence

---

[74] CH 2, 3, 140CD.
[75] CH 2, 3, 140D-141A.
[76] MT 1, 2, 100B.
[77] 1, 5, 23.
[78] 8, 3, 321.
[79] 7, 2, 314
[80] 2, 3, 37.
[81] René Roques, La Hiérarchie Céleste, Introduction, pp. xxvi-vii.

which it is itself unable to express. Attaining to the utmost limits of
rational knowledge with the removal of all intelligible concepts, we
assert the radical incommensurability of our cognitive capacity *vis-à-vis*
the goal of our quest. Having purified our notions of creaturely
perfection in such a way that they might refer to their transcendent
source, we ascertain that what is denoted so infinitely surpasses the
signification of our concepts, that it is more proper to deny them of
the Transcendent. We best celebrate the Transcendent, according to
Dionysius, therefore, by abandoning all intellectual activity and
submitting in a learned and innocent un-knowing to the mystery
of the absolute. The highest achievement of reason, thus, is to affirm
its own inadequacy.

The transcendent mystery which infinitely surpasses both the perfection
of being and the clarity of intellection, Dionysius paradoxically terms
the 'Divine Darkness' (θειᾶτον σκότος);[82] he elaborates a symbolism of
darkness and light in an attempt to convey the superabundance of its
intelligibility. Like the owl in Aristotle's *Metaphysics*, blinded by the
radiance of the sun, we are unable to behold the transcendent divinity,
according to Dionysius, not because of any defect but due to the
brilliance of 'the very darkness which is beyond intellect' (ὑπὲρ νοῦν
γνόφος).[83] Its transcendence is unapproachable, so that compared with
our intellectual vision it remains shrouded in impenetrable darkness.
But truly speaking, as Dionysius points out in his letter to the monk
Gaius, this ineffable darkness is such only in contrast to the relative
'clarity' of our knowledge. By refraining from all intellectual activity
we enter into the darkness which is above intellect, where we may be
illumined by a deep and silent darkness which is none other than a
superplenitude of light and intelligibility.

> Darkness becomes invisible to the light and all the more so, according as the
> light is more abundant. Knowledge also hinders unknowing, especially the
> greater it is. But if this is taken, not in a defective but in a superlative sense,
> it must be asserted in a manner beyond all truth, that the un-knowing
> surrounding God remains hidden for those who possess the light of reality
> and the knowledge of beings. His transcendent darkness is concealed to every
> light and obscures all knowledge.[84]

The ultimate ground for the incapacity of our knowledge to understand
God is to be sought in the abyss-like infinity which lies between the
transcendent and the beings which are the domain of our knowledge.

---

[82] *MT* 1, 1.
[83] *MT* 3, 1033B.
[84] *Ep.* 1, 1065A.

Dionysius warns against mistaking such knowledge of beings for a knowledge of God:

> If someone sees God and understands what he has seen, then he has not seen him, but one of the beings which are from him and which may be known. He himself is established beyond both knowledge and being. Wholly unknowable, *he is not*, but is in a manner beyond Being and is known beyond intellect.

Dionysius concludes, therefore, that 'A complete un-knowing is the knowledge par excellence of that which is beyond all known things.'[85] Accordingly, in the *Divine Names*, having vindicated the mutually complementary value of the ways of affirmation and negation in naming God, he proceeds to emphasise that the 'most divine' knowledge of God is received through un-knowing, in a union which transcends the mind. To prepare itself for this union the mind must first free itself of all things, and then, ever withdrawing from itself, become united to the 'brilliant rays which illumine it from the unfathomable depth of wisdom'.[86]

In this union, it is the inspiration of the transcendent which assumes primacy. Dionysius begins his *Mystical Theology* with a request to the transcendent God who is beyond Being and Goodness to guide his path to the

> highest peak of mystic inspiration, eminently unknown yet exceedingly luminous, where the pure, absolute and unchanging mysteries of theology are veiled in the dazzling obscurity of the secret silence, outshining all brilliance with the intensity of their darkness, and surcharging our blinded intellects with the utterly impalpable and invisible splendour surpassing all beauty.[87]

Dionysius advises Timothy (the novice being initiated to mystical theology) to relinquish the senses and the operations of the intellect, all sensible and intellectual things, the things which are not and the things which are; in this way he may 'rise, in so far as possible, through an unknowing, towards union with him who is beyond all Being and knowledge.' Through renunciation of the self, and freedom from all things, he will ascend to the 'ray of divine darkness which transcends all existence'.[88]

The Good, which is cause of all things (ἡ ἀγαθὴ πάντων αἰτία), is most eloquent but makes no utterance itself, being transcendent to thought and speech. It reveals itself, according to Dionysius, in its pristine truth only to those who, having passed beyond all things both

---

[85] *Ep.* 1, 1065A.
[86] 7, 3, 323.
[87] *MT* 1, 1, 997AB.
[88] *MT* 1, 1, 998B—1000A.

pure and polluted, and leaving behind all divine lights, sounds and
utterances, 'plunge into the darkness where, as Scripture says, truly
dwells he who is beyond all things.'[89] Entering the 'darkness of un-
knowing' (γνόφον τῆς ἀγνωσίας), the soul renounces all cognitive
apprehension and encounters that which is intangible and invisible,
belonging thereby neither to itself nor to any other but to him who is
beyond all things. Through the repose of all cognitive operation it is
united in a most supreme manner to him who is wholly unknowable;
of whom knowing nothing, it knows in a manner beyond understanding.[90]
Dionysius prays, therefore, 'that we may enter into this darkness which
is beyond light, and, without seeing and without knowing, to see and
to know that which is beyond vision and knowledge; for it is through
not-seeing and by un-knowing that we have true vision and knowledge.'[91]

This passage towards silent union with the transcendent, Dionysius
understands as the necessary sequence to both positive and negative
theology. Positive attribution descends from more elevated and general
perfections to particular ones, while negative abstraction proceeds
upwards from the lower to the more all-embracing:

> The higher we ascend, the more our words are limited to general aspects of
> what is intelligible; just as now, when we plunge into the darkness which is
> beyond intellect, we encounter not merely a shortage of speech, but a
> complete loss of words and thought ... And after the complete ascent we
> are wholly voiceless, being fully united to the ineffable.[92]

Dionysius' entire work is a sustained and arduous effort to express the
inexpressible; to communicate by means of words and concepts that
which by definition can neither be uttered nor understood. His strategy
is to impose negation upon affirmation and affirmation upon negation,
increasing both in a super-eminent union of intention and intensity
which aims only to transcend itself. But in the end, all attempts bear
witness to their own insufficiency. The pre-eminent cause of all things
is so transcendent to our ways of reflection that they must both,
whether negative or affirmative, be denied, so as to be understood in a
pre-eminent sense. Truly speaking, God may neither be denied, nor
affirmed; he is a realm utterly other than the poverty which constitutes
the world of human measure. 'God is the affirmation of all and the
negation of all, being beyond both all affirmation and negation.'[93] This

---

[89] *MT* 1, 3, 1000BC.
[90] *MT* 1, 3, 1001A.
[91] *MT* 2, 1025A.
[92] *MT* 3, 1033BC.
[93] 2, 4, 42.

is perhaps the last word of Dionysius on the discovery of God. And in this spirit he concludes his *Mystical Theology:*

> There is no speaking of it, nor name nor knowledge of it. Darkness and light, error and truth—it is none of these. It is beyond assertion and denial. We make assertions and denials of what is next to it, but never of it, for it is both beyond every assertion, being the perfect and unique cause of all things, and, by virtue of its preeminently simple and absolute nature, free of every limitation, beyond every limitation; it is also beyond every denial.[94]

---

[94] *MT* 5, 1048AB, Luibheid, p. 141.

CHAPTER TWO

DIONYSIAN ELEMENTS IN AQUINAS' DISCOVERY OF GOD

REASON AND REVELATION

From the outset Aquinas recognises the biblical background of Dionysius' endeavour to elucidate the divine names. He begins the introduction to his Commentary by stating that in order to understand these works, we must note that Dionysius artificially divides into four the things contained about God in the sacred writings:[1] he thus discerns Scripture as in a sense the subject matter of the entire body of Dionysius' writings. The division, while it coincides with the titles of four of Dionysius' works, derives from Aquinas and is significant for his interpretation of Dionysius. Through it he gives a hermeneutic of the principles which pervade and sustain the multiform vision of the Pseudo-Areopagite.

The first radical division in Aquinas' scheme of Dionysius' doctrine is that concerning the very nature of God's intimate unity and distinction, revealed as such only in revelation. For this, no sufficient similarity can be found in created things: it is a mystery which transcends every faculty of natural reason.[2] This subject matter has been treated by Dionysius, Aquinas states, in a book reportedly entitled *De Divinis Hypotyposibus*, i.e. *On Divine Characters*. The three remaining divisions which Aquinas enumerates are concerned in different ways with those names of God for which some similitude or likeness may be discovered in creatures. This is the work of natural reason in its investigation of created reality. Its aim, nevertheless, is to elucidate the names of God which are given in Scripture. To these three aspects of naming God through the power of reason we shall return. It will be

---

[1] *In DN Prooemium*, I: Ad intellectum librorum beati Dionysii considerandum est quod ea quae de Deo in Sacris Scripturis continentur, artificialiter quadrifariam divisit.
[2] Ibid.: Cuius unitatis et distinctionis sufficiens similitudo in rebus creatis non invenitur, sed hoc mysterium omnem naturalis rationis facultatem excedit.

useful to examine first how Aquinas, in his interpretation of Dionysius, relates the work of reason to the primacy of revelation.

A key notion which Aquinas introduces at the beginning of Chapter 1, and which governs the entire theory of human knowledge of God throughout his Commentary, is the principle of proportion and the participated nature of knowledge, i.e. the due and harmonious measure which must exist between a knowing subject and its object. He expresses the proportionate relation of subject and object in knowledge: *Semper enim oportet obiectum cognitivae virtutis, virtuti cognoscenti proportionatum esse.*[3] That is to say, the object of knowledge, in so far as it is to be known, must be in due proportion to the cognitive capacity of the knower. This proportionate relation of knowledge is further grounded in the participated nature of being. There is for St Thomas a close relation between the inherent perfection of an individual being, its cognitive capacity, and its degree of cognoscibility or intelligibility. There is, in other words, a correspondence on the ontological level between beings and (a) the objects which they may know and (b) the knowing subjects by which they may in turn be known. This is most clearly manifest in the distinction between finite and Infinite Being: 'Created substance is the object commensurate with created intellect, just as uncreated essence is proportioned to uncreated knowledge.'[4] Even when divine truths are revealed by God, they are bestowed in proportion to the measure of those to whom they are revealed: 'But it is beyond the proportion of finite intellect to know the infinite.'[5] Our knowledge is commensurate with finite reality,[6] bound to created things as that which is connatural to us.

Aquinas also considers the proportioned nature of the cognitive capacity and knowability of beings—both determined by their excellence of being—as restricting our ability to reason from one level of reality to another: 'A superior grade of beings cannot be comprehended through an inferior.'[7] Having given this principle himself, Aquinas repeats as examples the instances noted by Dionysius: intelligible realities cannot be understood 'perfectly' by means of the sensible (here he lightens the negative emphasis of Dionysius); the simple by means of the composite, or the incorporeal through the bodily. Applied to our

---

[3] I, i, 14.

[4] I, i, 14: . . . super ipsam substantiam creatam quae est obiectum commensuratum intellectui creato, sicut essentia increata est proportionata scientiae increatae.

[5] I, i, 19: Divina revelantur a Deo secundum proportionem eorum quibus revelantur: sed cognoscere infinitum est supra proportionem intellectus finiti.

[6] I, i, 29: Cognitio autem nostra commensuretur rebus creatis.

[7] I, i, 23: Superior gradus entium comprehendi non potest per inferiorem.

enquiry into God, this means that since God is beyond every order of beings whatsoever, he cannot be understood through the mediation of any being.[8]

St Thomas summarises the reasoning of the Areopagite: 'His intention is to show not only that God cannot be understood by any cognitive power—or made perfectly manifest in any utterance—but that neither can he be known through any created object nor through any created likeness.'[9] This is due not to any defect in God but to a supreme eminence of Being and intelligibility:

> God is incomprehensible to every created intellect since he is beyond every mind and reason, having in his essence more clarity of truth pertaining to his cognoscibility than any creature has the capacity to know. Hence no creature can arrive at a perfect manner of knowing God, to comprehend him whom (Dionysius) has named supra-substantial knowledge.[10]

In other words, God himself is infinitely knowable, whereas created intellect has but a limited capacity to know. Our want of knowledge concerning the divinity beyond being is due to a superabundance of truth which of our nature we cannot receive: 'According to Dionysius, therefore, it is necessary to say that God is incomprehensible to every intellect and cannot be contemplated by us in his essence so long as our knowledge is bound to created things as what is connatural to us.'[11] Aquinas concludes, therefore, that to God alone belongs a perfect knowledge of himself as he is: he remains hidden and no one can speak or think of him except in so far as is revealed by God.[12]

For Aquinas as for Dionysius, despite the utter transcendence of God beyond being, and his immeasurable luminosity which (in contrast

---

[8] I, i, 23: Sed Deus est super omnem ordinem existentium; ergo per nihil existentium comprehendi potest.

[9] I, i, 25: Non solum intendit ostendere quod Deus non possit per aliquam virtutem cognoscitivam comprehendi aut locutione perfecte manifestari, sed quod neque per aliquod obiectum creatum vel per quamcumque similitudinem creatam.

[10] I, i, 27: Sic, igitur, Deus incomprehensibilis quidem est omni intellectui creato, quia est super omnem mentem et rationem, utpote plus habens de claritate veritatis in sua essentia, quod ad Eius cognoscibilitatem pertinet, quam aliquod creatum de virtute ad cognoscendum. Unde nulla creatura potest pertingere ad perfectum modum cognitionis Ipsius, quem nominavit supersubstantialem scientiam, et hoc esset eum comprehendere. See also I, i, 11: (occulta Deitas) . . . est super omnem substantiam, et per hoc est occulta nobis quibus creatae substantiae sunt proportionae ad cognoscendum. Also *In Boeth. de Trin.*, 1, 2, ad 3.

[11] I, i, 27: Secundum rationem Dionysii oportet dicere quod Deus et incomprehensibilis est omni intellectui et incontemplabilis nobis in sua essentia, quamdiu nostra cognitio alligata est rebus creatis, utpote nobis connaturalibus.

[12] I, i, 13: De eo quod ab aliquo solo scitur, nullus potest cogitare vel loqui, nisi quantum ab illo manifestatur. Soli autem Deo convenit perfecte cognoscere seipsum secundum id quod est. Nullus igitur potest vere loqui de Deo vel cogitare nisi inquantum a Deo revelatur. I, i, 17: Deus soli sibi notus, nobis autem occultus.

to man's intellect) veils him in a shroud of divine darkness, God does not remain entirely unknown. Dionysius had suggested that it is through his benevolence that God reveals his supernatural splendour to creatures—to each in due proportion.[13] Aquinas is even more emphatic in explaining why a knowledge of the hidden God is bestowed: 'It would indeed be against the nature of divine goodness that God should retain for himself all his knowledge and not communicate it to anyone else in any way whatsoever, since it belongs to the nature of the good that it should communicate itself to others.' Dionysius can therefore, according to Aquinas, reconcile the reserved nature of divine knowledge with the possibility of man's participation in the knowledge of God: 'He says, therefore, that although the supersubstantial knowledge of God may be attributed to God alone, nevertheless, since God is Goodness itself, it cannot be that he should not communicate himself to some existing beings.'[14]

Aquinas emphasises that God bestows such knowledge, 'not through necessity but as a favour',[15] freely as a gift, to each being in the measure of its merits. According to the principle of proportion, God does not reveal himself according to the fullness of his own knowledge but enlightens each being according to its nature. Aquinas summarises: 'The nature of his goodness signifies that, while reserving a certain mode of knowledge as unique to himself, he communicates as a favour (*ex sua gratia*) to inferior beings some mode of knowledge, illuminating them according to the proportion of each.'[16] He even interprets this proportionate revelation as an instance of 'distributive justice' within the universal order of salvation.[17]

Our knowledge of divine realities, Aquinas further explains, is not by abstraction, as in the case of sensible things which possess in themselves a less simple mode of existence than in the intellect, but by way of participation. 'Divine realities are more simple and perfect in themselves than in our intellect or in any of the other things known to us: hence our knowledge of divine things is said to be achieved not by abstraction,

---

[13] I, 2, 9.

[14] I, i, 36 : . . . manifestat quomodo occultae Deitatis cognitio aliis communicatur. Esset enim contra rationem bonitatis divinae, si cognitionem suam sibi retineret quod nulli alteri penitus communicaret, cum de ratione boni sit quod se aliis communicet. Et ideo dicet quod licet supersubstantialis Dei scientia soli Deo attribuenda sit, tamen, cum Deus sit ipsum bonum, non potest esse quod non communicetur alicui existentium.

[15] I, i, 37: Quasi non ex necessitate sed ex gratia.

[16] I, i, 37: Suae bonitatis ratio hoc habet ut, reservato sibi quodam cognitionis modo qui sibi est singularis, communicet inferioribus ex sua gratia, aliquem modum cognitionis, secundum suas illuminationes, quae sunt secundum proportionem uniuscuiusque.

[17] I, i, 22.

but by participation.'[18] Our intellect participates in the intellectual power and light of divine wisdom, and in contemplating God becomes in a manner one with him, is assimilated to him, being 'informed' by him. In a brief parenthesis Aquinas also expresses this intimate cognitive union in terms of his own noetic, applying the fundamental principle that the intellect in act (*intellectus in actu*) is somehow identical with the object of knowledge as it is actually known (*intellectum in actu*).[19]

Because of the divine authority required by all truth concerning God, Aquinas, in agreement with Dionysius, notes that Scripture above all must be believed, since it is granted by God who is truth itself.[20] By faith we unite ourselves to realities which are more elevated than those which reason can know or speak, and adhere to these with even greater certainty. Dionysius proceeds in this work, therefore, says Aquinas, not by relying on human reason, but by drawing strength and security from the authority of Scripture.[21] The truth of revelation, in the words of Aquinas, is as it were an illumination radiating from primordial Truth; which light indeed does not extend sufficiently that we may behold the essence of God, but to a certain limit or measure—namely to those divine truths which, when illumined with the light of revelation, become intelligible to understanding (*veritates intelligibiles divinorum, intelligibilia divinorum*).[22] The divine ray of truth itself transcends and comprehends the boundaries of all knowledge whatsoever: these pre-exist more eminently within their primordial cause. And since no finite power can attain to the infinite, we can neither express this fontal ray nor contemplate it perfectly in any way: not because it is deficient but

---

[18] II, iv, 176: Sunt autem quaedam cognoscibilia, quae sunt infra intellectum nostrum, quae quidem habent simplicius esse in intellectu nostro, quam in seipsis, sicut sunt omnes res corporales, unde huiusmodi res dicuntur cognosci a nobis per abstractionem. Divina autem simplicia et perfectiora sunt in seipsis quam in intellectu nostro vel in quibuscumque aliis rebus nobis notis, unde divinorum cognitio dicitur fieri non per abstractionem, sed per participationem.

[19] II, iv, 177: ... divina in ipso intellectu participantur, prout scilicet intellectus noster participat intellectualem virtutem et divinae sapientiae lumen. See also I, i, 38: Et quia qui contemplantur Ipsum quodammodo unum cum Ipso efficiuntur (secundum quod intellectus in actu est quodammodo intellectum esse in actu) et per consequens Ei assimilantur utpote ab Ipso informati. See *ST*, I, 87, 1, ad 3.

[20] I, i, 21.

[21] I, i, 6-8.

[22] I, i, 15: Veritas enim sacrae Scripturae est quoddam lumen per modum radii derivatum a prima veritate, quod quidem lumen non se extendit ad hoc quod per ipsum possimus videre Dei essentiam aut cognoscere omnia quae Deus in se ipso cognoscit aut angeli aut beati eius essentiam videntes, sed usque ad aliquem certum terminum vel mensuram, intelligibilia divinorum lumine sacrae Scripturae manifestantur.

because, distinct from all things and transcending all existence, it is unknown to all.[23]

The limit measuring man's share in divine knowledge is determined by his response of piety and temperance.[24] He may not aspire to a knowledge beyond that apportioned to him or seek what is inferior, but attend resolutely to that superior illumination of truth and respond with love and reverence towards the divine realities which are revealed.[25] We venerate the hidden things of God, Aquinas remarks, by seeking not to investigate them, and those which are ineffable by remaining silent.[26] But, St Thomas emphasises, we honour divine realities best of all by uniting ourselves to the truths revealed in Scripture and by seeking to know the divine names by which God is praised.

Now, among the names which, according to Aquinas, are revealed by Scripture, most frequent are those which disclose God as cause and principle of all things, especially of the metaphysical perfections which proceed from God to creatures: Being, Goodness and Life. It is indeed striking that these are truths which may also be discovered by reason through a metaphysical reflection on the relation of beings to God.[27] Aquinas even asserts that from the names given in Scripture we have already a twofold knowledge regarding the diffusion of goodness or perfection into each thing and of the principle itself of this diffusion. The name 'Living God', for example, manifests the diffusion of life to creatures and the principle of this diffusion as God.[28]

Aquinas recognises Dionysius' exhortation that we should aspire to the *intelligible* truths of divine things according as they are manifested

---

[23] I, i, 72: Nulla virtus finita extendit se in infinitum, sed ad aliquem certum terminum concluditur; unde, cum omnis virtus cognoscitiva creaturae sit finita, cuiuslibet cognitionis creaturae est certus terminus ultra quem non tendit. . . Supersubstantialis autem radius, idest, ipsa divina veritas, excedit omnes terminos et fines quarumcumque cognitionum eminentius praeexistunt in ipso radio, sicut in causa primordiali, modo ineffabili nobis, propter suam eminentiam. Unde relinquitur quod praedictum radium non possumus cogitare inquirendo neque exprimere loquendo neque perfecte contemplari quocumque modo; non propter sui defectum, sed propter hoc quod est ab omnibus distinctus et, per consequens, ignotus omnibus, quasi super omnia existens. See also I, i, 73.

[24] I, i, 16; see I, iii, 3, 105.

[25] I, i, 39; see III, 233.

[26] I, ii, 44: Occulta per hoc veneramur quod ea non scrutamur et ineffabilia per hoc quod ea silemus; et hoc quidem ea sanctitate et castitate animi provenit non se extra suas metas extendentis.

[27] I, ii, 44: Per haec enim scimus laudare Deum viventem, bonum et alia huiusmodi, quae hic nobis de Deo in Scripturis sacris traduntur; see also I, ii, 53-4.

[28] I, ii, 45: Per divina igitur nomina, quae nobis in sacris Scripturis traduntur, duo cognovimus, scilicet: diffusionem sancti luminis et cuiuscumque bonitatis seu perfectionis, et ipsum principium huius diffusionis, utpote cum dicimus Deum viventem, cognoscimus diffusionem vitae in creaturis et principium huius diffusionis esse Deum.

through the light of sacred Scripture.[29] It is as dependent on revelation for its original inspiration and sustaining guidance that Aquinas understands the role of 'divine philosophy' for Dionysius. Reason may respond to revelation when presented with those truths of God for which a likeness may be found in finite beings. Since these are the proper object of human cognition we may rely in this domain upon the principles of human wisdom.[30] Because they are grounded in a profound and intimate relationship with God as cause and principle, this ontological resemblance allows us to validly conceive and speak of God.

This is the principle which Aquinas employs in the introduction to his Commentary in order to distinguish in the works of Dionysius between the fruits of reason and revelation. As we have noted, the first division which he makes concerns the hidden and intimate nature of God, which is in no way reflected in creatures. No adequate similitude is found in finite reality to reveal the unity and distinction of the divine persons. It surpasses in its mystery the natural faculty of reason.[31]

It is according to the varying values of similitude and their cognitive import that Aquinas proceeds to make his secondary distinction between the works of Dionysius in which reason reflects upon the divine realities revealed in Scripture. The things spoken of God and of which some likeness is found in creatures can relate towards him in either of two ways. First and most importantly, the similarity expressed in divine names may be attained in virtue of something—perfection or participation—which derives from God to creatures; since whatever perfection belongs to a being is a reflection of its fullness as it pre-exists in God as principle.[32] Thus from the primary Good are derived all good things, from the principle of life every living thing, and similarly with other such perfections.[33] These perfections belong primordially, in their plenitude, to God and may properly speaking be attributed to him as such. When Aquinas says that they are 'intelligible perfections', he means that we discover them by intellectual abstraction from creatures and know them through simple concepts signifying pure

---

[29] I, i, 15.

[30] I, i, 7.

[31] *In DN*, *Prooemium*, I.

[32] I, ii, 50: Quaecumque est propria rei perfectio, principaliter praeexistet in Deo.

[33] *In DN*, *Prooemium*, I: Quae vero dicuntur de Deo in Scripturis, quarum aliqua similitudo in creaturis invenitur, dupliciter se habent. Nam huiusmodi similitudo in quibusdam quidem attenditur secundum aliquid quod a Deo in creaturas derivatur. Sicut a primo bono sunt omnia bona et a primo vivo sunt omnia viventia et sic in aliis similibus. Et talia pertractat Dionysius in libro 'de divinis Nominibus', quem prae manibus habemus.

perfections: their content can be conceived as such without limitation or restriction and may therefore be attributed to God. They are thus 'metaphysical', i.e. do not imply any physical character or finite connotation. Now, it is with this first kind of name, Aquinas remarks, that Dionysius deals in his treatise *On Divine Names*, i.e. titles of perfections which, unfolding through experience to intelligence, are discovered as proper in the first place to God and in a derivatory, causal, manner to creatures as gifts or participations:

> In this book he aims at an exposition of the 'intelligible' names of God, that is, those which are not taken symbolically from sensible things but from the intelligible perfections which proceed from him into creatures, such as 'Being', 'Life' and suchlike.[34]

In the case of other names, however, the likeness conveyed is transferred from creatures to God. The quality or perfection pertains primarily to the creature, i.e. it necessarily signifies something of a creaturely nature and is not, properly speaking, compatible with the divine plenitude; for example the nature of 'lion', 'stone' and 'sun' may not be referred to him as a real likeness, but secondarily, in a symbolic or metaphoric manner (*symbolice vel metaphorice*).[35] We may indeed praise God with visionary images (*imaginativis visionibus*), attributing symbolically the forms and characters of sensible things, human honours, etc.[36] Such names themselves, however, express in the first place specific determinations pertaining to individuals of a limited essential perfection unlike those of Good, Being and Life. They co-signify simultaneously an inherent limitation in the reality which they express. Of the symbolic attribution to God of these concepts which denote finite, even sensible realities, Dionysius has treated in his book *On Symbolic Theology*.[37]

Having distinguished between the perfections revealed in beings as proper in their primary signification either to God (intelligible perfections) or to finite beings (sensible), and which are therefore attributed unequally to God due to their disparate similitude towards him, Aquinas now brings a radically significant reflection to bear on the very status of *similitudo*, whether sensible or intelligible: *Omnis*

---

[34] I, iii, 104: Dicit ergo primo quod nunc procedendum est, in hoc libro, ad manifestationem divinorum nominum intelligibilium, idest quae non sumuntur a rebus sensibilibus symbolice, sed ex intelligibilibus perfectionibus procedentibus ab Eo in creaturas, sicut sunt esse, vivere, et huiusmodi. See I, iii, 105.

[35] *In DN, Prooemium*, I: In quibusdam vero similitudo attenditur secundum aliquid a creaturis in Deum translatum. Sicut Deus dicitur leo, petra, sol vel aliquid huiusmodi; sic enim Deus symbolice vel metaphorice nominatur.

[36] I, iii, 102; See *De Potentia*, 7, 6, ad 8; *Contra Gentiles*, 1, 29.

[37] On the value of representing spiritual realities by the sensible, see *ST*, I, 1, 9; *In Boeth. de Trin.*, 6, 2, ad 1.

similitudo creaturae ad Deum deficiens est. That which God is, exceeds everything which may be found in creatures. Regardless of what our intellect, guided by creatures, can conceive, God himself remains hidden and unknown: *Hoc ipsum quod Deus est remaneat occultum et ignotum.*[38] This is true, St Thomas emphasises, not only of the immediate objects of sense experience, which are referred to God metaphorically, but also of the more intimate attributes such as 'life' and 'being'—those pure and simple perfections which may be disengaged by the intellect. 'For not only is God not "stone" or "sun", which are apprehended by sense, but neither is he such life or essence as may be conceived by our intellect; that itself which God is, therefore, remains unknown to us, since he exceeds all that which is apprehended by us.'[39] In order that our knowledge of God may become *less inadequate*, therefore, whatever we know in creatures is 'removed' from God according as it is found in creatures. Concerning these 'remotions', through which God remains hidden and unknown to us, Aquinas notes that Dionysius has written another book entitled *On Mystical—Hidden—Theology.*

Already in the *Prooemium,* therefore, Aquinas presents a comprehensive approach to the mystery of God. Our knowledge of God unfolds through the twofold medium of divine revelation and the natural discovery of human reason. In his Commentary, Aquinas presents an interesting concordance between these two sources. Rational knowledge is grounded in the senses and directed towards an autonomous understanding of the intelligible or metaphysical truth revealed in Scripture. In this research it follows a threefold approach, which Aquinas aptly illustrates through the individual works of Dionysius. The *via causalitatis* consists in attributing to God the metaphysical perfections which primarily belong to him and which devolve through causality to creatures—this path is traced in the *Divine Names.* The *via symbolica* refers to God in a metaphoric sense the characters and qualities of the sensible or physical universe, which are treated of in the *Symbolic Theology.* Finally, and for Aquinas most

---

[38] *In DN, Prooemium,* I.

[39] *In DN, Prooemium,* I: Sed quia omnis similitudo creaturae ad Deum deficiens est et hoc ipsum quod Deus est omne id quod in creaturis invenitur excedit, quicquid in creaturis a nobis cognoscitur a Deo removetur, secundum quod in creaturis est; ut sic, post omne illud quod intellectus noster ex creaturis manuductus de Deo concipere potest, hoc ipsum quod Deus est remaneat occultum et ignotum. Non solum enim Deus non est lapis aut sol, qualia sensu apprehenduntur, sed nec est talis vita aut essentia qualis ab intellectu nostro concipi potest et sic hoc ipsum quod Deus est, cum excedat omne illud quod a nobis apprehenditur, nobis remanet ignotum. De huiusmodi autem remotionibus quibus Deus remanet nobis ignotus et occultus fecit alium librum quem intitulavit 'de Mystica' idest occulta 'Theologia'.

significantly, the *via negationis* is effected through the negation or removal (*remotio*) of every creaturely mode of perfection from God as transcendent. This is done by Dionysius in the *Mystical Theology*.[40]

This division itself according to which Aquinas understands the ensemble of Dionysius' works, with its systematic optic and organic architecture, bears witness to the vast and profound perspective of his own searching and synthetic spirit. In this panorama the vision of Dionysius comes into clear depth and relief. With his distinctions of theological and rational, of intelligible and imaginatory, and of the positive and negative predication of God, Aquinas brings the various insights of Dionysius into close focus and contributes to a better appreciation of his vision. Inspired by Dionysius' remarks, Aquinas weaves together, elucidating according to their priority, these manifold relations of revelation and reason, divine providence and human response, gathering them around the unifying and focal point of participation which obtains between finite and infinite.

The *Triplex Via* of Divine Names

The influence of Dionysius in the formation of Aquinas' natural theology is only reflected in part in the *tria genera Dei nominationum* just outlined. More important for St Thomas is the *triplex via* which he discerns as underlying Dionysius' discovery of God in *De Divinis Nominibus*. The knowledge of God is attained by three steps—*per causalitatem, per remotionem, per eminentiam*. The first step of the threefold path is the affirmation of God as cause by way of the 'intelligible processions' (*per intelligibiles processiones*) which derive from God. Aquinas notes that Dionysius deals in the *Divine Names* exclusively with these 'intelligible perfections'; the symbolic transference of sensible qualities plays no role in the treatise and does not form a major part of Aquinas' debt to Dionysius. In making more explicit the content and manner of attribution, however, Aquinas is led to disengage as a third stage, distinct from that of outright negation, the way of eminent or transcendent attribution. To the role and significance of these 'intelligible perfections', which are the medium of the divine discovery, we shall return in the course of our enquiry. We turn our attention

---

[40] A passage from chapter I of *De Divinis Nominibus* gives Aquinas the occasion to summarise these three ways of naming God: Cum enim praemissa sint tria genera Dei nominationum, de primo, qui est per remotionum, agitur in Mystica Theologia; de secundo, qui est per intelligibiles processiones, in hoc libro; de tertio, qui est per sensibiles similitudines, in libro de symbolica Theologia (I, iii, 104).

now more directly to the function of Dionysius' positive and negative theology as transformed by Aquinas according to the structure of the *triplex via*.

The text which evokes Aquinas' exegesis of a *triplex via* is the noted passage from DN 7, 3, according to which we ascend to God ἐν τῇ πάντων ἀφαιρέσει καὶ ὑπεροχῇ καὶ ἐν τῇ πάντων αἰτίᾳ, i.e. through the removal and excess of all things and in the cause of all things. (In the translation of Sarracenus, which Aquinas follows: *in omnium ablatione et excessu et in omnium causa*.) This phrase among all his works indicates perhaps Dionysius' most commonly recognised influence upon Aquinas. Surprisingly, perhaps, Aquinas in his Commentary on the *Divine Names* does not deal at any great length with this threefold path. Throughout his writings it recurs with incessant frequency as a constant principle of method; it is not presented, however, as a unique theory or single statement. The *triplex via* is rather a threefold variation on the dominant and underlying theme of causality: the variants reveal how we may approach a knowledge of God by three paths which merely reflect differing moments of the causal relation between God and creatures. In the following paragraphs we shall first observe Aquinas' brief reaction to the present passage in his Commentary on Dionysius and review its various applications in his other works. Then we shall look in greater depth at the disproportionate similitude at the heart of the causal relationship of beings to God, which gives rise to the need for both positive and negative predication concerning the divine mystery.

Commenting on *DN*, 7, 3, Aquinas re-echoes even more strongly the problem posed by Dionysius: while God knows all things through his essence, beyond intellect and sense and surpassing all beings, it remains to be asked how we can know God. He himself is neither intelligible nor sensible but beyond all intelligible and sensible things; nor is he any of the things which exist but is beyond all beings. All our knowledge, however, is received through the intellect or senses, and we do not know anything except things which exist.[41] (Note that for Aquinas the determination of human knowledge towards finite existing things is a positive ground for knowledge rather than a restriction, as it tends to be for Dionysius.)

---

[41] VII, iv, 728: Dicit ergo primo quod, cum dictum sit quod Deus cognoscit omnia per essentiam suam quae est super intellectum et sensum et super omnia existentia, restat quaerendum quomodo nos possumus cognoscere Deum, cum Ipse non sit intelligibilis, sed supra intelligibilia; neque sensibilis, sed supra sensibilia; neque est aliquid de numero existentium, sed super omnia existentia: omnis autem cognitio nostra est per intellectum vel sensum, nec cognoscimus nisi existentia.

We know God therefore, not by contemplating his essence (this is the nature of divine self-knowledge) but by reflecting on the order of the entire universe (*ex ordine totius universi*). Aquinas comments that when God produces things into being (*esse*), he not only gives them being, but rather produces being together with order in things (*esse cum ordine in rebus*).[42] Going further than Dionysius, Aquinas claims indeed that the very universe of creatures is offered to us by God, in order that through it we may know him. He explains this by the concept of exemplarity (itself grounded in causality), saying that the well-ordered universe has certain imperfect 'images and likenesses of divine things'; such divine realities are compared to the universe as primary exemplars to their images.[43]

Concerning the manner and method by which we ascend to God, Aquinas gives to the text his own nuanced interpretation. Where Dionysius, speaking of procedure, says that we ascend to God in an orderly way—ὁδῷ καὶ τάξει—(Sarracenus: *via et ordine*), Aquinas adopts this in a more metaphysical sense: that we ascend from the order of the universe as by a kind of pathway to God, *sicut quadam via et ordine*. He notes, furthermore, that it is by means of the *intellect* that we attain to this knowledge of God.

Our ascent to God is effected, continues Aquinas, in a threefold manner. In illustrating the procedure by which the discovery is fulfilled he follows here the sequence given by Dionysius: *in omnium ablatione et excessu et in omnium causa*—'First and principally, through the removal of all things, namely in so far as we judge none of those things which we observe in the order of creatures to be God or fitting of God.' Commenting that we ascend to God *secundario vero per excessum*, Aquinas explains that we remove from God the perfections of creatures such as life, wisdom etc., not because of any defect of God, but because he surpasses every perfection of created being. Finally, we know God, 'according to the causality of all things, since we consider that whatever is in creatures proceeds from God as from their Cause.'[44] In conclusion

---

[42] VII, iv, 733: Ipsa divina sapientia est omnium causa effectiva, inquantum res producit in esse et non solum rebus dat esse, sed etiam esse cum ordine in rebus.

[43] VII, iv, 729: Non ergo cognoscimus Deum, videntes Eius essentiam, sed cognoscimus Ipsum ex ordine totius universi. Ipsa enim universitas creaturarum est nobis a Deo proposita ut per eam Deum cognoscamus, inquantum universum ordinatum habet quasdam imagines et assimilationes imperfectas divinorum quae comparantur ad ipsas sicut principalia exemplaria ad imagines.

[44] Ibid.: Sic ergo ex ordine universi, sicut quadam via et ordine, ascendimus per intellectum, secundum nostram virtutem ad Deum, qui est super omnia; et hoc tribus modis: primo quidem et principaliter in omnium ablatione, inquantum scilicet nihil horum quae in creaturarum ordine inspicimus, Deum aestimamus aut Deo conveniens: secundario vero per excessum: non enim creaturarum perfectiones ut vitam, sapientiam et huiusmodi,

Aquinas comments that our knowledge operates in a reverse manner to that of divine cognition: God knows creatures by his nature, whereas we know God through creatures.

It has been suggested that the discernment of a *threefold* path of knowing God corresponds in fact to Aquinas' own reading of the text,[45] and that in the present passage Dionysius speaks only of two means of knowing God: the removal of all things from God as transcendent and the attribution of all things to him as cause. In other words what for Aquinas are two operations—the removal of all things from God, and his affirmation as eminently transcending them all—are regarded by Dionysius as one; their intention is identical. The 'removal' has meaning only if complemented by transcendent attribution. Causal reflection, on the other hand, and its discovery of God as origin of all things, may operate as an independent rational activity, even though it must be followed by a movement of thought towards the transcendence of the cause, which is purified through the removal of every finite manner of perfection.

We have seen earlier that Dionysius presents what he takes to be two ways: an affirmative path, which follows primarily the power of causal reasoning, and a negative path, also grounded in causality but which brings into focus the intransgressible distance between finite and infinite by denying of God all manner of perfection inherent in creatures while, in a thrust of hyperbole, identifying with God these perfections themselves in their transcendent intensity. We stressed the fundamental unity of these ablative and eminent moments of the negative path for Dionysius.

Aquinas, however, bringing refined metaphysical insight to bear in an almost verbatim consideration of the text, distinguishes more adequately within the theory of Dionysius between the remotive and transcendent moments of the negative approach. He discerns among the perfections revealed in beings those which connote, on the one hand, some specific limitation and, on the other, those which, being free from such restriction, may be present in God according to an infinite degree. He is thus able to distinguish between concepts which must be removed from God absolutely and those which are denied only in their creaturely mode in order to be attributed to him in a pre-

---

Deo auferimus propter defectum Dei, sed propter hoc quod omnem perfectionem creaturae excedit, propterea removemus ab Eo sapientiam, quia omnem sapientiam excedit: tertio, secundum causalitatem omnium dum consideramus quod quidquid est in creaturis a Deo procedit sicut a Causa.

[45] Jean Vanneste, *Le mystère de Dieu*, p. 113; Vladimir Lossky, *Théologie négative et connaissance de Dieu chez Maître Eckhart*, pp. 21-2, n. 31.

eminent manner (life, wisdom etc.). He brings thus to the text of Dionysius a profound and valuable clarification.

Another interesting transformation which the Dionysian theme undergoes as it is incorporated into Aquinas' thought is the variety of sequences according to which the three moments are presented throughout his works. In his Commentary Aquinas follows the sequence given in the text of Dionysius. We have seen the prime importance which Dionysius gives to the negative and transcendent knowledge of God. He grounds both ablative and transcendent attribution clearly, however, in the causal relation of beings to God. Predication is affirmative or negative (either ablative or transcendent) depending on whether creatures are understood as revealing or concealing God. This primacy of causality is also adopted by Aquinas in the triptych tableau with which he presents Dionysius' doctrine. It will be of interest to examine the various models according to which Aquinas in his own speculation arranges the ways of causality, negation and eminence.

The present instance, where Aquinas in the immediate context of his Commentary enumerates the importance of the three ways according to their appearance in the text, is an example of his recurring desire to interpret Dionysius in a spirit sympathetic even to the letter. Thus he accepts here what we might call the mystical priority according to which Dionysius treats God, respectively, as Non-Being, Transcendent Being and Cause of Being. Viewing Dionysius' works as an ensemble in the Introduction to his Commentary, he displays his own commitment to a metaphysical method in seeking the foundation of reality; natural reasoning begins with causality; affirmation precedes negation and advances in its knowledge of God via the proper attribution of metaphysical perfections and the symbolic transference of sensible imagery. Having been attributed in a human sense such determinations are subsequently removed: absolutely in the case of sensible attributes and, in the case of metaphysical perfections in respect of their creaturely character, as a prelude to their transcendent identification with God who is their full subsistence. This schema corresponds indeed to some extent to Dionysius' fundamental reliance on causality.

Similarly, in his very early Commentary on the *Sentences*, where a profound debt to Dionysius is already evident, Aquinas adapts the formula of *DN*, 7, 3 to his own logical and metaphysical method in the discovery of God: *Dicit enim quod ex creaturis tribus modis devenimus in Deum: scilicet per causalitatem, per remotionem, per eminentiam.*[46] Etienne Gilson has suggested that Aquinas has here reversed the entire

---

[46] *In I Sent.*, 3, divisio primae partis textus, p. 88.

doctrine of Dionysius.⁴⁷ This is somewhat of an exaggeration. It is indeed an inversion of the text from *DN*, 7, 3, but we have indicated that Dionysius himself, in the broader perspective of his philosophic thought, grounds both negative and eminent predication alike in causality. Because of its comprehensive character, pithily summarising his approach to the mystery of God, there has been a tendency to reduce Dionysius' theology to this phrase of the *triplex via*—even though it is not fully explicit as a threefold path. However, in pointing out that Aquinas is in no way servile to the formula of Dionysius, it is worth remembering that neither is Dionysius bound to rigid formulae in expressing his thought. Thus in contrasting, for example, human cognition with the transcendence of God's nature, he may give primary significance to negation and eminence; in the order of discovery, however, causality is given priority, since it is immediately accessible. It is in this context of discovery that Aquinas here arranges the steps of the *triplex via*.

The adaptation of the threefold principle in this passage of the Commentary on the *Sentences* corresponds indeed more adequately to the *via inventionis* leading from beings to God. It presents a natural and logical succession, and reflects the metaphysical penetration of human enquiry which commences with finite things and proceeds to disclose the existence and intimate presence of the creative origin at the centre of beings. It is according to the measure of this presence and interiority that Aquinas distinguishes the steps of the *triplex via*, discovering the immediacy of creative causality in the *esse* of finite beings, and assessing according to its different degrees the intensity of their participation in divine Being. He thus explains the structure of the *triplex via* according to the sequence of causality, remotion and eminence:

> The reason is that the being (*esse*) of a creature derives from another. We are led accordingly, therefore, to the cause by which it is. Now this may occur in two ways: either with respect to that which is received: and here we are guided by the way of causality (*per modum causalitatis*); or with regard to the manner in which it is received (*modum recipiendi*), since it is received imperfectly. And here we have two ways, (firstly), according to the removal of imperfection from God and, (secondly), according as that which is received in a creature is more perfect and noble in the creator: this is the way of eminence.⁴⁸

---

⁴⁷ Etienne Gilson, *Le Thomisme*, p. 165. Gilson's cursory comments are based, in fact upon a misreading; he quotes *vita* instead of *via*, indicating mistaken reliance on a Latin version rather than the text of Dionysius.

⁴⁸ *In I Sent.*, dist. 3, div. primae partis textus: Harum autem diversitas sumitur secundum vias deveniendi ex creaturis in Deum, quas Dionysius ponit, VII cap. De div.

This is, moreover, the order of method which Aquinas adopts in the *Summa Theologiae*. The entire philosophic treatment of the question of God in this monumental synthesis is profoundly characterised by a method and principles deriving from Dionysius: both in the manner of affirming God's existence and of naming him in virtue of his relation to beings—more correctly, the relation of beings to God. This will become evident in more detail when we consider Q. 13, where Aquinas relies on Dionysius for his theory of the names of God. The following text, summarising his speculative approach to the existence of God, will be sufficient evidence of the thoroughgoing influence of Dionysius. It is worth citing at length; the question which Aquinas raises in Q. 12, art. 12 is the very one raised by Dionysius in *DN*, 7, 3: How can we know God since we only experience finite beings? The response too reflects the triple way of Dionysius, although the order is that preferred by Aquinas. We may also detect here a less agnostic nuance within his usual position that we can know of God only *that* he is—not *what* he is, but rather what he is *not*. From the existence of sensible things, he asserts, we know of God firstly that he is; but secondly, from his relation to creatures, we may discover what must belong to him in order to be their cause and to transcend them. We note the inspiration of Dionysius in Aquinas' solution to the question of how we know God:

> Our intellect cannot be led by sense so far as to see the essence of God; because sensible creatures are effects of God which do not equal the power of God, their cause. Hence from the knowledge of sensible things the whole power of God cannot be known; nor therefore can his essence be seen. But because they are his effects and depend on their cause, we can be led from them so far as to know of God that he exists and that he has whatever must belong to the first cause of all things which is beyond all that is caused. Thus we know about his relation to creatures: that he is the cause of all things; also that creatures differ from him since he is none of the things which are caused by him; and that these are removed from him not through any defect, but because he transcends them.[49]

Nom. Dicit enim quod ex creaturis tribus modis devenimus in Deum: scilicet per causalitatem, per remotionem, per eminentiam. Et ratio huius est, quia esse creaturae est ab altero. Unde secundum hoc ducimur in causam a qua est. Hoc autem potest esse dupliciter. Aut quantum ad id quod receptum est; et sic ducimur per modum causalitatis: aut, quantum ad modum recipiendi, quia imperfecte recipitur; et sic habemus duos modos, scilicet secundum remotionem imperfectionis a Deo et secundum hoc quod illud quod receptum est in creatura, perfectius et nobilius est in Creatore; et ita est modus per eminentiam.

[49] *ST*, I, 12, 12: Ex sensibilibus autem non potest usque ad hoc noster intellectus pertingere, quod divinam essentiam videat: quia creaturae sensibiles sunt effectus Dei virtutem causae non adaequentes. Unde ex sensibilium cognitione non potest tota Dei virtus cognosci, et per consequens nec eius essentia videri. Sed quia sunt effectus a causa

We find a slight variation on this order, together with a more detailed statement of methodic principle concerning the itinerary leading from sensible things to God, in Aquinas' Commentary on the Epistle to the Romans. Here again the tableau begins with causality, but the emphasis is on knowledge through negation. Once more the passage is worth reviewing in its entirety:

> There is something with regard to God which is entirely unknown to man in this life, namely, what God is (*quid est Deus*)...And this is so because man's knowledge begins with those things which are connatural to him, namely, sensible creatures, which are not adequate to represent the divine essence. Nevertheless man can know God from creatures of this sort in three ways, as Dionysius says in the *Divine Names*: first through causality; for since such creatures are imperfect and changeable, they must be reduced to some unchangeable and perfect principle. And from this we know that God exists (*de Deo an est*). Secondly, by way of excellence (*per viam excellentiae*); for all things are reduced to a first principle, not as to a proper and univocal cause, as man begets man, but as to a universal and transcendent cause. And from this we know that he is above all things. Thirdly, by way of negation because if he is a transcendent cause nothing which is in creatures can belong to him.[50]

The same sequence of the three moments is given in the Commentary on Boethius' *De Trinitate*, where Aquinas outlines the epistemological principles required for the divine things transcending sense and imagination:

> We come to know them from what is apprehended by the sense and imagination. This we do either by way of causality, as from an effect we come to know a cause which is not commensurate with the effect but surpasses it; or by transcendence or by negation, as when we separate from

---

dependentes, ex eis in hoc perduci possumus, ut cognoscamus de Deo an est; et ut cognoscamus de ipso ea quae necesse est ei convenire secundum quod est prima omnium causa, excedens omnia sua causata. Unde cognoscimus de ipso habitudinem ipsius ad creaturas, quod scilicet est omnium causa; et differentiam creaturarum ab ipso, quod scilicet ipse non est aliquid eorum quae ab eo causantur: et quod haec non removentur ab eo propter eius defectum, sed quia superexcedit. See also *ST*, I, 13, 1; I, 13, 10 ad 5; I, 87, 7, ad 3; *In I Sent.*, 22. 1. 2.

[50] *In Epistolam ad Romanos* I, lect. 6: Sciendum est ergo, quod aliquid circa Deum est omnino ignotum homini in hac vita, scilicet quid est Deus . . . et hoc ideo, quia cognitio hominis incipit ab his quae sunt ei connaturalia, scilicet a sensibilibus creaturis, quae non sunt proportionatae ad repraesentandam divinam essentiam. Potest tamen homo ex huiusmodi creaturis Deum tripliciter cognoscere, ut Dionysius dicit in libro de divinis nominibus. Uno quidem modo per causalitatem; quia enim huiusmodi creaturae sint defectibiles et mutabiles, necesse est eas reducere ad aliquod principium immobile et perfectum: et secundum hoc cognoscitur de Deo an est. Secundo per viam excellentiae: non enim reducuntur omnia in primum principium sicut in propriam causam et univocam, prout homo hominem generat; sed sicut in causam communem et excedentem: et ex hoc cognoscitur quod est super omnia. Tertio per viam negationis: quia si est causa excedens, nihil eorum quae sunt in creaturis, potest ei competere.

such beings whatever the sense or imagination apprehends. These are the ways of knowing divine things from the sensible world laid down by Dionysius in his *Divine Names.*[51]

On the same question of the knowledge of immaterial forms, Aquinas repeats in the subsequent article his reliance on the *triplex via*, giving primacy to the role of negation: 'We know *that* they exist, and instead of knowing *what* they are we have knowledge of them by way of negation, by way of causality and by way of transcendence.'[52] And in his Commentary on the *Sentences*, he pursues the threefold path to prove the intelligence of God, *per remotionem, per causalitatem, per eminentiam.*[53]

Yet another very valuable expression of the threefold discovery is given by Aquinas in the same Commentary on Boethius (Q 1, art. 2), where attention is directly focused on the unequal relation of cause and effect between God and creatures. From the existence of an effect whose likeness does not equal in measure the power of its cause (as it does, for example, in the case of one member of a species begotten by another), we can only know *that* a cause exists. Such is the knowledge, says Aquinas, which we may have of God. However, he adds, a cause is more perfectly known when the relation of the cause to its effect is better revealed through the effect. Such a relation may be considered azccording to three aspects. Firstly, according to the emanation or emission (*secundum progressionem*) of the effect from its cause; secondly in so far as the effect resembles its cause, and finally according as it fails to resemble its cause perfectly. Thus, says Aquinas, the human mind advances under three aspects towards a knowledge of God, although it does not succeed in knowing what he is, only that he is. God is known in the first place according as his power and efficacy are more perfectly known in creating beings (*in producendo res*). Secondly, his eminence is praised all the more perfectly in so far as he is known as the cause of more noble effects, since these bear greater likeness to

---

[51] *In Boeth. de Trin.*, 6, 2: Sed tamen ex his, quae sensu vel imaginatione apprehenduntur, in horum cognitionem devenimus vel per viam causalitatis, sicut ex effectu causa perpenditur, quae non est effectui commensurata, sed excellens, vel per excessum vel per remotionem, quando omnia, quae sensus vel imaginatio apprehendit, a rebus huiusmodi separamus; quos modos cognoscendi divina ex sensibilibus ponit Dionysius in libro De divinis nominibus. Translation, A. Maurer, *The Division and Methods of the Sciences*, p. 64.

[52] *In Boeth. de Trin.*, 6, 3, p. 223: Ita ergo de formis immaterialibus cognoscimus an est et habemus de eis loco cognitionis quid est cognitionem per negationem, per causalitatem et per excessum, quos etiam modos Dionysius ponit in libro De divinis nominibus.

[53] *In I Sent.*, 35, 1, 1, p. 809. As examples of the procedural primacy of negation, we may cite: *In I Sent.*, 35, 11; *De Potentia* 9, 7; *De Malo* 16, 8. ad 3; *Super ad Rom.*, 1, 6.

him. But thirdly, God is known even more and more as removed from everything which is manifest in effects. Dionysius notes, therefore, according to Aquinas, that from the excess and negation (of the perfection apparent in beings) we know God as cause of all things, i.e. through the transcendent attribution of perfection and the removal of all limitation (*cognoscitur ex omnium causa et excessu et ablatione*).[54]

Although in the majority of his references to the triple way of discovery, Aquinas gives primacy to either causality or negation, there is in *ST*, I, 13 a unique and singularly appropriate adaptation in order to denote God's absolute transcendence. St Thomas is here considering God in his absolute pre-eminence as source of beings. As their creative origin he resides untouched by beings, subsisting in supreme and removed transcendence. According to Aquinas this is precisely the meaning intended by those who name God—He who is beyond all being, the principle of all, removed from all.

> From the divine effects we cannot know the divine nature in itself, so as to know what it is; but only by way of eminence, causality, and negation. It is in this way that the name God signifies the divine nature. For this name was imposed to signify something existing above all that is, which is the origin of all things and is removed from all. This is what those who name God intend to signify.[55]

To the question of divine transcendence we shall return. In concluding our review of the many occasions where Aquinas adapts to his own thought the triptych tableau of Dionysius, let us conclude with a brief but dense text where the influence of Dionysius for Aquinas' entire philosphy of God is plainly evident. It occurs early in his Commentary on the *Sentences* of Peter Lombard, where Aquinas asks whether God may be known through creatures:

---

[54] *In Boeth. de Trin.*. 1, 2, Resp., p. 66: Quae quidem habitudo in effectu non pertingente ad aequalitatem suae causae attenditur secundum tria, scilicet secundum progressionem effectus a causa et secundum hoc quod effectus consequitur de similitudine suae causae et secundum hoc quod deficit ab eius perfecta consecutione. Et sic tripliciter mens humana proficit in cognitione dei, quamvis ad cognoscendum quid est non pertingat, sed an est solum. Primo, secundum quod perfectius cognoscitur eius efficacia in producendo res. Secundo, prout nobiliorum effectuum causa cognoscitur, qui cum eius similitudinem aliquam gerant, magis eminentiam eius commendant. Tertio in hoc quod magis ac magis cognoscitur elongatus ab omnibus his, quae in effectibus apparent. Unde dicit Dionysius in libro De divinis nominibus quod cognoscitur ex omnium causa et excessu et ablatione.

[55] *ST*, I, 13, 8, ad 2: Sed ex effectibus divinis divinam naturam non possumus cognoscere secundum quod in se est, ut sciamus de ea quid est; sed per modum eminentiae et causalitatis et negationis. Et sic nomen Deus significat naturam divinam. Impositum est enim nomen hoc ad aliquid significandum supra omne existens, quod est principium omnium, et remotum ab omnibus. Hoc enim intendunt significare nominantes Deum.

Since a creature proceeds by exemplarity from God himself as from a cause which is by analogy in some way similar (because every creature imitates him according to the possibility of its nature), it is possible to arrive at God from creatures by three ways: causality, remotion and eminence.[56]

Here are interfused all the metaphysical dimensions involved in the mysterious relation of beings to God: causation and exemplarity, participation and analogy, a nexus of relations which are opened up to us along a three-line path of discovery. Regardless of the order followed by Aquinas, it is significant that St Thomas should consider the diverse ways of arriving at a knowledge of God as best articulated according to the fundamental structure of the threefold way of Dionysius. He judges the three moments to be an adequate and exhaustive programme for all metaphysical reflection implied in 'revealing' or 'demonstrating' God. The various arrangements of the three functions point only to the organic unity and the interpenetrated character of their movements in seeking a knowledge of God. The ease with which Aquinas frequently adapts and transforms the triune structure, according to the nuance he wishes to accentuate, shows the freedom and alertness of his thought and its vibrant openness to the ever profound mystery of finite reality in the intimacy of its divine origin.

Having considered the epistemology of this threefold itinerary, we proceed to examine more closely from a metaphysical point of view one of the essential relations between God and creatures: their similitude. This will give a clearer understanding of the fundamental meaning of positive and negative theology in light of the absolute transcendence of God.

THE PRINCIPLE OF SIMILITUDE

The notion of 'similitude' is itself dependent on that of causality, and fundamentally presupposes the principle *Omne agens agit sibi simile*: every cause necessarily produces an effect bearing a resemblance to itself.[57] Efficient causality implies exemplarity; similitude is a necessary mode of presence of causal action. Effects proceed from their causes

---

[56] *In I Sent.*, 3, 1, art. 3, p. 96: Respondeo dicendum, quod, cum creatura exemplariter procedat ab ipso Deo sicut a causa quodammodo simili per analogiam, (eo scilicet quod quaelibet creatura eum imitatur secundum possibilitatem naturae suae), ex creaturis potest in Deum deveniri tribus illis modis quibus dictum est, scilicet per causalitatem, remotionem, eminentiam. The phrase in parentheses is not given in the text by Mandonnet. It appears in the Parma edition and is recognised by the editors of the *Index Thomisticus*.

[57] III, 227.

through a process of similitude or assimilation, says Aquinas, and in so far as it possesses within itself the likeness of its effects, a cause may be known and named by virtue of this exemplarity.[58] This is the rationale of all divine nomination. However, the similitude of the exemplar is present differently within its effect, depending on the kind of causality involved. By the same token, a cause may contain variously within itself the likeness of its effect according to the manner in which it is cause. Thus Aquinas distinguishes various kinds of causality, such as the generation of natural species and the activity of artistic creation.[59] As distinct from these, God causes the existence of beings not by reason of a specific nature (as man generates man) or through a relation of artisanship which is added to his nature, but *per ipsum esse*. He emphasises that the causality of creation derives from God by virtue of his total being—divine intellect and will are identical with God's Being. It proceeds from the plenitude of his essential goodness and affects the creature radically in all its reality. God prepossesses, therefore, within himself the likeness of all his effects.[60] The effect also bears in its totality a similarity to its divine origin. This relation of causality, more precisely the status of beings as creatures, is indeed their most intimate and fundamental determination. The creative presence of God pervades wholly and completely, begetting beings into existence at their innermost core. Beings are inconceivable, independent of their creative cause.

Disclosing this relation of dependence at its origin, and the manner in which it is effected, we may, therefore, from his effects come to a knowledge of the creative cause. 'Transfusing his similitude in some manner to all things, he may thus be named from the names of creatures.'[61] Since all perfections emanate to creatures from God, he may be named from each effect which derives from his goodness: 'God is named from his effects since the effects pre-exist super-eminently in him.'[62] This is what Aquinas himself calls the *regula magisterialis*, which he adopts from Dionysius: 'All names designating effects in creatures belong to the Divine Essence.'[63]

---

[58] I, iii, 86: Considerandum est quod cum effectus procedant per quamdam assimilationem a suis causis, secundum modum quo aliquid est causa, praehabet in se similitudinem sui effectus. I, iii, 89: Omnis autem causa intantum potest nominari ex nomine sui effectus, inquantum habet in se similitudinem eius.

[59] I, iii, 86.

[60] I, iii, 88: Quia igitur Deus est bonus, non quidem bonus quasi bonitatem participans, sed sicut ipsa essentia bonitatis, non per aliquam dispositionem creatam est causa rerum, sed 'per ipsum esse' suum 'est causa omnium existentium'; nec per hoc excluditur quin agat per intellectum et voluntatem, quia intelligere Eius et velle est ipsum esse Eius. Sic igitur in Ipso sua causa praehabet similitudinem omnium suorum effectuum.

[61] I, i, 30: Et ipse quidem est causa existendi omnibus, transfundens in omnia aliqualiter suam similitudinem, ut sic ex nominibus creatorum nominari possit.

[62] VII, ii, 708: Deus nominatur a suis effectibus, quia effectus super eminenter praeexistunt in Ipso.

[63] II, i, 126: . . . connumeranda sunt omnia nomina causalia, idest quae designant

It is by this exemplarity or similitude, Aquinas repeatedly stresses, that God proceeds into and is present within his effects.[64] The assimilation of creatures to divine Being is, however, necessarily deficient,[65] and since human cognition is properly speaking concerned with creatures, the knowledge we have of their cause is valid only according to the analogy of finite reality, i.e. in proportion to its participation in divine Being. God's similitude is in each case 'proportioned' to the finite measure of beings. According to the principle of analogy continually affirmed by Aquinas, beings thus reveal God in the measure that each receives a participation in his infinite perfection.

Aquinas expresses as follows both the positive and negative aspects of our divine knowledge through creatures:

> It is evident that whatever (perfections) are found in creatures pre-exist more eminently in God. But creatures are manifest to us; God, however, is hidden. According, therefore, as the perfections of things derive from God to creatures through a certain participation, that which was hidden is brought into openness; and this occurs according to the determined proportion of each thing.[66]

God, who is their infinite cause, remains in his nature unparticipated by creatures; this revelation of his perfection through creatures nevertheless constitutes the positive measure of our knowledge of him— apparently a paradox, more properly a mystery. 'We know God only in the measure in which we know the participations of his goodness.'[67] But since he so utterly transcends them, God remains in his nature ineffably unknown; the divine likenesses impressed in things are infinitely deficient in revealing their source and exemplar.

This twofold value of creation, both revealing and restricting our knowledge of God's perfection, which, as we saw, is underlined by Dionysius, finds a resounding echo in Aquinas' works and especially in

---

Deum ut principium processionis perfectionum quae emanant ab Ipso in creaturas, scilicet: bonum, pulchrum, existens, vitae generativum, sapiens et quaecumque alia per quae Causa omnium bonorum nominatur ex dono suae bonitatis. Et ex hoc potest accipi regula magisterialis quod omnia nomina designantia effectum in creaturas, pertinent ad divinam Essentiam. See *ST*, I, 5, 2.

[64] II, i, 136; II, iv, 178, 185f.; II, vi, 220; V, iii, 672-3.

[65] I, i, 29: Esse autem rerum creatarum deductum est ab Esse divino secundum quamdam deficientem assimilationem.

[66] I, ii, 51: Manifestum est enim quod quaecumque in creaturis sunt, in Deo praeexistunt eminentius. Sed creaturae quidem manifestae sunt nobis, Deus autem occultus. Sic igitur, secundum quod rerum perfectiones a Deo per quamdam participationem derivantur in creaturas, fit traditio in manifestum eius quod erat occultum; et hoc fit . . . secundum proportionem determinatam uniuscuiusque.

[67] II, ii, 135: Intantum Deus potest a nobis cognosci, inquantum participationes suae bonitatis cognoscimus; secundum autem quod est in se, est nobis occultus. See also II, iv, 178.

his Commentary on the *Divine Names*. In clarifying, for example, Dionysius' assertion that God is known both in all things and apart from all things, through both ignorance and knowledge, Aquinas adopts with equal emphasis Dionysius' twofold approach of, on the one hand, positive divine attribution through causality and, on the other, the transcendence of God by way of negation. God is known in all things, says Aquinas, as in his effects; and apart from everything, since he is removed from all things and surpasses them. Likewise, God is known through knowledge, since whatever falls within our knowledge has been brought forth by him; and he is equally known through ignorance in so far as we best know God in the knowledge that we are ignorant of what he really is.[68] Aquinas summarises the solution to the twofold value of knowledge by disclosing the profound relation binding beings to God: 'Causally God is all in all, but essentially he is none of the things which are in reality.' Aquinas provides here a metaphysical explanation for the profound contrast between our positive and negative knowledge of God: rooted in the relation which God bears to creatures, it is marked on the one hand by an intimate causal or virtual presence and on the other by a radical metaphysical transcendence or independence. God may thus be known as cause from any reality and in any manner whatsoever, but more profoundly, i.e. essentially, in no manner and from no being such as he is.[69] Directing in turn our attention specifically to the positive and negative knowledge of God, let us consider first in what sense God may be named affirmatively from creatures. We will examine this in Aquinas' Commentary and in parallel passages which point to the constant influence of Dionysius in this teaching.

PARTICIPATION: GROUND OF PREDICATION

The key inspiration in Aquinas' theory of divine nomination is the fundamental theory, inherited from Dionysius, of the participation and

---

[68] VII, iv, 731: Deus cognoscitur in omnibus, sicut in effectibus et sine omnibus, sicut ab omnibus remotus et omnia excedens; et propter hoc etiam cognoscitur Deus per cognitionem nostram, quia quidquid in nostra cognitione cadit, accipimus ut ab Eo adductum; et iterum cognoscitur per ignorantiam nostram, inquantum scilicet hoc ipsum est Deum cognoscere, quod nos scimus nos ignorare de Deo quid sit.

[69] VII, iv, 731: Rursus Deus est omnia in omnibus causaliter, cum tamen nihil sit eorum quae sunt in rebus essentialiter: et ideo, quidquid in rebus existens cognoscatur vel intellectu vel sensu vel quocumque praedictorum modorum, in omnibus istis cognitis quodammodo cognoscitur Deus, sicut causa, cum tamen ex nullo cognoscatur sicut est. See I, iii, 96, 98.

pre-eminent presence of all perfection in God. The perfections of all creatures are comprehended and anticipated by their creator according to an infinite degree of intensity. From among the numerous passages which we might cite as evidence of Dionysius' primary influence, a brief paragraph from the *Divine Names* will suffice:

> It is as Cause of all and as transcending all that he is rightly nameless and yet has the names of everything that is . . . For the unnamed goodness is not just the cause of cohesion or life or perfection . . . but it actually contains everything beforehand within itself—and this in an uncomplicated and boundless manner—and it is thus by virtue of the unlimited goodness of its single all-creative Providence.[70]

This teaching is echoed by Aquinas when he expresses the perfection of God and creatures according to their distinct manner of presence: 'The perfections which pre-exist in God in a unified and simple manner are received in creatures as divided and multiple.'[71] This is in turn the axis of his theory of divine names. Aquinas remarks: 'That which is said both of God and creatures is said because of the relation which binds the creature towards God, as its principle and cause, in whom pre-exist excellently all perfections of existing things.'[72] Through the divine similitude present in each, they participate in infinite goodness and reveal, each in its measure, the providence and perfection of God.

It follows that God may be praised by a plurality of names, which attribute to him as origin the perfections granted as participations.[73] All names may be attributed to God since he pre-possesses the fullness of perfections distributed in a limited measure among beings and known under a diversity of names. God may be named in an infinite number of ways.[74] Aquinas stresses, however, that he is called 'good', 'living', 'wise' and other such names, not due to a multiplicity or diversity in his nature—since all perfections are unified in him—but because it is from various perfections of creatures that we adopt the names which we attribute to God as the diffusive principle of all perfection.[75] This is indeed, he suggests, implicit in our very method of attribution. While

---

[70] 1, 7, 25-26, Luibheid, p. 56.

[71] *ST*, I, 13, 4: Quae quidem perfectiones in Deo praeexistunt unite et simpliciter: in creaturis vero recipiuntur divise et multipliciter.

[72] *ST*, I, 13, 5: Non enim possumus nominare Deum nisi ex creaturis. Et sic, eo quod dicitur de Deo et creaturis, dicitur secundum quod est aliquis ordo creaturae ad Deum, ut ad principium et causam, in qua praeexistunt excellenter omnes rerum perfectiones.

[73] II, iii, 160.

[74] XII, 941: . . . qui infinitis modis nominari potest in suis effectibus.

[75] I, ii, 54: Quod enim Deus dicatur bonus, vivus, sapiens et multis aliis nominibus nominetur, non est ex aliqua multitudine seu diversitate in eius natura existente (quia omnia haec in Eo unum sunt), sed ex diversis perfectionibus creaturarum accipimus diversa nomina, quae attribuimus Deo sicut primo Principio omnium horum processuum.

our intellect knows God, who is absolutely one and simple in himself, according to different conceptions, it is nevertheless aware that to all of these conceptions there corresponds a single and simple reality.[76]

St Thomas summarises the parallel relations of implication between God and the multiplicity of creatures, both on the level of participation in being and of attribution:

> As to the diverse perfections of creatures there corresponds a unique and simple principle, represented by the diverse perfections of creatures in a varied and multiple manner, similarly, to the various and multiple conceptions of our intellect there corresponds something absolutely one and simple, which is understood imperfectly according to these conceptions.[77]

Here we have an expression of the balanced realism of Aquinas' theism: God is known and named through creatures, albeit in an imperfect manner.

A further conclusion imposes itself regarding the nature of divine attribution: the perfections which are drawn from creatures are referred to God not only in a causal manner, but according to their full and essential signification. Names attributing perfections to God signify these in their unlimited intensity. Names which refer to perfections which are limited and composite in beings, signify in God a unified and unlimited reality. Specific names, Aquinas notes in his Commentary, signify in creatures something determinate and distinct from all else; employed in divine predication they indicate such a perfection not as finite but infinite. The name 'wisdom' signifies among created things a perfection distinct from justice, confined to a determinate genus and species. Referred to the divine it does not signify a reality restricted to genus or species, distinct from other perfections, but something infinite.[78]

The innumerable variety of perfections apparent throughout the universe are present in divine Being not finitely or disparately but in an infinite and unified manner. 'All things pre-exist in God, since he is the

---

[76] *ST*, I, 13, 12: Sed quamvis intelligat ipsum sub diversis conceptionibus, cognoscit tamen quod omnibus suis conceptionibus respondet una et eadem res simplex. *In DN*, II, ii, 135: Cum omnis multitudo rerum a Principio primo effluat, primum Principium, secundum quod in se consideratur, unum est.

[77] *ST*, I, 13, 4: Sicut igitur diversis perfectionibus creaturarum respondet unum simplex principium, repraesentatum per diversas perfectiones creaturarum varie et multipliciter; ita variis et multiplicibus conceptionibus intellectus nostri respondet unum omnino simplex, secundum huiusmodi conceptiones imperfecte intellectum.

[78] I, iii, 101: Cum singula nomina determinate aliquid significant distinctum ab aliis venientia in divinam praedicationem, non significant illud finite sed infinite: sicut nomen sapientiae prout in rebus creatis accipitur significat aliquid distinctum a iustitia, ut puta in determinato genere et specie existens, sed cum in divinis accipitur, non significat aliquid determinatum ad genus et ad speciem seu distinctionem ab aliis perfectionibus, sed aliquid infinitum.

origin of all; he produces all substances according to a power which exceeds all substances, from which it follows that all things pre-exist in God substantially and according to a single virtue.'[79] As the pre-eminent cause of all beings, the names of such perfections pertain, therefore, more properly to God. This is the background to the key pronouncement of Aquinas' positive theology in the *Summa Theologiae*: 'Such names are spoken of God not only causally, but moreover essentially. When God is called good, or wise, it is signified not only that he is the cause of wisdom or goodness, but that these pre-exist in him more eminently.'[80]

Such perfections pre-subsist in God, Aquinas notes, in a manner more eminent than we can understand or express.[81] God is the unlimited actuality of all perfections. He embodies the full signification of their terms even though when used in his regard their full sense exceeds our comprehension. Thus we have the marvel of names which are applied to God but which denote him precisely as beyond their signification. Aquinas expresses this well: 'The name "wise" when said of man somehow circumscribes and comprehends the reality signified: not when it is said of God; it leaves the reality signified as uncomprehended and exceeding the signification of the name.'[82] How may perfections which surpass reality, reflection and language be named validly by terms which place a restriction upon their infinite nature?

The key to Aquinas' solution and the manner by which he arrives, moreover, at a proper foundation of Dionysius' theory, is the distinction to which he points between such a reality or perfection in itself and the manner in which it is signified by us. This teaching is best summed up in the following passage from the *Summa Theologiae*:

> In those names which we attribute to God, two things are to be considered: namely the perfections themselves which are signified (*ipsas perfectiones significatas*), such as 'goodness', 'life' and suchlike; and our manner of signifying them (*modus significandi*). That which such names signify befits God properly, indeed more properly than creatures themselves and is spoken with priority of him. In their manner of signification, however, they may not be spoken properly of God: since they have a mode of signifying which belongs to creatures.[83]

---

[79] V, ii, 662: Sic enim omnia praeexistunt in Deo, sicut Ipse omnium est productivus; producit autem omnes substantias secundum virtutem quae excedit substantias omnes; unde sequitur quod omnia in Deo praeexistant, secundum virtutem substantialiter unam.

[80] *ST*, I, 13, 6: Huiusmodi nomina non solum dicuntur de Deo causaliter, sed etiam essentialiter. Cum enim dicitur quod Deus est bonus, vel sapiens, non solum significatur quod ipse sit causa sapientiae vel bonitatis, sed quod haec in eo eminentius praeexistunt.

[81] *ST*, I, 13, 2, ad 2: . . . in eo praeexsistit vita, licet eminentiori modo quam intelligatur vel significetur.

[82] *ST*, I 13, 5: Et sic, cum hoc nomen sapiens de homine dicitur, quodammodo circumscribit et comprehendit rem significatam: non autem cum dicitur de Deo, sed relinquit rem significatam ut incomprehensam, et excedentem nominis significationem.

[83] I, 13, 3: In nominibus vero quae Deo attribuimus, duo est considerare: scilicet ipsas

Because of its manner of signification there is thus an imperfection implicit in every name which we predicate, although the reality signified is proper to God in a manner which transcends the mode of signification. Names are therefore attributed to God only in respect of the reality which they denote and not according to their manner of signification. Aquinas articulates the doctrine of Dionysius around this distinction: 'Such names may therefore, as Dionysius teaches, be both affirmed and denied of God: affirmed indeed due to the meaning of the name; denied, however, due to its mode of signification.'[84]

The distinction allows Aquinas to make more precise what may be affirmed of God and what must be denied. Affirmed are the perfections themselves which are strictly proper to God alone; denied is the manner in which these perfections are experienced and understood by us—their *modus significandi*, which befits creatures alone. This is the pivotal point around which revolves the relation between positive and negative theology, grounding their unity and pointing their reciprocal progression towards transcendent or eminent predication. Aquinas thus sets in relation the limited value of positive theology and the positive value of negation. Having established the validity and truth of causal predication he proceeds to show that God is so immeasurably more than all we know, that he is best known through the removal of all our knowledge. Having advanced along the positive path and affirmed the unlimited perfection of divine Being we must retrace this path in order to remove the limiting measures of our own knowledge and experience.

Primacy of Negative Knowledge

Negative theology thus assumes for Aquinas a greatly superior role in understanding God. He indicates the limitations of positive theology

---

perfectiones significatas, ut bonitatem, vitam et huiusmodi; et modum significandi. Quantum igitur ad id quod significant huiusmodi nomina, proprie competunt Deo, et magis proprie quam ipsis creaturis, et per prius de eo dicuntur. Quantum vero ad modum significandi, non proprie dicuntur de Deo: habent enim modum significandi hunc qui creaturis competit. See *ST*, I, 13, 6; also *In DN*, V, iii, 673: Et omnia ista quae de Deo affirmantur [The Marietti edition gives 'affirmans'], possunt etiam ab eo negari, quia non ita conveniunt Ei sicut inveniuntur in rebus creatis et sicut intelliguntur a nobis et significantur. *De Potentia* 7, 2, ad 7; *In I Sent.*, 22, 1, 2.

[84] *Contra Gentiles* 1, 30: Et sic in omni nomine a nobis dicto, quantum ad modum significandi, imperfectio invenitur, quae Deo non competit, quamvis res significata aliquo eminenti modo Deo conveniat . . . Et quantum ad hoc nullum nomen Deo convenienter aptatur, sed solum quantum ad id ad quod significandum nomen imponitur. Possunt igitur, ut Dionysius docet, huiusmodi nomina et affirmari de Deo et negari: affirmari quidem, propter nominis rationem; negari vero, propter significandi modum.

and presents as its consequence the need for negative and transcendent theology. The intention of the latter is in no way negative; its purpose is not to diminish our appreciation of what knowledge we have gained, but to place God beyond all our estimation.

Early in his Commentary on the *Divine Names*, Aquinas notes with approval that, for Dionysius, granting the names gained through causal reflection, 'that itself which God is remains hidden.'[85] We know God, according to Aquinas, only as first principle of all perfection and as cause through his goodness in all participations; what he is in himself remains inscrutable and ineffable. God diffuses his perfection by way of similitude, but abides himself unparticipated, beyond all things, in his unique singularity.[86] He subsists superior to his participations— Being, Life and similar gifts which are shared by creatures; and since it is connatural to created intellect to understand and express these, it can neither understand nor express God himself.[87] Within the scope of our intellect, says Aquinas, falls only created and finite being which is totally deficient in contrast to uncreated and infinite Being; we must therefore understand that God is beyond all that we can apprehend by intellect.[88] He concludes: 'God is greater than all we can say, greater than all that we can know; and not merely does he transcend our language and our knowledge, but he is beyond the comprehension of every mind whatsoever, even of angelic minds, and beyond the being of every substance.'[89] We find a comment which is unusual for Aquinas: 'It seems indeed ridiculous to wish to treat of the names of something which cannot be named.'[90]

---

[85] I, ii, 41: Ostendit quomodo, post huiusmodi cognitionem, hoc ipsum quod Deus est remanet nobis occultum.

[86] I, ii 45: Et hoc quidem principium non cognoscimus per divina nomina sicuti est, hoc enim est indicibile et inscrutabile, sed cognoscimus Eum ut principium et ut causam. II, ii, 135: Intantum Deus potest a nobis cognosci, inquantum participationes suae bonitatis cognoscimus; secundum autem quod est in se, est nobis occultus; 'inegressibilem' autem dicit quia secundum quod in seipso est primum Principium nulli communicatur et sic quasi a seipso non egreditur. See II, iv, 178; VII, iv, 731.

[87] XI, ii, 897: Deus enim est supra omne esse et supra omnem vitam et supra omnia huiusmodi quae a creaturis participantur; et ita, cum connaturale sit intellectui creato quod intelligat et dicat Dei participationes, ipsum Deum, qui super omnia huiusmodi est, neque perfecte intelligere neque perfecte dicere potest.

[88] II, iv, 180: Non enim cadit in visionem intellectus nostri, nisi aliquod ens creatum et finitum quod omnino deficit ab Ente increato et infinito et ideo oportet quod Deum intelligamus esse supra omne id quod intellectu apprehendere possumus.

[89] I, iii, 77: Deus est potior omni nostra locutione et omni cognitione et non solum excedit nostram locutionem et cognitionem, sed universaliter collocatur super omnem mentem etiam angelicam et super omnem substantiam.

[90] I, iii, 77: Ridiculum enim videtur velle tractare de nominibus rei quae nominari non potest.

The way of negation imposes itself, therefore, as most worthy and here the influence of Dionysius is particularly evident:

> The most perfect to which we can attain in this life in our knowledge of God is that he transcends all that can be conceived by us, and that the naming of God through remotion is most proper . . . The primary mode of naming God is through the negation of all things, since he is beyond all, and whatever is signified by any name whatsoever is less than that which God is.[91]

Our knowledge awakens amidst the material things which are presented connaturally to our soul; but when we discover that God is nothing sensible or corporeal, the soul ascends by way of negation, according to Aquinas, through the ascending grades of reality to the outermost limits of the universe of beings. In this manner it becomes united with God in the manner which is possible in this life, i.e. when it knows him to transcend immeasurably even the most excellent of creatures.[92]

Aquinas frequently repeats Dionysius' statement: 'Negations are true of divine realities, whereas affirmations are inconsistent with the secret nature of the mysteries.'[93] This is because we know of God more truly that which he is not than what he is.[94] Concretely, the reason is again best articulated in terms of Aquinas' distinction between the perfections themselves signified as proper to God, and the finite mode according to which they are realised and signified in our experience. Predicates may be denied of God in both respects; they may be affirmed, however, only with respect to the perfection intended, the *res significata*, since its

---

[91] I, iii, 83-4: Hoc enim est ultimum ad quod pertingere possumus circa cognitionem divinam in hac vita, quod Deus est supra omne id quod a nobis cogitari potest et ideo nominatio Dei quae est per remotionem est maxime propria. . . . Hic igitur est primus modus Dei nominationum per abnegationem omnium, ea ratione quod Ipse est super omnia et quidquid est quocumque nomine signatum, est minus eo quod est Deus, quia excedit nostram cognitionem, quam, per nomina a nobis imposita, exprimimus. In his *Expositio Super Librum Boethii de Trinitate*, 6, 3, Aquinas puts forward the view that our knowledge of immaterial substances proceeds by way of negation rather than through the determination of genus and difference. According as negations are imposed and intensified, previous negations become more contracted and determinate—as genera through the addition of their differences—and so our knowledge becomes more precise: Sed loco cognitionis generis habemus in istis substantiis cognitionem per negationes. . . . Et quanto plures negationes de eis cognoscimus, tanto et minus confusa est earum cognitio in nobis, eo quod per negationes sequentes prior negatio contrahitur et determinatur, sicut genus remotum per differentias. See *Contra Gentiles* 3, 39 and 49.

[92] XIII, iii, 996: Unde haec coniunctio nostri ad Deum, quae nobis est in hac vita possibilis, perficitur quando devenimus ad hoc quod cognoscamus Eum esse supra excellentissimas creaturas.

[93] *CH* II, 3, 141A: εἰ τοίνυν αἱ μὲν ἀποφάσεις ἐπὶ τῶν θείων ἀληθεῖς, αἱ δὲ καταφάσεις ἀνάρμοστοι τῇ κρυφιότητι τῶν ἀπορρήτων. In *de Causis*, I, 6: Negationes in divinis sunt verae, affirmationes vero incompactae vel inconvenientes. (Pera, 161; Saffrey, 43); see *De Potentia* 7, 5, ad 2; ibid., 9, 7; for other references, see Durantel, pp. 73-4.

[94] *In I Sent.*, 34, 3, 1.

modus significandi is inconsistent with the plenitude of the perfection in God. Thus negations are absolutely true while affirmations, although not false, are only relatively true. The perfection signified is somehow present in God; but to be truly affirmed it must be conceived according to its supreme degree, free of its finite condition. Affirmations are true of God only under qualification. On the one hand we say that God is of his essence good and wise, etc.; but on the other hand we remove these names in respect of their mode of signification. Each of these words ('wisdom', 'goodness' and so on) expresses, according to our manner of conceiving, a definite manner of being which, limited and separated, is unbefitting of God in whom all perfections subsist in the unified and absolute subsistence of divine essence.[95]

Through the dialectic of affirmation and negation there thus emerges the transcendent sense of the names applied to God. As cause of everything, and according as they bear a resemblance to their origin, the names of all things may be spoken of him; but in the measure that they fail to represent him, we remove from God the names we have imposed and pronounce their opposites.[96] Affirmative names, Aquinas emphasises, are applied to God not according to the same measure as to creatures, but in a pre-eminent sense to him as cause.[97] And, on the other hand, names are removed from God not by reason of any deficiency, but *per quemdam excessum*,[98] because he possesses their perfection in a more excellent manner. 'Names such as "good" and "wise" are more truly denied than affirmed of God, says Dionysius, because that which is signified by the name does not agree with God in the manner signified by the name, but in a more excellent manner; whence Dionysius says that God is beyond substance and life.'[99] Both

---

[95] See *In I Sent.*, 22, 1, 2, ad 1: Cum in nomine duo sint, modus significandi, et res ipsa significata semper secundum alterum potest removeri a Deo vel secundum utrumque; sed non potest dici de Deo nisi secundum alterum tantum. Et quia ad veritatem et proprietatem affirmationis requiritur quod totum affirmetur, ad proprietatem autem negationis sufficit si alterum tantum desit, ideo dicit Dionysius, quod negationes sunt absolute verae, sed affirmationes non nisi secundum quid: quia quantum ad significatum tantum, et non quantum ad modum significandi. Also Ibid., 4, 2, 1, ad 2 and *De Potentia* 7, 5, ad 2 and 9, 7.

[96] I, i, 30: Sicut autem nomina a nobis imposita, de Deo dici possunt secundum quod aliqua similitudo est creaturarum ad Deum, ita secundum quod creaturae deficiunt a repraesentatione Dei, nomina a nobis imposita a Deo removeri possunt et opposita eorum praedicari.

[97] I, iii, 89: Si vero non sit similitudo secundum eamdem rationem, sed sit supereminentius in causa, non dicetur nomen de utroque secundum unam rationem, sed supereminentius de causa, sicut calor de sole et igne. I, i, 29: Nomina a nobis imposita de Deo dici possunt, non quidem sic sicut de creaturis, sed per quemdam excessum. See V, i, 610-11.

[98] I, i, 29.

[99] *ST*, I, 13, 3, ad 2: Huiusmodi nomina (bonus, sapiens, et similia) Dionysius dicit

positive and negative theology are therefore properly aimed towards
the absolute transcendence of God. In human thought and utterance
this eminently positive value of transcendence is most effectively
expressed by negative predication.

In a passage of *De Potentia*, Aquinas presents the movement of
reflection from creatures to God according to the threefold intentionality
of human predication:

> According to the teaching of Dionysius, these names are pronounced of God
> in three ways. First affirmatively, as when we say 'God is wise'; which must
> be said of him because there is in him a likeness of the wisdom which derives
> from him. Since, however, wisdom is not found in God such as we understand
> and name, it may be denied, so it is said 'God is not wise'. But wisdom is
> not denied of God because he is lacking in wisdom, rather it is present in
> him more supereminently than is spoken or understood; it is moreover
> necessary to say that God is 'superwise': he possesses it more excellently than
> the human intellect can grasp or word may signify.[100] Thus by this threefold
> way of speaking according to which God is said to be wise, Dionysius gives
> to understand perfectly how such names are attributed to God.[101]

It is proper, says Aquinas, that God be known as the 'Unnameable' ,
yet given the names of all beings; because he is separated from all
things, is nonetheless the cause of all.[102] More significant than both
affirmation and negation is God's pre-eminence; all manner of
predication, affirmative and remotive, is fundamentally incommensurable
vis-à-vis the divine transcendence. All things may both be affirmed and
denied of God, but truly speaking, he is beyond the operations of
attribution and negation; these are characteristic of human reflection

---

negari a Deo, quia id quod significatur per nomen, non convenit Deo eo modo quo
nomen significat, sed excellentiori modo. Unde ibidem Dionysius dicit, quod Deus est
super omnem substantiam et vitam.

[100] See *De Potentia* 9, 7: Sicut dicit Dionysius, sapientia et vita et alia huiusmodi non
removentur a Deo quasi ei desint, sed quia excellentius habet ea quam intellectus
humanus capere, vel sermo significare possit; . . . Et ideo de Deo, secundum Dionysium,
non solum dicitur aliquid per modum negationis et per modum causae, sed etiam per
modum eminentiae.

[101] *De Potentia* 7, 5: Et ideo, secundum doctrinam Dionysii, tripliciter ista de Deo
dicuntur. Primo quidem affirmative, ut dicamus, Deus est sapiens; quod quidem de eo
oportet dicere propter hoc quod est in eo similitudo sapientiae ab ipso fluentis: quia
tamen non est in Deo sapientia qualem nos intelligimus et nominamus, potest vere negari,
ut dicatur, Deus non est sapiens. Rursum quia sapientia non negatur de Deo quia ipse
deficiat a sapientia, sed quia supereminentius est in ipso quam dicatur aut intelligatur,
ideo oportet dicere quod Deus sit supersapiens. Et sic per istum triplicem modum
loquendi secundum quem dicitur Deus sapiens, perfecte Dionysius dat intelligere qualiter
ista Deo attribuantur.

[102] I, iii, 96, 98: Deus est segregatus ab omnibus et tamen est causa omnium. . . Ita
igitur Deo, qui est omnium causa et tamen super omnia existens, convenit et esse
innominabile, inquantum super omnia existens, et tamen conveniunt Ei omnia nomina
existentium, sicut omnium Causae.

and cannot be brought to bear upon divine being, which in its excellence outmeasures the categories of human thought. Affirmation and negation, therefore, are not mutually exclusive for the very reason that neither is properly commensurate with the mystery of the divinity. God is most faithfully known not simply through negation, but as the unknown. Aquinas expresses this as follows:

> It pertains to this excellence that it be unknown to us because of the very excellence of its light and that to no created intellect is it perfectly intelligible or comprehensible; furthermore all things may be affirmed and denied of God, since he is beyond all affirmation transcending, as he does, every human intellect by which affirmations and negations are composed.[103]

Having followed the threefold path of causality, removal and transcendence, Aquinas concludes that our most noble knowledge is to know that God is wholly unknown: 'We do not see of God what he is, but what he is not.'[104] The silent mystery enshrouding God, Aquinas emphasises in full agreement with Dionysius, derives from his most eminent intelligibility. 'The divine essence is unknown, not by virtue of his obscurity, but through an abundance of clarity.'[105] God remains unknown, since to know him we should require a cognitive virtue of infinite capacity. The only obstacle in understanding God's supereminent intelligibility is our infirmity of intellect.

Aquinas concludes: 'The most perfect knowledge of God is by remotion; we know God through unknowing, in a union with the divine beyond the nature of mind.' He notes with approval Dionysius' view that the mind, turning from all things and abandoning even itself, is united to the super-resplendent rays of the divinity and even suggests that negative knowledge is itself the fruit of divine illumination.[106]

St Thomas agrees with Dionysius that it is through silence that we best honour the divine secrets which transcend our natural understanding.

---

[103] II, ii, 143: Ad hanc etiam excellentiam est et quod a nobis ignoratur propter excellentiam sui luminis et quod a nullo intellectu creato est perfecte intelligibilis, idest comprehensibilis et quod de Eo omnia possunt affirmari et omnia negari . . . cum tamen Ipse sit super omnem affirmationem et negationem; est enim super omnem intellectum nostrum, qui affirmationes et negationes componit.

[104] *De Veritate* 8, 1, ad 8: Tantum cognoscitur quod Deus est super illud quod de ipso intellectui repraesentatur; unde illud quod est, remanet occultum. Et hic est nobilissimus modus cognitionis ad quem pervenire possumus in via; et ideo non videmus de Deo quid est, sed quid non est.

[105] I, iii, 82: Non enim est ignota propter obscuritatem, sed propter abundantiam claritatis. See *Ep.* 5, 1073A.

[106] VII, iv, 732: Rursus autem est alia perfectissima Dei cognitio, per remotionem scilicet, qua cognoscimus Deum per ignorantiam, per quamdam unitionem ad divina supra naturam mentis. . . . Et sic cognoscens Deum, in tali statu cognitionis, illuminatur ab ipsa profunditate Divinae Sapientiae, quam perscrutari non possumus.

He is cautious, however, in indicating that God is honoured by our
silence, not because we can say nothing about him, or are ignorant of
him, but because we *know* our understanding of him to be deficient.[107]
Since God is beyond all participation and remains, therefore, unknown,
we are best united to him, says Aquinas, through the removal of all
things and by the stilling of every intellectual operation.[108] While
Aquinas repeatedly refers to Dionysius' view that at the most perfect
level of knowledge we are joined to God as unknown, he is careful in
his appraisal of the doctrine. Indeed initially he cites it purposely among
the objections advanced in favour of agnosticism. He explains however
its proper sense:

> At the end of our knowledge we know God as unknown (*tamquam ignotum*),
> since the mind has most progressed in knowledge when it knows his essence
> to be beyond all that it can apprehend in this life; thus, although it remains
> unknown what he is, it is nevertheless known that he is.[109]

The silence of unknowing, as one author remarks, falls after and not
before, the exercise of 'proving, naming and knowing God'.[110]

There is, therefore, no difficulty in harmonising Aquinas' teaching
regarding the unknown nature of God with his dedication in seeking to
unfold his existence, and to contemplate the sublime mystery in so far
as humanly possible. The influence of Dionysius for both aspects is
beyond doubt. It is conveyed summarily in the following paragraph
from the *Summa Contra Gentiles*. Aquinas here compares the knowledge
of man with that of separate substances, who, he says, know through
their own substance that God is, that he is the cause of all things, that
he is eminent above all and set apart from all. He continues:

> Even we are able to reach this knowledge of God in some sense; for we
> know through his effects, that God is, and that he is the cause of other
> beings, that he is super-eminent over other things and set apart from all.
> And this is the ultimate and most perfect limit of our knowledge in this life,
> as Dionysius says in the *Mystical Theology*, 'We are united with God as the
> unknown.' Indeed, this is the situation, for, while we know of God *what he
> is not*, what he is remains wholly unknown. Hence, to manifest his ignorance

---

[107] *In Boeth. de Trin.*, 2, 1 ad 6: Deus honoratur silentio, non quod nihil de ipso
dicatur vel inquiratur, sed quia quidquid de ipso dicamus vel inquiramus, intelligimus
nos ab eius comprehensione defecisse. See *CH*, 15, 9, 340B (Ed. Heil, p. 191): τὴν ὑπὲρ
ἡμᾶς κρυφιότητα σιγῇ τιμήσαντες.
[108] I, iii, 83; II, iv, 180.
[109] *In Boeth. de Trin.*, 1, 2 ad 1: Dicendum quod secundum hoc dicimur in fine nostrae
cognitionis Deum tamquam ignotum cognoscere, quia tunc maxime mens in cognitione
profecisse invenitur, quando cognoscit eius essentiam esse supra omne quod apprehendere
potest in statu viae, et sic quamvis maneat ignotum quid sit, scitur tamen quia est. See
In IV Sent., 49, 2, 1; *In de Causis*. VI, 160.
[110] See C. B. Daly, 'The Knowableness of God', p. 132.

of this sublime ignorance, it is said of Moses that 'he went to the dark cloud in which God was.'[111]

Aquinas draws here on the doctrine of Dionysius to confirm that we have a real and valid knowledge of God's existence. Admittedly, of God's nature we have knowledge primarily only in respect of what he is not; the awareness of our own 'ignorance of this most sublime knowledge' is for Aquinas the most worthy of knowledge; the minimum that we can discover concerning God is of infinitely greater value than all other knowledge we can attain. The negative language which Aquinas employs is an attempt to surmount the incommensurability between knowledge and the infinite source of all illumination.

Aquinas rejects, however, an outright negativism or agnostic attitude. The aim and intention of his negative theology is eminently positive and requires initially a positive foundation.[112] St Thomas thus reduces at every opportunity the negative or "agnostic' character of Dionysius' thought where this appears exaggerated. Thus, referring to the *Mystical Theology* where Dionysius states that we are united to God τῷ παντελῶς δὲ ἀγνώστῳ—translated by both Eriugena and Sarracenus as *OMNINO autem ignoto*—Aquinas modifies the negative tone: *QUASI ignoto coniungimur*. A similar correction is introduced in the *Summa Theologiae*.[113] Such a modification indicates an important reappraisal of the role of negative theology and presents a more balanced theory of our knowledge of God.

Dionysius' theory undergoes, however, an even more radical metamorphosis in its adoption into Aquinas' system. With St Thomas there is a fundamental reinterpretation of the relation of knowledge and reality which transforms in turn the value and status of our

---

[111] *Contra Gentiles* 3, 49: Cognoscit tamen substantia separata per suam substantiam de Deo quia est, et quod est omnium causa, et eminens omnibus, et remotus ab omnibus non solum quae sunt, sed etiam quae mente creata concipi possunt. Ad quam etiam cognitionem de Deo nos utcumque pertingere possumus; per effectus de Deo enim cognoscimus quia est, et quod causa aliorum est, aliis supereminens et ab omnibus remotus. Et hoc est ultimum et perfectissimum nostrae cognitionis in hac vita, unde Dionysius dicit in libro De Mistica Theologia (c. 2) quod Deo quasi ignoto conjungimur. Quod quidem contingit dum de Deo quid non sit cognoscimus, quid vero sit, penitus manet incognitum. Unde et ad hujus sublimissimae cognitionis ignorantiam demonstrandam, de Moyse dicitur (Exod. 20: 21) quod accessit ad caliginem in qua erat Deus.

[112] *De Potentia* 7, 5: Intellectus negationis semper fundatur in aliqua affirmatione: quod ex hoc patet, quia omnis negativa per affirmativam probatur; unde nisi intellectus humanus aliquid de Deo affirmative cognosceret, nihil de Deo posset negare. Non autem cognosceret, si nihil quod de Deo dicit, de eo verificaretur affirmative.

[113] *ST*, I, 12, 13: Dionysius' authority is invoked for the objection that: ille qui melius unitur Deo in hac vita, unitur ei sicut omnino ignoto. Aquinas responds: Dicendum quod, licet per revelationem gratiae in hac vita non cognoscamus de Deo quid est, et sic *quasi ignoto* conjungimus.

knowledge of God. This is rooted in the new meaning which Aquinas discovers in the notion of being or *esse*. We have seen that for Dionysius knowledge has as its proper object the being of finite reality; and since God is *non-existens*, he therefore cannot be known. Being is limited and therefore presents, according to Dionysius, a restriction to our knowledge of God. With Aquinas the notion of being acquires an all-transcendent and infinite value. It is thus, he believes, the concept most appropriate to denote the infinity of God. And as an analogous notion, revealed in each reality, it is furthermore, the key to our reflection leading from beings to God. It is precisely as Being Itself, transcendent and unlimited, *Ipsum Esse Subsistens*, that God is in himself radically unknown; by the same token it is also because he is Being that we have analogous knowledge of his existence, and relation with creatures. Thus, whereas for Dionysius it is a hindrance to our discovery of God that human knowledge is oriented towards finite beings, this for Aquinas is the very foundation of our natural disclosure of God. Through the notion of being, and via its analogous value, our certitude of his existence is existentially grounded.

   This profound transformation in signification may be clearly witnessed in Aquinas' treatment of the question whether created intellect can know the essence of God. One of the objections is drawn from Dionysius: 'Created intellect can only know existing things (*non est cognoscitivus nisi existentium*), indeed that which first falls under the apprehension of intellect is being (*ens*). God, however, is not an existing thing (*non est existens*) but is beyond beings (*supra existentia*), as Dionysius says. He is therefore not intelligible, but is beyond all intellection.' Aquinas' response presents a profoundly conceived reformulation of this relation of knowledge and reality, and establishes above all the primacy of Being and its intelligibility, safeguarding both the validity of our knowledge concerning God and the transcendence of the divine mystery:

> When we say that God is non-existent, this does not mean that he does not exist in any manner whatever: but that he transcends everything which exists, in so far as he is his own being (*esse*). From this it does not follow that he cannot in any way be known but that he exceeds all knowledge; there cannot be a comprehensive knowledge of him.[114]

---

[114] *ST*, I, 12, 1: Intellectus creatus non est cognoscitivus nisi existentium: primum enim quod cadit in apprehensione intellectus, est ens. Sed Deus non est existens, sed supra existentia, ut Dionysius dicit. Ergo non est intelligibilis, sed est supra omnem intellectum. . . . Ad tertium dicendum quod Deus non sic dicitur non existens, quasi nullo modo sit existens: sed quia est supra omne existens, inquantum est suum esse. Unde ex hoc non sequitur quod nullo modo possit cognosci, sed quod omnem cognitionem excedat: quod est ipsum non comprehendi.

Each thing, Aquinas explains in the same question, is intelligible in so far as it is actual being or is 'being in act' (*ens actu*). *Esse* is the very principle or act of intelligibility within beings; God therefore, whose Being is infinite, is infinitely knowable but cannot be known by created intellect.[115] The indeterminate act of *esse* cannot be grasped as such by human intelligence; it can be received only as proportioned to its capacity. We can only grasp the perfection or intelligibility of *esse* as it is present in beings through the medium of essence. The composition of essence and the act of being, distinct but inseparable, is a prerequisite of human knowledge. The unlimited *esse* of God, identical with his very essence, cannot be comprehended by finite intellect. Yet, as the fullness of Being, God is infinitely knowable. Aquinas reconciles the dual aspects of the divine mystery: God is in himself eminently knowable, but to us remains sublimely unknown.[116]

As a final example both of the intimacy of Dionysius' influence which is deeply present within Aquinas' thought, and of the transformation which it undergoes, we quote from the Commentary on the *Sentences* a passage which shares something of the lyrical tone of the Neoplatonist. The language and movement of thought are unmistakably Dionysian, but oriented in a radically different direction and resting upon a wholly distinct metaphysical terrain. Aquinas argues in a sense which is at variance with Dionysius that Being is the proper and primary name of God:

---

[115] *ST*, I, 12, 7: Unumquodque enim, sic cognoscibile est, secundum quod est ens actu. Deus igitur, cuius esse est infinitum infinite cognoscibilis est. Nullus autem intellectus creatus potest Deum infinite cognoscere.

[116] I do not accept Vladimir Lossky's reading (*Théologie négative et connaissance de Dieu chez Maître Eckhart*, p. 23) that, commenting on the passage where Dionysius claims it is proper for the transcendent cause both to be without name and to receive all names (*DN*, I, 7, 25: . . . et innominabile conveniet et omnium existentium nomina), Aquinas transforms the meaning simply by adding the word *esse* before *innominabile*: Ita igitur Deo, qui est omnium causa et tamen super omnia existens, convenit et esse innominabile, inquantum super omnia existens, et tamen conveniunt ei omnia nomina existentium, sicut omnium Causae (I, iii, 98). Lossky aptly remarks: 'Tous les noms des existants peuvent convenir à Dieu qui est leur Cause; cependant, considéré en Lui-même, Dieu qui existe au-dessus de tous les existants est l'ÊTRE innommable. Ainsi, pour saint Thomas, l'ineffabilité qui convient à Dieu, en tant qu'il est *segregatus ab omnibus*, n'exclut pas l'être.' It is not simply as deprived of every name that God is known but praised as nameless and unfathomable BEING. According to St Thomas, it is as Being itself in its endless infinity that God is transcendent and nameless. Lossky, however, is mistaken, in my view, in reading '*esse*' in this passage as a noun rather than a verb: 'Le substantif *Esse* que le commentateur ajoute à l'Innominabile de Denys, transformant ainsi ce dernier terme en adjectif, est une correction prudente de saint Thomas à l'apophase dionysienne. Il s'agit bien d'une correction introduite ici en pleine conscience, car le texte du présumé disciple de saint Paul n'admettait que trop facilement une interprétation qui désexistentialisait la notion de Dieu. Cela nous paraît hors de doute.'

The name *qui est* expresses 'Being' (*esse*) as absolute and not determined
through any addition; and Damascene says, therefore, that it does not signify
what God is but as it were an infinite ocean of substance which is without
determination. When therefore we proceed towards God by the way of
remotion, we first deny of him anything corporeal; and then we even deny
of him anything intellectual, according as these are found in creatures, such
as 'goodness' and 'wisdom'; and then there remains in our minds only the
notion that he is, and nothing more: wherefore he exists in a certain confusion
for us. Lastly, however, we remove from him even 'being' itself as it is found
in creatures; and then he remains in a kind of shadow of ignorance, by which
ignorance, in so far as it pertains to this life, we are best united to God, as
Dionysius says, and this is the cloud in which God is said to dwell.[117]

* * *

Ultimately for Dionysius, the task of philosophy is to seek vestiges of
divine presence in the universe of creatures. In this, says Aquinas, God
has given to man a longer way to divine truth (*longior via*). In
philosophical contemplation man attains the happiness proper to the
human state—'a wayfaring happiness (*felicitas viae*), to which is directed
the whole of philosophical knowledge, stemming from what is knowable
in creatures.'[118]

We fashion our knowledge of God according to our cognitive
capacity: *ad modum cognoscentis*. Having regard for this status we
perceive the real but limited value of such knowledge. Is it not
appropriate that we should attribute to God, as does Dionysius, not
only that which we best know but also the best of what we know: the
personal perfections of life and love, knowledge and nobility, freedom,
goodness, and truth? Recognising the analogical value of our concepts
we safeguard the real validity of our knowledge. Here the dialectic
within language of positive and negative is indispensable. Positive and
negative nomination are interpenetrated and intensified, rising in a
crescendo of testimony to God's mystery. As light and dark in a

---

[117] *In I Sent.*, 8, 1, 1, ad 4: Sed hoc nomen 'qui est' dicit esse absolutum et non
determinatum per aliquid additum; et ideo dicit Damascenus, quod non significat quid
est Deus, sed significat quoddam pelagus substantiae infinitum, quasi non determinatum.
Unde quando in Deum procedimus per viam remotionis, primo negamus ab eo corporalia;
et secundo etiam intellectualia, secundum quod inveniuntur in creaturis, ut bonitas et
sapientia; et tunc remanet tantum in intellectu nostro, quia est, et nihil amplius: unde est
sicut in quadam confusione. Ad ultimum autem etiam hoc ipsum esse, secundum quod
est in creaturis, ab ipso removemus; et tunc remanet in quadam tenebra ignorantiae,
secundum quam ignorantiam, quantum ad statum viae pertinet, optime Deo coniungimur,
ut dicit Dionysius, et haec est quaedam caligo, in qua Deus habitare dicitur.
[118] *In I Sent.*, Prol., 1 ad 1.

landscape or painting do not stand still but set each other off, leading the eye in constant movement to deeper penetration and insight, so the interplay of positive and negative language traces the mosaic of the universe and focuses the vision of thought towards the infinity of divine being. Our knowledge of God has a real value; feeble though it be, it is of crucial importance as the only path open to us. The guarantee of its validity is the evidence of existence itself, the *nervus probandi* of all our affirmations and negations concerning God. Being is known first and last in all: the horizon of every question and the foundation of each affirmation, it is the thread which leads thought through the labyrinth of phenomena within our experience. And yet being is for us ultimately unknowable. What this means is that, penetrating to the intrinsic existence of things our insight is true and valid but not exhaustive or comprehensive. Following the current of causality, human thought is launched by the simple and clear power of existence towards the depths of the divine. The crowning achievement of human reason is to affirm the unfathomed depths of divine reality.

A contemporary English philosopher has written in praise of Aquinas: 'No passage in the writings of Thomas Aquinas is more often quoted today than the one in which, speaking of natural knowledge of God, he says that "Of God we know that he is, what he is not, and what relation everything other than himself has to him." The very healthy agnosticism of the passage is rightly emphasised and it might well be claimed that when we speak of omnipresence, omniscience, omnipotence, we are indeed speaking, not of God but of the relation to him of that which falls outside his being, its relation, or more accurately, the discriminable aspects of its fundamental dependence.'[119] But by removing all human concepts from God—those very concepts which are clear and familiar—are we not in danger of falling into deeper obscurity? This is, however, the very condition of such knowledge; it is indeed the only knowledge appropriate to divine reality. There is a dissymetry between our knowledge and the ultimate intelligibility of reality. The relative clarity of human cognition is at odds with the absolute illumination and luminosity proper to the plenitude of existence. Divine light bathes creation throughout its vast circumference in a mysterious radiance,[120] but itself remains in obscurity. Considered in themselves, in respect of their origin, creatures are shadow and darkness compared to God who is light itself. To human vision, light itself appears as darkness; the world which appears clear is in itself opaque and in need

---

[119] D. M. Mackinnon, *The Problem of Metaphysics*, p. 118.
[120] See W. Macneile Dixon, *The Human Situation*, p. 229

of illumination. The strategy must thus be to refocus the direction of our knowledge, to withdraw from the objects of relative clarity and radically transform the very intention of our insight. Our knowledge of God is eclipsed by the divine brightness, so that it appears as darkness. Blinded by its brilliance, all appears in darkness. But light dwells in darkness and only in darkness can the light be seen.

The greatest difficulty in affirming the mystery of God lies in the greatness of its truth. God remains hidden, that he may be known as God. The great unknown is an unknown greatness. It is almost too difficult for the mind to accept that there should exist a person, infinite in being, unceasing in goodness and love, whose nature is simply to be—to be *absolutely*—such that it is impossible for him not to exist; whose goodness is so generous as to generate the universe and all it contains. It is almost natural for the intellect to balk before a truth so wonderful and sublime, since it is at ease only with what it can dominate and calculate. The alternative to mystery, however, is absurdity or contradiction: to claim the world of our experience, which is insufficient in each of its aspects, is in need of nothing beyond itself. 'By accepting the freedom of the first cause, we make the contradiction disappear, but in its stead we find an ineffable and inscrutable mystery. Yet despite its obscurity this mystery is the light in which the whole of all finite beings, the world, becomes to some extent intelligible.'[121]

The visions of Dionysius and Aquinas alike are infused from the start and sustained throughout by a sense of sacred marvel before the divine origin of the world. Their works are characterised by an openness to what is unknown and undiscovered, inspired by the desire to comprehend—not necessarily to fully explain, but to contemplate and ponder; to accept and appreciate, and to articulate as best possible according to the deficient modes at their disposal. The question of the universe, aroused in wonder at the most humble of beings, is refined and purified, restored to its source, with the conclusion that it is a gift of divine Goodness and Being. With this response, however, the question is not just somehow answered; it has become enlarged and invested with an infinite dimension. It is absorbed into a mystery and has no longer need of answer. There has not only occured a change in the question, but with it a change in the enquirer and in the relation to what is contemplated: the mystery of infinite Goodness and Being. Man cannot now place the question before him, but stands himself within the mystery of its greatness. Wonder at the first mystery of being now gives way to a love for the goodness of Being which has given creation

---

[121] John A. Peters, *Metaphysics. A Systematic Survey*, p. 466, n. 157.

to man for his own sake. The response of Dionysius and Aquinas is not merely ἀπόφασις but ἀφασία, a devout and learned silence. Such is the summit to which saint, poet, philosopher and mystic aspire: 'In wonder all philosophy began; in wonder it ends: and admiration fills up the interspace. But the first wonder is the offspring of ignorance: the last is the parent of adoration.'[122]

---

[122] S. T. Coleridge, *Aids to Reflection*, p. 185.

PART TWO

TRANSCENDENCE OF BEING AND THE GOOD

CHAPTER THREE

THEARCHIA: THE TRANSCENDENT GOOD

Having seen the approach which must be adopted in seeking a knowledge of God, namely through positive (causal) and negative (transcendent) attribution, let us ask what understanding of God Dionysius acquires through such twofold nomination. We shall note accordingly Dionysius' understanding of the divine principle,[1] firstly in positive terms as the transcendent and pre-eminent fullness of Being and, secondly, as superior to Being, i.e. viewed in a transcendent sense as 'Non-Being'. Both paths denote the divinity as absolute and unlimited perfection itself.

Ultimately, God is named both in a positive and negative manner as the primary Good. In the manner of our discovery, his goodness is most evident and understood most meaningfully through his diffusion of gifts to all creation; in the generosity which moves him to generate all beings and in the providence with which he foresees and cares for all, maintaining each and establishing in harmony the hierarchy of being. We observe the felicitous if not fortuitous agreement of Christian orthodoxy with Neoplatonist metaphysics; God is named in the first place and principally as very Goodness itself. This is all the more convincing since Dionysius is following the principle adopted at the beginning of his treatise: we may conceive of God and speak of him only as he is revealed in Scripture. On three occasions Dionysius appeals to the sacred writers to portray goodness as the first name of God. He introduces the theme emphatically in Chapter 2 of *Divine Names*, where he begins his quest in plain reliance upon Scripture: 'The absolute Goodness is celebrated by the Scriptures as revealing and defining the entire and essential divine essence.'[2] This is what is signified by the proclamation 'None is good but God alone'[3]—the total and exclusive identification of the nature of God with Goodness itself.

---

[1] For clarity and convenience, I retain in transliterated form the Greek word used by Dionysius: Θεαρχία, 'Thearchia'.
[2] 2, 1, 31.
[3] Luke 18: 19.

A noteworthy passage in which Dionysius speaks of 'Good' as the
first name of God occurs in the penultimate paragraph of the *Divine
Names*, where having treated of the many names given to the thearchy
he places the entire enterprise in its total perspective. He sums up the
value of the treatise and shows its accord with the holy writings:

> We do not attribute to it the name of Goodness as appropriate, but through
> a desire to know and say something of that ineffable nature we first consecrate
> to it this most sacred of names. In this we shall be in agreement with the
> sacred writers, although the truth of the reality transcends us.[4]

While Dionysius stresses that no name whatsoever is of itself adequate
to reflect the transcendent divinity, he suggests that 'Goodness' is the
most proper, even though we are still far from the truth.

The most important of the passages where Dionysius agrees with
Scripture in naming God as Goodness is the opening paragraph of
Chapter 4, a chapter which deals specifically with the Good, and which
constitutes more than one fourth of the entire work. Dionysius begins
by remarking that the sacred writers have given the name of 'Good'
(ἀγαθωνυμίαν) to the 'supra-divine divinity' in a pre-eminent manner,
separating him from all things, portraying him as transcendent to all.
Significant is the sense which Dionysius, for his part, attributes to this
teaching: 'They say, as I think, that the divine essence is goodness itself
and that simply by its being the Good as the subsisting essence of the
Good (ὡς οὐσιῶδες ἀγαθόν) extends its goodness to all beings.'[5] This
is of course the language of Neoplatonism but we observe how
Dionysius introduces and sustains this theory on the authority of
Scripture. From the point of view of a metaphysics of being, it can be
observed that Dionysius relies upon the very notion of being to express
his stated primacy of the Good. We may summarise the Neoplatonist
concept of the Good encountered in the writings of Dionysius: God is
Goodness itself and merits in an exclusive way the honour of this
singular name. Beings are 'good', but their goodness is not self-
sufficient. It is a participation in essential goodness beyond good things.[6]
God's divinity is identical with his very goodness; he is at once both
God and Good (ὁμόθεον καὶ ὁμοάγαθον).[7]

In its first metaphysical significance, therefore, it is as its own infinite
and subsistent plenitude, wholly autonomous and self-sufficient, that
the Absolute is uniquely and exclusively called the Good. In the order
of knowledge, however, the transcendent Good is disclosed only as

---

[4] 13, 3, 452.
[5] 4, 1, 95.
[6] 4, 2, 105-6: ἀγαθὰ διὰ τὴν ὑπεραγαθότητα ... ἐπὶ τὴν πάντων ἀγαθῶν ἀγαθαρχίαν.
[7] 1, 5, 22.

origin of goodness in beings. It is superior to Being as its originating principle and as such embraces within its superabundance all the perfection of beings. For Dionysius God is the unlimited essence of Goodness, the One and Beautiful, who transcends all Being and embraces within his unity and simplicity the fullness of perfection manifested partially and disparately throughout the universe.

It is as the cause of beings, defined first in terms of their goodness, therefore, that the absolute is known philosophically as the subsisting Good. Beings *are* because of the value infused into them by the Good. It is at the heart of this realm of 'things made perfect' which share in varying degrees in the riches of goodness that, in the mind of Dionysius, we seek orientation towards ultimate significance, truth and value. It is because the universe manifests itself as a hierarchy of values that the absolute is praised as the unlimited presence of perfect goodness in itself. We will therefore seek indices throughout the work of Dionysius which may justify philosophically the doctrine which is stated at the outset on the authority of Scripture: that the Good is the name par excellence for the 'supra-divine divinity'. All knowledge regarding the goodness of God is grounded in the mediating role of reality. In accordance firstly with the positive approach of human discovery, God is affirmed to be Good as the plenary and pre-eminent perfection of Being itself. We shall treat specifically of this positive appreciation and examine in particular the Goodness of the thearchy as the plenitude of Being.

As we have seen, all naming is founded, according to Dionysius, upon the similitude which holds between cause and effect; the principle of discovery rests in turn upon the underlying principle of causal participation: 'what are in effects pre-exist abundantly and substantially in their causes.'[8] This universal principle is operative at its most profound in the bond whereby creatures inhere in God: a quality or perfection is present in a finite being only because it derives from and thus shares in the full presence of that perfection which is its source. The perfections of all finite things abide pre-eminently in God. Dionysius summarises this by pointing out that not only is God the cause of being for all things, constituting the source of life and perfection, but that he embraces all by anticipation 'simply and absolutely' (ἁπλῶς καὶ ἀπεριορίστως).[9] 'He precontains all things within himself in a unique and transcendent simplicity.'[10] Significant here is that all things are

---

[8] 2, 8, 58: περισσῶς καὶ οὐσιωδῶς προένεστι τὰ τῶν αἰτιατῶν τοῖς αἰτίοις.
[9] 1, 7, 26.
[10] 5, 9, 284: πάντα μὲν ἐν ἑαυτῇ προέχει κατὰ μίαν ἁπλότητος ὑπερβολήν.

present unitively or simply and in an absolute or plenary manner; the thearchy 'embraces all things in advance in the perfect goodness of its one and all-creative providence ... embracing and unifying, comprehending and anticipating all things.'[11] The goodness of creatures is the manifestation of the Divine Good; the creature is by participation that which its cause is primarily and causally.[12] It is as cause that God in the transcendent fullness of his Being pre-contains the perfections and qualities of all things.[13]

Dionysius' first *point de repère* in seeking to understand the divine nature from finite creatures is to affirm the pre-existent presence of all things in their supra-ontological source. Proceeding further, he discloses their mode of presence: not only are they caused, and forecontained in their transcendent origin, but are present in an infinite and unified manner—they subsist supra-ontologically. They are exhaustively subsistent in their source; the source is identical with their plenitude, more properly, he is infinitely more than their very fullness. All perfections are ultimately rooted in the common and unique source where all are identical. At its origin, Dionysius points out, each perfection arises in the same source so that, despite an evident diversity, 'it may not be said—for example—that Goodness is one and that Being is another, life or wisdom another.'[14]

TRANSCENDENCE OF GOD AS BEING

The thearchy therefore, considered in itself, is first understood philosophically—in so far as possible—as the superabundant fullness of all of those perfections manifest in the universe of Being. It is conceived according to the manner whereby it anticipates and pre-embraces to an endless degree the riches it confers upon reality. 'Nothing is self-perfect or lacking in complete perfection except that which is really self-perfect (ὄντως αὐτοτελές) and prior to all perfection.'[15] The goodness of God is known, therefore, in the first instance in terms of the participation and anticipation within it of all reality. In a word we may say, according to the positive mode of discourse, that from the perspective

---

[11] 1, 7, 26 and 1, 5, 21.
[12] 4, 22, 210.
[13] 4, 6, 130: ἀγαθὸν ... πάντας περιέχουσα τῷ ὑπερτετάσθαι καὶ πάντων ὑπερέχουσα τῷ ὑπερκεῖσθαι.
[14] 5, 2, 258.
[15] CH 10, 3, 273.

of reality God is Good as the plenary and pre-eminent perfection of Being itself.

The fullness of Being—the plenary presence of the perfection of all reality in God—forms the theme of Chapter 5 of the *Divine Names*. Although Being is for Dionysius of itself finite, it is the first of the divine gifts and thus the most significant with which to denote God's perfection. 'God is properly and principally praised above all else as Being (ὡς ὄν), from the most excellent of all his gifts, since as pre-containing and embracing all being—I mean (absolute) Being in itself—superabundantly in its origin and its transcendence, he has pre-established being itself, and through being has established all that is, whatever its manner of existing.'[16] Again: 'The transcendent Goodness itself, pouring forth the first gift of being itself (τοῦ αὐτοῦ εἶναι), is named from this venerable and primary participation.'[17] Dionysius sums up the aim of Chapter 5: 'Let us praise the Good as that which really is (ὡς ὄντως ὄν) and as the cause of existence for all beings.'[18]

We must remember that for Dionysius the word 'Being' is of itself inadequate to denote the divine nature of the thearchy; here he is employing the name to convey God's perfection in so far as possible from the evidence of finite reality. In whatever way we use the term, our language is always bound to our experience of the finite world. Nevertheless, rooted and restricted as it is within the finite horizon, the following denotation of God in terms of 'Being' emerges as significant: 'He neither was, nor will be; nor became, nor is becoming; nor will become, rather he is not; but he is the Being (τὸ εἶναι) of all beings.'[19] God embraces the fullness of Being, is yet beyond all Being. Again Dionysius' appreciation accords with Scripture: 'He who truly pre-subsists (ὁ ὄντως προών) is named by Scripture in many ways, according to every conception of being; thus he is rightly praised by "Was", "Is", "Became", "Becomes" and "Will become". Such terms signify that God *is* supra-existentially (ὑπερουσίως) and is the cause of every mode of existence.'[20] Dionysius praises God as 'He who truly is' (ὄντως ὄν),[21] a name which carries all the resonance of Exodus 3, 14. For him the name is a résumé of God's causal presence in beings. 'He who is (ὁ ὄν) is through his power beyond being the substantial cause of all being; creator of being, of subsistence, substance, essence and

---

[16] 5, 5, 266.
[17] 5, 6, 267.
[18] 5, 4, 261.
[19] 5, 5, 264.
[20] 5, 8, 280.
[21] 5, 1, 257.

nature ... he is the Being (the 'to be', τὸ εἶναι) of all things, whatever
their manner of being.'[22] Dionysius cautiously establishes a distinction:
'Moreover, God is not somehow something which is (οὐ πώς ἐστιν ὄν),
but rather he exists in a simple or absolute and unlimited way (ἁπλῶς
καὶ ἀπεριορίστως), embracing and pre-containing the whole of being
in himself.'[23] He brings out further God's fullness of Being: 'For he is
not this, but not that; nor does he exist in one way and not in another;
rather, he is all things as cause of all, embracing and anticipating in
himself the beginnings and ends of all things. And he is beyond all as
supra-existentially transcending all that is (καὶ ὑπὲρ τὰ πάντα ἐστὶν ὡς
πρὸ πάντων ὑπερουσίως ὑπερών).'[24]

Ontologically the root characteristic of the Good in its excellence as
the fullness of Being lies in its identity; it is the One par excellence:
unique and immutable, the total, exhaustive and simple plenitude of all
perfection in a unique presence, not only of that perfection which is
present in limited measure in created being, but all perfection whatsoever.
Briefly, the full plenitude of the Good is characterised by its identity in
and with itself, its fullness and presence beyond division or dependence.
Herein reside its self-sufficiency, self-rootedness and selfsameness. As
the source of Being, the thearchia is beyond the diversity of being; as
the source of multiplicity, it is transcendent unity: there is no division
or dispersion, decrease or increase within its nature (axiomatic for
Neoplatonist metaphysics). 'To it, then, must be attributed all things in
an all-transcendent unity ... It pre-contains all things in itself and in a
unique and transcendent simplicity excludes all duality, embracing all
things equally in its supra-simple infinity.'[25]

God is the One and the Good beyond Being. And while this notion
of the thearchia is unmistakably of Neoplatonist provenance, Dionysius
again appeals to Scripture in favour of his explication: 'Theology praises
the whole thearchia as the cause of all by the name of the One—for all
things are pre-contained and enclosed uniformly in the One itself.'[26] It
is, indeed Dionysius claims, the most powerful of all names
(καρτερώτατον). 'Theology predicates all things of the universal cause,
both singly and together, and praises him as the Perfect itself and as
the One.'[27] The epithets of 'Perfect' and 'One' are most closely related.
The thearchia is perfect because it is all in one; it is the fullness of

---

[22] 5, 4, 262.
[23] 5, 4, 262.
[24] 5, 8, 280.
[25] 5, 9, 284.
[26] 13, 3, 446-7.
[27] 13, 1, 435.

Being in a unified presence; it is fulfilled in its own totality, complete and replete within itself. It is its own end and the end for all (τέλειον).

The perfection of the One consists in its most consummate selfhood, in the unique and transcendent manner in which it enjoys and exercises the wealth of all beings in the intimacy of its self-constitution beyond all manner of being. 'The cause of all is the supra-plenitude of all, according to a single transcendent superfulness of all.'[28] Negatively, it can be appreciated that 'no duality can be a principle.'[29] Diversity for Dionysius is a sign of limitation, indicating a lack of completeness or absence of total perfection and goodness. Unity, simplicity and identity are hallmarks of perfection. They may be interpreted fundamentally as perfections, qualities or characteristics of Being. They were indeed identified by Parmenides, and Dionysius echoes the portrayal of the One as 'the all-embracing and undivided whole', expounded by Plato in the dialogue named after the father of ontology.[30] Such aspects of the perfect Goodness of the thearchia, its transcendence beyond difference, change, diversity and time etc., are illustrated throughout the treatise. Remarkable for its richness indeed is the variety of names used by Dionysius to praise the complete and exhaustive perfection of the thearchia, the singular fullness and excellence of the divine Good. Almost all of these names are, however, so many variations on the fundamental unity and identity in the Being of the primordial One. The total and exclusive perfection of God, his plenitude, autonomy and independence as the Primary Good, are expressed positively in terms of what is most extensive and radical in the sphere of our experience, namely Being in its various aspects. It will be of interest to examine Dionysius' appreciation of the positive dimension of the divine transcendence and elaborate upon some of the names which he attributes to the thearchia.

The perfect subsistence in Being of the thearchia is indeed stressed by Dionysius' references to the constancy of the Good, named equally as the Beautiful. In a litany of phrases, increasing and intensifying the expression of perfection, Dionysius extols the glory of God as goodness and beauty.

It is (called) Beautiful because it is all-beautiful (πάγκαλον) and more than beautiful (ὑπέρκαλον), being always and in the same manner beautiful, subject neither to generation nor corruption, increase nor decrease; not beautiful in one part and in another ugly, nor beautiful in relation to one

---

[28] 12, 4, 433: ὑπερπλήρης πάντων ἐστὶν ὁ πάντων αἴτιος, κατὰ μίαν τὴν πάντων ὑπερέχουσαν ὑπερβολήν.
[29] 4, 21, 205: πᾶσα γὰρ δυὰς οὐκ ἀρχή.
[30] *Parmenides* 137 C, D; 145A.

thing and not to another, nor beautiful in one place and not in another, as
though it were beautiful to some and not beautiful to others; but it is itself
beautiful, in itself and by itself, uniquely and eternally beautiful, containing
in advance and pre-eminently within itself the original beauty of all that is
beautiful.[31]

The characteristics of identity and totality, eternity and immutability
are clearly pronounced. The fact that the aspects denoted in this
passage—which Dionysius adapts from Plato—are those which
Parmenides prescribes for Being, gives it a twofold historical value.[32]

The absolute self-perfection and autonomy of the thearchia within
itself is again highlighted by Dionysius in Chapter 9, where he considers
the application to God of the quality of 'sameness'. Here the mark of
identity is made the specific object of praise. Dionysius writes:

The Same is supra-ontologically ($\dot{\upsilon}\pi\varepsilon\rho o\upsilon\sigma\dot{\iota}\omega\varsigma$) eternal, immutably abiding in
itself, having always the same manner of being, present to all things in the
same way; it is itself firmly and purely established through itself and of itself
in the most beautiful limits of its identity beyond Being ($\tau\tilde{\eta}\varsigma$ $\dot{\upsilon}\pi\varepsilon\rho o\upsilon\sigma\dot{\iota}o\upsilon$
$\tau\alpha\upsilon\tau\dot{o}\tau\eta\tau o\varsigma$); without change, unfailing, unwavering, abiding, pure and
immaterial, perfectly simple, without lack, with neither increase nor decrease;
it is ungenerated—not in the sense of being as yet unborn, nor as still
incomplete, nor as unengendered by this or by that, nor that it does not exist
in any manner or not at all—but as wholly and absolutely ungenerated, as
eternal Being, as Being perfect in itself ($\dot{\alpha}\varepsilon\dot{\iota}$ $\ddot{o}\nu$ $\kappa\alpha\dot{\iota}$ $\alpha\dot{\upsilon}\tau o\tau\varepsilon\lambda\dot{\eta}\varsigma$ $\ddot{o}\nu$), the same
in and according to itself, uniformly and identically determining itself.[33]

God, Dionysius continues, 'abides within himself, unmoved within his
own identity'.[34] This is repeated when Dionysius considers the terms
'standing' or 'sitting' as pronounced of God ($\sigma\tau\dot{\alpha}\sigma\iota\varsigma$, $\kappa\alpha\theta\dot{\varepsilon}\delta\rho\alpha$); they
likewise convey Dionysius' appreciation of the divine permanence and
subsistent self-sufficiency, the stability of the thearchia. 'God remains
himself in himself, abiding stably in his unmoved identity, transcendently
established in his power and acting in the same way according to the
same. He is altogether self-subsistent in his own stability and wholly
immovable in his immutability: and this in a supra-ontological manner.'[35]
Another aspect of the thearchia's consummate identity is indicated
when Dionysius describes God as 'without parts and inflexible' ($\dot{\alpha}\mu\varepsilon\rho\tilde{\eta}$
$\kappa\alpha\dot{\iota}$ $\dot{\alpha}\pi\alpha\rho\dot{\varepsilon}\gamma\kappa\lambda\iota\tau o\nu$).[36] The names 'sameness', 'unmoving' etc., applied to
God, denote his self-sufficiency, a characteristic par excellence of Being.

---

[31] 4, 7, 136-8.
[32] *Symposium* XXIX; 211AB. See Pera, *S. Thomae Aquinatis. In Librum Beati Dionysii
de Divinis Nominibus Expositio, Observationes*, pp. 115-16.
[33] 9, 4, 366-8.
[34] 9, 5, 370.
[35] 9, 8, 377-8.
[36] 9, 10, 381.

To be, without condition, is *to be fully*, without indigence but replete and autonomous within the self.

The 'consistency' of the thearchia, another word for its unity and identity in activity, is illustrated in respect both of its own constancy in causing good things and in causing moreover only what is good:

> Either he is not good, or he works goodness and produces good things; and not sometimes but not at other times, nor certain things and not all things, for thus he would undergo change and difference in what is most divine of all, namely his causality.[37]

Indeed the subsequent passage is a most forceful statement of the nature of God before all else as the Good—*ἐν θεῷ τἀγαθὸν ὕπαρξίς ἐστιν . . .* :

> If the Good is in God his very substance, then in changing from the Good, God will sometimes be and at other times will not be. And if he possesses the Good by participation, he will have it from another, and will sometimes have it and sometimes not.[38]

Here, two elementary aspects of great significance are outlined: God himself is very Goodness itself, by his very essence and not by reception or participation. Furthermore, his Goodness precedes his existence, in such a way that were he conceived at any time as anything less than his own goodness, it would be implied in effect that he would not exist.

An elegant presentation of the self-rootedness of the thearchia is to be found in Dionysius' exposé of its identity with its own goodness. This is given in Chapter 4, 14, where Dionysius explains why theologians have called God 'Love' and 'Loving-Kindness' (*ἔρως, ἀγάπη*). In brief but graphic outline, Dionysius meditates upon the infinite depth of the divine source and sketches the universal expanse of its activity—which emerges from itself and returns for its own sake upon itself.

First and foremost, 'it alone is beautiful and good through itself' (*τὸ μόνον αὐτὸ δι' ἑαυτὸ καλὸν καὶ ἀγαθόν*).[39] This is the most significant pronouncement which Dionysius makes concerning the thearchia as the very essence and identity of the Good itself. God's Being *is* his Goodness; we may say that God's 'Being' is one with his Goodness, although his Goodness is infinitely more. All else is good by participation; the thearchia alone is good of itself; and its communication of goodness, moreover, to creatures is ultimately for its own sake.

> . . . for in the end what is he if not Beauty and Goodness, the One who of himself reveals himself, the good procession of his own transcendent unity?

---

[37] 4, 21, 208-9.
[38] 6, 21, 209.
[39] 4, 14, 176.

He is yearning on the move, simple, self-moved, self-acting, preexistent in the Good, flowing out from the Good onto all that is and returning once again to the Good.[40]

The motif and élan underlying this abiding of the Good, the blossoming forth and return, its continual self-donation and response, is the love of the divine for itself. It is its own source and end; its diffusion unfolds, proceeds and returns entirely within its own realm. Its origin is identical with its final end. It enjoys pure and replete identity within its own self-love.

In this divine yearning shows especially its unbeginning and unending nature traveling in an endless circle through the Good, from the Good, in the Good and to the Good, unerringly turning, ever on the same centre, ever in the same direction, always proceeding, always remaining, always being restored to itself.[41]

The eternal dialogue and self-love of the divine Good is the best appreciation we can attain of the goodness and perfection of the thearchia: its fathomless indwelling and self-abiding, rooted in its transcendent unity, its self-diffusion for its own sake and return to its original identity.

Dionysius expresses God's absolute primacy in Being with regard to time in a variety of ways which praise him as the all-embracing ground and transcendent source of all things temporal and eternal. This is what is signified, he suggests, by the biblical name 'Ancient of Days' (Dan. 7, 22): God is both 'the eternity and time of all things, is yet before every day, beyond time and eternity.'[42]

According to Dionysius, 'time' denotes that which is affected by generation, corruption and change.[43] Now God, needless to say, is beyond all such change. His Being is simple and absolute, without limit of time or change since he pre-contains the plenitude of all that is. 'He neither was, nor will be, nor became, nor is becoming, nor will become... He is the being of all beings.'[44] His Being cannot be measured; he is beyond all measure and is himself the measure of all. 'He is the source and measure of the ages ($\dot{\alpha}\rho\chi\dot{\eta}$ $\kappa\alpha\dot{\iota}$ $\mu\dot{\epsilon}\tau\rho\nu$), the being ($\dot{o}\nu\tau\dot{o}\tau\eta\varsigma$) of temporal things, the eternity of that which is, the time of things which become, the existence of all beings whatsoever.'[45]

God is called 'King of Eternity',[46] Dionysius suggests, 'since all being exists and subsists'[47] in him and around him who remains 'unchanged

---

[40] 4, 14, 176-178, trans., Luibheid, 82-3.
[41] 4, 14, 178; trans., Luibheid, 83.
[42] 10, 2, 388.
[43] 10, 3, 395.
[44] 5, 4, 264.
[45] 5, 4, 262.
[46] I Tim. 1, 17.
[47] 5, 4, 263.

and unmoved with respect to every movement, abiding within himself in his eternal movement.'[48] Eternity is the 'measure of universal being' (τὸ καθόλου τὸ εἶναι μετρεῖν),[49] of 'that which is incorruptible and abides in sameness'.[50] Here Dionysius suggests the twofold aspect of God's immutability, together with his unending activity. Timelessness does not imply a static nature; God is eternally active within himself but in his nature transcends all change. He is so exhaustively and intensely active that all change is impossible. God is fully actual; change indicates a potency which has yet to be actualised. Significant, moreover, is Dionysius' remark that 'eternity' principally and most properly refers to 'beings which are' (τὰ ὄντα), while time indicates those things which are in a state of becoming (τὰ ὄντα τῷ αἰῶνι καὶ τὰ ἐν γενέσει τῷ χρόνῳ καὶ λεγόμενα καὶ δηλούμενα).[51] There is here a suggestion of Being as the most all-embracing and fundamental of perfections. Eternity is a characteristic of Being itself (τοῦ αὐτοεῖναί ἐστιν αἰών).[52]

The names 'ancient' and 'young' both signify in diverse ways the pre-eminence of God (τὴν ἀρχαιότητα τὴν θείαν), that he proceeds through all things from beginning to end.[53] He is named 'ancient', signifying that he is primary and from the beginning, as preceding and transcending time (ὡς πρὸ χρόνου καὶ ὑπὲρ χρόνον);[54] the term 'young', on the other hand, means that he does not grow old.[55]

Even more characteristic of Dionysius' approach, however, is his description of God as prior even to eternity itself (πρὸ αἰῶνος),[56] and beyond the eternal. Thus he argues that God lies beyond all manner of human denomination, even that which has been refined and purified of the limits of time and Being. He does not, however, venture so far as to say that God is the 'non-eternal'. To the meaning, method and scope of such negative hyperbole we now turn, in order to examine the transcendence of the Good beyond Being as portrayed by Pseudo-Dionysius.

---

[47] 5, 4, 263.
[48] 10, 2, 389.
[49] 10, 3, 394.
[50] 10, 3, 396.
[51] 10, 3, 397.
[52] 6, 1, 285.
[53] 10, 2, 391.
[54] 10, 3, 398.
[55] 10, 2, 391.
[56] 10, 3, 389.

TRANSCENDENCE OF GOD BEYOND BEING

From what we have seen, we can say that Dionysius praises God positively as Being itself. More characteristic, however, is his denomination of God as *other* than Being, as *prior* to Being, and ultimately even as *Non-Being*. For Dionysius, the transcendence of God beyond beings, considered both positively and negatively, is again indicated primarily through the relation of causality. In the positive sense God constitutes the plenitude of such perfection as is apportioned to creation in finite measure. As causal origin the thearchia surpasses and excels all beings. 'The Beautiful and Good is above all things that are'.[57] The original Platonist phrase ἐπέκεινα τῆς οὐσίας,[58] is re-echoed in various forms: The Good is: πάντων οὖσαν ἐπέκεινα,[59] ἔξω καὶ ἐπέκεινα τῶν ὅλων,[60] τοῦ πάντων ἐπέκεινα,[61] πάντων ἐστὶν ἐπέκεινα πάντων αἴτιος ὤν,[62] ἐπέκεινα τῶν ὅλων.[63]

Negatively, this fullness or transcendence is most clearly expressed as follows: 'The cause of all things that are is itself none of these but *supra-ontologically transcends them all* (ὑπερουσίως ἐξῃρημένον)'.[64] In other words, not only does the thearchia surpass all things but is 'free of' or 'exempt from' all beings.[65] It is 'supra-essentially separated from all things'.[66] As de Gandillac points out, ἐξῃρημένης is the classical Neoplatonist term to indicate the transcendence of the One.[67] This is clearly stated in the *Celestial Hierarchy*: 'The hidden thearchy is supra-essentially separated from all, abiding transcendently in itself (ὑπεριδρυμένης); and none among beings can be properly and fully called by a name similar to his.'[68] More significant, however, both here and elsewhere, is the word ὑπερούσιος, -ως. Not only does the thearchia transcend all beings: it transcends even Being itself and all modes of Being. God is 'supra-existential' or 'supra-essential', ὑπερούσιος; He 'is' beyond all manner of existence; 'existing supra-essentially beyond all beings' (ὑπὲρ τὰ ὄντα ὑπερουσίως εἶναι).[69] 'The cause of all is truly

---

[57] 4, 9, 148.
[58] *Republic*, VI, 509B.
[59] 11, 1, 405.
[60] *Ep.* 9, 5, 1112C.
[61] 9, 5, 371.
[62] *Ep.* 5, 1076A.
[63] *MT* 5, 1048B.
[64] 1, 5, 23.
[65] 2, 11, 73.
[66] *CH* 13, 3.
[67] *La Hiérarchie Céleste*, p. 150 n. 3.
[68] *CH* XII, 3, 293B.
[69] *MT* 1, 2, 1000A.

beyond all, and he who is supra-essential and supernatural entirely
transcends all things (ὑπερέχῃ), whatever their being and nature.'[70]
Dionysius is incongruously constrained by a language proper to beings
to speak of the thearchia which 'really is (ὄντως ἐστίν) the one beyond
all things'.[71] His writings abound with such phrases denoting the
transcendence of God as 'existing' beyond all manner of existence. In
brief, 'God transcends Being and is "supra-essentially" (καὶ οὐσίας ὁ
θεὸς ἐξῄρηται καὶ ἔστιν ὑπερουσίως).'[72] This might well be taken to
mean that God himself has no essence, that his Being is not
circumscribed by any finite measure or limitation. This understanding
would indeed be correct, since Dionysius uses the word οὐσία to refer
to beings both in their essence and to the reality of their existence. The
transcendence of the thearchy beyond Being is, therefore, not totally
conveyed by ὑπερούσιον—although it could be held that, because he
does not distinguish between the essence and existence of beings, in
denoting God as 'super-essential', Dionysius also understands him as
beyond existence itself. Because of an as yet undifferentiated vocabulary,
the interpretation of God as 'supra-existential' would be legitimate and
I believe this is the author's intended meaning. That it is so, i.e. that
he considers God 'to be' beyond all existence, is, moreover, clear from
Dionysius' letter to Titus, where God is said to be ὑπὲρ αὐτὸ τὸ εἶναι.[73]
And in a pithy phrase he writes that 'the "to be" (εἶναι) of all things
is the *divinity beyond being*.'[74] God, therefore, transcends existence itself.
He is more than Being; he is other than Being.

The total ontological priority and transcendence of the thearchy is
also expressed in the term προών. The cause of all beings precedes and
anticipates Being itself. Being may well be the first participation but
the Good itself exceeds and is anterior to Being.[75] 'Being itself is never
deficient in any being, but Being (the self-existent) is from the Pre-
existent (ἀυτὸ δὲ τὸ εἶναι ἐκ τοῦ προόντος).'[76] Beings come to be
because they participate in self-existing Being, but they are caused by
the Pre-existent. 'All beings and all ages have their being from the Pre-
existent.'[77] Dionysius emphasises, moreover, that the Pre-existent is both
the beginning and end of all things.[78] 'The Pre-existent is the principle

---

[70] 11, 6, 426.
[71] *MT* 1, 3, 1000C.
[72] 4, 20, 201.
[73] *Ep.* 9, 5, 1112C.
[74] *CH* IV, 1, 177D: τὸ γὰρ εἶναι πάντων ἐστὶν ἡ ὑπὲρ τὸ εἶναι θεότης.
[75] 5, 5, 266.
[76] 5, 8, 278-279.
[77] 5, 5, 265 : πᾶσι τοῖς οὖσι καὶ τοῖς αἰῶσι τὸ εἶναι παρὰ τοῦ προόντος.
[78] 5, 10, 284: πάντων οὖν ἀρχὴ καὶ τελευτὴ τῶν ὄντων ὁ προών.

and cause of every kind of being . . . if anything whatsoever is, it is and
is thought and is preserved in the Pre-existent.'[79]

The pre-eminent and pre-ontological causation of the thearchy is
again forcefully expressed in a passage, referred to already, where
Dionysius uses the words προεῖναι and ὑπερεῖναι together with προέχων
and ὑπερέχων, suggesting more adequately by the verbal form the
intense activity and presence, yet the transcendence of the supra-original
Good. '(That which is) pre-existence and supra-existence (τὸ προεῖναι
καὶ ὑπερεῖναι), pre-embracing and transcending all Being (προέχων καὶ
ὑπερέχων τὸ εἶναι πᾶν), has pre-established . . . Being itself (αὐτὸ καθ᾽
αὐτὸ τὸ εἶναι) and through this Being established all being, whatever
its manner of existence.'[80]

In another striking phrase Dionysius states that 'He who is really
pre-existent' is cause and source of all.[81] The very phrase ὁ ὄντως
προών, literally 'beingly before Being', appears almost as a contradiction.
Dionysius is here straining against the limits of language. Similarly we
find the statement that 'God is Being supra-existentially' (ὤν ἐστιν ὁ
θεὸς ὑπερουσίως).[82] And Dionysius even speaks of the Good as really
(i.e. in its being) beyond Being (τῷ ὄντως ὑπερουσίῳ).[83]

In Dionysius we meet the basic Neoplatonist principle that the cause
of all beings is itself necessarily beyond, or prior to its effects. 'Only
Being itself beyond being is the source, being and cause of the being of
all beings.'[84] And he notes that all beings have 'their being and their
well-being from the pre-existent'.[85] God, it is emphasised, 'is infinite in
power (ἀπειροδύναμος), not becauses he produces all power, but
because he is above and beyond all power, even self-subsistent power
itself (αὐτοδύναμις).'[86] God produces power, therefore, only because he
is himself beyond all Power. His creative causality stems from his utter
transcendence as the Good beyond Being itself, which in turn is elevated
beyond all that shares in Being. Only with the prefatory remark, 'If it
is proper to say so', does Dionysius remark that 'Being itself has the

---

[79] 5, 5, 265.
[80] 5, 5, 267.
[81] 5, 8, 280.
[82] 2, 11, 73.
[83] 4, 3, 111 Cf. 5, 8, 280: ὑπερουσίως εἶναι.
[84] 11, 6, 424: μόνον γὰρ τοῦ εἶναι πάντα τὰ ὄντα καὶ αὐτὸ τὸ εἶναι ὑπερούσιον ἀρχὴ
καὶ οὐσία καὶ αἴτιον.
[85] 5, 8, 277: τὰ ἄλλα πάντα ὄντα . . . καὶ τὸ εἶναι καὶ τὸ εὖ εἶναι ἔχει καὶ ἔστι καὶ εὖ
ἐστι ἐκ τοῦ προόντος.
[86] 8, 2, 333.

power to be from the power beyond Being' (παρὰ τῆς ὑπερουσίου δυνάμεως).[87]

GOD AS NON-BEING

In order to emphasise even further the otherness and transcendence of the thearchia beyond Being, Dionysius conceives of the divinity even as Non-Being! 'He abides transcendently beyond mind and being . . . he is not, but is supra-essentially.'[88] The 'non-being' or 'non-existence' of God is needless to say in no manner a depreciation of the divine and Dionysius makes the distinction: 'For nothing is completely a non-being, unless it is said to be in the Good in the sense of beyond-Being.'[89] According to Dionysius, reason will even dare to say that 'Non-Being is beautiful and good when celebrated supra-essentially of God by the removal of all things.'[90] We have here an eloquent example of Dionysius' apophatic discourse indicating the transcendence and pre-eminence of the divine.

The negation of Being in God, as of all perfections, is the indication of its transcendent and pre-eminent presence according to a wholly distinct mode within the divine thearchy. 'In no manner like any being, yet the cause of Being to all things, it is itself Non-Being as beyond all Being.'[91] We find this doctrine outlined with some detail in DN 4, 3 where Dionysius writes: 'Since the Good is above all beings, as indeed it is, as formless it creates all forms, and in it alone is Non-Being a super-excellence of Being.'[92] The Good is Non-Being precisely because it is an excess or superabundance of Being. Significantly the principle established by Plotinus comes to the fore: a cause must be free from limit and must transcend whatever it causes. The Good is cause of Being only because it is itself other than Being, i.e. Non-Being. As formless it can of its limitless power create all forms and so determine all beings. Only as Non-Being is it the superabundant source of Being.

---

[87] 8, 3, 334.

[88] Ep. 1, 1065A: αὐτὸς δὲ ὑπὲρ νοῦν καὶ ὑπὲρ οὐσίαν ὑπεριδρυμένος . . . μηδὲ εἶναι, καὶ ἔστι ὑπερούσιος.

[89] 4, 19, 190.

[90] 4, 7, 141: τολμήσει δὲ καὶ τοῦτο εἰπεῖν ὁ λόγος ὅτι καὶ τὸ μὴ ὂν μετέχει τοῦ καλοῦ καὶ ἀγαθοῦ· τότε γὰρ καὶ αὐτὸ καλὸν καὶ ἀγαθὸν ὅταν ἐν θεῷ κατὰ τὴν πάντων ἀφαίρεσιν ὑπερουσίως ὕμνηται.

[91] 1, 1, 7: κατὰ μηδὲν τῶν ὄντων οὖσα· καὶ αἴτιον μὲν τοῦ εἶναι πᾶσιν, αὐτὸ δὲ μὴ ὂν ὡς πάσης οὐσίας ἐπέκεινα . . .

[92] 4, 3, 111: εἰ δὲ καὶ ὑπὲρ πάντα τὰ ὄντα ἐστίν—ὥσπερ οὖν ἐστι—τἀγαθὸν καὶ τὸ ἀνείδον εἰδοποιεῖ καὶ ἐν αὐτῷ μόνῳ καὶ τὸ ἀνούσιον οὐσίας ὑπερβολή.

It is the source of life only because as non-living it is the superabundance of Life (καὶ τὸ ἄζωον ὑπερέχουσα ζωή). Without intellect it is itself transcendent wisdom (καὶ τὸ ἄνουν ὑπεραίρουσα σοφία). In summary, 'Whatever is in the Good is a supereminent formation of the formless.'[93] Here we have not merely a theory of negative discourse which serves to highlight the absolute transcendence of the Good but more radically a theology of Non-Being itself. The same doctrine also appears in the *Mystical Theology*, where Dionysius states that 'The cause of all, being beyond all, is not without Being, or life, or without reason or intelligence.'[94] This triad of created perfection—Being, Life and Wisdom—is a fundamental theme in Neoplatonism and recurs as a constant refrain in the writings of the Pseudo-Dionysius.

GOD BEYOND BEING AND NON-BEING

Not yet content with his definition of the thearchy as beyond Being, or even as Non-Being, Dionysius seeks to advance still further in his attempt to express the supremacy of God. The highest to which he attains is to say that the Good even transcends both Being and Non-Being; the things which are and the things which are not. Here he formulates in terms of reality the principle that the Good is beyond both affirmation and negation.

This is an even more remarkable aspect of the relation between the Good and Being. Not only must the primary Good be understood as Non-Being, precisely as the transcendence and supereminence of Being itself; its primacy before Being also means that even *that which is not* is contained within the Good. Not only do all beings derive from the transcendent Good and are therefore embraced in it by anticipation but, moreover: 'All the things which are not abide supra-essentially in the Beautiful and the Good.'[95] Dionysius reasons: 'If all beings are from the Good, and the Good is beyond beings, then even non-being has its being in the Good.'[96] He gives some indication of what this may signify by placing it in the context of the finality of causation. 'The Beautiful and the Good is desired, sought and loved by all; even non-being desires it and strives somehow to be in it . . . and through it that which is not is affirmed and exists supra-ontologically.'[97]

---

[93] 4, 3, 111.
[94] *MT* 4, 1040D.
[95] 4, 10, 155: πάντα τὰ οὐκ ὄντα ὑπερουσίως ἐν τῷ καλῷ καὶ ἀγαθῷ.
[96] 4, 19, 190.
[97] 4, 18, 184: εἰ πᾶσίν ἐστι τὸ καλὸν καὶ ἀγαθὸν ἐραστὸν καὶ ἐφετὸν καὶ ἀγαπητόν—

Dionysius suggests that prior to existing, things which are as yet uncaused desire the Good in some way: 'If it is lawful to say so, even non-being itself aspires to the Good beyond all beings and strives through the denial of all things somehow to exist within the Good which is really beyond Being.'[98] They come into being in fulfilment of their love for the Good. In this way, whereas 'Being' embraces things which have being, the Good has dominion both over things which are, as well as over things which do not yet exist. The Good is understood by Dionysius, therefore, not only as the fullness of Being but as preceding and superseding Being itself, not merely as Non-Being but even as transcending Being and Non-Being. The thearchy is Non-Being itself as surpassing both Being and that which has not Being.

Dionysius appears to be quite aware of the magnitude and ambition of his enterprise: 'All things desire the Beautiful and the Good according to every cause and there is not any among beings which does not participate in the Beautiful and Good. Indeed, our discourse will even *dare* to say that non-being (τὸ μὴ ὄν) participates in the Beautiful and the Good.'[99] He believes, however, that he has equalled the magnitude of the task. Concluding Chapter 4 of the *Divine Names*, Dionysius claims that he has 'adequately celebrated the Good as truly admirable, as the principle and end of all . . . as perfect Goodness transcending both beings and non-beings.'[100] The significance of the name 'Good' and its transcendence beyond Being is again given in résumé at the start of Chapter 5: 'The divine name of Good, revealing all the processions of the universal cause, is extended to beings; it is beyond both beings and non-beings. The name of Being, however, is extended to all beings and is beyond beings.'[101] The name of Being when attributed to God praises him as the Cause of Being and as transcending, therefore, all things which are. The name of the Good praises him, however, as embracing not only the things which are, but those which are not; these participate in anticipation of their existence, as it were, already in the Good. The transcendence of the Good, its primacy

---

ἐφίεται γὰρ αὐτοῦ καὶ τὸ μὴ ὄν, ὡς εἴρηται, καὶ φιλονεικεῖ πως ἐν αὐτῷ εἶναι . . . καὶ ἐπ' αὐτοῦ καὶ τὸ μὴ ὄν ὑπερουσίως λέγεται καὶ ἔστι.

[98] 4, 3, 111: εἰ θεμιτὸν φάναται, τἀγαθοῦ τοῦ ὑπὲρ πάντα τὰ ὄντα καὶ αὐτὸ τὸ μὴ ὄν ἐφίεται καὶ φιλονεικεῖ πως ἐν τἀγαθῷ καὶ αὐτὸ εἶναι, τῷ ὄντως ὑπερουσίῳ κατὰ τὴν πάντων ἀφαίρεσιν.

[99] 4, 7, 141.

[100] 4, 35, 256: νῦν δέ, ὡς καθ' ἡμᾶς ἀρκούντως ὕμνηται τἀγαθὸν ὡς ὄντως ἀγαστόν, ὡς ἀρχὴ καὶ πέρας πάντων, . . . ὡς πρόνοια καὶ ἀγαθότης παντελὴς καὶ ὑπερβάλλουσα τὰ ὄντα καὶ τὰ οὐκ ὄντα.

[101] 5, 1, 257: καὶ γὰρ ἡ τἀγαθοῦ θεωνυμία τὰς ὅλας τοῦ πάντων αἰτίου προόδους ἐκφαίνουσα, καὶ εἰς τὰ ὄντα ἐκτείνεται καὶ ὑπὲρ τὰ ὄντα καὶ ὑπὲρ τὰ οὐκ ὄντα ἐστίν· ἡ δὲ τοῦ ὄντος εἰς πάντα τὰ ὄντα ἐκτείνεται, καὶ ὑπὲρ τὰ ὄντα ἐστί.

before Being, arises from its dominion not only over beings, but also over non-being.

The Meaning of 'Non-Being' for Dionysius

For Dionysius, God is beyond the very distinction of Being and Non-Being.[102] His transcendence is evident from the greater universality of his causal power which extends beyond the domain of being to embrace non-being.[103] In his scholion to the *Divine Names*, Maximus sums up well the uniqueness of Dionysius' position. To the objection 'How can that which is non-being participate in the Good?', the Confessor tellingly remarks: 'This holy man understands "non-being" differently' (τὸ μὴ ὂν διαφόρως νοεῖ ὁ θεῖος ἀνήρ),[104] and he gives an accurate summary of Dionysius' doctrine: 'non-being' refers to God who is beyond beings and to matter which, being formless, cannot properly be said to be but which, participating in the Good, acquires form and therefore being. The interpretation of non-being as referring to God and to formless matter is generally espoused by Dionysius' commentators and would appear to be correct. To non-being as matter Aquinas apports a more fundamental perspective which we shall examine. First it will be informative for our enquiry to recall the context of Dionysius' doctrine with reference to his own text.

Nowhere does Dionysius explicitly identify non-being with matter. We find passages, however, where non-being and 'formless' are associated and where the non-being of what is formless through an absence of being is juxtaposed with the Good which through superabundance is without form and existence. In 4, 3, 111, for example, we read: τἀγαθὸν καὶ τὸ ἀνείδεον εἰδοποιεῖ καὶ ἐν αὐτῷ μόνῳ καὶ τὸ ἀνούσιον οὐσίας ὑπερβολή. The same relation between these two distinct kinds of non-being is repeated in 4, 18, 184; here again we find the contrast between non-being which desires the Good, and the supra-existential Good which gives form and being to the formless and non-existent: τὸ καλὸν καὶ ἀγαθὸν ἐραστὸν καὶ ἐφετὸν καὶ ἀγαπητὸν— ἐφίεται γὰρ αὐτοῦ καὶ τὸ μὴ ὄν, ὡς εἴρηται, καὶ φιλονεικεῖ πως ἐν αὐτῷ εἶναι καὶ αὐτό ἐστι τὸ εἰδοποιὸν καὶ τῶν ἀνειδέων καὶ ἐπ' αὐτοῦ καὶ τὸ μὴ ὂν ὑπερουσίως λέγεται καὶ ἔστι.

---

[102] *MT* 1, 997B.
[103] 5, 1, 257.
[104] *PG* IV, p. 254.

Indeed, not only is the Good supra-existential in itself, embracing all things that are, but more significantly, as the ground of all things which it inaugurates into existence from non-being, all things which are not are anticipated supra-existentially in the Beautiful and the Good.[105] Dionysius sums this up in the last lines of the chapter on the Good: 'The Good is praised as embracing the things which are, and as creating the forms of non-beings, transcending beings and non-beings.'[106] Here again what is without form is equated with non-being.

We may safely conclude, therefore, that by 'non-being' Dionysius understands matter which is devoid of form and which cannot thus be said properly to be. He does not, however, characterise the non-being of matter as something which is completely non-existent. Absolute non-being is predicated of God alone; speaking in another context—that of evil—Dionysius affirms: 'Nothing is wholly non-existent unless this is said supra-substantially of the Good.' The transcendent Good alone is non-existent in a supra-existential manner. From the phrase 'If all beings are from the Good, and the Good is beyond beings, even non-being has its being in the Good,' we may conclude that matter falls within the domain of non-being which abides within the Good. Of the Good, Dionysius states forcefully: 'The Good transcends by far and is greatly prior to what simply is and what is not.'[107] And of evil he declares that it is even more distant from the Good than non-being.[108] Thus we have three senses of non-being: (1), the transcendent Non-Being of the absolute Good which exceeds both Being and non-being, (2), the relative non-being of matter deprived of form which has however a disposition towards determination and existence and (3), evil, which is even more distant from being than matter and of which Dionysius declares 'it is not itself in any manner whatever existent ($\kappa\alpha\grave{\iota}$ $\alpha\grave{\upsilon}\tau\grave{o}$ $\mu\eta\delta\alpha\mu\tilde{\omega}\varsigma$ $\mu\eta\delta\alpha\mu\tilde{\eta}$ $\mu\eta\delta\grave{\varepsilon}\nu$ $\check{o}\nu$).'[109] Thus while Dionysius considers matter to be without form—and therefore less than fully existent—he never asserts that it is wholly non-existent. Indeed in *DN* 4, 28, Dionysius emphasises that matter has a certain share in beauty, order and form, and while matter cannot act without these and is therefore incomplete in itself, it is nevertheless necessary for the complete perfection of the universe.[110] Without form and order, matter is not complete in its being; it is nevertheless more than non-being. Dionysius

---

[105] See 4, 10, 155.
[106] 4, 35, 256.
[107] 4, 19, 190.
[108] See Pera's note, p. 166.
[109] 4, 32, 245.
[110] 4, 28, 232 and 234.

considers indeed the possibility of the non-existence of matter as well
as its existence, indicating that in either case matter cannot be a source
of evil; he rejects, however the conclusion that matter does not exist.
To the contrary, in the *Celestial Hierarchy*, Dionysius states that 'matter
also has received existence from him who is truly beautiful'.[111] Thus,
whereas for Plotinus, the last trace of divine power is to be found in
living things,[112] Dionysius in this unique passage attributes existence to
matter and refers it to the divine Good. More characteristic is the
affirmation that matter is a remote echo, the most distant and most
feeble of all the realities which proceed from God.[113]

We may note that Dionysius once uses the term πρώτη ὕλη,[114] not
in the sense of Aristotle, but as referring to the objects in the material
world which first receive the rays of the sun. He is using the image to
illustrate the degrees in which the divine power is received by the
angelic orders. In this analogy, Dionysius indeed suggests that there are
degrees of nobility in the material world itself; sunlight passes easily
'through first matter' but diminishes when received and reflected by
more dense and opaque matter. In accordance with this meaning,
Corderius translates πρώτη ὕλη as *materia proxima*.[115]

This is, in brief, the meaning which Dionysius attaches to the notion
of matter, which is significant for his understanding of the priority of
Goodness beyond Being. Before reviewing Aquinas' response to
Dionysius' theory of being and non-being, and the latter's affirmation
of the priority of the Good, it will be of benefit to take a preliminary
look at Aquinas' understanding of the nature of goodness.

---

[111] *CH* 2, 144B.
[112] de Gandillac, *La Hiérarchie Céleste*, p. 83, n.1.
[113] 4, 20, 198: κατ᾽ ἔσχατον ἀπήχημα πάρεστι τἀγαθόν.
[114] *CH* 13, 3, 301A, ed. Heil, p. 151.
[115] *CH* 13, 301A.

CHAPTER FOUR

AQUINAS: BEING, NON-BEING AND THE GOOD

THE NOTION OF THE GOOD

In his understanding of the good, Aquinas is initially guided by the teaching of Aristotle. It is not surprising, therefore, that much can be learned from the first *lectio* of his Commentary on the *Nicomachean Ethics*. To Aristotle's well-known phrase, 'The Good is what all things desire',[1] Aquinas adds valuable insight and elaboration. He begins with a remark which is important for the entire treatment, namely, that 'the good' is a notion which is ultimate or primary in itself. It is interesting that even within this context Aquinas allowed this as a reason why the Platonists could hold that the good is prior to being; he states summarily, however, that they are more properly convertible. Goodness, along with being, is one of those fundamental characteristics which cannot be analysed into concepts anterior to itself. It cannot be reduced to elements which are simpler or more ultimate; however, it becomes manifest through the things which derive from it, as a cause is revealed by its effects. Since the effect proper to the good is that it moves the appetite or will, this is how it may be described. The good is thus defined as that which all things desire.[2]

Desirability, however, is a consequence or result of goodness. To describe the good as that to which all things tend, Aquinas notes, is to indicate by means of a characteristic the presence of goodness rather than disclose its essence or ground. Aristotle's definition indicates what we may term the 'phenomenological' content of goodness—its

---

[1] *Nic. Eth.* I, i, 1094 a: καλῶς ἀπεφήναντο τἀγαθὸν οὗ πάντα ἐφίεται.
[2] *In Ethicorum*, 1, 1, 9: Considerandum est, quod bonum numeratur inter prima: adeo quod secundum Platonicos, bonum est prius ente. Sed secundum rei veritatem bonum cum ente convertitur. Prima autem non possunt notificari per aliqua priora, sed notificantur per posteriora, sicut causae per proprios effectus. Cum autem bonum proprie sit motivum appetitus, describitur bonum per motum appetitus, sicut solet manifestari vis motiva per motum. Et ideo dicit, quod philosophi bene enunciaverunt, bonum esse id quod omnia appetunt.

manifestation to the desiring subject—but does not penetrate to that which fundamentally constitutes it as such. In Plotinus' phrase: 'The good must be desired; but it is not good because it is desirable; it is desirable because it is good.'[3] It is thus necessary to go beyond the *ratio boni* which allows us to recognise goodness, to the *natura boni*, its ontological ground.[4] In question 5 of the *Summa Theologiae*, Aquinas gives such a foundation to goodness by indicating its identity with being, more exactly with being conceived as actuality.

In this question Aquinas establishes that while *ens* and *bonum* are identical in reality they differ in their meaning for reason, i.e. in what they expressly signify to knowledge.[5] Being expresses the reality that something exists; goodness signifies its relation to the will and denotes being as desirable. Goodness thus adds to being the character of appetibility. Now Aquinas declares that each thing is clearly desirable in so far as it is perfect, since what all things desire is necessarily their own perfection.[6] We shall see that this is the case both where something is loved directly for its own sake, being perfect in itself, or desired as an indirect means for the perfection of another. Beings are desired, that is, either as fully perfect or as perfective of another. Perfection is thus the goal towards which desire is directed. The good is what as such is perfect; perfection is of the essence of goodness. This definition of the good as the desired contrasts with that of Plato, for whom the good is known primarily, not because of its desirability but through its generosity. Tò ἀγαθόν, for Plato, is at the summit of the intelligible world and is the source of all being and value. Moreover, Goodness, in the Platonist tradition, exercises efficient rather than final causality.[7]

Seeking the ground of perfection as such, Aquinas in turn states that anything is perfect only in so far as it is in act,[8] inasmuch as it is actually and really endowed with, i.e. determined or perfected by, the qualities or resources which constitute it as an object of desire. That which is in potency is lacking in perfection.[9] Actuality alone fundamentally endows or grants value. Only that which is real can be desired. What is only possible or merely potential cannot be in any way

---

[3] *Enneads* VI, 7, 25.

[4] See Joseph de Finance, *Connaissance de l'être*, pp. 161-2, *Essai sur l'agir humain*, p. 79.

[5] *ST*, I, 5, 1: Dicendum quod bonum et ens sunt idem secundum rem, sed differunt secundum rationem tantum.

[6] *ST*, I, 5, 1: Manifestum est autem quod unumquodque est appetibile secundum quod est perfectum, nam omnia appetunt suam perfectionem.

[7] See de Finance, *Connaissance de l'être*, p. 160.

[8] *ST*, I, 5, 1: Intantum est autem perfectum unumquodque inquantum est actu.

[9] *ST*, I, 5, 1 ad 1.

the term of tendency or desire, or be perfective of another. What grounds perfection is its very reality or existence itself. Now, the first and fundamental actuality of each being is its very act of existing (*esse*), i.e. the act whereby it really exists and in virtue of which all its determinations are made actual. *Esse* or the act of being is thus the actuality of every thing and something is good inasmuch as it exists.[10] A thing is perfect only because it exists and possesses in reality the determinations which are the modes of its being. In summary, therefore, being or existence is the source of goodness in all things. They have actuality to the extent to which they have being; to be actual is to be perfect, thus desirable, and this for Aquinas is precisely what is signified by goodness. It is clear, therefore, states Aquinas, that being and good are the same in reality, although *bonum* makes explicit the note of 'desirability' not expressly pronounced in the notion of *ens*.

Thus while Dionysius, in accordance with the Platonic tradition, defines goodness through its generosity or efficiency, and Aristotle describes it as the term of desire, we encounter in Aquinas an example of the masterly way in which these complementary points of view may be harmonised through a discovery of their common ground.[11] St Thomas succeeds in fusing the final and efficient viewpoints of Aristotle and Dionysius. This he does by deepening Aristotle's own notion of act so as to ground all actuality in the primary perfection of being. (We shall observe later how Dionysius' influence in this discovery is significant). The perfection of actuality is the foundation of goodness both as origin and end. Something is said to be good because it is desired; but it is desired only because it can further perfect the reality of that which seeks it. Now, this it can do only if it is itself in act— having the resources to actualise what is potential in the other, and more radically if it is *actu esse*, in actual existence. Furthermore, at their fundamental and universal level all beings seek God in so far as they strive towards their own perfection. The reason is that God is first cause, which is possible only if he is the pure and plenary actuality of Being, *Ipsum Esse Subsistens: purus actus absque permixtione alicuius potentiae*.[12] So, whether loved in a disinterested manner as fully perfect in itself, as is the case with God, or indirectly solicited as a means of perfecting another, goodness is grounded in the actuality of existence. The good is sought either as the perfect plenitude of actual being, or

---

[10] *ST*, I, 5, 1: Unde manifestum est quod intantum est aliquid bonum inquantum est ens: esse enim est actualitas omnis rei.
[11] See Heinrich Weertz, *Die Gotteslehre des Ps. Dionysius und ihre Wirkung auf Thomas von Aquin*, p. 15.
[12] *ST*, I, 9, 1.

relatively as perfective of the being of another. Existence is the common source of goodness in both senses.

Aquinas indeed adopts from Dionysius many phrases which are close to Aristotle's definition of *bonum*. In *De Veritate* 22, 1, for example, while discussing the question *utrum omnia bonum appetunt*, even before citing Aristotle he first refers to Chapter 4 of *Divine Names* and paraphrases a number of texts: *Dionysius dicit, cap. IV de divinis Nominibus: Existentia pulchrum et bonum desiderant; et omnia quaecumque faciunt, propter hoc quod videtur eis bonum, faciunt; et omnium existentium intentio principium et finem habet bonum.*[13] Only in second place does he invoke the authority of Aristotle: *Praeterea, Philosophus dicit, I Ethicorum, quod quidam bonum bene definierunt, dicentes, quod bonum est quod omnia appetunt.*[14] And it is again with reference to *DN*, 4, 10 that Aquinas writes in *ST*, I-II, 27: *Cum enim bonum sit quod omnia appetunt, de ratione boni est quod in eo quietetur appetitus.*[15] In *Contra Gentiles* 3, 3, we find a similar juxtaposition of the views of Dionysius and Aristotle on the nature of the good. Having expounded on the good as the perfection towards which action is directed, Aquinas concludes: *Hinc est quod Philosophi definientes bonum dixerunt: Bonum est quod omnia appetunt. Et Dionysius, IV Cap. de Divinis Nominibus, dicit quod omnia bonum et optimum concupiscunt.*[16]

Perhaps the most profound rapprochment between Dionysius and Aristotle in this matter is to be found in *ST*, I, 6, 1, where Aquinas wishes to show that goodness belongs pre-eminently to God. He begins with Aristotle's definition that a thing is good inasmuch as it is desirable and recalls that each thing desires its own perfection. But the perfection of whatever is caused consists in a likeness to its source, since it is in the nature of every agent to produce an effect which resembles itself

---

[13] *De Veritate* 22, 1, sed contra; Durantel, p. 156, citation 73, refers this passage to 4, 7. In fact the first part is from 4, 10 (Pera 158) where, according to Sarracenus' translation, Dionysius writes: Omnia pulchrum et bonum desiderantia faciunt et volunt quaecumque faciunt et volunt. The last phrase of Aquinas' passage is a summary of a number of lines from 4, 7 (Pera 140-1) which, again according to Sarracenus, read as follows: Est principium omnium pulchrorum, sicut effectiva causa et movens tota ... et finis omnium sicut finalis causa, etenim pulchri causa cuncta fiunt ... quoniam bonum et pulchrum secundum omnem causam cuncta desiderant. Durantel only refers to the last phrase of this passage from 4, 7.

[14] *De Veritate* 22, 1.

[15] *ST*, I-II, 27, 1 ad 3.

[16] This passage seems to have been adapted from Eriugena's translation of 4, 7, 704B (Pera 140-1): Ideo et id ipsum est optimo bonum, quia bonum et optimum juxta omnem causam omnia concupiscunt. It is curious that Aquinas here follows Scotus' translation of τοῦ καλοῦ καὶ ἀγαθοῦ as *bonum et optimum*, while Sarracenus more accurately renders *pulchrum et bonum*. Other references to Aquinas' citation of 4, 7 and 4, 10 are given by Durantel, pp. 156 and 159-60. He neglects, however, to note *Contra Gentiles* 3, 3.

(*cum omne agens agat sibi simile*).[17] In desiring its own perfection, therefore, every effect seeks to participate more fully in the likeness of its cause. Aquinas declares that since God is the first efficient cause of all things, he is pre-eminently desirable for all and therefore universally good. He concludes 'It is for this reason that Dionysius in *The Divine Names* attributes goodness to God as the primary efficient cause, saying that God is called good "because from him all things subsist in their being." '[18]

AQUINAS' INTERPRETATION OF DIONYSIUS' NON-BEING

Matter as Non-Being

Aquinas does not hesitate to immediately identify the non-being of Dionysius with 'prime matter' (*ipsum non-existens, idest materia prima*;[19] *non-existens, idest materia prima*;[20] *id quod non-est, scilicet materia prima*),[21] and it is in keeping with the Platonist concept of matter that he interprets in turn the priority of the Good beyond Being in the scheme of Dionysius:

> To understand why God is named as good, it should be considered that the Platonists, not distinguishing matter from privation, placed it in the order of non-being, as Aristotle states in *Physics* I.[22] Now the causality of being extends only to the things which are (*entia*). Thus according to the Platonists, the causality of being did not extend to prime matter, to which, on the contrary, the causality of the good extends. A sign of this is that prime matter most of all seeks the good. It is indeed proper to an effect to turn through desire towards its cause. Thus the Good is a more universal and supreme cause than Being, since its causality extends to more things.[23]

---

[17] The obverse of this principle also holds true: nihil autem appetit nisi simile sibi. (*ST*, I, 5, 2 ad 1).

[18] *ST*, I, 6, 1: Dicendum quod bonum esse praecipue Deo convenit. Bonum enim aliquid est secundum quod est appetibile. Unumquodque autem appetit suam perfectionem; perfectio autem et forma effectus est quaedam similitudo agentis, cum omne agens agat sibi simile. Unde ipsum agens est appetibile et habet rationem boni, hoc enim est quod de ipso appetitur ut eius similitudo participetur. Cum ergo Deus sit prima causa effectiva omnium, manifestum est quod sibi competit ratio boni et appetibilis. Unde Dionysius in libro de Div. Nom. attribuit bonum Deo sicut primae causae efficienti dicens quod bonus dicitur Deus sicut ex quo omnia subsistunt. Cf. *DN*, 4, 4, 121.

[19] IV, ii, 298.

[20] IV, v, 355.

[21] IV, xiii, 463.,

[22] *Physics* I, ix, 192a.

[23] III, 226. See *In de Causis*, IV, 101: Causa autem prima est latior, quia extendit se etiam ad non-entia. *In de Causis*, lect. IV, Prop. XXI, 724b: Materia non participat ens, sed tamen participat bono.

Aquinas attributes this view of matter also to Dionysius: *Unde tam ipse (Plato) quam sui sectatores materiam appellabant 'non-ens', propter privationem adiunctam. Et hoc modo loquendi etiam Dionysius utitur.*[24] In his Commentary on the *Liber de Causis*, Aquinas provides the following explanation:

> According to the Platonist viewpoint, the more general something is, the more they posited it as separate—as something prior, participated by posterior things, and therefore as cause of the posterior. In the order of those things which are affirmed most generally they placed the one and the good, which are more general even than being, since the good or the one is predicated of that of which being is not predicated, namely prime matter which Plato classed with non-being, not distinguishing between matter and privation, as is stated in Physics I; yet he attributed unity and goodness to matter, in so far as it is ordained to form. The good is spoken not only of the end, but of that which is ordered towards end.[25]

Aquinas attributes the Platonist identification of matter with non-being to Plato's failure to distinguish between matter and privation.[26] The concept of privation is indispensable for an understanding of the material world. Plato had already made the distinction between matter and form, thereby correcting, as Aquinas notes,[27] the view of the ancients that matter was the sole principle of movement in the corporeal world. He failed, however, to discover the third principle of material being which is necessary to explain the process of becoming, namely, στέρησις, i.e. the privation of form. Aristotle's concept of privation allows matter to be viewed as potency towards form rather than as simple non-being. Matter never exists without form; form is the co-principle together with which it alone receives existence. Yet, informed by a specific determination, it is not of necessity restricted for once and forever to that particular form. Determined by a single form it excludes and is deprived of all others; these are, however, not totally beyond the bounds of its existence: they are not excluded to the very limits of absolute non-being but reside to a greater or lesser degree within its potential resources.

---

[24] IV, ii, 295.

[25] *In de Causis*, IV, 98: Secundum positiones platonicas ... quanto aliquid est communius, tanto ponebant illud esse separatum et quasi prius a posterioribus participatum et sic esse posteriorum causam. In ordine autem eorum quae de rebus dicuntur communissimum ponebant unum et bonum, communius etiam quam ens, quia bonum vel unum de aliquo invenitur praedicari de quo non praedicatur ens: scilicet, de materia prima, quam Plato coniungebat cum non-ente, non distinguens inter materiam et privationem, ut habetur in I Physic. et tamen materiae attribuebat unitatem et bonitatem, inquantum habet ordinem ad formam. Bonum enim non solum dicitur de fine, sed de eo quod est ad finem.

[26] See also *ST*, I, 5, 2 ad 1 and *In DN*, IV, ii, 295.

[27] IV, ii, 295.

Thus, for Aristotle too, matter is also associated with privation, but is not identical with privation. Privation of form is correlative to a receptivity or openness towards further enrichment through the medium of form. Plato did not have at his disposal the concepts of potency and privation, and neglecting to differentiate between matter and privation, equated the privation of form with an absence of existence. He was thus obliged to define matter as non-being. It is in this sense that Aristotle writes, in that paragraph of his *Physics*, to which Aquinas frequently alludes: 'We say, however, that matter and privation are different, that matter is accidentally non-being while privation is in itself non-being; matter is proximate to being and is in a way being, but privation is in no way real.'[28] The distinction is clear for Aristotle: matter may not be confused with privation and although not fully existent, it is infused with a desire and tendency towards being. Of this desire for Being Aristotle himself writes: 'Being is something divine and good and desirable and whereas privation is the contrary of being, it is in the nature of matter to seek and desire it according to its own nature.'[29]

There is in fact a striking parallel here with Dionysius. One has the impression that Aristotle and Dionysius differ only in the terms employed. Aristotle speaks of matter as potential and therefore in some manner existent, seeking actuality and perfection through form; Dionysius understands matter as non-being which, since it desires existence as its primary good even before entering the realm of reality, is embraced under the reign of the universal Good. As Aquinas notes, according to the Platonists the more superior a cause, the more universal its power.[30] Now, that which undergoes causal influence primarily and most universally is prime matter, since of itself it is devoid of all actuality and determination. It can be the effect of the prime cause alone, i.e. the Good, since the causality of secondary causes does not extend to it. 'Because everything which is caused turns through desire towards its cause, prime matter desires the Good; since desire is

---

[28] *Physics* I, ix, 192a: ἡμεῖς μὲν γὰρ ὕλην καὶ στέρησιν ἕτερον φαμὲν εἶναι, καὶ τούτων τὸ μὲν οὐκ ὂν εἶναι κατὰ συμβεβηκός—τὴν ὕλην—τὴν δὲ στέρησιν καθ' αὑτήν, καὶ τὴν μὲν ἐγγὺς καὶ οὐσίαν πως—τὴν ὕλην—τὴν δὲ στέρησιν οὐδαμῶς.

[29] *Physics*, I, ix, 192a: ὄντος γάρ τινος θείου καὶ ἀγαθοῦ καὶ ἐφετοῦ, τὸ μὲν ἐναντίον αὐτῷ φαμὲν εἶναι, τὸ δὲ ὃ πέφυκεν ἐφίεσθαι καὶ ὀρέγεσθαι αὐτοῦ κατὰ τὴν ἑαυτοῦ φύσιν. See Aquinas, *In DN*, IV, ii, 295: Secundum Aristotelem necessarium sit materiam a privatione distinguere, quia materia quandoque invenitur sub forma, quandoque sub privatione; unde privatio adiungitur ei per accidens. Cf. *De Veritate* 21, 2.

[30] See *Contra Gentiles* 3, 74: Quanto autem aliqua causa est superior, tanto est maioris virtutis: unde eius causalitas ad plura se extendit. Also *ST*, I, 65, 3; Cf. Proclus, *Elements*, Props. 57 and 70; *De Causis*, Prop X (95); *In de Causis* X, 251. Cf. *In de Causis* I, 29.

but the disposition of a being towards the actualisation of what it is deprived of (*privatio et ordo ipsius ad actum*).'[31]

The primal propensity of matter towards the perfection of form is thus a theme common to Aristotle, Dionysius and Aquinas. For Aristotle, matter is simultaneously characterised by its privation of form and a native orientation towards its acquisition. To escape the void of sheer indeterminacy, matter strives for form and is ever in need of new formation; it is continually impelled towards new perfection within its appropriate sphere of potential. This indigenous orientation is the root of the dynamism and continual renewal within the world. For Dionysius, form is the first-sought goal of matter and thus its primary good. Through the influence of form, matter is first inaugurated into the realm of reality. Without form, matter is of itself non-being and strives to attain form as its good, not—as Albertus Magnus has appropriately remarked, in the manner of an activity—but through the natural desire for what is proper to it and of which it is deprived.[32]

In his commentary on the passage from Aristotle cited above, that being (*ens*) is desirable, Aquinas curiously writes: *FORMA est quoddam divinum et optimum et appetibile*. Every form is a certain participation in the likeness of divine being who is pure act, and each thing is actual in so far as it possesses form. Form is good because it is the perfection of potency, and therefore desirable since each thing desires its perfection.[33] Later he remarks that natural desire is nothing other than the disposition of beings towards their end in accordance with their nature. Most relevant for our discussion is Aquinas' assertion: 'But not only is that which is in act through an active power directed towards its end, but matter too in so far as it is in potency, since form is the end of matter. For matter to seek form is for it to be directed towards form as potency to act.'[34] Aquinas perceives the concordance of Dionysius and Aristotle in respect of this doctrine: 'Matter, existing in itself without quality and form, is not capable of anything, since the principle of acting is form through which something is in act; since each thing acts in as far as it is in act.'[35] For Aristotle, Dionysius and Aquinas alike, matter is inscribed with a need and predisposition for

---

[31] IV, ii, 296.

[32] *Super Dionysium de Divinis Nominibus*, IV, 235: Certare non dicitur hic per modum alicuius actionis, sed dicitur materia certare ad bonum propter desiderium, quod habet boni, ad quod est apta nata propter privationem adiunctam.

[33] *In Physic.*, I, 7.

[34] *In Physic.*, I, 10.

[35] IV, xxi, 560: Materia autem secundum seipsam existens sine qualitate et forma non potest aliquid, quia principium agendi est forma per quam aliquid est actu; unumquodque autem agit secundum quod actu est.

form, towards which of its nature it tends as its initial good. For Aristotle and Aquinas matter thereby comes into actuality; for Dionysius it comes into being; and since prior to acquiring existence it is already related to it as a good, matter falls within the sphere of goodness. Since before existing, it participates in goodness by desire, Dionysius attributes a more universal causality to the Good, exerting as it does causal influence beyond the range of being, embracing through anticipation the unformed matter in its desire for perfection. Because matter, although it is 'non-being', seeks its own perfection and determination, it comes under the influence of the Good. The Good is the ultimate goal of every desire. Hence we may conclude: *finis et bonum convertuntur*. The highest and final goal, namely Goodness itself, must also be the object of the deepest, most primordial desire and need.

Matter is subject to the causality of the Good through desire; it is the primary subject of universal causality since as formless it is disposed towards being as its first determination. Being is sought as a good, and since each thing in pursuing its good seeks a resemblance with its cause, the universal cause is the absolute Good itself. To say that existence is desired by matter bears a twofold implication for Dionysius: since being is precisely what is sought by matter as its primary good, it is by that token clear that matter does not fall within the domain of being; and secondly, since being is sought as an instance of the good, i.e. as an approximation towards the primary Good, the ultimate goal is the Good itself, first and universal cause of all. Being is seen, by Dionysius, not as the foundation of perfection or goodness, but as an approximating measure or instance of the Good which embraces Being as something desired.[36]

---

[36] Matter retains what Aquinas terms a *debile esse*. See *De Veritate*, 3, 5, ad 1: Quamvis materia prima sit informis, tamen inest ei imitatio primae formae: quantumcumque enim debile esse habeat, illud tamen est imitatio primi entis; et secundum hoc potest habere similitudinem in Deo. Cf. *In VIII Phys.*, 1, 2, 974: Unde hoc ipsum in potentia quod habet materia prima, sequitur derivatum esse a primo essendi principio, quod est maxime ens. For further references to Aquinas' view of the ontological status of prime matter, see William J. Hoye, *Actualitas Omnium Actuum*, p. 113, n. 112. Hoye remarks: '*Ens in potentia* is situated at the bottom of the hierarchy of being, but it still has a real place in this hierarchy.' In *Contra Gentiles* 3, 20, 2012, Aquinas notes that matter holds the lowest grade in goodness, just as it holds the lowest grade in being. (Possidet igitur haec substantia ultimo modo dicta, sicut ultimum gradum in esse, ita ultimo gradum in bonitate.) *In I Sent.*, 36, 2, 3 ad 2: Esse autem perfectum, materiae non convenit in se, sed solum secundum quod est in composito; in se vero habet esse imperfectum secundum ultimum gradum essendi, qui est esse in potentia. *De Spirit. Creat.*, Q. 1, p. 370: (Materia prima) est incompletissimum inter omnia entia. For an interesting discussion of matter, see William E. Carlo, *The Ultimate Reducibility of Essence to Existence in Existential Metaphysics*, pp. 117-36; also the excellent pages on the positive character of matter in Fabro's *Participation et Causalité*, pp. 413-16.

God as Non-Being

Maximus had remarked that by non-being Dionysius understands both God and prime matter. For Aquinas there is suggested even a unique similarity between prime matter and the Good. Moreover, the twofold principle that every agent causes something resembling itself, and that every effect seeks a likeness to its cause, is operative in Dionysius' view and receives special comment from Aquinas. The non-existence of prime matter bears a certain resemblance towards the beauty and goodness which is praised in God through the removal of all things. 'In prime matter their removal is considered through defect, but in God through excess, inasmuch as he exists supra-substantially.'[37] Prime matter is conceived as non-being because it lacks all character and determination of being and cannot, therefore, exist of its own accord; the Good, on the other hand, is viewed as non-being because it possesses none of the determinations of beings but transcends them universally, while embracing them virtually in its superabundance. Aquinas recognises that 'by a certain remote resemblance, a likeness of the first cause is found in prime matter.'[38] Prime matter and the primary Good are both without form, the former through deficiency, the latter by excess. Both pure potency and pure act are devoid of determination: pure potency as prior to all determination, pure act as beyond all determination. All of the forms which are lacking in matter are virtually and eminently present in the transcendent cause. And matter, ordered necessarily by a fundamental need towards the acquisition of form, is thus implicitly oriented towards the primary Good in whom are preserved all forms and perfections. When Dionysius says that 'even non-being desires the good beyond all being and strives itself to be somehow in the Good',[39] he is referring, according to Aquinas, to 'prime matter, in so far as it desires a form which is a similitude of divine *esse*.'[40] In this manner it aims to be in the Good and to resemble it, while for its part the Good communicates to prime matter the inclination towards form. Goodness and being are predicated essentially of the substantial Good 'by the denial of all things'—not through any defect, as with prime matter, but due to its excess. Aquinas summarises his understanding of Dionysius' view:

---

[37] IV, v, 355.
[38] IV, ii, 297.
[39] 4, 3, 111: τἀγαθοῦ τοῦ ὑπὲρ πάντα τὰ ὄντα καὶ αὐτὸ τὸ μὴ ὂν ἐφίεται καὶ φιλονεικεῖ πως ἐν τἀγαθῷ καὶ αὐτὸ εἶναι.
[40] IV, ii, 298.

Non-being is affirmed of the supreme Good and is moreover present in it, not by defect, as is said of prime matter and pure negation or sheer privation, but supra-substantially. God is indeed called non-existent, not because he is lacking in existence, but because he is beyond all existing things.[41]

It is significant that Aquinas here writes *super omnia existentia* rather than *super omne esse*. For St Thomas, although God surpasses all existing things, he cannot be said without qualification to transcend *esse* as such, as Dionysius holds, because it is his nature to be *ESSE* itself.[42]

Potency as Non-Being

In his Commentary on the *Divine Names* Aquinas is anxious to present a plausible interpretation of Dionysius' view that God's nature is Goodness itself which transcends the status and scope of Being. In the face of this position it is interesting, as we have seen, to observe his reading of non-being as matter, but, more importantly in broader terms his equation of non-being with being-in-potency. It is in terms of causality, therefore, allied with the distinction of actual and potential being that Aquinas' exegesis of Dionysius' theory is set out. By situating the discussion within the Aristotelian framework of potency and act, Aquinas provides a broader metaphysical perspective for an understanding of Dionysius.

In the opening paragraph of his commentary on Chapter 5, Aquinas states that Dionysius deems the Good prior to Being, and therefore treats of it firstly, because, according to the Platonists, goodness 'somehow' extends beyond being (*quia bonum quodammodo ad plura se extendit, ut Platonici dixerunt*). This view Aquinas straightaway translates into his own metaphysical terms: 'For that also which does not exist in act, but is being in potency, because it is ordained towards the good,

---

[41] IV, xiii, 463.

[42] We find occasionally in Aquinas' Commentary an attenuation of Dionysius' sense of 'non-being', to the point where it seems almost to lose its intended meaning. In IV, xiv, 478, he writes: 'That which is beyond all beings must be non-being, just as that which is beyond all bodies is non-corporeal.' Here he understands non-being as signifying simply that which transcends the existence of finite beings. This is the meaning which he apparently gives to 'suprasubstantial', thereby agreeing with Dionysius' assertion that 'nothing is fully non-existent, unless non-existence is said of the supreme good according as it is beyond substance' (4, 19, 190). And Dionysius' statement 'The Good is established far beyond that which is both simple being and non-being' (Ibid.) is toned down by Aquinas who adds that the Good transcends non-being 'according as it is found in things'. This presentation of Dionysius' conception of Goodness, being and non-being is at once an underestimation of Dionysius' own intention and an implicit revelation of its inherent limitation.

has, from this very fact, the nature of goodness; but it participates in
the causality of being only when it becomes actual being.'[43] Potential
being, therefore, according to Aquinas in his exposé of Dionysius, lies
outside the scope of being but is comprehended by the Good. Potency
towards existence is itself portrayed as a good. 'The name of the
Good . . . extends both to things which exist as well as to things which
do not exist, in so far as non-beings have something of the good
according as they are in potency to being.'[44] The name Goodness
expresses the complete and universal providence of God, whereas
'Being' denotes only a determinate effect.[45]

The interpretation of non-being as that which is itself not in existence,
but which as potentially existent is pre-ordained towards being and
therefore good, is proper to Aquinas' Commentary and is nowhere
suggested by Dionysius. Its significance, however, is crucial for Aquinas
because it allows a plausible interpretation of the Dionysian primacy of
the Good. Ingenious is the manner in which Aquinas marshals in its
favour an interpretation of a passage from Dionysius concerning the
relation of angels towards the Good. Dionysius has stated that divine
minds (οἱ θεῖοι νόες) have both a greater desire for the Good and a
more perfect participation than other things in the Beautiful and the
Good.[46] From this Aquinas concludes that angels not only have a
greater participation in the Good, 'possessing actually a more perfect
goodness', but that having a greater desire for the Good, they are
'more perfectly ordered towards it'. Taking this passage as a statement
regarding the twofold relation of angels towards goodness, namely
through desire and by actual possession, Aquinas claims to discern in
Dionysius the view that goodness is found in creatures in two ways,
namely 'according to an actual participation of the good or through a
disposition towards the good.'[47] This, suggests Aquinas, is in accordance
with Dionysius' fundamental principle that the Good also extends to
what is not actually in being.[48] Angels are thus more perfectly ordered
towards goodness, he states, 'through a certain "approximation"
(*appropinquatio*) towards it'. Aquinas' reading of Dionysius is as follows:

---

[43] V, i, 606 see also VII, i, 697: Bonum autem, secundum quod prius dictum est,
quantum ad causalitatem est prius quam ens, quia bonum etiam ad non entia suam
causalitatem extendit..

[44] V, i, 610.

[45] V, i, 613.

[46] 5, 3, 260: παρὰ πάντα τὰ ὄντα τοῦ καλοῦ καὶ ἀγαθοῦ ἐφίενται καὶ μετέχουσιν,
αὐτοὶ μᾶλλόν εἰσι περὶ τἀγαθὸν οἱ περισσῶς αὐτοῦ μετέχοντες καὶ πλείους καὶ μείζους
ἐξ αὐτοῦ δωρεὰς εἰληφότες.

[47] V, i, 616: His enim duobus modis, bonum in creaturis invenitur: aut secundum
participationem actualem boni aut secundum ordinem ad bonum.

[48] V, i, 616: Bonum se extendit etiam ad non-ens actu.

angels share in goodness according to the measure in which they are actually good, i.e. in proportion to their actual being. They desire, furthermore, such goodness as they do not possess. Goodness thus holds dominion both over the actual possession of perfection—the measure of its being—and its privation, i.e. its lack of being understood as potency.

BEING AS FIRST DESIRED

Now, whereas for Dionysius the Good is beyond Being because it moves non-being to seek its first determination and good in existence, for Aquinas existence is itself the first and final good sought by all things. Existence is of itself in its own character of finality the primary good sought by all things. He interprets the causality, which according to Dionysius is exerted by the transcendent Good upon non-being to be the final causality imparted by existence to potential being in its tendency towards actualisation. *Esse*, the act whereby anything exists, is its first and fundamental good; the basic and initial perfection of each thing is that it should actually be. By definition, the good is what all things desire. But manifestly all things primarily desire actuality, since each thing pursues its own preservation and resists corruption; moreover, what is potential tends towards its realisation. It is thus actuality which constitutes the very nature of goodness. More basically, it is *esse*, the actuality of being, which constitutes the good; the good of each thing is its act and perfection of being: *Esse igitur actu boni rationem constituit . . . naturaliter enim bonum uniuscuiusque est actus et perfectio eius.*[49] For every thing, it is the same to be and to be good: *Esse enim actu in unoquoque est bonum ipsius.*[50]

This has for Aquinas the importance of a fundamental law: a principle regarding the nature of value—and the value of reality—which had already been formulated: *Melius esse quam non esse*: ἄμεινον εἶναι πολλῷ τὸ εἶναι τοῦ μὴ εἶναι.[51] Each thing in its own way strives for actuality: that which has existence in act seeks to preserve its being and what is potential is oriented dynamically through a native impulse to attain actuality. Although Aquinas in the following passage from *De Veritate* does not have Dionysius in mind, it clearly illustrates his view that existence is the primary good and serves as a strategic counterpoint

---

[49] *Contra Gentiles*, 1, 37.
[50] *Contra Gentiles*, 1, 38.
[51] Clement of Alexandria, *Stromata* VI, 17, cited by Pera, p. 79.

to the Pseudo-Areopagite. Beginning with Aristotle's definition, he outlines as follows how *esse* is the primary and fundamental good of all things.

> Since the essence of good consists in this, that something be perfective of another in the manner of an end, everything which has the character of an end also has the nature of goodness. Now two things belong to the nature of end: it must be sought or desired by things which have not yet attained the end, and loved by the things which share the end, as something which is lovable. For it is essentially the same to tend towards an end and in some way to repose in it (just as it is by one and the same nature that a stone moves towards the centre and rests there). Now these two properties (tendency and rest) are found to belong to the very act of being (*ipsum esse*). For those things which do not yet participate in the act of being tend towards it by a certain natural appetite. In this way matter tends to form, according to the Philosopher in *Physics* I. But all things which already have existence, however, naturally love that existence and preserve it with all their power . . . The act of existing itself has the nature of a good. Thus, just as it is impossible that there be any being which does not have existence, so too it is necessary that every being be good from the very fact that it has existence, although in certain beings many aspects of goodness are added over and above the act of being whereby they subsist.[52]

Aquinas is here referring to the initial act of being, understood in an unqualified sense, as distinct from the intensive, perfective value of being which embraces all the subsequent goodness of each entity.

Aquinas may remark, therefore, that while the phrase *Omnia bonum appetunt* does not suggest that there is a unique good to which all things aspire, but that each thing naturally tends to a good suitable to itself, nevertheless, if reduced to a particular good, this unique good desired by all would be the act of being. 'Nor is this prevented by the fact that all things have existence, since whatever has being desires its continuance, and what has being actually in one way only has it potentially in another . . . and thus what does not have being in act desires to be actually.'[53]

Esse is thus universally the unique good sought by all. All things are animated by a zeal for being: *omnibus delectabile est esse*.[54] When Aquinas notes with Aristotle, therefore, that goodness does not present a unique or single meaning but shares rather in a diversity of meaning similar to that of the categories of being, this means that goodness is universally grounded through the actualisation of existence; being is analogously the perfection of each entity. 'Every action and movement are seen to be ordered in some way toward being (*esse*), either that it

---

[52] *De Veritate* 21, 2.
[53] *De Veritate* 22, 1 ad 4.
[54] *De Veritate* 22, 1 ad 7.

may be preserved in the species or in the individual, or that it may be newly acquired. Now, the act of being is itself good, and so all things desire to be. Therefore, every action and movement are for the sake of the good.'[55] Aquinas is thus echoing Aristotle's view: τὸ εἶναι πᾶσιν αἱρετὸν καὶ φιλητόν.[56] And referring to existence as the primary good sought universally by all, he transforms the view of Plotinus: 'All things inasmuch as they do not possess the Good, wish to change; as soon as they have it, they wish to be what they are.'[57] As the actualising principle of all existential richness, *esse* is the term of desire: sought by things which are not fully in act, loved and preserved by those which already exist.

Moreover, whereas for Dionysius, potency is primarily good from the mere fact that prior to its existence it has through desire a tendency towards the Good, for Aquinas whatever tends as potential towards its goal does so in so far as it has in real existence a likeness towards its goal (*similitudo secundum esse naturae*). Now, in so far as the form of one thing is present in another with perfect actuality, there is no such tendency but rather repose. But in so far as something has potentially within itself the form of its good, it desires it and tends towards it as end. In this manner matter is said to desire form, as form resides potentially within it. For Aquinas, therefore, the dynamism of tendency and actualisation arises from this similitude in real existence: 'The more that potentiality is achieved and brought closer to act, the more vigorous is the inclination which it causes. This is why any natural motion is intensified near the end when the thing tending to the end is more like that end.'[58] This is another instance of the fecundity of being as actuality, which for Aquinas is the principle and origin of all acquisition and communication of perfection. The closer the proximity in being, all the more intense is the impulse of what is in progress towards perfection and the more fruitful is the bestowal by its source.

GOODNESS, BEING AND CAUSALITY

The question is also raised repeatedly in the other works of Aquinas, which is more fundamental: *Ens* or *Bonum*, and which perfection is more suitable to denote the nature of God? It is principally with

---

[55] *Contra Gentiles* 3, 3, 1881.
[56] *Nic. Eth.*, IX, 7, 1168a 7-8.
[57] *Enneads* VI, ix.
[58] *De Veritate* 22, 1, ad 3.

Dionysius in mind that Aquinas raises this question; the difficulties
which he registers against his own view are drawn from Dionysius. It
is objected, firstly, that in the *Divine Names* Dionysius treats in the first
place of the Good, suggesting thereby that it is also prior of itself to
existence. Secondly, it also seems that what is more general is also
prior, and since goodness according to Dionysius is more universal than
Being—extending beyond the things which partake of being, to non-
being which it calls into existence—goodness is therefore prior to
being.[59]

Aquinas' standard reply is that being and goodness are in reality
identical; in the order of knowledge being is primary, whereas in respect
of causality the good is prior. *Bonum* is more expressive of divine
causality, in particular of God as the final end and perfection of all
creatures. It is to God as cause, therefore, Aquinas states, that Dionysius
attributes the transcendence of the Good. He is treating of the divine
names according as they express the nature of causality (*secundum
rationem causalitatis*). 'The Good extends to beings and non-beings not
by predication but according to its causality.' Moreover, by non-beings
in Dionysius' thought, Aquinas understands 'not those things which do
not exist absolutely and totally, but those things which are potential
and not actual.'[60] The Good exerts a final causality over those things
which are potential, since they are in motion towards it, whereas being
(*ens*) exerts at most a formal causality in respect of things which
actually exist.

But whereas for Dionysius the Good is more universal than Being,
since it embraces (to use Aquinas' terms), both beings which are actual
and in potency, according to Aquinas, everything is good precisely
inasmuch as it is in being—either in actual existence or because as
potency it tends towards actuality of being. It is in their proportion to
esse that all things are good, whether actual or potential.

> Being is divided by act and potency. Now, act as such is good, for something
> is perfect according as it is in act. Potency too is a good thing, for potency
> tends towards act, as is clear in every change; potency is proportionate to
> act and belongs in the same genus with act; privation does not belong to it,
> except accidentally. So everything which exists, whatever its mode of existence,
> is good inasmuch as it is a being.[61]

In *De Veritate* 21, 2, Aquinas also explains the causal priority of
goodness in the light of the distinction between predication and
causality. The act of existing only extends in causality to those things

---

[59] *ST*, I, 5, 2; also *De Veritate* 21, 2.
[60] *ST*, I, 5, 2 ad 2.
[61] *Contra Gentiles* 3, 7, 1917.

which actually exist. Goodness on the other hand, while it is not predicated of things which do not exist, extends its causality to them inasmuch as through desire they fall under its influence.[62] Aquinas thus concedes that things which do not exist in actuality may participate through desire in the nature of the Good. In *De Malo* 1, 2, this conclusion is given more validity: potency as such is good in itself. Discussing here the question *Utrum malum sit in bono*, St Thomas points out that the good may be considered in two ways: either in general, in an unrestricted, absolute sense (*de bono absolute*) or according to a particular aspect (*bonum hoc*). Now, considered absolutely, Aquinas seems to agree with the Platonists that the good has a most universal extension (*amplissimam*), greater even than being. The good is that which is desired, and what is in itself desirable as an end is thereby also in itself good. But whatever is ordered towards an end, by its very relation towards end, thereby becomes desirable too and acquires the status of a good. Moreover, what is in potency towards the good has also a relation towards goodness, since to be in potency is precisely to be ordered towards act. Aquinas concludes, therefore, that whatever is in potency shares by that very fact in the nature of goodness. This reasoning he then applies to the Platonist view of matter.

> Every subject, thus, inasmuch as it is in potency with respect to any perfection whatsoever, even prime matter, from the fact that it is in potency, has the nature of goodness. And since the Platonists did not distinguish between matter and privation, but classed matter together with non-being, they stated that the good extends more widely than being (*quod bonum ad plura se extendit quam ens*). Dionysius seems to have followed this way of thinking in his book *On the Divine Names* when he ranked the good as prior to being. And although matter is to be distinguished from privation and is non-being by accident only, this view, nevertheless, is to some extent true, since prime matter is only potentially being and through form acquires being as such; but it has potency through itself alone; and since potency belongs to the nature of the good, it follows that goodness belongs to it *per se*.[63]

What is perhaps remarkable about this passage on the nature of the good considered simply or absolutely as it is in itself, in which Aquinas concedes a measure of truth to Dionysius' view on the wider extent of the good, is that this agreement is not strictly required by the context. Nor does it occur in response to any objection from the authority of Dionysius which would call for a favourable interpretation. Aquinas wishes to argue that evil can only be found in what is good, since, considered absolutely, evil has no existence in itself. He points out that

---

[62] *De Veritate* 21, 2 ad 2.
[63] *De Malo* 1, 2.

evil may reside only in what is good as potential being: it is but the absence of a perfection in a subject which has a due and natural potency towards such perfection. St Thomas explains that evil cannot coincide with the good in its primary concrete state—the perfection itself of a thing (*ipsa perfectio rei*)—since they are contraries. Here of course he is revealing his own doctrine that the real goodness of a thing consists in its possession of perfection through actual existence, i.e. it derives from its actual being. Aquinas could indeed have expressed the fact that evil can exist only in the good, by saying that evil is the absence of a potential good in an existing being (which is thus good) in so far as it remains yet unfulfilled and potential in some sense. For the sake of emphasis no doubt, he invokes the Neoplatonist view of goodness beyond existence, thus allowing a greater charge of meaning to the term 'good' than is necessary and than can be ultimately sustained in his own metaphysics of value, as we shall later see.

In the *Summa Contra Gentiles* 3, 20 also, Aquinas attributes goodness to matter in virtue of its potency towards form and its impulse towards existence. Whereas form is good in itself, and composite substances receive their goodness and actuality through form, matter is good in so far as it is in potency for form. Aquinas however affirms that although any thing is good inasmuch as it is a being, it does not follow that matter, which is being purely in potency is thereby only potentially good.

> For 'being' is said absolutely, whereas 'good' also involves a relation (*bonum autem etiam in ordine consistit*), for something is said to be good not only because it is an end or has achieved its end, but just as it is ordered towards an end (*ordinatum in finem*) which it has not yet attained, by this very relation itself it is called good. Matter, therefore, cannot simply be called being as such, because it is potential being and is predicated in relation to actual existence (*ordo ad esse*); it can, however, because of this relation, be called good without qualification. It appears thus that the good is, in a way, of wider scope than being. For this reason, Dionysius in Chapter 4 of *The Divine Names* states that 'the good extends to existing things and non-existing things.' For even the non-existent, i.e. matter understood as privation, desires a good, since nothing desires the good except that which is good.[64]

Aquinas suggests here that goodness embraces the promise as well as the possession of perfection.

What at first appears to be a literal reversal of this position occurs in *De Veritate* 21, 2. Aquinas writes: 'Just as prime matter is being potentially and not actually, so it is potentially perfect and not actually,

---

[64] *Contra Gentiles* 3, 20, 2013; Cf. *Contra Gentiles* 3, 7, 1917.

and good potentially and not actually.'[65] What is remarkable about the denial of the unqualified goodness of matter on this occasion is that it occurs immediately after a response[66] in which Aquinas has conceded a greater universality to goodness through causality if not by predication. Noteworthy, however, is that on the one hand, Aquinas is dealing with a difficulty raised from the perspective of Algazel and, on the other, with a statement from Dionysius which has the approval of Maximus. We observe again Aquinas' reluctance to contradict the fundamental doctrine of the writer whom he believed to be the disciple of St Paul.

The same modification in the explanation of the goodness of matter is found in *ST*, I, 5, 3 ad 3, where Aquinas declares emphatically: *Dicendum quod materia prima, sicut non est ens nisi in potentia, ita nec bonum nisi in potentia.* Again of interest is that he makes this assertion immediately before claiming support from Platonism against the objection that not everything in existence is good, since prime matter as such is not desirable but only desires. In defence Aquinas cites the view held by the Platonists that because of its privation matter is properly speaking non-being, although by its predisposition to the good it 'partakes something of the good.' There is of course no conflict or contradiction between these various texts. For Aquinas, only that which has actual existence can enjoy goodness in reality; but whatever is in potency, by the fact that it is oriented towards a fuller actuality of being, comes under the influence of *esse* which it seeks as final end.

It is because goodness has for Aquinas the nature of end, attracting beings beyond their state of actual perfection to their plenitude of goodness, i.e. their fullness of being, that he may concede that the Good is in a sense prior to Being. Ultimately grounded in the actuality of being, the good as such always has reference to end. From the outset, therefore, Aquinas discusses the question of the primacy of the Good within the context of final causality. From this perspective, and in the light, moreover, of the distinction between actual and potential being, Aquinas is able to read Dionysius' view in a manner wholly in harmony with his own metaphysics. Aquinas simply understands Dionysian non-being as signifying potential being; *ens* is equivalent to the existential perfection present formally and actually in beings, whereas *bonum* is the final end and total perfection of all things: it comprehends both actual and potential being. This is indeed a refined rearrangement and profound transformation of the Dionysian universe according to a new ontological hierarchy in which Being is transcendent.

---

[65] *De Veritate* 21, 2 ad 3: Sicut materia prima est ens in potentia et non in actu; ita est perfecta in potentia et non in actu, et bona in potentia et non in actu.

[66] *De Veritate* 21, 2 ad 2.

What Aquinas is here making Dionysius say is that in its finality, as the fullness of perfection sought by all beings, Being as end precedes and surpasses the actuality of Being which is exercised by finite beings.

Most revealing in this regard is Aquinas' explanation of the dialectic of meaning between the concepts of being and goodness. *Ens* signifies simply and primarily that something is in act (*esse in actu*) so that 'being' may be pronounced as such without qualification of all that simply exists in its initial distinction from mere potency. Any further perfection in being, beyond the first act whereby something exists, is predicated of it, not in the unqualified sense of basic existence, but is added to it as denoting a certain aspect. *Bonum*, on the other hand, signifies what is desirable as perfect and thus suggests the idea of something complete as fully attained or realised. Something is called 'good' without qualification only when it is completely and perfectly actualised. If its perfection is not so complete as it should be, then although it has the initial perfection of existence, it cannot simply be called good without qualification, but only in a certain respect. 'To exist without qualification is to achieve an initial actuality; to be good without qualification is to achieve complete actuality.' (*Secundum primum actum est aliquid ens simpliciter et secundum ultimum, bonum simpliciter.*)[67] This inverse relation between the signification, *simpliciter*, of 'being' and 'goodness' reveals from a unique point of view the distinction between being in its general, extensive meaning, denoting that which simply is, and its intensive or all-comprehensive sense as the plenary perfection of all which is. While being is in both senses identical in subject with goodness, only in its full and intensive meaning is it identical in both connotation and denotation with the good and may be predicated interchangeably with it.

The notion of goodness is more expressive than the mere statement of existence; it gives not only the fact, but the ultimate reason why, the purpose for which things are. As W.K.C. Guthrie remarks with respect to Plato: 'Even when one knows that something *is* or exists, there is always the further question, What is it for? What is the good of it? The good of a thing is the final explanation of its existence.'[68] As convertible with goodness, Being also, in its infinite and intensive sense—in the case of divine Being—has this final and gratuitous character.

The Good is prior from the point of view of causality, because finality takes precedence in the order of causes. Introducing in his Commentary the question of the primacy of the Good, Aquinas explains

---

[67] *ST*, I, 5, 1 ad 1.
[68] *A History of Greek Philosophy*, Vol. IV, p. 507.

that it was Dionysius' intention in *The Divine Names* to consider those names which reveal the emanations of creatures from God in so far as he is cause of things. As such, God is best named as Good, since first and universally it is the Good which has the nature of cause.[69] Aquinas adduces two reasons for attributing causal superiority to *Bonum*, reflecting respectively the two aspects of causation, final and efficient. 'The good, firstly, has the nature of an end; but end has primarily the nature of cause.'[70] This is of course a translation of the principle: *omne agens agit propter finem*—each thing acts for the sake of its own good. The corollary of this, *omne agens agit sibi simile*, expresses the second ground for the priority of *Bonum*, signifying, according to Aquinas, that a cause acts, not in so far as it simply exists in some manner or other, but inasmuch as it is perfect; the perfect, namely, has the nature of goodness.[71] Perfection is thus the ἀρχή and τέλος of all. Each thing acts in view of its own full and final perfection, but acts only in so far as it is itself already in some measure perfect. Efficient and final causality stand thus in a reciprocal relation. Aquinas brings them into clear counter-focus as belonging to the same universal causality of Being. Considered as both final and efficient cause, therefore, the Good seems to take precedence over Being. This is, however, the only occasion where Aquinas attributes primacy also to *Bonum* with regard to efficient causation. He usually declares the Good to be primary as final cause. (Aquinas completes his exposé of the Neoplatonist order of causes according to the Aristotelian division by remarking that, for its part, form is cause inasmuch as it makes matter actual, while matter only becomes actual under the influence of the agent or efficient cause.)

In attributing primacy to the Good as final cause, Aquinas in no way jeopardises his own position. In agreeing with Dionysius that from a causal point of view, the notion of goodness is prior to that of being, Aquinas need not abandon his own view of God as transcendent Being for a divine transcendence beyond Being. As Etienne Gilson remarks, St Thomas merely places the thought of Dionysius within the context where it is fully true, namely that of finality. Reinterpreted from this perspective it reinforces indeed Aquinas' theory of God as the plenitude of Being.[72]

---

[69] III, 227: Id autem quod habet rationem causae, primo et universaliter est bonum.

[70] III, 227: Bonum habet rationem finis; finis autem, primo, habet rationem causae.

[71] III, 227: Agens agit sibi simile, non inquantum est ens quocumque modo, sed inquantum est perfectum. Perfectum enim, ut dicitur in IV Meteorologicorum, est quod potest sibi simile facere. Perfectum autem habet rationem boni.

[72] Etienne Gilson, *The Elements of Christian Philosophy*, p. 169.

Finality constitutes according to the vision of Aquinas a profound dimension of the reality of things, marked as they are by potency, inserted into the order of causes and thereby oriented dynamically towards their complete perfection. The principle *omne agens agit propter finem* means that each efficient cause is directed towards a specific end, acting for the sake of a goal, i.e. a good which does not yet exist *in actu* but which is perceived as real. Such an end is real in two ways: it must be present virtually (*virtualiter*) within its cause since an effect is a certain participation in the nature and actuality of its cause; in this sense it is said to exist already although not precisely as end. But precisely as end it is present to an intelligent agent through its *esse intentionale*, where it is perceived exactly as real and not merely as a concept. It is not the concept of goodness which moves the efficient cause but the end grasped as real in its potency and capable of fulfilment.

The absolute primacy of finality follows, as we shall see, from the unity of all things in divine being which is efficient and final cause. However, the priority of finality may be verified at the finite level from the transcendental character of being as convertible with the good. For Aquinas there is no distinction in reality between being and goodness. What has being is thereby good; everything is good because it is being. Finality as such is a characteristic of being. The good is, by definition, the real in so far as it is desired. Gilson remarks:

> Precisely because it is essentially desirable, goodness is a final cause. Not only this, but it is both prime and ultimate in the order of purposiveness. Even being is only because it is for the sake of something, which is its final cause, its end. In the order of causality, then, goodness comes first, and it is in this sense that Platonism receives from Thomas Aquinas all the credit to which it is entitled.[73]

The intentional character of the good as final cause is the cornerstone of its priority. The relation between *ens* and *bonum* becomes clear through a comparison of the orders of efficient and final causality. In the order of efficiency existence is anterior, while in respect of finality or intention goodness is primary.[74] The origin or motivation of all causal purpose is the effect not yet attained but envisaged as a reality worthy of pursuit. Perceived thus as an end desirable in itself the good releases an influence of attraction upon the agent, moving in turn the latter to bestow form on the material cause and communicate existence to it in actuality. Everything happens for the sake of an end. All causal

---

[73] E. Gilson, Ibid.

[74] *De Potentia* 7, 2, ad 10: Finis autem licet sit primum in intentione, est tamen postremum in operatione, et est effectus aliarum causarum.

action derives from the desirability of the good. Aquinas remarks: 'As the efficient cause influences by acting, so the final cause influences as tended towards and desired.'[75] And in the order of purposiveness this influence is primary. The good is thus, for Aquinas, the *causa causarum* since it moves the other causes to exert their causal function.[76] Already in one of his earliest works, Aquinas stated that, while the end is not the cause of the efficient cause, it is the cause of its causality: it causes it to be efficient: *Finis etiam non est causa illius quod est efficiens, sed est causa ut efficiens sit efficiens . . . unde finis est causa causalitatis efficientis, quia facit efficiens esse efficiens.*[77]

Aquinas illustrates the distinction between these two orders by contrasting the order of perfections as they are attained within the effect (*in causato*) with the sequence of influence emanating from the final cause in the act of causation (*in causando*). Now what is primary in the process of causation is attained as last within the effect: *Videmus quod primum est in causando ultimum esse in causato.* In causation, the end or good is primary and moves the efficient cause to action; there follows the action of the agent and finally the form in that which is caused. The reverse order is observed in the reception of perfections within the effect: first arises the form whereby the effect is given existence; secondly emerges the operative power (*virtus effectiva*) which perfects it in existence; finally the thing attains the nature of good whereby it in turn pours out perfection within being.[78] From a dymamic point of view, therefore, goodness or end is the primary cause moving the agent, which in turn moves the subject to its new form and mode of being. In the process of causation, goodness and the action of the first cause extend to what does not exist in actuality—non-being in that sense—whereas *ens* as inherent or exemplary form extends to things which are already in act. From a static or formal point of view, *esse* is primary because it is the foundation of every other formality which can

---

[75] *De Veritate* 22, 2: Sicut autem influere causae efficientis est agere, ita influere causae finalis est appeti et desiderari.

[76] *De Veritate* 21, 3 ad 3: Finis est prior in causando quam aliqua aliarum causarum.

[77] *De Principiis Naturae*, IV, 356.

[78] *ST*, I, 5, 4: Cum bonum sit quod omnia appetunt, hoc autem habet rationem finis; manifestum est quod bonum rationem finis importat. Sed tamen ratio boni praesupponit rationem causae efficientis, et rationem causae formalis. Videmus enim quod id quod est primum in causando, ultimum est in causato . . . In causando autem, primum invenitur bonum et finis, qui movet efficientem; secundo, actio efficientis, movens ad formam; tertio advenit forma. Unde e converso esse oportet in causato: quod primum sit ipsa forma, per quam est ens; secundo consideratur in ea virtus effectiva, secundum quod est perfectum in esse (quia unumquodque tunc perfectum est, quando potest sibi simile facere, ut dicit Philosophus in IV *Meteor.*): tertio consequitur ratio boni, per quam in ente perfectio fundatur.

be the object of desire: 'Life, wisdom and so on are desired according
as they are in act; so that what is desired in all things is existence of a
certain mode. Nothing therefore is desirable except being, and in
consequence nothing is good unless it exists.'[79] From this point of view
Aquinas may affirm: 'That which is desirable in itself is *esse*.'[80] All
formal perfections are desirable in relation to being.

From the dymamic aspect of causality, goodness precedes being due
to its nature of end. End is primary in the order of causality (*in ratione
causalitatis*);[81] it is *causa causarum*, the first among causes, since it is
the purpose for which anything becomes, and in view of which all other
aspects are viewed as causes. Through it, matter first receives the status
of material cause and because of it form exerts its determination.
Matter acquires form, and form perfects matter only in view of an end:
*Unde dicitur quod finis est causa causarum, quia est causa causalitatis in
omnibus causis.*[82] An agent acts only for the sake of an end or goal; as
the fruit of its desire it communicates form and existence to what is
potential, thus causing it to actually be. The good exerts a final causality
over those things which are potential, since they are in movement
towards it, while being exerts at most a formal causality in the things
which are in act.[83] In the process of causation, therefore, notes Aquinas,
'the good precedes being as end precedes form.'[84] In *De Veritate* we
find the contrast summarised as follows:

> Good expresses the diffusion of a final and not an efficient cause: both
> because the agent, as such, is not the measure and perfection of a thing, but
> rather its initiator, and because the effect participates in the efficient cause

---

[79] *ST*, I, 5, 2 ad 4: Dicendum quod vita et scientia et alia huiusmodi sic appetuntur,
ut sunt in actu, unde in omnibus appetitur quoddam esse. Et sic nihil est appetibile nisi
ens, et per consequens nihil est bonum nisi ens. See Cornelio Fabro, *La nozione metafisica
di partecipazione*, 2nd ed., pp. 95-6.

[80] *ST*, I, 5, 2 ad 3: Illud igitur quod per se est appetibile est esse.

[81] *In I Sent.*, 8, 1, 3.

[82] *De Principiis Naturae*, IV, 356. *Contra Gentiles* 3, 17, 1997: Finis inter alias causas
primatum obtinet, et ab ipso omnes aliae causae habent quod sint causae in actu: agens
enim non agit nisi propter finem.

[83] *ST*, I, 5, 2 ad 2.

[84] In his Commentary on the *Posterior Analytics* Aquinas portrays as follows the
relation between the four causes: Causae autem ad invicem ordinem habent: nam ex una
sumitur ratio alterius. Ex forma enim sumitur ratio materiae: talem enim oportet esse
materiam, qualem forma requirit. Efficiens autem est ratio formae: quia enim agens agit
sibi simile, oportet quod secundum modum agentis sit etiam modus formae, quae ex
actione consequitur. Ex fine autem sumitur ratio efficientis: nam omne agens agit propter
finem. *In I Poster. Anal.*, lect. 16, 5. See also *ST*, I-II, 1, 2; *De Veritate* 28, 7; *Contra
Gentiles* 3, 17: Finis etiam posterior est causa quod praecedens finis intendatur ut finis:
non enim movetur aliquid in finem proximum nisi propter finem postremum. Est igitur
finis ultimus prima omnium causa.

only in an assimilation of its form, whereas a thing pursues its end according to its total being. And this is the nature of goodness.[85]

The good is thus more universal, states Aquinas, not through the extent of its predication, since in this respect it agrees with being, but in the manner of its causality. Efficient, exemplary causality extend only to those things which actually participate in the form of an exemplary cause; the causality of being, therefore, extends only to beings, just as the causality of life to living things. But final causality is extended also to those things which do not participate in form, since imperfect things, while not yet participating in the nature of their end, desire and tend towards their end since they are under way towards it.[86]

PRIMACY OF BEING

Aquinas' view of the absolute primacy of Being before Goodness is summed up with admirable clarity in his brief response to the objection that *Bonum* rather than '*Qui est*' is a more appropriate name for God since, in Dionysius' words, 'the name Good reveals everything which proceeds from God.' Aquinas replies: *Hoc nomen bonum est principale nomen Dei inquantum est causa non tamen simpliciter. Nam esse praeintelligitur causae.*[87] It is because Being is a pre-condition for the efficacy of any cause whatsoever that it is in itself absolutely primary.[88] It is universally the most fundamental of all notions and, more radically, is primary among all perfections. To be understood as cause, something

---

[85] *De Veritate* 21, 1, ad 4.

[86] *In I Sent.*, 8, 1, 3, ad 2.

[87] *ST*, I, 13, 11 ad 2.

[88] Etienne Gilson, in *The Elements of Christian Philosophy*, misplaces Aquinas' view on the priority of existence: 'Hence in the Thomistic account of reality, although everything is there because of the good and for the sake of some good, the existence of everything first presupposes an efficient cause and a formal cause, for these causes are the actual and intrinsic constituents of being.' (p. 169) The passage from *ST*, I, 5, 4, however, which Gilson has in mind (*Ratio boni praesupponit rationem causae efficientis, et rationem causae formalis*) refers to the primacy of efficient and formal causality from the point of view of the effect (*in causato*). But as Aquinas continues, finality is prior in the order of causation, and it is with this contrast that he is here concerned and not with the absolute primacy of Being. It is not because in the thing itself which is caused form and efficient cause precede in their existence the intended end, that being precedes goodness, but because, simply speaking, *esse absolute praeintelligitur causae*: to exert either efficient or final power any cause, of whatever order, must first BE. More pertinent is Gilson's remark: 'On ne redira jamais trop que ce primat de l'être est la ligne de partage qui divise le thomisme d'une métaphysique du bien. Pour être bon, il faut d'abord être. Pour être cause, ce qui est propre à ce qui est bon et diffusif de soi, il faut d'abord être.' ('Elements d'une métaphysique thomiste de l'être', p. 10).

must first be conceived as in some manner existing. To exert the power of causality a cause must already be, even if in the case of a final cause only by an intentional existence. Considered simply, being is primary: in knowledge it precedes all other concepts and is in reality the ground of all perfections. Conceptually, 'being' is the most universal of all notions, the first intelligible aspect under which any object is grasped. A thing is implicitly apprehended and affirmed as 'something which is' and recognised subsequently as exercising a causal activity. This epistemological primacy merely reflects the ontological priority of being in the original constitution of things. A thing first exists and from its existential resources diffuses its perfection, whether efficient or final. 'What does not exist cannot be the cause of anything. Hence, each thing must stand in the same relation to the fact that it is a cause, as it does to the fact that it is a being.'[89] More profoundly, 'Nothing gives being except in so far as it is an actual being.'[90]

These two ways of appreciating being—as the first and universal *concept* within which all others are generated or as the primary *perfection* which embraces all others in origin—are expressed by Aquinas in a question of his Commentary on the *Sentences* to which we have already referred: *Utrum hoc nomen 'Qui est' sit primum inter nomina divina.*[91] He first declares that *Ens, Bonum, Unum* and *Verum* are prior to the other divine names by their universality. They can, however, be compared either with regard to their subject, in which respect they are convertible, having an identical subject. Or they may be compared in meaning (*intentiones*), in which case being is simply and absolutely prior to the others. 'The reason for this is that being is included in the meaning of the others but not conversely. That which first falls within the conception of intellect is being (*ens*) without which nothing can be apprehended by intellect.'

In *ST*, I, 5, 2, where he asks *Quid sit prius secundum rationem, utrum bonum vel ens*, Aquinas states that 'A more fundamental idea is one which fructifies earlier within the grasp of the intellect. But being is what first occurs in mental conception, since each thing is knowable in so far as it is actual.' Aquinas indicates that not only is the notion of being primary in the order of knowledge, but that being itself precedes the domain of knowledge as its very foundation. Only that which exercises the act of being can awaken and make actual the intentional virtuality of intellect and provide an object of knowledge. 'Being,

---

[89] *Contra Gentiles* 3, 74, 2498: Quod non est, non potest esse alicuius causa. Unde oportet quod unumquodque, sicut se habet ad esse, ita se habet ad hoc quod sit causa.
[90] *Contra Gentiles* 3, 66, 2408: Nihil enim dat esse nisi inquantum est ens actu.
[91] *In I Sent.*, 8, 1, 3.

therefore, is the proper object of intellect; it is that which is first understood, just as sound is what is first heard; being, therefore, is in meaning prior to the good.'[92]

This primacy of reality is also attained by an analysis which proceeds in an inverse direction to that of the genesis of knowledge: 'What is final in analysis is first in the order of existence (*primum in esse*). Being (*ens*), however, is what is last attained by intellect, since when everything else has been removed, being remains as final. It is, therefore, first in the natural order.'[93] When all other aspects have been taken away, we are left merely with the existence of that which is apprehended. The assertion of existence, therefore, is the implicit ground of all judgments purporting to attain the real. *Quia est*, that something exists, is the foundation and condition for all subsequent knowledge about the object. It is in this judgment that the concept of *ens*, which has been born through the intentional openness of the intellect towards reality, is restored and united to the concretely existing real from which it has arisen.

Such a concept of being is fundamental in the order of cognition and reveals that being is itself prior to the order of knowledge. Being, however, according to Aquinas is prior in a much more profound sense, namely, as the first perfection of reality, embracing within itself in a concentrated and anticipated manner all the subsequent qualities and riches of beings. Here there is an advance in appreciation from being viewed as the fact of existence affirmed in the judgment, to being discovered as the primary and interior principle of all perfection.

Of interest to us is that it is under the inspiration of Dionysius that Aquinas passes, as Fabro puts it, from the semantic, existential meaning of *esse* to *esse* in its intensive signification, a step which, according to Fabro, would constitute more and more profoundly the central axis of his metaphysics,[94] presenting one of the most powerful reasons for the primacy of Being as the divine perfection par excellence. Aquinas adopts from Dionysius the view that being is the first of the perfections which participate in divine goodness, containing within itself all other perfections such as life and knowledge, and that it is, therefore, the most appropriate with which to name God.

That 'He who is' is the most proper name of God among other names . . . is taken from the words of Dionysius, who says that among all other participated

---

[92] *ST*, I, 5, 2.
[93] *In I Sent.*, 8, 1, 3, Contra: Illud quod est ultimum in resolutione, est primum in esse. Sed ens, ultimum est in resolutione intellectus: quia remotis omnibus aliis, ultimo remanet ens. Ergo est primum naturaliter.
[94] *Participation et Causalité*, p. 220.

perfections of divine goodness, as life, intelligence and such like, being (*esse*) is first—the principle, as it were, of the others, pre-containing all these as somehow united within itself.[95]

Astounding indeed is the fact that, in answer to the objections formulated here under the authority of Dionysius against Being as the first name of God, Aquinas cites Dionysius himself in return: We know the divine attributes only through God's participations, as they are shared by creatures.[96] And among all perfections, according to Dionysius, being is primary: *ante alias ipsius participationes, esse positum est.*[97] Aquinas appeals, moreover, to a cognate source, the *Liber de Causis*, (although at the time he still believed it to be the work of Aristotle): *Prima rerum creatarum est esse.* From these he concludes that *esse* is anterior to all other divine attributes and that '*Qui est*' is God's first name. In *In DN*, V, i, 632 also, Aquinas exploits this primacy of existence at the finite level in order to name God essentially as '*Qui est*'. St Thomas of course is here making Dionysius and the writer of *De Causis* say something quite different to their intention. For both of these Neoplatonist writers, being is indeed the first creature and most excellent divine participation, but does not constitute the divine nature as it is in itself. Existence is as such of necessity an effect which has been created and, therefore, but a finite perfection and attribute. It is, to be sure, the most excellent and divine participation, but is no more than a participation. Aquinas exloits the Neoplatonist doctrine regarding the primacy of being among creatures but reinterprets and reinstates it at a transcendental level according to a deeper and universalised dimension of being, infused with an infinite value and elevated to an infinite status.

Summarising Aquinas' view at this point: Being is the primary and ultimate object of knowledge; existence grounds all cognition. It is the foundation and horizon of the intentional order. What it is for something to be a cause is understood only because it is first affirmed that it is. *Quia est* is the first fruit of knowledge; *aliquid est* is the foundation and primary principle of all cognition: being is, and must be affirmed. Being is the cradle of all meaning and from it emerges the

---

[95] *In I Sent.*, 8, 1, 1: Quod qui est est maxime proprium nomen dei inter alia nomina . . . sumitur ex verbis Dionysii, qui dicit, quod esse inter omnes alias divinae bonitatis participationes, sicut vivere et intelligere et huiusmodi, primum est, et quasi principium aliorum praehabens in se omnia praedicta, secundum quemdam modum unita. Without reference to Dionysius, but clearly in his spirit, Aquinas writes, two articles later: Omnia alia includuntur quodammodo in ente unite et indistincte, sicut in principio (*In I Sent* 8, 1, 3).

[96] *In I Sent.*, 8, 1, 3. See *DN*, 1, 4.

[97] 5, 5, 266. See also *ST*, I, 5, 2, Sed Contra.

intelligibility of all subsequent objects of thought. To a phenomenology of desire, being is revealed, moreover, as the primary goal of all pursuit. Existence, implicitly, is what is first sought by all things, a fact witnessed by the impulse of all things towards self-preservation and the actualisation of what is possessed in potency. Being thus has the nature of a good as final cause. (*Ad esse autem pertinet et principium essendi et finis.*)[98] That 'something should be' is the first principle in the order of desire, of the will in its encounter with reality. Being is good and is to be loved: such is the principle in the dynamic order of ends and value.

With the affirmation of being as *primum cognitum* and its evaluation as *primum desideratum*, we have not yet, however, attained to the fundamental meaning of being. In an extension and penetration of *esse* as the value initially desired, *esse* is further revealed, not merely as the good which is first sought, but as the actuality of all acts and perfection of all perfections. This is the so-called 'intensive' meaning of being. And it is precisely in the advance towards this appreciation that Dionysius exerts on Aquinas a profound influence. It is to the background and context of this doctrine that we now turn our attention.

---

[98] V, i, 650.

PART THREE

TRANSCENDENT CAUSALITY AND EXISTENCE

CHAPTER FIVE

UNITY OF DIVINE CAUSATION IN DIONYSIUS

There are two closely related aspects of Dionysius' view regarding the relation of the Good to creatures which exerted considerable influence on Aquinas' understanding both of existence in general, and of divine being and goodness. The Good is, namely, the *unique and immediate cause of all beings*, and it causes, moreover, all things through the *first and primary perfection of being itself*. Being is thus its first effect and participation, and includes all subsequent perfections as particular determinations of itself. In contrast to the *Platonici*, who maintained a plurality of universal principles, Dionysius restores the exclusive causality of the universe to a unique and transcendent Good. The Good causes all things directly in their being; all that it produces is constituted as being, although he holds that the Good itself transcends the plenary perfection of Being. Aquinas exploits and deepens Dionysius' view of the primary role of being in creation and establishes in turn its universal and absolute priority. In the light of this deepened meaning of existence, he reinterprets the nature of the universal first cause as infinite *Esse* rather than as *Bonum*.

The unification by Dionysius of all separate and secondary causes into the one, singular and absolute thearchic cause is an advance towards the immediacy and simplicity of causality which is fully realised in Aquinas' theory of creation as the immediate gift by absolute Being of itself to beings. Dionysius clears the metaphysical regions of the diversity of divine principles which Plotinus and Proclus believed necessary for the gradual emanation and descent of creatures from the One. Dionysius unites all creative principles in the single transcendent Good which, he affirms, acts immediately and intimately at the heart of created reality. By affirming the unique and universal causality of God through the removal of all intermediary principles, he attains a purer and more transcendent notion of God. Moreover, by attributing the mediation of all created perfection to the unique though created perfection of εἶναι, Dionysius reaches a unique view of the immanent and intensive richness of being. With the intuition of being as the primary participation and first creature comes a radical transformation in the relation of beings to God. Through *esse*, God is immediately active throughout each and every being at its most radical and interior origin. It remains for Aquinas to remove the distance between these two principles of perfection—finite and infinite—and proclaim the identity of the divine Good with the absolute fullness of Being itself.

Central to the formation and significance, moreover, of Aquinas' notion of *esse commune*, i.e. being as the intensity and fullness of finite perfection, which points beyond itself as participating in the simple plenitude and intensity of infinite Being, is Dionysius' doctrine of the immediate and total character of the causal relation between God and beings. Drawing a more profound conclusion, this radical causation of all beings, considered universally, reveals for Aquinas the nature of the first cause as infinite Being itself. As cause of all things, God must contain within his power the perfection of all. And since being (*esse*) is the primary perfection of all that is created, according to Aquinas the creator is most properly named as Being.

A number of themes must be distinguished in order to appreciate the integral inspiration of Dionysius in Aquinas' synthesis: the unity and immediacy of divine causation, being as the primary and all-comprehensive perfection, and God as infinite and subsisting in himself. I suggest that the unity and immediacy of creation, while not explicitly reflected upon by Dionysius, is itself an advance towards the primacy, universality and immediacy of Being. Dionysius' view of the unicity and immediacy of divine causality is repeatedly praised by Aquinas as a major correction to the theory of the multiple universal causes held by the Platonists. As Aquinas explains it, the *Platonici* had wished to 'reduce all composite and material things to simple and abstract principles',[1] i.e. to reduce 'universal effects to more intelligible causes'.[2] According to this view, the more universal a perfection, the more transcendent it is, i.e. the more separated from individual things, while it is also participated as cause by subsequent beings with greater priority. In the order of perfections they placed unity and goodness as the most universal, since these are also predicated of prime matter.

The 'Platonists', therefore, posited the separate One or Good as supreme and primary principle of all things. 'But after unity and goodness, nothing is found which is so common as being (*ens*) and thus they assumed separated being itself (*ipsum ens separatum*) as something created inasmuch as it participates goodness and unity; they ordered it, however, as the first among all created things.'[3] They also posited the

---

[1] *In DN, Prooemium.*
[2] V, i, 612.
[3] *In de Causis* IV, 98.

other universal forms of things to subsist separately in themselves. These principles they seem to have conceived, however, according to their strictly formal character, since rather than reduce all things to an all-embracing and universal unity, they attributed them to a diversity of ultimate causes:

> They believed that the same thing could not be the cause of many, i.e. of the proper natures in which they differ but only of what they have in common. They posited, therefore, certain secondary causes by which things are determined in their proper natures; these receive being in common from God and are called the exemplary causes of things. Thus the exemplar of man is *homo separatus*, who is cause of humanity in all individual men, and similarly with other natures.[4]

These exemplars, separate realities existing in themselves, are the source of unity and simplicity preceding the division and composition of participated things of a similar kind and in which composite things participate. 'Similarly, they said that prior to composite living things there is a certain separated life, by participation in which all living things are alive, and which they called life *per se*. Likewise with wisdom *per se* and *esse per se*.'[5] The Platonists placed all of these mutually diverse principles beneath the One or Good, which is their primary principle.[6]

In his Commentary on the *Liber de Causis*, Aquinas gives a clear outline of both positions: 'Plato posited the existence of universal forms of things which subsisted separately in themselves. And because such universal forms have, according to him, a certain universal causality over particular beings which participate in them, he thus called all forms which subsist in this manner "gods", since the name "God" expresses a certain universal providence and causality.'[7] Aquinas explains that Plato placed a certain order among these forms, whereby the more universal a form the greater its simplicity and priority as cause: it is participated by subsequent forms, as if we were to suppose that animal is participated by man, life by animal and so forth.

> But what is participated finally by all, while itself partaking of none, is the separate One or Good in itself which, he said, was the supreme God and first cause of all. Proclus, therefore, in his book introduces Proposition 116: 'Every god is participable except the One.'[8] Dionysius corrects this position which supposed an order of different separate forms called gods—as if

---

[4] V, iii, 664.

[5] V, i, 634.

[6] Cf. *Super Ep. S. Pauli ad Coloss.*, I, 4, and *In DN, Prooemium*.

[7] *In de Causis* III, 65.

[8] *In de Causis* III, 66. Here Aquinas explains *participabilis* as *id quod participat*, which is incorrect in light of the proposition referred to.

goodness itself were other than being itself and similarly life and the other perfections. It is necessary to say that all these perfections are essentially identical with the very first cause of all from which things participate all perfections; thus we do not posit many Gods but one. And this is what Dionysius says in Chapter 5 of *De Divinis Nominibus*.[9]

For Dionysius, although there are many names for God, indicating the many divine emanations, these all refer to the one God who is the single source of all divine processions. For the *Platonici*, each name indicated a distinct origin, a separate transcendent principle. According to Dionysius, Goodness holds indeed priority of rank, denoting the most universal providence from which all things proceed. But he emphasises:

> Goodness is not one thing and Being another nor are Life and Wisdom distinct; nor are there many causes and different divinities producing other perfections, some superior and others inferior. Rather, all the good emanations and divine names which we praise are of the one God. The first name (Good) reveals the perfect providence of the one God, while the others reveal it according to various degrees of universality or particularity.[10]

While he regarded it as a great merit that Dionysius abandoned the Platonist order of separate causes and transcendent principles, uniting them all within the primal unity of a unique divine principle, Aquinas seems to have simplified the views of Plotinus and Proclus too summarily for accuracy. Although Proclus, whom Aquinas mainly has in mind in his critique, differentiates between various intelligible essences and indeed multiplies such distinctions without need, he does not consider such distinctions as a separation from the sensible. They do not constitute a χωρισμός, a duplicate world, a view which Aquinas seems to have received from Aristotle's portrayal of Platonism.[11]

Perhaps more significant is Dionysius' rejection of the graded procession through emanation of distinct ontological and intelligible principles from God, which had been axiomatic for Neoplatonism. Dionysius replaced this view, which had ordered the polytheism of ancient thought into a stratified system, with the Christian doctrine that, despite differences of rank, all reality derives directly from, and is caused immediately by the one creator of the universe. As well as

---

[9] *In de Causis* 3, 72-3. Durantel, *Saint Thomas et le Pseudo-Denis*, p. 229, writes: 'Certains platoniciens n'attribuaient aux causes universelles que des effets universels, établissant une échelle de causes hiérarchisées pour produire la série correspondante des effets. Au-dessus de tout, le bien répandant sur tout sa bonté, l'être sur tous les êtres, la vie sur les vivants, etc. Denis écarte cette erreur et soutient que le même principe est à la fois l'auteur du bien, de l'existence, de la vie, etc.'

[10] 5, 2, 258.

[11] See Klaus Kremer, *Die Neuplatonische Seinsphilosophie*, p. 293.

rejecting all multiplicity of divine causation, Dionysius also denies every mediation in the causal relation of God to beings. He interprets the Neoplatonist principle, that the superior is transmitted to the inferior via an intermediary, as meaning that this communication is a co-operation subsequent and subordinate to the first creative gift of God. As René Roques notes, 'Le rôle des intermédiaires dionysiens est plus humble, car ils ne possèdent pas un vrai pouvoir de génération, mais strictement une fonction de mediation.'[12] All beings, ranging from the celestial natures to the most lowly earthly creatures are caused immediately by the one God and embraced within his providence.[13] In place of measured grades of mediating causality, Dionysius praises the multiplicity of ways in which beings reflect within the world of finite natures the infinite riches of Divine Being through their interaction and mutual co-operation in the perfection of creation. As each being partakes—in its own measure—in divine perfection, it also shares in a parallel manner in God's creative activity, but is itself continually sustained and maintained by God's universal presence.

In response to a query supposedly raised in a letter by his fellow-presbyter Timothy, Dionysius clarifies in Chapter 11 of *Divine Names* the meaning and status of universal perfections considered in themselves as such, i.e. Being itself, Life itself and Wisdom itself (τί ποτε ἄρα φημὶ τὸ αὐτοεῖναι τὴν αὐτοζωὴν τὴν αὐτοσοφίαν).[14] It is asked why, for example, God is sometimes called Life itself, and sometimes the substance of Life (πῶς τὸν θεόν ποτε μὲν αὐτοζωήν φημι, ποτε δὲ τῆς αὐτοζωῆς ὑποστάτην).[15] There is here no contradiction, Dionysius stresses: God is called Life or Power in itself from beings, especially primary beings, in so far as he is *cause* of all beings; he is called the very substance of Life as *transcending* all things supra-essentially, even the primary beings (ὡς ὑπὲρ πάντα καὶ τὰ πρώτως ὄντα ὑπερὼν ὑπερουσίως).[16]

Dionysius contrasts two senses in which these perfections, 'Being Itself', 'Life Itself' and 'Divinity Itself' may be taken. As signifying origin (ἀρχικῶς μέν) and understood in a divine and causal sense (θεικῶς καὶ αἰτιατικῶς), they refer to the unique origin and cause of all, which is itself beyond all origin and being. Signifying participation (μεθεκτῶς δὲ) they denote the providential powers proceeding from the

---

[12] *L'Univers dionysien*, p.78; See also pp. 68-81. Cf. *CH* III, 3, 168A; XIII, 4, 305 C-D. See E. Von Ivanka, *Von den Namen zum Unnennbaren*, pp. 17-19.

[13] *CH* VII, 4, 212C, Ed. Heil, p. 119.

[14] 11, 6, 421.

[15] 11, 6, 421.

[16] 11, 6, 422.

unparticipated God. These are the powers themselves bestowing being, life, or wisdom in which beings individually participate. Considered separately in themselves, these perfections do not constitute independent and distinct divine principles; they are not separate divinities apart from the transcendent principle and supra-ontological divine cause of all things. 'We do not say that Being itself (τὸ αὐτοεῖναι) is some divine or angelic substance which is the cause by which all things are. For supra-ontological Being in itself alone (αὐτὸ τὸ εἶναι ὑπερούσιον), is the principle, substance and cause by which all things are.'[17] Nor is there a life-generating divinity distinct from the transcendent God (ὑπερθεόν) which is cause of the life of all living things and of very life itself; nor any other essences or substances which are origins and creative principles of beings such as have been called gods and creators of beings.[18] One can well understand the significance which the passage just quoted might have for Aquinas. Although αὐτὸ τὸ εἶναι ὑπερούσιον transcends Being to the extent of also embracing non-being, and surpasses every ontological reference and meaning, translated into the perspective of Aquinas, it expresses faithfully the absolute transcendence of God as Being itself beyond that-which-is. God alone, the transcendent cause beyond Being, is the unique and universal cause of all: he is thus, moreover, the immediate cause also of every being.

Dionysius' distinction here between the perfections considered ἀρχικῶς and μεθεκτῶς is parallel to that made by Aquinas in his commentary on Chapter 5 between the *separatio realis* and *separatio rationalis* of the universal perfections. Considered in themselves as really separate from the individual things in which they inhere, such perfections subsist only in the unity and identity of God. As really abiding in creatures they can be considered independently only according to a mental separation. This signifies for Dionysius a commitment to the primacy of reality over knowledge, i.e. of that which is known, before the manner of cognition; also to the anteriority of the essence and source of perfection before that which only shares in it.

Dionysius thus overcomes the error which vitiates the Platonist view of universal participation and causality—that things exist in the same abstract, separate or independent manner according to which they are conceived. According to Aquinas, the Platonists supposed that what existed as an idea, i.e. what could be conceived in itself as abstract, also subsisted in itself as an independent reality, as the cause, moreover,

---

[17] 11, 6, 424.
[18] Cf. Aquinas, *ST*, I, 44, 4, ad 4: Sicut dicit Dionysius, *per se vitam* et *per se sapientiam* quandoque nominat ipsum Deum, quandoque virtutes ipsis rebus datas: non autem quasdam subsistentes res, sicut antiqui posuerunt.

according to a certain universal order, of particular individuals.[19] In his own *Treatise on Separate Substances* Aquinas declares: 'The basis of this position is found to be without foundation, for it is not necessary that what the intellect understands separately should have a separate existence (*esse*) in reality. Hence, neither should we posit universals subsisting outside singulars . . . for universals are the essences of particular things themselves.'[20]

This manner of conceiving the ultimate nature and ground of individual things further impedes the discovery of the ultimate and universal unity of all beings, since the transcendent ideas are diverse principles of perfection in which beings respectively participate. While, for the Platonists, a single principle is cause of a similar perfection in many beings, it cannot be the source of the many perfections within even a single being, much less of the multiple perfections dispersed throughout the variety of beings, since for the *Platonici* the same cause cannot be the source of that by which things differ, but only of what they have in common. Such transcendent pluralism Dionysius overcomes by denying forthright the need for distinct and separate sources in favour of an all-embracing, unique and universal transcendent causality. In doing so, Dionysius is only taking with more profound consequence the Platonist principle which Aquinas in turn espouses and cites with frequency—in St Thomas' formulation: *Quanto aliqua causa est altior, tanto ad plura se extendit eius causalitas.*[21] Or again, *quanto virtus alicuius causae est perfectior, tanto ad plura se extendit.*[22] The more superior a cause, the more universal its causal exercise; inversely, the more universal a common effect, the more transcendent is its source. Aquinas remarks that although Dionysius suppressed the order of separate causes, he retains the same order of priority held by the *Platonici* among the perfections which inhere in the world of existing things. For Aquinas this is laudable in so far as Dionysius places all perfections—such as life and wisdom—within Being, but unacceptable since he places God as goodness beyond the fullness of Being.[23]

---

[19] XI, iv, 931: Platonici, ponentes ideas rerum separatas, omnia quae sic in abstracto dicuntur, posuerunt in abstracto subsistere causas secundum ordinem quemdam; *ST*, I, 50, 2: Supponit enim quod quaecumque distinguntur secundum intellectum, sint etiam in rebus distincta.

[20] *De Subst. Separ.* I; ed. Spiazzi, 50; ed. Lescoe, p. 8.

[21] IV, 2, 296.

[22] *In de Causis* I, 29; See Proclus, *The Elements of Theology*, Props. 57, 70.

[23] *In de Causis* IV, 99: Dionysius autem ordinem quidem separatorum abstulit, ponens eumdem ordinem quem et Platonici, in perfectionibus quas ceterae res participant ab uno principio quod est Deus: unde in IV cap. de Divinis Nominibus praeordinat nomen boni in Deo, omnibus divinis nominibus et ostendit quod eius participatio usque ad non-ens extenditur, intelligens per non-ens materiam primam.

Dionysius does not attribute universal causality, therefore, to God in so far as he is Being, but rather as transcending Being.

Aquinas adopts from Dionysius, however, the metaphysical architectonic of the finite universe. The principle governing the order of priority is the universality of perfection and its causal power. The more universal a perfection the more superior its cause, and the more powerful and intimate its causal presence within its effects. Aquinas endorses fully the Platonist view of the primacy of Being before Life, and of Life before wisdom, as perfections which inhere within beings; precisely that such perfections are immanent to beings rather than transcendent realities is for Aquinas the great advance made by Dionysius in the metaphysics of participation. Moreover, that such perfections are subsumed into the comprehensive perfection of Being (although it is finite) is a unification and intensification of the process of causation.

Aquinas, therefore, encounters already in Dionysius a significant advance towards the absolute nature of the perfection of Being; although Being is for Dionysius finite in comparison with the transcendent Good, it is infinite or transcendent in relation to everything which participates in it. It is finite as caused but infinite as embracing exhaustively within itself the perfection of all things caused. Being is the fundamental actuality and presence of all things, their universal and indeterminate perfection. Being contains within its fullness every perfection which is determined in the individual according to a particular mode.

This grasp of the unity of causes is undoubtedly a refined and deepened reflection upon reality—a closer appreciation of the transcendental relations which constitute and permeate each being in its uniqueness and totality, and an intuition of its profound dimensions and principles. It is an advance to the primacy and transcendence of Being. Because he recognises this universal nature of existence as what is first enjoyed by all things, Dionysius can speak of a single universal causality. Following the Platonist leitmotif that what things have in common must derive from a single source, and reducing all determinations to modes of being, Dionysius could thus affirm a unique transcendent cause. Dionysius overcomes what was for the Platonists a hindrance to the unicity of divine causation, namely that a single cause cannot be source of the diversity found in many things but only of what they have in common,[24] by highlighting the all-embracing value of Being as

---

[24] V, iii, 64: Considerandum est quod Platonici, ponentes Deum esse totius esse causam, quia credebant quod idem non posset esse causa plurium, secundum propria in quibus differunt, sed solum secundum id quod est omnibus commune, posuerunt quasdam secundas causas per quas res ad proprias naturas determinantur et quae communiter esse

the primary and ubiquitous effect of divine creation which is the anticipated fullness of every subsequent mode of being. In giving rise to Being, God causes all things wholly and immediately and is intimately efficacious throughout the universal texture of reality. This immediate and universal presence is summed up for Aquinas in Dionysius' words, referring to God as *principalis substantia omnium* (πάντων ὑποστάτις ἀρχηγική),[25] a phrase which Aquinas is careful to recast significantly: '... *inquantum est principium existendi omnibus.*'[26] Aquinas is also anxious to bring out the harmony between the corrected Neoplatonist view and the teaching of Aristotle, which is *magis consona fidei christianae.*[27] He shows, moreover, how the unknown writer of *De Causis* expounds the same teaching as Dionysius on the unity of divine causes.[28] The difference with Aquinas is that, for the Neoplatonist writers there is, beyond the plenitude of Being, One who is even greater than existence. Being is for them indeed identical with God, but God is in himself infinitely more than the fullness of Being.[29]

---

a Deo recipiunt et has causas exemplaria rerum vocabant, sicut exemplar hominis dicebant quemdam hominem separatum, qui esset causa humanitatis omnibus singularibus hominibus; et similiter de aliis. Sed Dionysius, sicut dixerat Deum esse causam totius esse communis, ita dixerat eum esse causam proprietatis uniuscuiusque, unde consequebatur quod in ipso Deo essent omnium entium exemplaria.

[25] 1, 7, 26.

[26] I, iii, 100: Fuerunt enim quidam Platonici qui processiones perfectionum ad diversa principia reducebant, ponentes unum principium esse vitae, quod appellabant primam vitam, et aliud principium esse intelligendi, quod appellabant primum intellectum et aliud existendi quod appellabant primum ens et bonum. Et ad hoc excludendum, dicit quod Deus vere laudatur ut principalis substantia omnium, inquantum est principium existendi omnibus.

[27] *In de Causis* X, 241; also XIII, 289 and XVIII, 344.

[28] *In de Causis* IV, 121.

[29] Interpreting the Platonist stratification of causes in a manner which might be acceptable, it is fascinating to observe how Aquinas fuses the predicamental perspective of Aristotle with the transcendental optic of Neoplatonism. According to the writer of *De Causis*, the effect of the first cause precedes in existence the effect of the second cause, and receives more universal diffusion (*In de Causis* III, 82). The second cause can only bestow its effect upon what already exists as an effect of the first cause. Now, in all things being is first caused by the primary principle of all and is most commonly diffused, whereas intellection presupposes existence and is communicated by Intelligence only to certain beings. This position, notes Aquinas, *si non sane intelligatur* (Ibid. 83), contradicts the view of Aristotle and truth itself. Arguing against the Platonist order of separate causes (*Metaphysics* III, 6, 1003a 11ff.), Aristotle suggests, according to Aquinas, that in such a view, Socrates would consist of three individuals, namely: himself, *homo separatus* and *animal separatum*. He cannot be a single being if he receives his individuality, his humanity, and his animality from three distinct causes. But since intellectual being (*esse intellectuale*) belongs to the very nature of the soul, if the soul had its *esse* from one cause and its intellectual nature from another, it could not be perfectly one. The soul must, accordingly, receive its intellectual nature from the same first cause from which it has its essence: Et hoc concordat sententiae Dionysii ... quod non aliud sit ipsum bonum, ipsum esse et ipsa vita et ipsa sapientia, sed unum et idem quod est Deus, a quo derivatur

Aquinas applies with even greater rigour than Dionysius the Platonist principle of the primacy of unity as the source of multiplicity, and of essential fullness as the ground of limited participations. Seeing all things as a multiplicity in being, he restores all through a fundamental and universal causality to the essential and transcendent presence of Being in *Ipsum Esse Subsistens*. All perfections, however diverse and distinct, or of whatever nature, have in common the universal perfection of being. Being is the universal effect and since, according to the principle of the *Platonici*, that which things have in common must originate from a single source, all things must have a unique, common cause, which is the unlimited and essential fullness of being. In causing being, God thus causes all things and since at the finite level, Being is the fullness of perfection, it is the most appropriate name with which to denote the divine nature. Aquinas thus employs Platonist principles to overcome the limits of Platonist participation. (The diversity of things in being he explains as arising from the ideas or exemplars in the divine intellect, namely the knowledge which God has of the things which exist virtually within his power and which he wishes to bestow on the objects of his creative generosity. We shall examine this theme in more detail.)

In response to the question *Utrum Deus sit tantum unus*, raised at the beginning of his Commentary on the *Sentences*, (which displays his strong debt to Dionysius, whom he then took in fact to be a follower of Aristotle), Aquinas makes appeal to the Platonist principle—cited from Dionysius—that all multiplicity must derive from unity: *omnis multitudo procedat ex aliqua unitate, ut dicit Dionysius* (οὐδὲν γάρ ἐστι τῶν ὄντων ἀμέτοχον τοῦ ἑνός, ἀλλ᾽ ὥσπερ ἅπας ἀριθμὸς μονάδος μετέχει),[30] and concludes: *Oportet universitatis multitudinem ad unum principium omnium entium primum reduci, quod est Deus*.[31] Moreover, Aquinas' reply to an objection immediately afterwards depends entirely on Dionysius' theory of eminent and intensive presence and the principle of unity:

> Although the goodnesses which are participated in by creatures are different in nature, they have nevertheless an order towards one another; one includes the other and is grounded upon the other, as life is included in intelligence and being in life; they are reduced, therefore, not to diverse principles but to one. Even if there obtained no such order, this would not exclude the unity

---

in res et quod sint et quod vivant et quod intelligant ut ipse ibidem ostendit. Significantly for Aquinas, this unity is present already in Aristotle's thought: Unde et Aristoteles in XII Metaphys. signanter attribuit Deo et intelligere et vivere, dicens quod Ipse est vita et intelligentia, ut excludat praedictas platonicas positiones (*In de Causis* III, 84).

[30] 13, 2, 440.

[31] *In I Sent.* 2, 1, 1.

of the primary principle: what is unified in the principle is multiplied in the effects, since what is in a cause is always more noble than in its effect. Wherefore, although a first principle may be unique and simple in reality, there are present within it many perfections which are distinct in nature such as wisdom, life and the like, according to which the various perfections which differ in reality are caused in creatures.[32]

From his Commentary on the *Liber de Causis*, we may iuxtapose passages which reveal Aquinas' individual perception and reception of the Platonist doctrine of participation. The principle is formulated: *Omne quod in pluribus invenitur oportet reducere ad aliquod primum quod per suam essentiam est tale, a quo alia per participationem talia dicuntur.*[33] Now, for Aquinas, as for Dionysius, it is *esse* which is *primum in pluribus*: *esse igitur, quod est primum, commune est omnibus.*[34] It is thus evident for Aquinas that the cause of all is the unique and transcendent essence of Being, which is primary: the One which is itself the fullness of existence and whose very nature it is to be. The unity of beings is attained, not by proceeding to infinity in the order of existing things, but by transcending this order to a primary ontological unity which is the infinite source of being: *Non est autem in aliquo rerum ordine in infinitum procedere. Igitur oportet in ordine entium esse aliquod primum quod dat omnibus esse.*[35] Freed from its separatist nature, Aquinas fully embraces the Platonist principle of causality and participation; in particular he makes his own much of the vision of the *Liber de Causis*, which he continously relates to the *Corpus Areopagiticum*.

The absolute primacy of Being as the plenary presence prior to participation may also be seen from the point of view of causality. A cause must possess in a more perfect and pre-eminent manner the perfection which it imparts;[36] and the greater or more perfect the power of a cause, the more extensive its effect.[37] Now, since *esse* is the primary perfection and the most universal effect, it must derive from the most perfect of all causes. Moreover, according to the principle of participation, *Ens per essentiam* alone can cause *entia per participationem.*

The unicity of creation, i.e. the identity of all perfections at their source within the single God who bestows existence, and the primacy of existence as the fullness of all subsequent determinations, are complementary aspects of the universal primacy and immediacy of

---

[32] *In I Sent.*, 2, 1, 1 ad 1.

[33] *In de Causis* XVI, 318.

[34] *In de Causis* XVIII, 339.

[35] *In de Causis* XVIII, 340.

[36] *In de Causis* I, 23: Eminentius convenit aliquid causae quam causato.

[37] *In de Causis* I, 29: Quanto virtus alicuius causa est perfectior, tanto ad plura se extendit.

Being, viewed respectively in its infinite and finite modes. What is universally caused is being, and this can only be caused by what has of itself the virtue or power of existence, i.e. Being itself, named by Aquinas as *Ipsum Esse Subsistens*. Obversely, the primacy of *esse* as the fullness of perfection derives from its unique and privileged status as the first of all creatures, and as containing all subsequent perfections. It is the unicity and immediacy of creation which determines being as the primary effect and fullness of all created perfection. Being is not simply the first perfection which is created, but universally and more profoundly the very fullness of all perfection whatsoever. Within the created gift of Being are contained in latent and superior presence every mode and determination of existence. Being is the plenitude of perfection. Although, according to Dionysius, God's nature consists in his essential Goodness which transcends the realms of both Being and Non-Being, God's first creature is Being itself. It has a central role as the primary perfection in which all others participate.

Dionysius proclaims the identity and unity of all perfections in their uncaused nature within the transcendent infinity of divine goodness and, in finite beings, their presence in the intensive and all-embracing perfection of Being. Referring to the universal causal principles, he affirms the identity of Goodness, Being, Life and Wisdom, whereby the Good holds primacy; in the created realm he attributes all perfections to the fullness of created being. Aquinas, taking this further, holds that since God is the unique and universal cause of all things, and because Being is revealed as the primary and principal perfection of all, God is also understood as Absolute Being itself.

In stressing the unity of God's causation, Dionysius overcomes the difficulties of Platonist participation: Being, Life and Wisdom are not diverse principles of causation which exist in themselves even as subordinate to God, nor are they distinct aspects of the unique divine nature; they are rather identical with the very plenitude of the divine nature in which there is no division but pure and perfect simplicity. The universality of God's presence is guaranteed. As unique creative cause of being, he is intimately and pervasively present throughout every form and determination of being. These abide wholly and exhaustively within his creative presence, nourished continually by his endless power.

Dionysius thus plays a profound role in preparing Plato's doctrine of the Good for its transformation and reception within Aquinas' vision, by identifying τὸ Ἀγαθόν unequivocally with the unique and supernatural God. In the foreword to his Commentary, Aquinas shows how much he follows Dionysius in discerning within Platonism what is in accordance with Christian teaching and what must be rejected. It is

clear that Aquinas can accept Plato's ʾΑγαθόν only if interpreted as
synonymous with the Christian God; for Aquinas also, God is the very
essence of goodness, unity and being, the first principle from which
everything else derives its goodness, unity and existence.[38] Now,
Dionysius prepares the way for Aquinas' identification of God with
Plato's Good by naming the first principle of all things indifferently
both as God and Good or Supra-Good: *Unde Dionysius Deum nominat
quandoque ipsum quidem bonum aut superbonum aut principale bonum
aut bonitatem omnis boni.*[39] In this light, the teaching of the *Platonici*
on the universal Good is readily harmonised with Christian teaching:
*Id quod dicebant de primo rerum principio, verissima est eorum opinio et
fidei christianae consona.*[40] Moreover, Aquinas finds already expressed
in Dionysius a rejection of that element of Platonism which disagrees
not only with faith, but which is out of harmony also with philosophical
truth, namely the existence of separately existing universal causes.[41]
Throughout his works, and in his Commentary on the *Liber de Causis*
in particular, Aquinas frequently appeals to the authority of the
Areopagite in criticising the multiplicity of divine principles.

Dionysius thus goes beyond Plato, Plotinus and Proclus in establishing
a monotheism in which the absolute Good is the unique and universal
source and goal of all, the provident creator who is honoured best by
the singular name of God. Pierre Faucon summarises the significance
of Dionysius' influence in St Thomas: 'Telle est donc l'évidence: c'est
en bénéficiant de l'enseignement dionysien que Thomas d'Aquin permet
au Platonisme de franchir une nouvelle étape par l'identification de
l'Idée du Bien au Dieu de l'Exode . . . L'idée première que Saint Thomas
reçoit de Denys est celle de la causalité du Bien. Il s'agit là d'un
principe qui domine le problème de la création.'[42]

---

[38] *In DN*, *Prooemium* II: Ponebant, enim, unum primum quod est ipsa essentia bonitatis
et unitatis et esse, quod dicimus Deum et quod omnia alia dicuntur bona vel una vel
entia per derivationem ab illo primo.

[39] *In DN*, *Prooemium* II.

[40] *In DN*, *Prooemium* II.

[41] *In DN*, *Prooemium* II: Haec igitur Platonicorum ratio fidei non consonat nec veritati,
quantum ad hoc quod continet de speciebus naturalibus separatis.

[42] Pierre Faucon, *Aspects néoplatoniciens de la doctrine de Saint Thomas d'Aquin*, pp.
40, 45; See p. 42: 'Nous sommes donc placés devant une evidence qui concerne
l'orientation fondamentale de la doctrine thomiste: Thomas d'Aquin bénéficie avec Denys
de l'héritage platonicien en exprimant son adhésion aux principes étiologiques des
dialogues du *Timée* et de la *République*. Ebauchée dans le *Commentaire des Sentences*,
l'option en faveur du platonisme prend forme dans le commentaire dionysien au moment
ou Saint Thomas résout la question de la causalité originaire en comparant la fonction
étiologique du Bien divin à l'irradiation de la lumière solaire.'

Dionysius, Aquinas and Exodus 3, 14

An interesting question concerns the reason for this advance in Dionysius' thought towards the unicity and immediacy of divine causation and the primacy of existence in reality. There are, I suggest, two factors which coincide in Dionysius' discovery of the unique relation between God and Being: namely, the biblical teaching of the uniqueness of creation and a philosophical appreciation of the primacy of being before all existential determinations—indeed as their very fullness.

There can be little doubt that the doctrine of creation revealed to both Dionysius and Aquinas, as well as to all Christian philosophers, the fundamental character of existence, which had remained concealed to classical Greek philosophy. For the Greeks, the radical origin of things within being held no mystery; existence posed no question since it was assumed eternal: the question was rather to explain the genesis of the world-order or cosmos. However, once the possibility of origin or radical beginning is raised, Being is put into question; it loses its transparent intelligibility and emerges as an endless mystery in need of illumination. In the absence of the eternal necessity of the universe, what most needs and merits questioning is existence itself. No longer may it be taken for granted. The Christian teaching of creation thus played, I suggest, a crucial and positive role in disclosing to philosophy the radical character of Being. This awakens, moreover, an appreciation that existence is what is fundamental in all things. Dionysius recognises indeed the primacy of Being, as Fabro remarks,[43] in an eminently realist manner: in order to live or know, something must first of all *be*. Even if the Platonist theory of individual transcendent causes is espoused, one must admit that such participations must first partake in the primary efficacy of existence.

Now, if there is but a single, all-perfect cause of all things and if the first and final perfection of each individual is that of being, it must be the nature of the cause to be the endless perfection of Being itself which is continuously and intimately operative at the core of each thing. Expressed philosophically, it is because all determinations are latent or implicit within the perfection of being that there is need of only a single source which causes through the power or *virtus* of being. To natural reflection and intuition, it is evident that Being is the first perfection of all, more universal than life or wisdom; God causes, therefore, all things through Being and is himself transcendent Being. The difference between

---

[43] *Participation et Causalité*, p. 226.

our two authors is that for Dionysius God excels even Being itself, whereas for Aquinas, God is subsisting Being and precisely as Being itself is absolutely transcendent.

In naming God as Being, i.e. ὁ ὤν, or 'Qui est', both authors refer to Exodus 3, 14. I do not wish to engage here in an extended discussion on the question of the so-called 'metaphysics of Exodus'. Much has been made of its importance by some interpreters and it has been disputed by other commentators with equal vehemence. Indeed in weighing up the significance of Exodus and the *Areopagitica*, respectively, on Aquinas, Van Steenberghen goes so far as to declare: 'Le sens des formules de l'*Exode* est très discuté et il paraît certain que S. Thomas doit sa métaphysique de l'*esse* à Denys et non à l'*Exode*; il a ensuite interprété le texte sacré à l'aide de sa métaphysique.'[44] In attaching importance, however, to the absence of any reference to Exodus in Dionysius' text confirming the primacy of Being, Van Steenberghen overlooks 5, 4, 262, where Dionysius, in keeping with his expressed aim of praising God only with names drawn from Scripture, names the universal cause as ὁ ὤν, which Pachymeres (long before Pera, who also notes it), already took as referring to the divine revelation of Moses.[45]

In highlighting the importance of Dionysius in the formation of Aquinas' philosophy of being, one must be cautious in attributing complete or exclusive influence to a single source. It is clear that perhaps Exodus, and certainly the revealed doctrine of creation, already exerted a decisive role in leading Dionysius to the central meaning of being and the unique and immediate character of creation. It is reasonable to accept that the text had for Aquinas a profound and far-reaching metaphysical impact. A distinct question is whether Aquinas arrived at his notion of *esse* through a reflection upon this passage, or discovered instead the existential significance of Exodus in the light of an independent, rational metaphysics—within the context of the historically available doctrine of creation. There is, however, strong reason for agreeing with Fabro's view that 'L'instrument principal et décisif de cette transformation métaphysique de l'*esse* biblique semble avoir été indubitablement le Pseudo-Denys.'[46] That is to say, Aquinas discovered in reliance upon Dionysius both the theological and ontological signification of this passage. There is a confluence of inspiration.

In a detailed and significant passage of *De Substantiis Separatis* (to which Durantel makes no reference), Aquinas even takes Dionysius'

---

[44] 'Prolégomènes à la *quarta Via*', p. 105, n. 13.
[45] PG III, 836C: κατὰ τὸν πρὸς Μωσῆν χρηματισμόν.
[46] *Participation et Causalité*, p. 217.

declaration of the unity or identity of Goodness, Being and Life in God, as stemming directly from Scripture:

> Accordingly it is said in Matthew 19, 'One is good, God'; and that he is being itself—therefore in Exodus 3, God answers Moses who asks what is God's name, 'I am who am'; and that he himself is the life of living beings—accordingly it is said in Deuteronomy 30, 'He is the life of the living.' And this truth, Dionysius most expressly teaches in the fifth chapter of the *Divine Names*, when he says that Sacred Scripture '. . . does not say that to be good is one thing and to be a being is another and that life or wisdom is something else'.[47]

At this point of our enquiry, we have seen that the unity of causation brings the primacy of being into focus as the first created perfection, and restores universal and absolute transcendence to God as unique creative cause. In the following chapters we take a closer look at the nature of being and its relation to God: firstly, the priority of being itself and its role within creation, as the primary creature of God, and as divine similitude par excellence. We shall then review the nature of God, understood by Aquinas as transcendent Being, and the process of creation itself. In each of these areas we shall observe the profound influence of Dionysius together with St Thomas' independence of thought.

---

[47] *De Subst. Sep.*, 17, ed. Lescoe, n. 93, p. 136: Unde dicitur Matth. XIX, 'Unus est bonus, Deus'; et quod sit ipsum esse, unde Exodi III Moysi quaerenti quod esset nomen Dei respondit Dominus, 'Ego sum qui sum'; et quod ipse est viventium vita; unde dicitur Deut. XXX 'Ipse est viventium vita'. Et hanc quidem veritatem expressissime Dionysius tradit V Capitulo De Divinis Nominibus dicens quod sacra scriptura 'non aliud dicit esse bonum et aliud esse ens, et aliud vitam aut sapientiam . . .' Spiazzi, p. 50, even includes *sacra scriptura* within the quotation from Dionysius. Aquinas also refers this doctrine of Dionysius to Scripture in *In de Causis* III, 73: Et hoc est quod dicit V cap. de Divinis Nominibus 'non aliud esse bonum dicit' scilicet sacra scriptura 'et aliud existens et aliud vitam . . .' It should be noted, however, that the word '*dicit*' in the line from Dionysius just cited refers, not to Scripture, but to his own discourse. (5, 1, 257: τῷ λόγῳ σκοπός . . . ταύτας οὖν ὁ λόγος ὑμνῆσαι ποθεῖ τὰς τῆς προνοίας ἐκφαντορικὰς θεονυμίας.) In his Commentary, Aquinas reads the passage correctly: 'Hoc ergo excludit ipse Dionysius, dicens quod praesens sermo *non dicit . . . Neque dicit praesens sermo . . .*' (V, i, 613). It is interesting, however, that on two occasions he states that Dionysius was directly motivated by Scripture in naming God as Being.

CHAPTER SIX

DIONYSIAN ELEMENTS IN AQUINAS'
NOTION OF BEING

UNIVERSAL BEING: THE FIRST CREATED PERFECTION

The most explicit statement by Dionysius on the nature and status of being is to be found in Chapter 5 of the *Divine Names*, where he treats of the name 'Being' as applied to God. While for Dionysius, in accordance with the Neoplatonist tradition, Goodness is the proper name of God, Being is primary among created perfections and is therefore the most excellent of names drawn from creation which may be pronounced in praise of God. For Aquinas, on the other hand, Being is not only the primary perfection of finite reality but also the very essence and proper name of God. In Dionysius' view, 'Good' is the universal and transcendent name which alone expresses God's nature; 'Being' expresses what is globally and primarily the first gift of creation. Of inestimable interest, however, is the significance which Dionysius gives to the value of being in itself as constitutive of the perfection of finite beings. This is found in his exposition of being as God's primary effect and first participation. We shall examine Dionysius' view in the context of Aquinas' Commentary, since there is here a close unity of meaning regarding this central and fundamental doctrine. (Indeed, as Van Steenberghen remarks, we find here, 'dans le commentaire de S. Thomas comme dans le texte de Denys, l'aspect le plus original de la doctrine de la participation à l'être.')[1]

As Aquinas notes, Dionysius gives two reasons why the name 'Being' or *'Qui est'* is applied most fittingly to God. These are in fact two aspects of the one relation of causality. Firstly, God is to be named according to his primary effect, i.e. from the most sublime perfection which he produces. (Dionysius must thus prove the paramount excellence of being within creation, in order to attribute Being to God before all other names.) Secondly, the argument is raised to the level of

---

[1] Fernand Van Steenberghen, 'Prolégoménes á la *quarta via*', p. 104.

participation through an intensification of the value of being which has been disclosed in the first step of the argument: 'He says that God himself has prior and pre-eminent being in a prior and eminent way',[2] i.e. he possesses in the unity and abundance of his Being the unlimited measure of every perfection. This conclusion rests upon the first justification of the primacy of being.

Granted God's causality, and that he is most appropriately named from his primary and most noble effect,[3] it is a matter of discovering which is his most noble effect and primary participation. The question whether being is the highest perfection because it is the first participation in God or rather the first divine participation by virtue of its supreme perfection is an artificial one. The distinction is superfluous since by the very nature of God's perfection and his creative communication, it is evident that the highest perfection of reality should be that which participates most intimately in him. The question which is at once the highest perfection and first participation is to be solved, thus, by reflection.

We find in Dionysius a rational justification of the primacy of being, albeit in a less radical and profound form than in Aquinas. Dionysius establishes summarily the excellence of being and, once this position is attained, defends the priority of being on the ground of its divine origin and its immediacy as the causal presence of God within beings. He begins thus with a natural appreciation of the radical value of being and argues that for something to be wise or living, it must first of all be.

> Being is laid down ($\pi\rho o\beta \dot{\epsilon}\beta\lambda\eta\tau a\iota$, propositum) or created before the other participations in God, and Being itself ($a\dot{v}\tau\dot{o}$ $\kappa a\theta$' $a\dot{v}\tau\dot{o}$ $\tau\dot{o}$ $\epsilon\dot{\iota}\nu a\iota$) is anterior to life itself, wisdom or divine likeness; and all the other principles in which beings participate, first participate themselves in Being. Moreover, all of the subsistent principles in which beings participate, themselves participate in subsisting Being; and there is no being whose essence and eternity are not Being Itself.[4]

Although the primacy of Being is attained by Dionysius through a natural insight and justified by reasoned reflection, this justification occurs within the context of creation. Being is the first perfection to be created and that which first participates in God.

---

[2] V, i, 636: Hoc ergo est quod dicit quod ipse Deus praeesse et superesse praehabet et superhabet. See DN 5, 5, 267: $\kappa a\dot{\iota}$ $\gamma\dot{a}\rho$ $\tau\dot{o}$ $\pi\rho o\epsilon\dot{\iota}\nu a\iota$ $\kappa a\dot{\iota}$ $\dot{v}\pi\epsilon\rho\epsilon\dot{\iota}\nu a\iota$ $\pi\rho o\dot{\epsilon}\chi\omega\nu$ $\kappa a\dot{\iota}$ $\dot{v}\pi\epsilon\rho\dot{\epsilon}\chi\omega\nu$.

[3] V, i, 633: Si qua causa nominetur a suo effectu, convenientissime nominetur a principali et dignissimo suorum effectuum.

[4] 5, 5, 266: $\kappa a\dot{\iota}$ $\pi\rho\dot{o}$ $\tau\hat{\omega}\nu$ $\ddot{a}\lambda\lambda\omega\nu$ $a\dot{v}\tauo\hat{v}$ $\mu\epsilon\tauo\chi\hat{\omega}\nu$ $\tau\dot{o}$ $\epsilon\dot{\iota}\nu a\iota$ $\pi\rho o\beta\dot{\epsilon}\beta\lambda\eta\tau a\iota$ $\kappa a\dot{\iota}$ $\ddot{\epsilon}\sigma\tau\iota\nu$ $a\dot{v}\tau\dot{o}$ $\kappa a\theta$' $a\dot{v}\tau\dot{o}$ $\tau\dot{o}$ $\epsilon\dot{\iota}\nu a\iota$ $\pi\rho\epsilon\sigma\beta\dot{v}\tau\epsilon\rho o\nu$ $\tau o\hat{v}$ $a\dot{v}\tauo\zeta\omega\dot{\eta}\nu$ $\epsilon\dot{\iota}\nu a\iota$ $\kappa a\dot{\iota}$ $a\dot{v}\tauo\sigma o\phi\dot{\iota}a\nu$ $\epsilon\dot{\iota}\nu a\iota$ $\kappa a\dot{\iota}$ $a\dot{v}\tauo o\mu o\iota\dot{o}\tau\eta\tau a$ $\theta\epsilon\dot{\iota}a\nu$ $\epsilon\dot{\iota}\nu a\iota$ $\kappa a\dot{\iota}$ $\tau\dot{a}$ $\ddot{a}\lambda\lambda a$ $\ddot{o}\sigma\omega\nu$ $\tau\dot{a}$ $\ddot{o}\nu\tau a$ $\mu\epsilon\tau\dot{\epsilon}\chi o\nu\tau a$.

Being is taken by Dionysius from the outset as the principal, most ancient and venerable of God's gifts. The priority of existence among all the participations of the Good stems from its privileged position as radix of all specific perfections, in which they must first participate in order to be and to effect their presence within beings. Not only is Being the plenitude of perfection from which all individual beings derive, but it is the source of all the perfections which they share. In Dionysius we re-encounter the Platonist concept of universal causes, i.e. transcendent principles of perfection in which finite beings participate according to the various qualities which they enjoy. For the Pseudo-Areopagite, however, it serves as a model of reflection in order to conceive of the causality of distinct perfections and their exemplary presence in the Creator. The so-called transcendent principles are not distinct from Being, separate and apart from it, as it were, but are themselves participations in Being itself. 'For, indeed, all the principles of beings through their participation in Being both are and are principles; they first of all are and are then principles.'[5]

Thus, according to Dionysius if we suppose, for example, that Life itself ($αὐτοζωή$) is the principle of living things, and Similarity itself the principle of all things which bear resemblance, and Unity and Order the principles of all things which are unified and ordered; and likewise if we call 'Participations per se' ($αὐτομετοχάς$) all the other principles in which beings participate, we will find that these participations first participate in Being; through Being they first of all subsist themselves and are subsequently principles of this or that. By participation in Being, therefore, they both subsist in themselves and permit things to participate in them. And if these principles exist through their participation in Being, much more so do those beings which in turn partake of them.[6] Through Being all things both are, and receive their determination as the kind of being which they are.[7]

This intensive unity of the qualities and perfections of a being in its very Being or its to be, and the superiority of Being, are illustrated by the reply to a hypothetical but interesting objection. If Being transcends life and life exceeds wisdom, why, it is asked, are living and intelligent beings superior to things which merely exist, i.e. beings whose highest perfection is their simple existence; and why do intellectual and spiritual natures surpass all others and come closer to God, rather than those

---

[5] 5, 5, 267: καὶ γοῦν αἱ ἀρχαὶ τῶν ὄντων πᾶσαι τοῦ εἶναι μετέχουσαι καί εἰσι καὶ ἀρχαί εἰσι καὶ πρῶτόν εἰσι ἔπειτα ἀρχαί εἰσι.

[6] 5, 5, 267: εἶναι πρῶτον αὐτὰς μετεχούσας καὶ τῷ εἶναι πρῶτον μὲν οὔσας, ἔπειτα τοῦδε ἢ τοῦδε ἀρχὰς οὔσας καὶ τῷ μετέχειν τοῦ εἶναι καὶ οὔσας καὶ μετεχομένας.

[7] 5, 7, 274: τὰ ἄλλα ὅσα τῷ εἶναι ὄντα, τὰ ὄντα πάντα χαρακτηρίζει.

which have the simple richness of being. Should not those which participate exclusively and solely in the most sublime gift of God, namely existence, be superior and therefore transcend the rest?[8] But as Dionysius points out in his response, the objection assumes that intellectual beings do not also share in life and existence, whereas it is precisely as beings that they are living and intelligent.[9] The perfections are not separate but spring from Being itself, are concentrated and rooted within it. Just as life includes virtually within itself as one of its possible determinations the perfection of wisdom, so does Being embrace life, although it extends beyond living things so as to contain also inanimate beings. Its extension is more universal, thus its perfection is more fundamental and creative. This text of Dionysius clearly illustrates the nature of virtual and intensive presence of all perfection in Being and is frequently invoked by Aquinas to explain both the intimate and intensive presence of *esse* throughout all things and the unified presence of all finite reality in God as the source of Being.[10] In a startling sentence, expressing what has recently been termed the 'ontological difference', Dionysius emphasises the distinction and primacy of Being with respect to beings, and the priority of Being itself in the divine causation of that which is: 'He is the Being of beings; and not only beings, but the Being itself of beings is from the Being before the ages.'[11]

In his Commentary, Aquinas points out that beings which are endowed with life and intellection do not lack, but 'possess being more excellently.'[12] In the words of Dionysius, not only do they desire God's beauty and goodness more but, actually partaking of these perfections, 'are closer to the Good, participating in it more abundantly and receiving from it more abundant and greater gifts.'[13] In the same manner, rational beings surpass those which have mere perception, while the latter are superior to mere living beings, and these in turn to inanimate reality.

It is noteworthy that, in commenting upon these lines of Dionysius, St Thomas introduces the concept of *act* to explain the distinction

---

[8] 5, 3, 259.
[9] 5, 3, 260: ἀλλ' εἰ μὲν ἀνούσια καὶ ἄζωα τις ὑπετίθετο τὰ νοερά, καλῶς ἂν εἶχεν ὁ λόγος.
[10] E.g. *ST*, I, 4, 2, ad 3.
[11] 5, 4, 264: ἀλλ' αὐτός ἐστι τὸ εἶναι τοῖς οὖσι καὶ οὐ τὰ ὄντα μόνον, ἀλλὰ καὶ αὐτὸ τὸ εἶναι τῶν ὄντων ἐκ τοῦ προαιωνίως ὄντος.
[12] V, i, 615: Sed divinae mentes Angelorum non carent esse, quinimmo habent excellentius super alia existentia creata. Living things are clearly 'more noble' than non-living bodies (*ST*, I, 3, 1).
[13] *DN* 5, 3, 260.

between the desire for the Good in beings and their actual and effective possession of it, which, ultimately, is the necessary keynote of existence: *et non solum magis desiderant, quasi perfectius ordinatae in ipsum, sed eo magis participant, perfectiorem bonitatem actu habentes.*[14] (For Dionysius, even non-being, i.e. matter without form, is 'ordained' towards goodness; beings come into existence and possess Being precisely through love of Goodness.) Here, Aquinas ingeniously attributes the multiplicity of perfections within a being to the unique excellence of its own act of *esse*. The excellence of being enjoyed by any reality is relative to its possession in act of a greater measure of goodness. *Esse habent excellentius* is equivalent to *perfectiorem bonitatem actu habentes.* Aquinas is thus able to draw advantage from Dionysius' limitation of being to the possession in act of goodness to illustrate the primacy of the act of being: what matters ultimately is the actuality of perfection.

As noted earlier, the central meaning of being in Dionysius cannot be fully discovered simply from a reflection on finite beings alone. We must refer to its divine origin and its privileged role in creation. Its primacy as a perfection among creatures stems from its immediacy as the creative medium by which God is present in and to all creatures. This is noted by Aquinas who comments that, for Dionysius, *nomen vero entis designat processum essendi a Deo in omnia entia.*[15] Being, *ipsum esse*, (αὐτὸ καθ᾽ αὐτὸ τὸ εἶναι), is for Dionysius the most dignified and privileged of creatures because it is the first participation in God. All perfections are perfections of Being and Being itself is the first perfection created. Thus it is in and through Being that all things participate in God.[16] As its first gift the absolute and self-subsisting Good brings forth Being itself.[17]

As Aquinas notes, the reason for Dionysius' view of the primacy of Being is its position as the principal and most worthy of God's effects and its role as mediatory focus of all subsequent effects. St Thomas

---

[14] V, i, 615. Pierre Faucon writes: 'Invité par Denys à concevoir l'être comme le fondement ou la source originelle de toutes les perfections, Thomas d'Aquin exploite le vocabulaire d'Aristote: l'être est l'acte actuant et fondamental d'où jaillissent les perfections à mesure qu'elles sont éduites de la potentialité. Cette explication de la pensée dionysienne en termes aristotéliciens manifeste l'originalité de l'exégèse thomiste: recueillant les doctrines de ses devanciers, Saint Thomas procède au moyen de confrontations doctrinales qui mettent en relief les complémentarités. La preuve est ainsi faite qu'au moment où il rédige son commentaire, Saint Thomas n'hésite pas à se servir de la philosophie d'Aristote pour soutenir son option en faveur du platonisme dionysien.' Pierre Faucon, *Aspects nèoplatoniciens de la doctrine de saint Thomas d'Aquin*, p. 235.

[15] V, i, 610.

[16] 5, 5, 266: καὶ πρὸ τῶν ἄλλων αὐτοῦ μετοχῶν τὸ εἶναι προβέβληται.

[17] 5, 6, 267: πρώτην οὖν τὴν τοῦ αὐτὸ εἶναι δωρεὰν ἡ αὐτοϋπεραγαθότης προβαλλομένη.

gives an interesting interpretation of Dionysius' phrase πρὸ τῶν ἄλλων αὐτοῦ μετοχῶν τὸ εἶναι προβέβληται. He writes:

> Being itself is offered to creatures to be participated in before all the other participations of God. Whatever perfection a creature may have, it receives through a participation in God, who is, as it were, offered to all beings that they may participate in him; but he is first participated in with regard to Being itself (*ipsum esse*) prior to any other perfection: thus Being itself *per se* is more ancient, that is, more primary and noble than Life itself.[18]

Aquinas claims to discern two arguments in Dionysius in favour of the primacy and superior dignity of Being as such over Life, Wisdom and other such exemplary perfections. Firstly, whatever shares in other participations must partake first of Being. To this Aquinas adds the simple logical consideration that something is known as a being before it is conceived as 'one', 'living' or 'wise'. What Aquinas calls the second argument for the primacy of being is a metaphysical explication of the first: Being is the first value participated in not only by individual beings, but is more immediately and profoundly the source of those perfections and princples of which, in the language of Neoplatonist metaphysics, each individual specifically partakes. Life and wisdom are certain ways of being; Being is, therefore, prior to and more simple than life and wisdom, and is related to them, according to St Thomas, both *sicut participatum ad participans* and *ut actus eorum*.[19] Being is thus the principle of all principles participated in by beings. Dionysius concludes: 'No being exists whose substance and eternity is not Being itself (τὸ αὐτὸ εἶναι)'[20] or, as Aquinas puts it, Being is the 'form' participated in by all things with respect to their subsistence and duration.[21]

---

[18] V, i, 633: Hoc est ergo quod dicit, quod ipsum esse propositum est creaturis ad participandum ante alias Dei participationes. Quamcumque enim perfectionem creatura habeat, fit per hoc in Dei participatione, qui quasi proponitur et offertur omnibus ad participandum; sed per prius participatur quantum ad ipsum esse, quam quamcumque aliam perfectionem: et ipsum per se esse est senius, idest primum et dignius eo quod est per se vitam esse.

[19] V, i, 635: Quod autem per se esse sit primum et dignius quam per se vita et per se sapientia, ostendit dupliciter: primo quidem, per hoc quod quaecumque participant aliis participationibus, primo participant ipso esse: prius enim intelligitur aliquod ens quam unum, vivens, vel sapiens. Secundo, quod ipsum esse comparatur ad vitam, et alia huiusmodi sicut participatum ad participans: nam etiam ipsa vita est ens quoddam et sic esse, prius et simplicius est quam vita et alia huiusmodi et comparatur ad ea ut actus eorum. Referring to this passage from the Commentary on Dionysius, Fabro writes: 'Saint Thomas, et lui seul, proclame l'émergence absolue de l'*esse* comme acte de tous les actes et de toutes les formes. Formes et actes "retombent" dans la condition de puissance ou de "capacité" receptive de l'acte d'être.' Ibid.

[20] 5, 5, 266.

[21] V, i, 635.

Here we have an example both of a major inspiration exercised by Dionysius and a masterly commentary by St Thomas. Dionysius uses neither the word 'act' nor 'perfection', but his sense is clear. The phrases πρὸ τῶν ἄλλων αὐτοῦ μετοχῶν τὸ εἶναι προβέβληται καὶ ἔστιν αὐτὸ καθ' αὑτὸ τὸ εἶναι πρεσβύτερον and τὰ ἄλλα ὅσων τὰ ὄντα μετέχοντα, πρὸ πάντων αὐτῶν τοῦ εἶναι μετέχει[22] could only have been interpreted by Aquinas in terms of participation in *esse* as the first perfection[23] and act of all beings.[24] Aquinas weaves together the causal principles of both Platonist and Aristotelian metaphysics, placing them under the primacy of being as their primary act which enriches, and the first perfection to be participated. Whether the form which determines a being is conceived as an immanent act or as a transcendent perfection which is participated, it must first be actualised by and participate in being. In perceiving the central value of Being, the supreme form and primary act, Aquinas discerns the focus and fulcrum uniting Platonist and Aristotelian metaphysics; Dionysius plays a significant role in this discovery.

For Dionysius, Being is the focal point, the radical and radial centre of God's action within beings. This is the ultimate source of its primacy. The power of creation touches most radically the central act of being and from here diffuses its presence and penetrates throughout all creation. This is the ontological primacy proper to the act of being. It is, as it were, the immediate and intimate medium through which God acts upon each being, actualising its essence and all its features. On the relation of being to creatures and creator respectively, and its role in creation, Dionysius gives a dense but clear statement, which is important not only in itself but more so for the commentary which it provoked in Aquinas. The text upon which Aquinas comments begins as follows: 'The most worthy (gifts) of being he bestows on the more exalted natures which Scripture calls eternal; yet Being itself, however, is never withdrawn from any being whatsoever.'[25] Aquinas adds: 'since nothing can be said to exist unless it possesses *esse*.'[26] Of particular interest is the new meaning which Aquinas introduces to this text. The point which Dionysius wishes to make here, according to Aquinas, is *quod etiam ipsum esse commune est a Deo*,[27] i.e. *quod Deus est causa ipsius*

---

[22] 5, 1, 266.

[23] V, i, 633.

[24] V, i, 635.

[25] 5, 8, 278: καὶ τὰ μὲν πρεσβεῖα τοῦ εἶναι νέμει ταῖς κρείττοσιν οὐσίαις, ἃς καὶ αἰωνίας καλεῖ τὰ λόγια τὸ δὲ εἶναι αὐτὸ τῶν ὄντων πάντων οὐδέποτε ἀπολείπεται.

[26] V, ii, 659: Nihil potest dici existens nisi habeat esse.

[27] V, ii, 653.

esse commune; et ... quod ipsum esse est omnibus commune.[28] Now,
when we compare this interpretation with the passage referred to we
discover, firstly, that Dionysius is in fact speaking in the first instance
of the most elevated of natures, which receive from God the most
dignified gifts of Being and which, being eternal, are distinct from other
beings, which—he is quick to add—also enjoy the perpetual presence
of Being. The interpretation of Aquinas may perhaps be implied but is
not the most obvious.

Secondly, and of greater importance, is that instead of the simple
ipsum esse (τὸ εἶναι αὐτὸ) which we find in Dionysius, Aquinas adopts
the expression *ipsum esse commune*. Why does Aquinas introduces this
adaptation? What is its significance? An incidental change of expression,
a deepening of Dionysius' intuition, or perhaps a transformation of the
very notion itself? St Thomas' approach to this text also seems directed
towards a certain interpretation which is not primarily evident.
Dionysius' phrase τὸ δὲ εἶναι αὐτὸ τῶν ὄντων πάντων οὐδέποτε
ἀπολείπεται[29] simply notes that Being is never absent from any being
whatsoever. Aquinas makes explicit the ontological significance: *ostendit
quod ipsum esse est omnibus commune.*[30]

Aquinas provides one significant indication later in his commentary
on Chapter 5, where he distinguishes Dionysius' view from the position
of the Platonists which we have already outlined. Although the latter
affirmed God to be *totius esse causa*, they also believed it necessary to
posit certain secondary causes which determine things according to their
proper nature. This was because they believed that a single cause could
not be the source of the variety whereby things differ, i.e. according to
their proper nature, but only of what is common to all. They posited,
therefore, certain causes which determine things in their proper natures,
which receive in common their being from God, calling these causes
the exemplars of things. 'But in saying that God was *causa totius esse
commune*, Dionysius stated that he was cause of what is proper to each
thing, from which it follows that the exemplars of all beings are in God
himself.'[31] For Dionysius, 'Being itself' is the universal and intimate
perfection at the foundation of each thing' particularity. This is the
meaning grasped by Aquinas in *ipsum esse* and which he finds
adumbrated in Dionysius. *Esse* is the distillation, fullness, and intensity

---

[28] V, ii, 658.
[29] 5, 8, 278.
[30] V, ii, 658.
[31] V, iii, 664: Sed Dionysius, sicut dixerat Deum esse causam totius esse communis, ita
dixerat eum esse causam proprietatis uniuscuiusque, unde consequebatur quod in ipso
Deo essent omnium entium exemplaria.

of all perfection and God is its ground and origin. Aquinas adds *commune* to emphasise the universal and all-pervasive character of *esse* as created wholly and uniquely by God. It would appear, therefore, that by explicitly adding the term *commune*, Aquinas wishes to exploit the profound sense of Dionysius' words and align it with his own notion of being.

Because of what some authors consider to be a certain divergence between the many texts of St Thomas on *esse commune*, a variety of theories has arisen regarding its specific meaning. It is worth considering the problem, therefore, in some detail. Let us first state the relation of being to God or the 'Pre-existent' (*προών*) according to Dionysius, and consider Aquinas' understanding of the passage, in particular the meaning which he attaches to *ipsum esse commune*. Secondly, a brief look at St Thomas' treatment of the topic elsewhere will help us appreciate the relation between the Dionysian texts and the ensemble of Aquinas' writings.

Dionysius exposes the relation of being to the Pre-existent in a brief litany of contrasts and distinctions:

> Being itself is from the Pre-existent; Being belongs to him, but he does not belong to Being; Being is in him but he is not in Being; Being receives him but he does not receive being; he is the eternity and principle of Being. He is the measure of all things prior to essence, Being and eternity. He is the creator (*οὐσιοποιός*) of all things, their principle, medium and end.[32]

Aquinas' commentary on this passage is of primary significance. As aready noted, to the *ipsum esse* by which Sarracenus translates *αὐτὸ εἶναι*, Aquinas adds the word *commune*. How does he understand the relation of Being to God, as presented in this passage by Dionysius? Aquinas first notes that since *ipsum esse commune* proceeds from God, who is the first Being, *esse commune* is related differently than other beings to God in three respects. He remarks observantly that the essential distinction between God and beings is already stated in the phrase *καὶ αὐτὸ δὲ τὸ εἶναι ἐκ τοῦ προόντος* and that from this distinction follows the nature of their relation. It is interesting that Aquinas does not literally follow Dionysius' terms of the distinction but gives to the context a colouring of his own; where Dionysius (in

---

[32] 5, 8, 279: *καὶ αὐτὸ δὲ τὸ εἶναι ἐκ τοῦ προόντος καὶ αὐτοῦ ἐστι τὸ εἶναι καὶ οὐκ αὐτὸς τοῦ εἶναι καὶ ἐν αὐτῷ ἐστι τὸ εἶναι καὶ οὐκ αὐτὸς ἐν τῷ εἶναι καὶ αὐτὸν ἔχει τὸ εἶναι καὶ οὐκ αὐτὸς ἔχει τὸ εἶναι καὶ αὐτός ἐστι τοῦ εἶναι καὶ αἰὼν καὶ ἀρχὴ καὶ μέτρον πρὸ οὐσίας ὢν καὶ ὄντος καὶ αἰῶνος καὶ πάντων οὐσιοποιὸς ἀρχὴ καὶ μεσότης καί τελευτή*. I have translated *ἔχει*, literally 'has', with 'receive', in order to avoid any misinterpretation of Being as 'possessing' the 'Pre-existent', which is the error in Rolt's translation, p. 29. Pachymeres (845C) renders *ἔχει* with *μετέχει*, i.e., participates: *ὁ δὲ θεὸς οὐ μετέχει τοῦ εἶναι, ἀλλ᾽ αὐτὸ τὸ εἶναι μετέχει τοῦ θεοῦ*.

translation) reads: *Et ipsum autem esse est ex praeexistente* (ἐκ τοῦ προόντος), Aquinas renders: *ipsum esse commune est ex primo ente, quod est Deus.*[33] There is indeed a sense in which God is the First Being, as the exemplar and principle of all Being. For Dionysius, however, he is more significantly before and beyond Being. Aquinas here, as frequently, interprets Dionysius in a sense harmonious with his own theory of the primacy of Being rather than of the Good.

We may also note that Aquinas' formulation does not correspond to the relation which Dionysius had outlined between God and beings. The distinction which Aquinas exposes is between God's relation to *esse commune* and that of finite beings to *esse commune*. He perceives three distinctions in the relationship of *esse commune* and *alia existentia* to God. Firstly, 'other beings depend on *esse commune*, but not God; rather does *esse commune* depend upon God.'[34] This he concludes from Dionysius' phrase *'et Ipsius est esse et non Ipse est esse'* (καὶ αὐτοῦ ἐστι τὸ εἶναι καὶ οὐκ αὐτὸς τοῦ εἶναι), taking the genitive as indicating the dependence of being on God. There is no reference here by Dionysius to the relation of Being to finite beings but this had already been exposed in detail, and Aquinas summarises it in contra-distinction to the relation of Being to *primum Ens*.

Secondly, *esse commune* is related to God in a manner different from beings, since all existing things are preserved or contained under *ipsum esse commune*, whereas God is not. *Esse commune* rather is itself contained under the power of God, *sicut contentum in continente*, since his divine power extends beyond created being. It is in this sense of the virtual and intensive presence of beings within Being and of Being within God that Aquinas interprets the phrase *'in Ipso est esse et non Ipse est in eo quod est esse'.*[35] Finally, Being differs from beings in its relation to God since, while beings participate in Being (*eo quod est esse*), God does not. Created being itself (*ipsum esse creatum*) is rather a certain participation in God and a similitude of him (*quaedam participatio Dei et similitudo Ipsius*). Dionysius' phrase *'Ipsum habet esse'* is clarified by Aquinas: *ut participans similitudinem Eius.*[36]

---

[33] V, ii, 660. Aquinas here is probably following his teacher Albertus Magnus: Et ipsum esse, creatum scilicet, est a praeexistente, idest a primo ente. *Super Dionysium De Divinis Nominibus,* p. 320.

[34] V, ii, 660: ... primo quidem, quantum ad hoc quod alia existentia dependent ab esse communi, non autem Deus, sed magis esse commune dependet a Deo.

[35] V, ii, 660: Secundo, quantum ad hoc quod omnia existentia continentur sub ipso esse communi, non autem Deus, sed magis esse commune continetur sub eius virtute, quia virtus divina plus extenditur quam ipsum esse creatum; et hoc est quod dicit, quod esse commune est in ipso Deo sicut contentum in continente et non e converso ipse Deus est in eo quod est esse.

[36] V, iii, 660: Tertio, quantum ad hoc quod omnia alia existentia participant eo quod

These three respects in which *ipsum esse* is related to God differently than beings—dependence, pre-eminent presence, and participation—are but specific explications of the distinction between God and beings. They clarify how its relation to God differs from its relation to beings, since the relation of beings to *esse commune* reflects how *esse commune* is related to God. What results most clearly from this paragraph of Dionysius and from Aquinas' commentary which confirms it is, on the one hand, the radical contingency of created being in relation to God (stressed by Dionysius) and, on the other, the radical position of Being itself as the source and intermediary of the dependence, presence and participation of beings. The latter emphasis is introduced by Aquinas, who undoubtedly wishes to highlight the dignity of the perfection of *ipsum esse*. For this reason also, presumably, he calls God *primum ens* rather than *praeexistens*. As created, Being is itself a 'participation and likeness of God'; it bears this title, however, before all beings and enjoys a radical primacy as the source of finite beings and all their perfections. Properly speaking, it is their source as mediator. 'Creatures participate in the unparticipated Being of God through the intermediary of *esse commune*.'[37] It is for this reason that Aquinas adds the title *commune* to the reality of *ipsum esse*. It conveys that it is general, not as the most barren of concepts, but that as primordial and pre-eminent perfection it is pregnant with universal being. It is intensely omnipresent in all things.[38]

The Meaning of *Esse Commune*

It would appear evident that as explained in the present context, *ipsum esse commune* is identical with St Thomas' notion of *actus essendi*, the

---

est esse, non autem Deus, sed magis ipsum esse creatum est quaedem participatio Dei et similitudo Ipsius; et hoc est quod dicit quod esse commune habet Ipsum scilicet Deum, ut participans similitudinem Eius, non autem ipse Deus habet esse, quasi participans ipso esse.

[37] André Hayen, 'Intentionnalité de l'être et métaphysique de la participation', p. 404: 'les creatures participent l'être imparticipé de Dieu par l'intermediaire de l'*esse commune*.' See also Hayen's work *L'Intentionnel selon saint Thomas*, p. 247, n. 2: 'Est-ce à dire que les êtres finis participent à l'*esse commune* participant lui-même à l'être incrée de Dieu? Oui, si l'on entend l'*esse commune*, non comme un intermediaire, mais comme un *principium quo*, intrinsèque à l'être participant, réellement distinct de cet être et de l'essence qui le restreint, mais intimement uni à cet être qu'il constitue être, et si des lors on affirme complementairement que ce *principium quo* est l'être crée lui-même, en tant qu'il participe l'*esse divin*.'

[38] IV, i, 263: Si autem ipsae res in se considerentur: primum et communius, quod in eis invenitur, est esse. *Comp. Theol.* I, 68: Primus effectus Dei in rebus est ipsum esse, quod omnes alii effectus praesupponunt.

intimate act of existing which is at the heart of every reality. The addition of *commune* to *ipsum esse*, however, presents a difficulty for some interpreters of this passage, who claim that in its usual sense *commune* denotes a concept which exists *in intellectu tantum*, a mere *ens rationis*, albeit founded on our experience of *entia*. Here, on the contrary, *esse commune* is shown to be that on which all things depend for their real existence—what is most perfect in reality and first created by God. It is portrayed as the very foundation of beings.

If we look carefully at the texts of *Contra Gentiles* 1, 26, we discover that Aquinas says: '*Multum igitur minus et ipsum esse commune est aliquid praeter omnes res existentes nisi in intellectu solum.*' Apart from and beyond existing things, *ipsum esse commune* indeed resides in the intellect alone. Implied is that it exists primarily within the multiplicity, not as an abstract unity but as a concrete perfection realised differently in the individual members of the many. It does not state that *esse commune*, understood as *esse naturale*, refers to no extramental reality whatsoever, but exactly the opposite; apart from the many, it enjoys merely mental status.[39] As common to many,[40] *esse* is not *praeter multa*, beyond the many, but inherent to them, *esse inhaerens*.[41] There is thus no contradiction between Aquinas' Commentary on Dionysius and his other works.

That *ipsum esse commune* may not be confused with the general concept of being is also evident from another passage of Aquinas' Commentary, where its distinction from Infinite Being is again stated. Aquinas specifically asks what Dionysius understands by *per se esse vel per se vita et huiusmodi*. He explains that these principles may be understood in two ways. Firstly, in so far as it signifies a real distinction or separation beyond the single beings which participate in it (and freed, therefore, from the limits of finite reality), such a principle, for example Life, is identical with God himself. Secondly, in so far as a principle or perfection *per se* is understood as involving a distinction or separation according to reason alone, it signifies the very principle as it

---

[39] Cf. L. Oeing-Hanhoff, *Ens et Unum Convertuntur*, pp. 85-6, n. 67: 'Mit dieser Formulierung ist nicht der Unterschied von Prinzip und Prinzipiat oder das Prinzipsein des *esse commune* geleugnet, vielmehr schliesst Thomas dadurch "die Meinung der Platoniker aus, die das Sein unter Gott gleichsam getrennt subsistierend ansetzen." (Div. Nom. 5, 1). Wie aber Thomas statt des *homo separatus* von der nicht subsistierenden *humanitas inhaerens* als *principium quo* spricht (vgl. Ver. 21, 4), so ist auch das *esse commune* nicht 'ausserhalb der Dinge', sondern *esse inhaerens* (vgl. de hebd. 2; Pot. 1, 1; 7, 2, 7; etc.).'

[40] V, ii, 658: Ipsum esse est omnibus commune.

[41] *De Potentia* 7, 2, ad 7: Intellectus autem noster hoc modo intelligit esse quo modo invenitur in rebus inferioribus a quibus scientiam capit, in quibus esse non est subsistens, sed *inhaerens*.

abides within things themselves, both singular and multiple, distinguished in thought but not in reality from things.[42] Thus, when Aquinas comments: *Hic autem per se vitam accepit pro vita quae inest viventibus*, emphasising that *loquitur enim hic de participationibus, vita autem per se existens non est participatio*,[43] we may conclude (since Aquinas himself groups *per se esse vel per se vita et huiusmodi*) that *per se esse* is to be understood as *esse quod inest entibus*. And since *vita per se existens* is not a participation, but God himself praised as the fullness and source of life, likewise *esse per se existens (participatum)*, involving a real separation from beings, signifies God as the plenitude of Being, while *ipsum esse* is the act of being immanent to things. This passage also dispels any confusion of *esse commune* with *esse divinum*, the other major pitfall in seeking to determine the signification of *esse commune*.[44]

Is it possible that St Thomas may have understood *esse commune* differently elsewhere? Quite unlikely, since in deliberately introducing the term of *esse commune* which is absent in Dionysius, it must be to indicate that what Dionysius calls αὐτὸ εἶναι, is identical with his own notion of *esse commune*.[45] In an attempt to define precisely what St Thomas means by *esse commune*, interpreters have perhaps done violence to his facility of thought by establishing an excessive rigidity with regard to this notion. According to some, *esse commune* refers strictly and exclusively to a logical concept alone; this, however, is to empty metaphysical reflection of its natural richness of reality. Others maintain that *esse commune* embraces God himself.

Each position can appeal to texts in its favour. Any effort to restrict the notion of *esse commune* to any one signification shall, however,

---

[42] V, i, 634: Cum ergo dicitur per se vita, secundum sententiam Dionysii, dupliciter intelligi potest: uno modo, secundum quod per se importat discretionem vel separationem realem et sic per se vita est ipse Deus. Alio modo, secundum quod importat discretionem vel separationem solum secundum rationem et sic per se vita est quae inest viventibus, quae non distinguitur secundum rem, sed secundum rationem tantum a viventibus. Et eadem ratio est de per se sapientia et sic de aliis.

[43] V, i, 634.

[44] Commenting upon another group of quotations, J. B. Lotz, in a superb article, speaks of these as the *zwei Fehlösungen* to which interpretation of Aquinas' *Seinsphilosophie* may fall prey: 'Die eine versucht, das Sein als *esse commune* vom Seienden zu trennen und zu einer *selbständig Grösse* zu machen; Thomas verwahrt sich dagegen: das kann es nur als Gedankending, nicht aber als etwas Wirkliches geben . . . Die andere setzt vorschnell das dem Seienden innewohnende Sein *mit dem göttlichen Sein* gleich, was der Aquinate auf das entschiedenste zurückweist.' ('Das Sein selbst und das subsistierende Sein nach Thomas von Aquin', p. 191) Lotz brings out the Dionysian provenance of Thomist *esse* (p. 189).

[45] Cf. L. Elders, *Revue Thomiste*, 1967, p. 612. De Vries believes, nevertheless, that there is a disparity between St Thomas' treatment of *esse commune* in his Commentary on Dionysius and in his other works. Cf. 'Das *esse commune* bei Thomas von Aquin', pp. 163-77.

inevitably neglect other explicit texts of Aquinas. More importantly, however, it is to overlook the special analogical nature of being, which is the hallmark of *esse commune*. It is not a simple or univocal notion. In seeking to establish the primary signification given by Aquinas to the term *esse commune*, it seems necessary to allow a certain freedom of terminology. It would be to deprive Aquinas of all facility and spontaneity of both thought and expression to presuppose a strict adherence to a rigidly defined vocabulary. It is not our present purpose to make an exhaustive study of all the uses made by Aquinas of *esse*. I suggest, however, that the primary signification intended by *esse commune* is *ipsum esse creaturae*, and that Aquinas is inspired in this regard by Pseudo-Dionysius.

In a passage of the Commentary on the *Sentences*, which seems to have been overlooked, Aquinas shows how the many senses of being are related and how, in each case, our knowledge proceeds from the being of the individual creature.[46] Besides (1), its individual and proper existence in actuality, (existence in the primary ontological sense), each being also has (2), a certain presence within the intellect by which it is known. More profoundly (3), it is said to be in God, its creative source and cause; its being abides in God, in a very real way more perfectly than within itself. In the first and third cases, *esse* has a real existence, an actual status; in the second it enjoys the status of an object of knowledge. Now, according to Aquinas, *esse creaturae* may also be considered (4), in a general way, apart from or independently of its other meanings: *communiter, prout abstrahit ab omnibus his*. It may be asked how we are to conceive of *esse creaturae* in this most universal cognitive modality possible, freed from the characteristics which determine its presence in itself, to the intellect, and as distinct from God.

It is with regard to this fourth mode of conceiving *esse creaturae in propria natura* that the first mode is compared with both the second

---

[46] *In I Sent.*, 36, 1, 3 ad 2: Dicendum quod esse creaturae potest quadrupliciter considerari: primo modo, secundum quod est in propria natura; secundo modo, prout est in cognitione nostra; tertio modo, prout est in Deo; quarto modo communiter, prout abstrahit ab omnibus his. Cum ergo dicitur quod creatura verius esse habet in Deo quam in seipsa, comparatur primum et tertium esse respectu quarti, quia omnis comparatio est respectu communis; et pro tanto dicitur quod in Deo habet verius esse, quia omne quod est in aliquo, est in eo per modum eius in quo est et non per modum sui; unde in Deo est per esse increatum, in se autem per esse creatum, in quo minus est de veritate essendi quam in esse increato. Si autem comparatur esse primum ad secundum respectu quarti, invenitur habere secundum excedentia et excessa; esse enim quod est in propia natura rei, in eo quod est substantiale, excedit esse rei in anima quod est accidentale; sed exceditur ab eo secundum quod est esse materiale et illud intellectuale. Cornelio Fabro cites this text in *Participation et Causalité*, pp. 370-1.

and third. Abstracted from the specific determinations of the three primary instances, this concept, like all others, is both general and ideal. As a term of comparison, which allows us to determine the degree of superiority between finite being *secundum quod est in propria natura* and *prout est in cognitione nostra* on the one hand, and *prout est in Deo* on the other, it necessarily refers to the real perfection of *esse*, but in a manner other than its actual mode of existence. It conceives the perfection of *esse* in a purely ideal manner and not as it inheres in finite reality, is present to cognition, or as it is within the power of the Absolute. Nevertheless it refers to *esse creaturae*.

We may be tempted to identify *esse commune* with this conception of *esse creaturae*—conceived separately from its real foundation *in propria natura*, from the intentional presence by which it is known and from the absolute foundation in which it is ultimately grounded. It is a concept common to multiple modes of being rather than as grasping the individual and universal perfection of being. However, it is more satisfactory to take *esse commune* as identical with *esse creaturae*. It is precisely this which is considered according to its various modes. Its primary modality is *secundum quod est in propria natura*, since even though *creatura verius esse habet in Deo quam in se*, each being exists in virtue of its *esse proprium*; *esse intentionale* is grounded in reality and the concept by which we compare all three is an ideal construction, abstracting from any actual presence, real or intentional.

This remarkably illuminating text from the early Commentary by St Thomas on the *Sentences* unites the various senses in which *esse commune* may be understood. Whether envisaged as immanent to the intellect, in its virtual presence in God, or as a logical term of comparison, the point of departure is always *esse creaturae*, i.e. being as the term of creation. The text does not speak explicitly of *esse commune*, but it is clear that what Aquinas understands by *esse commune* can be none other than *esse creaturae*. In his Commentary on Dionysius, he gives the name *esse commune* to *ipsum esse*, and uses *esse commune* and *esse creatum* synonymously. Here he shows how the many senses of being are related; in each case our knowledge begins with *esse creaturae*.

Such an interpretation is in total accord with the passages from the Commentary already noted. The common doctrine of the Pseudo-Areopagite and St Thomas may be summed up in the words of the Commentary: *Deus est causa ipsius esse commune . . . ipsum esse est omnibus commune.*[47] Aquinas expresses the central role of Being more

---

[47] V, ii, 658.

concisely: *Deus per ipsum esse omnia causat*.[48] As Cornelio Fabro
comments, 'God is the cause of *ipsum esse commune* in so far as *esse* is
at the summit of all perfections. *Esse commune* is neither an abstract
formality nor a unique act of being common to all beings, but is the
actualitas essendi which each being receives through the intermediary of
its own *esse* participated in God ... *Esse* is, therefore, the "weaving
together" (*plexus*) of all reality and the *coincidentia oppositorum*: that
which is most actual and most common, most intimate and most
present, most intense and most universal.'[49]

We may subscribe, therefore, to the view of André Hayen that,
granting the many aspects pertaining to St Thomas' doctrine of *esse
commune*, one conclusion seems to impose itself: '*Esse participatum a
creaturis*, in other words, *esse commune*, is not a simple reality which a
single concept can express. We can only have a synthetic knowledge of
it, since it is itself synthetic. *Esse commune* is the *esse* proper to each
creature in so far as it descends from God, in so far as it is intrinsically
constituted through its relation with God.'[50]

ESSE COMMUNE AND IPSUM ESSE SUBSISTENS

Esse may indeed be said in many senses. The τὸ ὂν λέγεται πολλαχῶς
of Aristotle belongs among the primary intuitions of metaphysics: the
unity and diversity alike of being. In Aquinas it finds its proper
application in the central value of *esse commune*. Λέγεται πολλαχῶς is
indeed another way of expressing that *esse* is common to the universal
many but distinct in each. We must be careful to distinguish between:
(1), *esse commune* in its first sense as the premier perfection inherent in
all finite beings; (2), the general concept of *esse* considered abstractly
in its perfection; and (3), the *Ipsum Esse Subsistens* of divine Being, in
which the perfection of *ipsum esse* is virtually and eminently present in
its full measure. All difficulties arise from a neglect of these distinctions
which are outlined by Aquinas in the Commentary on the *Sentences*. It
will be worth while taking a closer look at these differences, and in

---

[48] V, i, 639.

[49] *Participation et Causalité*, pp. 372 and 371. See also pp. 468, 486 and 507-8.

[50] *L'Intentionnel selon saint Thomas*, p. 246. See also Bernhard Lakebrink, *Perfectio omnium perfectionum*, p. 53: 'Das weit gestreute Sein in der Vielfaltigkeit dessen was je einzeln ist, begreifen wir zu Recht als *esse commune*, oder als *esse universale*, das gewirkt wird vom *esse divinum*. Während jenes seinem subsistenten Wesensgrunden "inhäriert", ist dieses an und fur sich selbst die Fülle des *esse per se subsistens*, das alles Begreifen übersteigt.' On the distinction between *esse commune* and *esse divinum*, see further pp. 142–3.

particular the advance made in reflection from the concept of being as *esse commune* to divine Being, whose nature is *Ipsum Esse Subsistens*.

The primary metaphysical signification of 'being' is *ipsum esse commune creaturae*. It is the datum from which all other notions are derived. Even *ens commune*, the logical concept of the entity of things, which provides the formal object of ontology, stands at the threshold of metaphysical reflection and does not penetrate to the inner principle sought by a deeper reflection upon reality. It is by a process of dialectic reflection that we arrive at the concept of *esse*, the source of being in each reality, the interior cause both of its distinction from, and unity with, all other beings. Our concept of *esse commune* (the perfection common to all particular beings), resides only within the intellect—a characteristic of all concepts. But it is grounded in concrete being. Just as the perfection of humanity exists in reality at the level of the individual, the perfection of *esse* is the primary perfection of each being. This act of *ipsum esse commune* is what the concept refers to.

From this universal concept of the perfection of being as act, predicable of all finite beings, we may draw a formal concept of being as act and perfection in itself, prescinding from the finitude which marks the object of the concept. This is *esse* considered *in abstracto*, independent both of its limited presence in beings and distinct from divine Being where it finds its proper ground and full signification. This concept, however, may not be confused with *esse commune*.[51] It is derived from and is a precision of our first concept in which *esse commune* is grasped. We need this concept, nevertheless, applicable in some sense to both finite beings and to God.[52] Otherwise we could not say with the Pseudo-Dionysius that 'Being' is the name drawn from creation which is most worthy of God. This is for Aquinas the analogical value of being.

Esse commune is the act of existing inherent in finite beings, in which being does not as such subsist in its fullness. Reflection upon these beings reveals the value of being as a perfection in itself. We can consider this value of being, in some way infinite in itself, in two ways:

---

[51] According to de Vries, 'ist also das *esse commune* das Sein ohne jeden bestimmenden Zusatz, das Sein schlechthin . . . Das *esse commune* ist also nicht bloß das geschaffene Sein, sondern das Sein in seiner ganzen uneingeschränkten Weite, das auch das göttliche Sein mitumfaßt.' ('Das *esse commune* bei Thomas von Aquin', p. 174). We must disagree with Gilson when he says that the object of the notion of *esse commune* 'n'existe que dans la pensée, à titre d'être de raison, et non pas, comme l'acte de l'étant, dans la réalité.' ('Propos sur l'être et sa notion', p. 10) Gilson interprets *esse commune* as 'le concept abstrait d'être en général, le plus universel des universaux. Comme tous les universaux, celui-là est un être de raison sans réalité autre que celle de l'intellect qui le conçoit.' ('Eléments d'une métaphysique thomiste de l'être', p. 19, n. 20.)

[52] In this sense, *Contra Gentiles* 2, 15, 953: Esse autem dicitur de omni eo quod est.

as it really exists in things and grasped beyond them in a concept according to reason alone; or we may consider the value and perfection of being as actually existing in itself, apart from and really transcending individual finite beings. So considered, this latter concept of being corresponds to the concept of God, whose very essence it is to subsist as Being Itself. While we attribute *esse* to God, the *esse* signified transcends the mode of signification, which is proper to the *esse commune* of beings.

We necessarily acquire our notion of God as absolute and infinite subsisting Being through the mediation and transformation of our concept of *esse commune*, the being common to his created analogues. The idea of God, however, infinitely transcends *esse commune* and refers beyond finite being to absolute and infinite subsisting Being which exists necessarily in itself as the plenitude of perfection. Reflection on the infinite value of *esse commune*, abstracted from finite beings, and expressing the perfection of being, unlimited in itself, reveals the necessity of the infinite perfection of Being as subsisting in itself.[53] The concept of divine being is attained, however, only at the end of a specific reasoning and is distinct from the concept of *esse commune*. Aquinas emphasises this distinction with frequency. In his Commentary on the *Divine Names* he is concerned above all with the distinction between *Ipsum Esse Subsistens* and *esse commune* on the metaphysical level. In his other works it is their difference in the order of concepts which generally attracts his attention.

It is the very subtlety of these notions as exposed by St Thomas, mysterious and strange in themselves, along with the need to distinguish between their various significations, metaphysical and intentional, which presents a difficulty for any interpretation. Since Being is in some sense 'infinite' there is a danger of confusing God with the very Being of things. The distinction between *discretio vel separatio realis* and *discretio vel separatio solum secundum rationem* is here of capital importance in determining the status of our general concept of Being and *Ipsum Esse Subsistens*, and in distinguishing both from *esse commune*. If we take, for example, the phrase *Ipsum esse absolute consideratum infinitum est: nam ab infinitis et infinitis modis participari possibile est*,[54] we may well ask whether it may not refer to God as well as to *esse commune*. If

---

[53] *De Potentia* 2, ad 7: Intellectus autem noster hoc modo intelligit esse quo modo invenitur in rebus inferioribus a quibus scientiam capit, in quibus esse non est subsistens, sed inhaerens. Ratio autem invenit quod aliquid esse subsistens sit; et ideo licet hoc quod dicunt *esse*, significetur per modum concreationis, tamen intellectus attribuens esse Deo transcendit modum significandi, attribuens Deo id quod significatur, non autem modum significandi.

[54] *Contra Gentiles* 1, 43.

esse is considered as subsisting apart from the beings in which it inheres, it necessarily denotes *esse divinum*. However, it is primarily intended to denote *esse commune*, which may be participated in according to an infinite multiplicity. *Esse commune* inheres in all things and is participated by all essences.[55]

The infinity of *esse commune* in relation to beings, yet its finitude before God are well reconciled in Aquinas' Commentary on the Pseudo-Dionysius: *Nam ipsum esse creatum non est finitum si comparetur ad creaturas, quia ad omnia se extendit; si autem comparetur ad esse increatum, invenitur deficiens et ex praecogitatione divinae mentis, propriae rationis determinationem habens.*[56] Created by God, *esse* is a participation and likeness of God. Compared to beings it is unlimited. It is not beings which determine *esse*. As their innermost act, rather, *esse* is the formal and determining principle in beings. All the perfections of beings participate in *esse* as their ground. *Esse* has, therefore, a formal and actualising infinity in relation to all creatures.[57] *Esse* is what is most formal in beings: *Nihil est formalius quam esse: esse est formalissimum.*[58] Aquinas is able to maintain, therefore, the infinity of *esse commune* and its primacy before beings, without confusing it with God. The infinity of *esse divinum* is absolute, however, transcending not merely what beings are but also their act of being.

The fundamental difference between *esse*, the *actus essendi* of finite beings, and *Ipsum Esse Subsistens* is that the act of *esse* does not itself subsist but is the act through which a being exists: *esse significat aliquid completum et simplex sed non subsistens.*[59] *Esse commune* cannot subsist by itself, precisely because it is *commune* and not *unum*, diversified as it is by the substances which receive it[60] and distinguished, therefore, from *Ipsum Esse per se subsistens*. We have the apparent paradox that *esse*, which is the source of what is real, the very perfection of being, does not itself exist: *non sic proprie dicitur quod esse sit, sed quod per esse aliquid sit.*[61] It does not subsist as such, unlimited in itself, but only as inhering within beings, realised in a multiplicity of essences and related to them as their act, and limited through its distinction from essence

---

[55] V, ii, 660: Omnia existentia participant eo quod est esse; *De Anima* VI, 2: Ipsum esse est . . . participabilis ab omnibus.

[56] XIII, iii, 989.

[57] On the notion of 'formal infinity', Cf. *De Potentia* 1, 2; *ST*, III, 10, 3, 1; I, 7, 1 and 2; *De Veritate* 2, 2, 5; 2, 9, 7; *Contra Gentiles* 1, 43; *In I Sent.*, 3, 1, 1, 4; 43, 1, 1

[58] *Contra Gentiles* 1, 23. '*Formalius* s'entend ici par opposition à *materiale* et *potentiale*. Le plus formel est aussi le plus acte, donc le plus parfait.' (E. Gilson, 'Eléments d'une métaphysique thomiste de l'être', pp. 9-10).

[59] *De Potentia* 1, 1.

[60] *De Potentia* 7, 2 ad 5.

[61] VIII, i, 751; *De Hebd.*, 2, 1: . . . non possumus dicere quod ipsum esse sit.

by their capacity to participate in its perfection.[62] There is, therefore, no conflict between the primacy and universality of Being in itself and its individuation in beings, both of which are greatly stressed by both Pseudo-Dionysius and Aquinas. Being as such is unique: *esse inquantum est esse, non potest esse diversum.*[63] At the level of finite reality, however, in the immediate objects of our knowledge, the perfection of being is diversified throughout the multiplicity of concrete substances: *esse est diversum in diversis.*[64] By analogy, however, it is common to all.[65] In finite reality being does not present itself as subsistent, but as inherent in beings, interior to all yet distinct in each.

Nor is there any contradiction between such phrases as '*Ipsum esse est communissimum*' and '*esse uniuscuiusque est ei proprium, et distinctum ab esse cuiuslibet alterius rei.*'[66] The individuation and limitation of *esse* by essence is subsequent to its reception into beings.[67] It follows, therefore, that all distinctions between beings are internal to the perfection of being itself; they are distinctions of being. Likewise, the concept of *esse commune* must implicitly contain all these individual determinations, neither including them explicitly nor excluding them. It is thus that St Thomas may distinguish between *esse commune* and *esse divinum* or *Ipsum Esse Subsistens.* A priori, the concept of divine Being excludes all addition, whereas the concept of *esse commune* is indifferent, neither including nor excluding the fact that *esse* is always particularised in reality. As the plenitude of perfection, nothing can be added to *Ipsum Esse Subsistens.* By his very essence, God can receive no addition; in his purity and fullness he is distinct from all being. On the contrary, the concept of *esse commune* neither includes nor excludes any further specification; otherwise nothing could be understood as existing, since in reality *esse* requires a specific determination and in a definition this must be added to the universal notion of being. The individuality of divine Being derives from the all-inclusive fullness of its perfection, that of *esse commune* from its limited reception in finite beings.[68]

---

[62] *ST*, I, 75, 5 ad 4: esse participatum quod comparatur ad participans ut actus eius . . . finitur ad capacitatem participantis. Cf. *In I Sent.*, 8, 5, 1, *Contra.*

[63] *Contra Gentiles* 2, 52, 1274.

[64] *De Ente et Essentia*, V.

[65] *ST*, I, 4, 3: Secundum aliqualem analogiam, esse est commune omnibus.

[66] *De Potentia* 7, 3.

[67] See L. Oeing-Hanhoff, *Ens et Unum Convertuntur*, p. 81, n. 29: 'Hier aber wird das Sein nicht als aufgenommen in den Wesenheiten, sondern an sich, freilich in seiner transzendentalen Relation zur Wesenheit und zum Prinzipiat betrachtet. Von sich aus ist aber das *esse* als Prinzip und Akt allgemein. Vgl. dazu: Pot. 7, 2, obi. 5: non sunt diversae res nisi quarum est diversum esse. Sed esse huius rei non est diversum ab esse alterius inquantum est esse, sed inquantum est in tali vel in tali natura. (Dieser Gedanke wird in der Antwort bestätigt.)'

[68] *De Ente et essentia* V: Hoc enim esse, quod Deus est, huius conditionis est, ut nulla

It can only be considered a serious misinterpretation, therefore, to identify *esse commune* in any sense with *esse divinum*. The interpretation of Klaus Kremer must be rejected as erroneous.[69] Aquinas is explicit: *Esse divinum, quod est eius substantia, non est esse commune, sed est esse distinctum a quolibet alio esse.*[70] Although we say that God is simply *esse*, we cannot infer that he is the *esse universale* through which every being formally exists. God's Being subsists in its own unity and is individuated by his infinity, i.e. by the absence of any determination. *Esse commune* or *universale* inheres in the multiplicity and is *diversum in diversis*. *Ipsum Esse Subsistens* rejects all diversity. In the *Summa Contra Gentiles*, Aquinas emphasises the distinction quite clearly: 'Divine *esse* is without addition, not only in thought but also in reality: not only without addition, but is, moreover, unable to receive any addition.' He concludes, therefore, *quod Deus non sit esse commune, sed proprium.*[71] And in *De Potentia* he writes:

> Being to which no addition is made is universal being, though the possibility of addition thereto is not incompatible with the notion of universal being: whereas the divine being is being to which no addition can be made and this enters into the very notion of the divine being: wherefore the divine being is not universal being (*esse commune*).[72]

Aquinas contrasts, therefore, *Ipsum esse per se subsistens et unum tantum* with *ipsum esse quod est communissimum.*[73] He distinguishes between two senses of *esse sine additione*, one indicating *esse divinum*—to which no addition is possible—the other expressing *esse commune*

---

additio sibi fieri possit; unde per ipsam suam puritatem est esse distinctum ab omne esse . . . individuatio primae causae, quae est esse tantum, est per puram bonitatem eius. Esse autem commune sicut in intellectu suo non includit aliquam additionem, ita nec includit in intellectu suo aliquam praecisionem additionis; quia si hoc esset, nihil posset intelligi esse, in quo super esse aliquid adderetur. Cf. *ST*, I, 3, 4 ad 1.

[69] *Die Neuplatonische Seinsphilosophie und ihre Wirkung auf Thomas von Aquin*, pp. 309-10. See in particular the reviews by Elders and Solignac. Van Steenberghen writes: 'L'*Esse subsistens* ne peut être confondu avec l'*esse commune*: l'*esse commune* est un universel, qui ne peut exister sans être reçu dans un sujet particulier; l'*Esse subsistens*, au contraire, est éminemment distinct, car il est individualisé par son infinité même, qui exclut tout sujet récepteur.' 'Prolégomènes à la *Quarta Via*', p. 110.

[70] *De Potentia* 7, 2 ad 4

[71] *Contra Gentiles* 1, 26, 247: Divinum autem esse est absque additione non solum in cogitatione, sed etiam in rerum natura: nec solum absque additione, sed etiam absque receptibilitate additionis. Unde ex hoc ipso quod additionem, non recipit nec recipere potest, magis concludi potest quod Deus non sit esse commune, sed proprium: etiam ex hoc ipso suum esse ab omnibus aliis distinguitur quod nihil ei addi potest. This is brought out again most clearly in Aquinas' Commentary on the *Liber de Causis*, IX, 233f.

[72] *De Potentia* 7, 2 ad 6: Ens commune est cui non fit additio, de cuius tamen ratio non est ut ei additio fieri non possit; sed esse divinum est esse cui non fit additio, et de eius ratio est ut ei additio fieri non possit; unde divinum esse non est esse commune.

[73] *De Substantiis Separatis*, ed. De Maria, III, p. 233

(*quod de omnibus praedicatur*)—to which no particular addition is necessary.[74]

It is of course only on the basis of *esse commune* that we may affirm the reality of divine being and it is in refining and determining our concept of *esse commune* that we come to define God as *Ipsum Esse Subsistens*. It is precisely because *esse commune* may receive determination that by adding the notion of infinite subsistence we arrive at a definition of God as *Esse Subsistens*. In this case, however, we add not to the concept of divine being, but to *esse commune*.[75] Our concept of *esse commune*, the act of existing which is the foundation of all that is found in beings and is thus infinite in relation to them, furnishes all the elements of thought necessary to elaborate our concept of infinite Subsisting Being. As the highest perfection of finite reality it is what is most worthy among creatures to name the divine. It requires, however, a profound transformation and enrichment; a refinement which is possible because of the distinction within our thought of the two aspects of *modus significandi* and *res significata*. In its signified nature, *esse* is extended to infinity in content and intensity and can no longer refer to finite common being, but is reserved exclusively for unique and absolute subsisting Being.

This seems to be the only interpretation of *esse commune* which is both faithful to St Thomas' Commentary on Dionysius and consistent

---

[74] *ST*, I, 3, 4, ad 1.

[75] See de Vries, 'Das *esse commune* bei Thomas von Aquin', pp. 174-5. The position of de Vries must be distinguished from that of Kremer. He refuses to identify God with *esse commune* in content and extension but claims that, undetermined, *esse commune* logically embraces not only created being but also divine being. *Esse commune* would, therefore, signify not merely created being, but being in all its unlimited logical extension, 'das Sein schlechthin, das umfassende Sein', including also divine Being. But as de Vries himself admits, this interpretation runs contrary to the many texts of Aquinas in the Commentary on Dionysius (pp. 167, 175). A more harmonious view, respecting both the progressive nature of metaphysical reflection and faithful to the explicit statements of Aquinas is to take *esse commune* as the being of finite beings, to the concept of which, as de Vries well points out, may be added the concepts of subsistence, infinity, unity etc. We cannot conclude, for example, from statements as *Esse autem dicitur de omni eo quod est* and *Omnibus autem commune est esse* (*Contra Gentiles* 2, 17), that *esse commune*, simply and purely, extends also to divine being. It is not at all clear from the context, as de Vries seems to think, that *esse* refers to both creator and creature. Quite on the contrary, God is said to be *causa omnium de quibus ens praedicatur*, and *omnia* is distinguished in the context from God (*Oportet igitur omnia quae sunt a Deo esse*). According to de Vries, 'ist also das *esse commune* das Sein ohne jeden bestimmenden Zusatz, das Sein schlechtin' (p. 174). But being, so considered, abstractly and without any further determination cannot exist. It is a mere *ens rationis*, a secondary concept derived from the primary reality of *esse commune*. Nor do the texts cited by A. Hayen, (*L'Intentionnel selon Saint Thomas*, pp. 243-4) in support of the argument *Deus cadit sub esse commune* convince. *Ens commune* and *ens universale* are not the same as *esse commune*.

with the great number of passages throughout his writings where the term occurs. We proceed now to take a closer look at another feature of this doctrine of being, derived in large measure from Dionysius, namely, *virtus essendi*, or the 'intensive' character of *esse*.

VIRTUS ESSENDI : INTENSIVE BEING IN DIONYSIUS AND AQUINAS

Although the term *esse intensivum* does not appear in the works of St Thomas, it expresses with admirable accuracy his notion of being as the exhaustive and comprehensive plenitude of the existential perfection of things. It has been coined by Cornelio Fabro after Aquinas' phrase *albedo intensive infinita*, which is used to illustrate the presence of a perfection in a cause which constitutes the essence and fullness of that perfection, in contrast to its limited participation by an effect.[76] It indicates the infinite intensity and simple fullness which precedes dispersion and division throughout any multiplicity. This is a pervasive background motif in both Dionysius and Aquinas: the cause possesses the perfection more eminently than that which has it as received. The effect is present *virtually*, i.e. according to a greater power; its perfection is contained *more intensely* in the source. Following from this is the pre-eminent presence of all perfections within the comprehensive plenitude of Being and, more originally and profoundly, their unlimited presence in absolute, infinite divine Being. Cornelio Fabro is the exponent of St Thomas whose work has contributed most to an appreciation of this aspect of Aquinas' original vision of being. Such an understanding of the profound significance of these texts, inspired in great measure by Dionysius, was closed to Durantel—who, in 1919 merely remarked: 'L'antériorité de l'être doit s'entendre naturellement d'une antériorité logique et non chronologique.'[77]

That the notion of the eminence or intensity of perfection as virtually present within the cause is derived from Dionysius is clear from the following sample passage:

> Predication according to essence is always more primary than predication by participation. For what is in an effect cannot be in the cause in the same manner but more eminently; and Dionysius explains this as follows: 'If

[76] *De Veritate* 29, 3: Si enim intelligatur corpus album infinitum non propter hoc albedo *intensive* infinita erit, sed solum extensive, et per accidens. This distinction between *intensive* and *extensive* corresponds to that between *virtualis* and *dimensiva*, which we will consider in detail in the following pages. See Cornelio Fabro, *Participation et Causalité selon S. Thomas d'Aquin*, p. 253, n. 18.

[77] *Saint Thomas et le Pseudo-Denis*, p. 180.

anyone should say that life itself lives or that light itself is enlightened, he would not in my view speak correctly, unless this is expressed differently: since what are in effects pre-exist abundantly and substantially in their causes.' He calls life or light the cause, and what is living or enlightened the effect.[78]

As we outlined, Aquinas praises Dionysius for rejecting the separate order of independent universal causes and for restoring all creative causality to the unique and universal cause. The Platonist motif, however, illustrates the fundamental principle that what is caused as an effect participates in its cause and that its perfection is preserved in it virtually according to a superior mode. A perfection which is received into a subject does not accrue or belong essentially to it of its own power. The key to Plato's affirmation of transcendent perfection is the recognition of the limited nature of the objects within our experience. A limited or incomplete measure of any perfection is unable to explain itself, to render reason for its existence. It is intelligible only through the indwelling presence of that fullness upon which, of its nature as finite, it places a limitation. A perfection embodied within an individual is measured to the capacity of that being. But such a limited measure is ultimately meaningful only in the light of a plenitude which, free from all restriction, is sufficient to itself and which is the source of its limited participations.

Virtual Quantity: the Language of Esse Intensivum

Aquinas adopts from Neoplatonism and in particular from Dionysius the doctrine of the intensity and plenitude of perfection; he recognises it as verified in a special way at the most intimate and ultimate level of *esse*. It is Dionysius' view of participation and pre-eminent presence which leads Aquinas to conceive of *esse* as the emergent fullness shared by all entitative characters. Aquinas' notion of intensive and emergent *esse* becomes in turn the core and foundation for his existential

---

[78] *In I Sent.*, 22, 1, expositio textus (ed. Mandonnet, p. 544-5): Semper autem principalior praedicatio est quae est per essentiam, quam quae est per participationem ... Non enim quid est in causato, oportet esse in causa eodem modo, sed eminentiori; et sic exponit Dionysius sic dicens: 'Vivere si quis dicat vitam, aut illuminare lumen, non recte secundum meam rationem dicit; sed secundum alium modum ista dicuntur: quia abundanter et substantialiter ea quae sunt causatorum, prius insunt causis'; dicit causam vitam vel lumen, causatum, vivens vel illuminatum. Dionysius' text: περισσῶς καὶ οὐσιωδῶς προένεστι τὰ τῶν αἰτιατῶν τοῖς αἰτίοις (2, 8, 58).

metaphysics of participation, as Fabro repeatedly emphasises.[79] Dionysius understands being, above all, as the focus of participation by all things in divine Goodness. All things are preserved in the created fullness of Being.

Aquinas indeed himself exploits the idea of virtual intensity to convey the inward nature of things and the varying degrees of their perfection, especially that of being. It will be revealing to take a closer look at the language employed. Especially noteworthy is the manner in which Aquinas draws upon elements from Aristotle's concepts of power and virtue in the moral and physical spheres. These he takes far beyond their setting in Aristotle, to the deeper level of ontological fullness and divine subsistence propounded by Dionysius.

The nature of intensity is most frequently elaborated in the context of theological discussions: the equality and relations of the divine persons, the divine gifts of grace, the nature of angels, the virtue of charity, or the ability of human and angelic knowledge to comprehend divine nature. Intensity expresses the manner of quantity characteristic of metaphysical or spiritual actions, powers and realities: a mode which must differ from the kind of quantity proper to corporeal reality. A passage which appropriately illustrates our theme is found in De Veritate, where Aquinas responds to the question whether or not the grace of Christ is infinite.[80] He begins by noting that 'finite' and 'infinite' refer to quantity, and that quantity is of two kinds: 'dimensional' (dimensiva), which indicates extension, and 'virtual' (virtualis) which signifies an intensity or degree of perfection (secundum intensionem):

---

[79] Participation et Causalité, p. 195: 'Cette "notion intensive" de l'esse . . . est le veritable fondement de la métaphysique thomiste de la participation.'

[80] De Veritate 29, 3: Est autem duplex quantitas: scilicet dimensiva, quae secundum extensionem consideratur; et virtualis, quae attenditur secundum intensionem: virtus enim rei est ipsius perfectio, secundum illud Philosophi in VII Physic: Unumquodque perfectum est quando attingit propriae virtuti. Et sic quantitas virtualis uniuscuiusque formae attenditur secundum modum suae perfectionis. Utraque autem quantitas per multa diversificatur: nam sub quantitate dimensiva continetur longitudo, latitudo, et profundum, et numerus in potentia. Quantitas autem virtualis in tot distinguitur, quot sunt naturae vel formae; quarum perfectionis modus totam mensuram quantitatis facit. Contingit autem id quod est secundum unam quantitatem finitum, esse secundum aliam infinitum. Potest enim intelligi aliqua superficies finita secundum latitudinem, et infinita secundum longitudinem. Patet enim hoc, si accipiatur una quantitas dimensiva, et alia virtualis. Si enim intelligatur corpus album infinitum, non propter hoc albedo intensive infinita erit, sed solum extensive, et per accidens; poterit enim aliquid albius inveniri. Patet nihilominus idem, si utraque quantitas sit virtualis. Nam in uno et eodem diversa quantitas virtualis attendi potest secundum diversas rationes eorum quae de ipso praedicantur; sicut ex hoc quod dicitur ens, consideratur in eo quantitas virtualis quantum ad perfectionem essendi; et ex hoc quod dicitur sensibilis, consideratur in eo quantitas virtualis ex perfectione sentiendi; et sic de aliis. Cf. In I Sent., 17, 2, 1: Quantitas autem dicitur dupliciter: quaedam virtualis, quaedam dimensiva.

'the excellence or power—*virtus*—of a thing is its perfection' (*virtus enim rei est ipsius perfectio*), since, as Aristotle teaches, 'anything is perfect when it attains its proper excellence (*virtus*)'.[81] Thus the virtual quantity of each form is determined by the measure of its perfection. While dimensional quantity comprises length, width, depth and number, 'virtual quantity' (*quantitas virtualis*) is distinguished into as many classes as there are natures and forms; it is their degree of perfection which determines their quantitative measure. Thus a white body, for example, has the virtual quantity of whiteness in so far as it embodies, or approximates to, the full perfection of whiteness; the virtual quantity of a sentient being is considered in respect of the perfection of sensation and so on. Thus, considered as a being, the virtual quantity of any thing is determined by its perfection of existing: *sicut ex hoc quod dicitur ens, consideratur in eo quantitas virtualis quantum ad perfectionem essendi.*[82] In one and the same object, distinct modes or measures of virtual quantity can be affirmed according to the different natures predicated of it. We can indeed conceive of a white body which is infinite in dimension, but its whiteness will not thereby be infinite in intensity, but only in extension and accidentally.[83] That which is infinite in dimensive quantity has nevertheless of itself a finite act of existence.[84] Even if we were to conceive of a sensitive soul, which has the full perfection of sensation, it would still be finite in essence, because its act of being (*esse*), even though infinite in its sentient power, is limited to a certain perfection of being, namely sensibility, which is exceeded by the perfection of intelligence.[85] We may note that while virtual quantity

---

[81] *Physics*, VII, 3, 246a 13-15: ἡ μὲν ἀρετὴ τελείωσίς τις—ὅταν γὰρ λάβῃ τὴν ἑαυτοῦ ἀρετήν, τότε λέγεται τέλειον ἕκαστον. Moerbeke translates: 'Virtus enim quaedam perfectio est: unumquodque enim tunc maxime perfectum est, cum attingit propriae virtuti.' See Aquinas, *In Physic.*, VII, vi, 920. The reference given in *De Veritate* 29, 3 of the Marietti edition to C. VIII is incorrect. This is reprinted in the Frohmann Holzboog *Opera Omnia*. See *In Metaph.*, V, xviii, 1037f. for an interesting explanation of the perfection of a natural being in terms of its proper measure of magnitude (*magnitudo naturalis*)—both of its continuous dimensions and of its natural ability or power. From Aquinas' example of a horse, it seems that with the first sense he has in mind some ideal physical range, admitting of variation, and determined no doubt by the form of the species. We can thus best understand Aquinas' statement that both forms of perfection (*quantitas dimensiva sibi naturaliter determinata* and *quantitas virtutis sibi debitae secundum naturam*) belong to the interior perfection of a being.

[82] *De Veritate* 29, 3.

[83] See also *De Veritate* 2, 9, ad 9: Si aliquod corpus infinitum ponamus esse album, quantitas albedinis extensiva, secundum quam dicitur quanta per accidens, erit finita; quantitas autem per se, scilicet intensiva, nihilominus esset finita.

[84] *De Veritate* 2, 9, ad 9: Illud quod est infinitum quantitate, habet esse finitum.

[85] *De Veritate* 29, 3: Si ergo intelligatur aliqua anima sensibilis quae habeat in se quidquid potest concurrere ad perfectionem sentiendi qualitercumque, illa quidem anima erit finita secundum essentiam, quia esse suum est limitatum ad aliquam perfectionem

is present in all things, dimensive quantity resides only in bodies; in God and angels virtual quantity alone is present.[86]

Now, with regard to the meaning or nature of being (*ratio essendi*), Aquinas affirms:

> Only what includes all the perfection of being (*omnis essendi perfectio*) can be infinite, since it is a perfection which may be diversified in an infinite number of different modes. And in this manner only God is infinite in his essence; because his essence is not limited to any determined perfection but embraces every mode of perfection to which the nature of being can extend; he is, therefore, essentially infinite.[87]

God alone has infinite intensity (*intensio infinita*).[88] The important notion of *quantitas virtualis* and the virtual perfection of being is thus given its maximum significance in referring to divine Being. (The virtual fullness and intensity of divine being will be examined in the following chapter.) And while Aquinas begins this passage of *De Veritate* with a phrase from Aristotle, his vision of God as the infinite perfection or comprehensive intensity of Being is unmistakably Dionysian, even in formulation. Almost continuous in both text and context are some brief lines from *De Malo* which resumes Dionysius' corrected view of the Neoplatonist theme of separated perfections. The separated form which is pure act, namely God, is not limited to any one species or genus but possesses the total power of being boundlessly, inasmuch as he is his own being. This is clear, states Aquinas, from Chapter 5 of *Divine Names*:

> The separate form which is pure act, namely God, is not determined to any species or genus, but has uncircumscribed the full power of being (*totam virtutem essendi*) since it exists as its own act of being, as is clear from Dionysius in Chapter 5 of *Divine Names*.[89]

---

essendi, scilicet sensibilem, quam excedit perfectio intelligibilis; esset tamen infinita secundum rationem sensibilitatis, quia eius sensibilitas ad nullum determinatum modum essendi limitaretur. The English version (*Truth*, Vol. 3, trans. Robert W. Schmidt, SJ, Chicago, 1954, p. 413) mistranslates the last phrase as 'any definite mode of *sensing*'.

[86] *In I Sent.*, 19, 3, 1: In Deo non potest esse quantitas nisi virtutis. Cf. Ibid., ad 3. *ST*, I, 8, 2 ad 1: Incorporalia non sunt in loco per contactum quantitatis dimensivae, sicut corpora: sed per contactum virtutis. *ST*, I, 52, 1: (Dimensiva quantitas) . . . in angelis non est; sed est in eis quantitas virtualis. Cf. *Quodlib.* 1, 3, 1. In the *Summa*, Aquinas makes a related distinction between quantitative and virtual totality or 'whole' (I, 76, 8; I, 8, 2 ad 3).

[87] *De Veritate* 29, 3: Quantum igitur ad rationem essendi, infinitum esse non potest nisi illud in quo omnis essendi perfectio includitur, quae in diversis infinitis modis variari potest. Et hoc modo solus Deus infinitus est secundum essentiam; quia eius essentia non limitatur ad aliquam determinatam perfectionem, sed in se includit omnem modum perfectionis, ad quem ratio entitatis se extendere potest, et ideo ipse est infinitus secundum essentiam.

[88] *De Veritate* 2, 9. The validity of referring this term to God may be extrapolated from the context.

[89] *De Malo* 16, 9 ad 6: Forma separata, quae est purus actus, scilicet Deus, non

From Dionysius, Aquinas attains the notion of the infinite and virtual intensity of perfection in God; being is the universal and fundamental power or perfection which comes to presence in individuals according to varied degrees. We encounter here a striking manner in which being is grasped as power or perfection, virtue or strength, which rather than possessing richness by way of extension or dominion beyond itself, is one of inner attainment, of self-actuality according to differing degrees of pitch or intensity.

The vocabulary and application of *virtus* is rich and extensive in itself. Most frequently it refers to the moral quality of human powers or faculties in their capacity to act. But it is clear that for Aquinas it is much broader. Following on Aristotle, the word *virtus* expresses for him the perfection of any power in relation to its final goal.[90] The following passage, although delivered in a discussion on human habits and dispositions, has a profound metaphysical meaning: 'Virtue denotes a determinate perfection of a power. The perfection of anything, however, is considered especially in relation to its end. Yet the end of a power is its act. A power is said to be perfect, therefore, in so far as it is determined to its act.'[91] Thus in its unqualified sense, *virtus* is the *ultimum potentiae*—the utmost to which a power can attain.[92] *Virtus*, however, also admits of degrees in relation to such an ultimate. Such quantity of virtue (*quantitas virtutum*) is most aptly exemplified in the domain of human habits and Aquinas again employs the vocabulary of participation and intensity. Greatness of virtue may be taken to refer to the intensity or slackness according to which it is shared by the subject.[93] Aquinas explains that the magnitude of *virtus* may be deemed greater or less (*major et minor*) in two ways: in itself, with respect to

---

determinatur ad aliquam speciem vel genus aliquod; sed incircumscripte habet totam virtutem essendi, utpote ipsum suum esse existens, sicut patet per Dionysium cap. V De divinis nominibus. *In de Caus.*, IX, 2, 232: Eius virtus excedit omnem virtutem et Eius esse omne esse. See Ibid., IV, 109.

[90] *De Caelo* I, 11, 281a, 10-19: δέον ὁρίζεσθαι πρὸς τὸ τέλος καὶ τὴν ὑπεροχὴν τὴν δύναμιν... ἡ δὲ δύναμις τῆς ὑπεροχῆς ἐστίν... διωρίσθω γὰρ κατὰ τῆς ὑπεροχῆς τὸ τέλος λεγόμενον τὸ κυρίως δυνατόν.

[91] *ST*, I-II, 55, 1: Dicendum quod virtus nominat quamdam potentiae perfectionem. Uniuscuiusque autem perfectio praecipue consideratur in ordine ad suum finem. Finis autem potentiae actus est. Unde potentia dicitur esse perfecta, secundum quod determinatur ad suum actum. *ST*, I-II, 55, 3: Virtus importat perfectionem potentiae. *In I Sent.*, 29, 3, 1: Virtus autem, secundum Philosophum, est ultimum in re de potentia.

[92] *ST*, I-II 55, 1 ad 1: Unde quando dicitur quod virtus est ultimum potentiae, sumitur virtus pro objecto virtutis. Id enim in quod ultimo potentia potest est id quod dicitur virtus rei.

[93] *ST*, I-II, 66, 2: Quantitas virtutum... potest attendi secundum participationem subjecti, prout scilicet intenditur vel remittitur in subjecto. For similar terminology, see *ST*, I-II, 52, 1, which treats 'de intensionibus habituum' (66, 1): intensio et remissio, magis et minus, plus vel minus, intensior et remissior.

the things to which it extends, or on the part of the subject by which it is participated. It will be participated variously by different persons or by the same person at different times.[94] This is intensive greatness, the magnitude which is proper and unique to *virtus*: the inner measure and density of its presence embraced and embodied concretely in the individual. As examples Aquinas mentions knowledge and health, which are received in greater measure by one subject than by another, according to its nature and aptitude. Such habits and dispositions vary in intensive greatness, he explains since, as Aristotle has pointed out, they are judged in relation to a subject which possesses them (*secundum ordinem ad aliquid*).[95] Aristotle's analogy of health springs easily to mind here and while its parallel with being is far from the present context, it is exactly what we are concerned with.

In a significant passage of the *Summa*,[96] Aquinas grounds the virtual quantity of a being's perfection in its form. Here he points out that the quantity proper to material beings is *dimensive* in nature. This may be either continuous (extension in the literal sense, characteristic of time or space)[97] or discrete, which constitutes the nature of number. We may

---

[94] *ST*, I-II 66, 1: Si vero consideretur virtus ex parte subjecti participantis, sic contingit virtutem esse majorem vel minorem, sive secundum diversa tempora in eodem, sive in diversis hominibus.

[95] *ST*, I-II 52, 1: Sic igitur patet quod, cum habitus et dispositiones dicantur secundum ordinem ad aliquid ut dicitur in VII Physic., dupliciter potest intensio et remissio in habitibus et dispositionibus considerari. Uno modo, secundum se: prout dicitur major vel minor sanitas; vel major vel minor scientia quae ad plura vel pauciora se extendit. Alio modo, secundum participationem subjecti: prout scilicet aequalis scientia vel sanitas magis recipitur in uno quam in alio, secundum diversam aptitudinem vel ex natura vel ex consuetudine. Cf. Aristotle, *Physics* VII, 3, 246b 3-4: ἔτι δὲ καί φαμεν ἁπάσας εἶναι τὰς ἀρετὰς ἐν τῷ πρός τί πως ἔχειν. Note that *virtus* translates both δύναμις and ἀρετή.

[96] *ST*, I, 42, 1 ad 1: Ad primum ergo dicendum quod duplex est quantitas. Una scilicet quae dicitur quantitas molis vel quantitas dimensiva, quae in solis rebus corporalibus est; unde in divinis personis locum non habet. Sed alia est quantitas virtutis, quae attenditur secundum perfectionem alicuius naturae vel formae. Quae quidem quantitas designatur secundum quod dicitur aliquid magis vel minus calidum inquantum est perfectius vel minus perfectum in tali caliditate. Huiusmodi autem quantitas virtualis attenditur primo quidem in radice, idest in ipsa perfectione formae vel naturae, et sic dicitur magnitudo spiritualis, sicut dicitur magnus calor propter suam intensionem et perfectionem. Et ideo dicit Augustinus, quod in his quae non mole magna sunt, hoc est maius esse quod est melius esse, nam melius dicitur quod perfectius est. Secundo autem attenditur quantitas virtualis in effectibus formae. Primus autem effectus formae est esse, nam omnis res habet esse secundum suam formam. Secundus autem effectus est operatio, nam omne agens agit per suam formam. Attenditur igitur quantitas virtualis et secundum esse et secundum operationem; secundum esse quidem inquantum ea quae sunt perfectioris naturae sunt majoris durationis; secundum operationem vero inquantum ea quae sunt perfectioris naturae sunt magis potentia ad agendum.

[97] See *ST*, I, 42, 1, obj. 1: In divinis autem personis non invenitur neque quantitas continua intrinseca, quae dicitur magnitudo; neque quantitas continua extrinseca, quae dicitur locus et tempus; neque secundum quantitatem discretam invenitur in eis aequalitas, quia duae personae sunt plures quam una.

also speak, however, of the 'quantity of power' (*quantitas virtutis*) or excellence of a being, its *virtual quantity*—its perfection in respect of any aspect or determination. (The analogy used by Aquinas here is that of heat: hot things are said to be 'more' or 'less', according as they are more or less perfect.) According to Aquinas, the virtual quantity of any being is first rooted in its nature or form; form confers upon it what Aquinas strikingly calls its 'spiritual greatness' (*magnitudo spiritualis*), endowing, on the analogy of heat, its intensity and perfection (*suam intensionem et perfectionem*).

Moreover, form further determines, as an effect, the virtual quantity of any being in two respects: inwardly, so to speak, it mediates or measures its act of being (*forma dat esse*), and outwardly it is the origin of the virtual quantity of a being's activities or operations, since in its action every agent acts in virtue of its form (*omne agens agit per suam formam*). In this passage Aquinas thus outlines summarily the three aspects under which we may speak of the 'virtual quantity' of beings: *esse* or the act of being, its form or nature, and its operations or activity. Form plays, moreover, a central role as in a sense the instrumental origin or source of the virtual perfection of the other two.[98] Aquinas states explicitly in *De Potentia* that the *virtus essendi* of each thing is proportionate to the measure and intimacy of its form.[99]

A similar threefold distinction is offered in *In I Sent.*, 19, 3, 1,[100] where Aquinas, faced with the question whether greatness can be

---

[98] In this regard see also *Contra Gentiles* 2, 55, 1299: Esse autem per se consequitur ad formam . . . unumquodque autem habet esse secundum quod habet formam. (References are to paragraphs of the Marietti edition.) *De Veritate* 29, 3 ad 4: Forma est principium actus. Secundum autem quod habet esse in actu, non est possibile quod a forma cuius est essentia finita, procedat actio infinita secundum intensionem. On the role of form, see Klaus Riesenhuber, *Die Transzendenz der Freiheit zum Guten*, Chapter 9: 'Die Form als Ursprung des Seins'; also Cornelio Fabro, *Participation et Causalité*, pp. 343-62.

[99] *De Potentia* 5, 4 ad 1: Nam quantum unicuique inest de forma, tantum inest ei de virtute essendi. See the texts cited in footnotes 130-2 below. Tomás Melendo Granados, *Ontología de los opuestos*, p. 186: '. . . hay que admitir un *magis et minus* en las formas sustanciales. *Magis et minus* que se origina, no por la intensificación o remisión de una misma forma, sino por la diversidad jerárquica entre las formas sustanciales, que provoca una mayor o menor intensidad en la posesión del acto de ser.' See *In I de Gen. et Corrupt.*, 8, 62.

[100] Respondeo dicendum, quod in Deo non potest esse quantitas nisi virtutis; et cum aequalitas attendatur secundum aliquam speciem quantitatis, aequalitas non erit nisi secundum virtutem. Virtus autem, secundum Philosophum, VI Ethic., c. II, est ultimum in re de potentia. Unde etiam dicitur in VII Physic., text. 18, quod virtus est perfectio quaedam, et tunc unumquodque perfectum est quando attingit propriam virtutem. Omnibus igitur illis modis quibus contingit pertingere ad ultimum est considerare virtutem rei. Hoc autem contingit tripliciter: primo in operationibus in quibus contingit gradus perfectionis inveniri. Unde dicitur habere virtutem ad operandum quod attingit completam operationem, prout dicitur II Ethic., cap. v, quod virtutis est quae bonum facit habentem, et opus eius bonum reddit. Secundo respectu ipsius esse rei, secundum quod etiam

applied to God, responds that in God there can only be quantity of power: *quantitas virtutis*. He follows Aristotle in saying that *virtus* is the ultimate achievement of a being, i.e. the attainment of its utmost potentiality. *Virtus* is synonymous with perfection: a thing is perfect when it attains its proper power or virtue. The virtue of a thing may be considered, therefore, with regard to every aspect in which it is open to attain fulfilment. This occurs in three ways: firstly, in those operations in which it is possible to find different degrees of perfection. Thus that which exercises a complete activity has the (full) virtue of action (*virtus ad operandum*). The virtue or power of a thing is also found 'with respect to the very existence of a thing' (*respectu ipsius esse rei*). Thus, in Aristotle's example, a thing may have the power to always exist.[101] Finally there is that virtue which is measured according to the plenitude of perfection with respect to the being itself (*respectu ipsius entis*), in so far as it attains the ultimate within its own nature—in other words, according to its form. The power of God is clearly supreme in all three respects: manifestly, God has the operative power to act; eternity is itself the very power of his existence; and the fullness of the perfection itself of divine nature is his greatness, a magnitude, which Aquinas stresses, is not one of dimension but of virtue alone.[102]

Aquinas refers to Augustine's view in Chapter 6 of *De Trinitate*, that in beings whose greatness is not one of bulk, *to be more*, or greater, is *to be better*: *In his enim quae non mole magna sunt hoc est maius esse quod est melius esse*. Augustine dealt with the distinction of material and bodily magnitude at some length in *De Quantitate Animae*. As with Aquinas, the greatness of being of spiritual realities resides, according to Augustine, in their *virtus*: 'When we hear and speak of a great and strong soul, we ought not to think of its size, but of its power (*quantum*

Philosophus dicit, I Caeli et mundi, text. 103, quod aliquid habet virtutem ut semper sit. Item secundum plenitudinem perfectionis respectu ipsius entis, secundum quod attingit ultimum naturae suae . . . Si igitur virtus divina consideretur secundum perfectionem ad opus, erit virtus potentiae operativae. Si autem consideretur perfectio quantum ad ipsum esse divinum, virtus eius erit aeternitas. Si autem consideretur quantum ad complementum perfectionis ipsius naturae divinae, erit magnitudo. Quod patet ex hoc quod ipse probat aequalitatem in magnitudine ex hoc quod tota plenitudo naturae Patris est in Filio; secundum quem etiam modum Augustinus dicit, VI De Trinitate, cap. viii, quod in his quae non mole magna sunt, idem est maius esse quod melius, secundum quod etiam dicimus aliquem hominem esse magnum, qui est perfectus in scientia et virtute.

[101] Aquinas frequently uses the phrase *virtus essendi* to express the power of some beings (heavenly bodies) to endure eternally in existence (*Contra Gentiles* 2, 33, 1098, *De Caelo et Mundo* I, vi, 62). Though related, this is not the full, intensive, meaning of *esse* as a virtual perfection. For the texts of Aristotle, *De Caelo*, see note 129 below.

[102] *In I Sent.*, 19, 3, 1 ad 3.

possit).'[103] Aquinas recognises the distinction in Aristotle's evaluation of the intellect which, 'though small in bulk, surpasses by far all else in power and value.'[104] In his commentary on this passage from the *Ethics* he simply notes that the magnitude of the intellect is one of virtual quantity, but does not elaborate.[105] In none of the passages where he outlines the distinction between virtual and dimensive quantity does Aquinas attribute the doctrine to a particular source.

The connection between the virtual quantity of beings and the intensive nature of perfection is brought out clearly by Aquinas when considering the intensity of action. Responding in *De Potentia* to the question whether the power of God is infinite,[106] Aquinas speaks of a certain intensity which belongs to the efficiency of action (*intensio secundum efficaciam agendi*), according to the manner whereby a being exercises its active powers.[107] A certain infinity may, he suggests, be ascribed to active power in a manner similar to that of quantity, both continuous and discrete. The 'quantity' of power is discrete when measured according to the number of its objects—whether they are many or few. This is called 'extensive quantity' (*quantitas extensiva*, which is of course synonymous with 'dimensive quantity'). The quantity of power is continuous when measured with respect to the slackness or intensity of its action. This is its 'intensive quantity' (*quantitas intensiva*). Extensive quantity refers to the *objects* of power, intensive quantity to its *action*; active power is the principle of both. The former determines

---

[103] *De Quantitate Animae*, 17: Non igitur magnum vel ingentem animum cum audimus aut dicimus, quantum loci occupet, sed quantum possit, cogitandum est.

[104] *Nic. Eth.*, X, vii, 8, 1178a: εἰ γὰρ καὶ τῷ ὄγκῳ μικρόν ἐστι, δυνάμει καὶ τιμιότητι πολὺ μᾶλλον πάντων ὑπερέχει. In the translation of William of Moerbeke: Si enim et mole parvum est, potentia et pretiositate multum magis omnibus superexcellit.

[105] *In Ethic.*, X, xi, 2107: Quamvis enim hoc optimum sit parvum mole, quia est incorporeum et simplicissimum, et per consequens caret magnitudine molis, tamen quantitate virtutis et pretiositatis multum excedit omnia quae in homine sunt.

[106] *De Potentia* 1, 2: In actione etiam invenitur quaedam intensio secundum efficaciam agendi, et sic potest potentiae activae attribui quaedam infinitas secundum conformitatem ad infinitatem quantitatis et continuae et discretae. Discretae quidem secundum quod quantitas potentiae attenditur secundum multa vel pauca obiecta; et haec vocatur quantitas extensiva: continuae vero, secundum quod quantitas potentiae attenditur in hoc quod remisse vel intense agit; et haec vocatur quantitas intensiva. Prima autem quantitas convenit potentiae respectu obiectorum, secunda vero respectu actionis. Istorum enim duorum activa potentia est principium. The reference given to *De Potentia* 1, 3 in Fabro, *Participation et Causalité*, p. 253, is incorrect.

[107] Aristotle compares the magnitude of powers in a somewhat similar manner, measuring them in terms of time: 'The greater power is always that which produces an equal effect in less time, whether it be heating, sweetening, throwing or, in general, effecting any kind of change.' *Physics*, VIII, 10, 266a29–31: ἔστω γὰρ ἀεὶ ἡ πλείων δύναμις ἡ τὸ ἴσον ἐν ἐλάττονι χρόνῳ ποιοῦσα, οἷον θερμαίνουσα ἢ γλυκαίνουσα ἢ ῥίπτουσα καὶ ὅλως κινοῦσα.

its extent (the number of its objects), the latter the measure of its presence, efficacy, and intimacy within them.

The powers and activities of the spirit, such as intellectual knowing and loving are thus measured in degrees of virtual, rather than dimensive quantity: they admit of greater or lesser levels of efficacy; they vary in the measure of their intensity. Intellectual comprehension, for example, admits only indirectly of dimensive quantity—inasmuch as it relies upon sensation for its object. Considered in itself, in its grasp of the intelligible, it varies in virtual quantity, according as it comprehends its object more or less perfectly and intimately.[108] Extensive quantity, Aquinas declares, is accidental to knowledge, whereas intensive quantity is essential to it.[109] (Note the identity of *quantitas virtualis* and *quantitas intensiva*.) Similarly, love is marked only extrinsically by extensive or dimensive quantity, i.e. as it attains to fewer or more numerous objects; intrinsically it is measured only by the intensity of its act (*secundum intensionem actus*), as it loves something to a greater or lesser degree. This is its virtual quantity and as such it varies *quantum ad intensionem actus*.[110] Now, divine power is infinite in both respects, since it never produces so many effects that it cannot produce more, nor does it ever act with such intensity that it cannot act even more intensely. Aquinas clarifies: 'The intensity of God's action is not measured according as it

---

[108] *De Veritate* 8, 2: Per se autem non comparatur ad intellectum intelligible secundum quantitatem dimensivam, cum intellectus sit virtus non utens organo corporali; sed per se comparatur ad ipsum, solum secundum quantitatem virtualem. Et ideo in his quae per se intelliguntur sine coniunctione ad sensum, non impeditur comprehensio intellectus nisi propter excessum quantitatis virtualis; quando scilicet quod intelligitur, habet modum intelligendi perfectiorem quam sit modus quo intellectus intelligit.

[109] *De Veritate* 20, 4 ad 14: Quantitas extensionis est scientiae accidentalis; quantitas autem intensiva est ei essentialis.

[110] *ST*, II-II, 24, 4 ad 1: Dicendum quod caritati non convenit quantitas dimensiva, sed solum quantitas virtualis. Quae non solum attenditur secundum numerum obiectorum, ut scilicet plura vel pauciora diligantur: sed etiam secundum intensionem actus, ut magis vel minus aliquid diligatur. Et hoc modo virtualis quantitas caritatis augetur. See also *In I Sent.*, 17, 2, 1, *Solutio* and ad 2: Quantitas autem dicitur dupliciter: quaedam virtualis, quaedam dimensiva. Virtualis quantitas non est ex genere suo quantitas, quia non dividitur divisione essentiae suae; sed magnitudo eius attenditur ad aliquid divisibile extra, vel multiplicabile, quod est obiectum vel actus virtutis... Quantitas virtutis attenditur dupliciter: vel quantum ad numerum obiectorum, et hoc est per modum quantitatis discretae; vel quantum ad intensionem actus super idem obiectum, et hoc est sicut quantitas continua; et ita excrescit virtus charitatis. Similarily, the spiritual gifts of love, knowledge, charity and grace are measured in terms of their virtual or intensive quantity—secundum maiorem et minorem perfectionem virtutis (*In I Sent.*, 17, 2, 1 ad 3). Cf. *De Veritate* 29, 3 ad 4: Forma est principium actus. Secundum autem quod habet esse in actu, non est possibile quod a forma cuius est essentia finita, procedat actio infinita secundum intensionem. Unde et meritum Christi non fuit infinitum secundum intensionem actus: finite enim diligebat et cognoscebat; sed habuit quamdam infinitatem ex circumstantia personae, quae erat dignitatis infinitae.

is in itself—because thus it is always infinite, since God's action is his essence—but according as it attains its effect; thus some things are moved by God more efficaciously, some less.'[111] God is equally present to all things, but not present to all in equal measure.

Since *esse* is what is most efficacious within each thing, grounding and actualising its every perfection, it is, in the light of this passage, most appropriate to speak of the intensity of the act of being at the inner heart of the individual, and of the comprehensive infinity of its existential intensity within *Ipsum Esse Subsistens*. From the many texts and varied contexts in which Aquinas elaborates the notions of virtual quantity, denoting the intensity of action and existential and formal perfection, we can conclude that it is both valid and enlightening to speak of the virtual intensity of being, and of *virtus essendi* as the intensive power or perfection of being. Cornelio Fabro does not seem to have exploited the wide wealth of texts by Aquinas on virtual quantity and the connection between *virtus* and intensity.[112] Perhaps this is not all too surprising, since it is indeed only *en passant* that Aquinas himself makes explicit the identity between 'virtual' and 'intensive' quantity (*Et similiter patet in quantitate virtuali vel intensiva*).[113] He does not dwell at any length on their fruitful association. These notions are present below the surface of his discourse; their profound kinship, their original and ultimate identity with respect to being, however, should be clear.

The text of *De Veritate* 29, 3 understands the notion of intensity in the Platonist sense of presence and plenitude of perfection; *De Potentia* I, 2 adopts it as a model for deepening the Aristotelian notion of

---

[111] *De Potentia* 1, 2: Utroque autem modo divina potentia est infinita. Nam nunquam tot effectus facit quin plures facere possit, nec unquam ita intense operatur quin intensius operari possit. Intensio autem in operatione divina non est attendenda secundum quod operatio est in operante, quia sic semper est infinita, cum operatio sit divina essentia; sed attendenda est secundum quod attingit effectum; sic enim a Deo moventur quaedam efficacius, quaedam minus efficaciter.

[112] Citing *De Veritate* 29, 3, he writes: 'En conclusion: de la quantité dimensive l'analogué métaphysique est passé à la *quantitas virtualis* qui est la perfection d'être, et il s'est placé au sommet dans l'Acte d'être comme plenitude de perfection.' (*Participation et Causalité*, p. 259). See note 176 below.

[113] *De Veritate* 29, 3 ad 5: Quod enim finitum aliquid per continuum augmentum possit attingere ad quantumcumque finitum, veritatem habet, si accipiatur eadem ratio quantitatis in utroque finito; sicut si comparemus lineam ad lineam, vel albedinem ad albedinem; non tamen si accipiatur alia et alia ratio quantitatis. Et hoc patet in quantitate dimensiva: quantumcumque enim linea augeatur in longum, nunquam perveniet ad latitudinem superficiei. Et similiter patet in quantitate virtuali vel intensiva: quantumcumque enim cognitio cognoscentis Deum per similitudinem proficiat, nunquam potest adaequari cognitioni comprehensoris, qui videt Deum per essentiam.

operation and actuality. In the *Summa*, Aquinas attributes virtual quantity to the mediation of form.

Virtual Intensity of Being

These passages, particularly revealing of Aquinas' concept of Being as intensive *virtus*, power and excellence which is present in graded measures, as an inner quantity—(one is tempted to speak of a 'qualitative quantity')—seem to have been overlooked by writers on thomistic being.[114] In an isolated remark Etienne Gilson draws attention to the Dionysian origin of the term.[115] In an article entitled precisely '*Virtus Essendi*', he identifies *virtus essendi* with the *actus essendi* of each thing, receives through form, but denies that it can be present in diverse degrees of intensity. This is because of his failure to advert to Aquinas' distinction between 'dimensive' and 'virtual' quantity. He writes as follows:

L'on ferait fausse route en cherchant dans saint Thomas une doctrine de l'être qui reconnaîtrait à l'*esse* une intensité intrinsèque variable à laquelle correspondraient, dans la nature, les degrés différents de perfection qui distinguent les êtres. Le mouvement comporte des degrés de quantité qui permettent de le dire plus ou moins grand, l'être n'en a pas... Pour l'imagination, une *virtus*, une *dunamis* est une force, et si on en parle comme de quelque chose qui peut être donné dans sa totalité, ou ne se rencontrer que sous forme de participation limitée, il est inévitable que nous l'imaginions

---

[114] An exception is James F. Anderson, who mentions it briefly in *The Bond of Being* pp. 295-6. By the same author, see *The Cause of Being*, pp., 122-3, for an outline of Aquinas' distinction between quantitative, essential and virtual totality. The present investigation is a partial response to the suggestion of L.-B. Geiger: 'Aristote s'était contenté, nous l'avons dit, de poser au-dessus des êtres *mobiles*, des substances *immobiles* et éternelles. Saint Thomas approfondit cette manière de voir en mettant en évidence une sorte d'intensité croissante ou de perfection en quelque sorte qualitative de l'*actus essendi*. Une étude de son vocabulaire, à cet égard, serait des plus révélatrices. L'*esse* comporte une *virtus*, une *perfectio* qui va croissant, à mesure qu'on s'élève dans l'échelle des êtres (idée qui eût sans doute paru inintelligible à Aristote). Et cette croissance n'est rien d'autre que la réalisation de moins en moins imparfaite, de plus en plus purement actuelle, de l'*actus essendi* lui-même, selon toute sa plénitude intensive, *secundum totum suum posse*. (*Philosophie et Spiritualité* I, pp. 149-50). See *La participation dans la philosophie de Saint Thomas d'Aquin*, p. 198, n. 2, where Geiger, with a reference to Dionysius, speaks of *virtus essendi*, 'sorte de plénitude intensive de l'*esse*. See p. 373, n. 2: 'Cette notion de: *nature de l'être (entitas, natura entis, virtus essendi)*, demanderait à être précisée. Elle suppose une vue de l'être, où de prime abord celui-ci apparaît comme doué d'une densité qualitative, qui permet de lui appliquer les données générales valables pour les formes ou les essences.' Geiger quotes *In DN*, V, i, 629 as an example of this understanding of being.

[115] *Le Thomisme* (Paris, 1972), p. 194, n. 8: 'La notion de *virtus essendi*, d'origine dionysienne, signifie l'aptitude intrinsèque de la forme à l'existence.'

comme une quantité variable. Le plus simple est de lui attribuer divers degrés d'intensité. C'est justement là que l'erreur d'interprétation guette le lecteur. Il convient de ne transposer les attributs du physique dans l'ordre du métaphysique. Au delà de la nature il n'y a plus de matière, ni d'étendue, ni de quantité, ni de plus ou moins. L'*esse* échappe à toutes ces déterminations, mais comme malgré tout il y a des différences d'être nous nous représentons des degrés de pureté et d'actualité formelle sous l'aspect de degrés d'intensité quantitative qui ne conviennent aucunement à l'être.[116]

I cite this passage at length to show how far from the mark Gilson's remarks are. He takes his cue from the pronouncement *esse autem non habet aliquam extensionem quantitatis* in *Contra Gentiles*.[117] Being has no *quantitative* extension; Gilson, however, seems unfamiliar with Aquinas' phrase: *ex hoc quod dicitur ens, consideratur in eo quantitas virtualis quantum ad perfectionem essendi*.[118] The distinction which Aquinas makes is between *extensio quantitatis* and *quantitas virtualis*. This is precisely the meaning of the paragraph which Gilson only quotes in part. Aquinas illustrates the contrast in the continuation of the passage: *non oportet quod virtus essendi sit infinita in corpore finito,*

---

[116] 'Virtus Essendi', *Mediaeval Studies* 26 (1964), pp. 8-9. Much of what I am attempting to convey here is brought out much more admirably by Gilson himself in *The Elements of Christian Philosophy*, pp. 210-12, where the influence of Dionysius on Aquinas' appreciation of being is highlighted. Gilson comes closest to affirming existence as a variable, virtual and intensive value when he speaks of quality and quantity as inseparable in reality: there is thus a 'quality of quantity'. However, only 'if we agree to *imagine* [his emphasis] essences as various quantities of actual being (will) the ontological density of each essence . . . determine a qualitative specification proper to it.' Gilson interprets Aristotle's view that 'a definition is a sort of number' to suggest that 'The Philosopher seems to have conceived (or imagined) each specific essence (stone, plant, animal, etc.) as a certain quantity of being . . . Translated into the language of Thomas Aquinas, this would mean that each essence represents the quantity of actual being (*esse*) participated in by a specifically defined substance . . . There is less being in a material form, limited to be itself only because of its matter, than in an intellectual substance capable of becoming any other given being.' My only disagreement with Gilson is that rather than a concession to imagination, such a view of being as a virtual quantity exhibiting varying degrees of intensity is conceptually compelling and is, moreover, textually based in the works of Aquinas. Indeed Joseph Owens considers that Aquinas' advance beyond Aristotle (whose philosophy of being is marked by 'the absence of any treatment of *existence*') may be expressed in Gilson's words from *Le Thomisme*, (1944, pp. 54-5): 'Chaque essence est posée par un acte d'exister qu'elle n'est pas et qui l'inclut comme son autodétermination . . . c'est donc la hiérarchie des actes d'exister qui fonde et règle celle des essences, chacune d'elles n'exprimant que l'intensité propre d'un certain acte d'exister.' (Joseph Owens, *The Doctrine of Being in the Aristotelian Metaphysics*, p. 466, n. 41). See A. Solignac, 'La doctrine de l'*esse* chez saint Thomas est-elle d'origine néoplatonicienne?', *Archives de Philosophie* 30 (1967), pp. 449-50: 'La densité d'être, si l'on peut dire, la densité de valeur de chaque acte d'*esse*, est variable selon chaque être; c'est pourquoi il y a une *scala entis*, une échelle des degrés d'être.'

[117] *Contra Gentiles* 1, 20, 175.

[118] *De Veritate* 29, 3.

licet in infinitum duret.[119] The inner power or virtue of being belongs to a dimension of beings other than that of quantitative measurement (spatial or temporal). This is what Aquinas means when he declares that the being of anything, considered in itself, is not a quantity (*non est quantum*); it has no parts, but is at once complete.[120] In this sense it is invariable; a thing either is or it is not. Moreover, each being is one; existence and unity are convertible. Quantity belongs to the being of a thing only accidentally—in so far as it is subject to time and change, or if the thing itself has a determined quantity. Thus Aquinas completes the paragraph of *Contra Gentiles* 1, 20: 'There is no difference whether something endures through that power [*virtus essendi*] for an instant or for an infinite time, since its changeless being is not touched by time except by accident.'[121] (In this sense we can understand Aquinas' profound statement: *Esse autem est aliquid fixum et quietum in ente.*)[122]

Even if it were extended without limit, what is of its nature finite could never attain to infinity.[123] Extended endlessly in space, a bodily being would still remain finite in nature; and what is temporal, even were it to endure without beginning or end, would likewise remain limited in its being. What is finite, were it to exist eternally, would be eternally finite. Infinity is not attained by multiplying finitude *ad infinitum*, nor eternity simply by endlessly extending time. The *virtual* quantity of being is the vertical source in which the perfection of each thing is intensified and grounded, whereas *dimensive* quantity is the level at which the perfection of material being is dispersed along the axes of space and time. Intensified to infinity, the former constitutes the unique subsistence of simple and absolute Being; extended beyond limitation the latter would be formless and ever-finite matter, of itself powerless and inert.[124] (Later in *Contra Gentiles*,[125] Aquinas contrasts

---

[119] *Contra Gentiles* 1, 20, 175.

[120] *De Caelo et Mundo* I, vi, 62: Ipsum autem esse alicuius rei secundum se consideratum non est quantum: non enim habet partes, sed totum est simul.

[121] *Contra Gentiles* 1, 20, 175.

[122] *Contra Gentiles* 1, 20, 179.

[123] For an interesting discussion on Aristotle's principle that an infinite power cannot reside in a finite magnitude (*Phys.*, VIII, 10, 266a27-8: οὐκ ἐνδέχεται ἐν πεπερασμένῳ μεγέθει ἄπειρον εἶναι δύναμιν), see Carlos Steel, '*Omnis corporis potentia est finita*. L'interprétation d'un principe aristotélicien: de Proclus à S. Thomas', *Philosophie im Mittelalter*, Ed. Jan. P. Beckmann et al., 213–24.

[124] See *De Potentia* 1, 2: Dicendum quod infinitum dicitur dupliciter. Uno modo privative; et sic dicitur infinitum quod natum est habere finem et non habet: tale autem infinitum non invenitur nisi in quantitatibus. Alio modo dicitur infinitum negative, id est quod non habet finem. Infinitum primo modo acceptum Deo convenire non potest, tum

the 'dimensive quantity' of material things with the *virtus* of immaterial beings. A body possessed of infinite dimensive quantity would spatially be everywhere; an immaterial being having infinite power would be everywhere present. Through the immensity of his power—*immensitate suae virtutis*—God touches all things, as the universal cause of all things.)[126] It is because Aquinas uses the language of measure and quantity, proper in our initial experience to dimensive extension but here adapted to a more profound and inner metaphysical dimension, that he can make the following assertion, which, moreover, provides the rule and founding principle for the inner and intensive measure and density of creatures: *Unumquodque tantum habet de esse, quantum [Deo] appropinquat.*[127] This is the language of quantity and distance, borrowed to express the participation of existence.

One cannot agree with M.-D. Philippe who, in his criticism of Gilson, states that by *virtus essendi* Aquinas means nothing more than *la capacité d'exister.*[128] Clearly, Aquinas does not simply attribute to God the 'capacity to exist', i.e. a possible existence. Aquinas does indeed speak of *potentia ad esse*, but this denotes something quite distinct. Referring to Aristotle's statement that some things have the power (δύναμιν) to exist always,[129]—and recalling that *virtus* denotes *quamdam perfectionem potentiae*—Aquinas notes that *potentia* can be understood either with respect to *esse* or to *agere*. *Potentia ad esse*, and the corresponding *virtus ad esse* belong to matter; *potentia ad agere* and *virtus ad agere* reside in form, which is the *principium agendi. Virtus ad esse* thus stands in counterpoint to *virtus essendi*; it signifies the *ens in*

---

quia Deus est absque quantitate, tum quia omnis privatio imperfectionem designat, quae longe a Deo est. Cf. *De Potentia* 1, 2 ad 5.

[125] *Contra Gentiles* 3, 68, 2424: Res enim corporea est in aliquo sicut in loco secundum contactum quantitatis dimensivae; res autem incorporea in aliquo esse dicitur secundum contactum virtutis, cum careat dimensiva quantitate. Sic igitur se habet res incorporea ad hoc quod sit in aliquo per virtutem suam, sicut se habet res corporea ad hoc quod sit in aliquo per quantitatem dimensivam. Si autem esset aliquod corpus habens quantitatem dimensivam infinitam, oporteret illud esse ubique. Ergo, si sit aliqua res incorporea habens virtutem infinitam, oportet quod sit ubique.

[126] *Contra Gentiles* 3, 68, 2430. On the nature of divine immensity, M. Curtin writes: 'God is not only beyond continuous quantity but also, by reason of his fullness of being, he is beyond the possibility of measurement; he is immeasurable, immense. What measure or independent standard could really be applied to him? His immensity, an absolute attribute, must be distinguished from his omnipresence which is a relative attribute; if God had not created the world, he would still be immense; but he would not be omnipresent because there would be no world for him to be present in.' 'God's Presence in the World. The Metaphysics of Aquinas and some Recent Thinkers', p. 129.

[127] *ST*, I, 3, 5 ad 2.

[128] Marie-Dominique Philippe, 'Analyse de l'être chez Saint Thomas', p. 28, n. 88.

[129] *De Caelo* I, 12, 281a 25-32: ἅπαν ἄρα τὸ ἀεὶ ὂν ἁπλῶς ἄφθαρτον... δυνατὸν τὸ ἀεὶ ὄν... δύναται εἶναι... δύνασθαι εἶναι.

potentia of matter, whereas *virtus essendi* is the actualising perfection of *ens in actu*, the integral and complete individual being.[130] In *Contra Gentiles* 1, 20, (the passage from which Gilson draws the disputed phrase referred to), Aquinas contrasts the 'passive potency for being' (*potentia quasi passiva ad esse*), which is the potency of matter, with what is a kind of active potency (*potentia quasi activa*) which is the power of being—*virtus essendi*.[131] This belongs primarily, he asserts, to the potency or power of form, since each thing is through its form.[132]

Another term which Aquinas uses synonymously with *virtus*, and which he invests with the same positive, 'quantitative', ontological significance is *posse*. It provides further confirmation of the qualitative measures which being may embody. 'Those things which merely exist are not imperfect because of any imperfection in absolute being. For they do not possess being according to its whole power (*secundum suum totum posse*); but rather they participate in it through a certain particular and most imperfect mode.'[133] Aquinas thus distinguishes between the *esse* of things which are devoid of any perfection beyond simple existence and those which have a higher ontological density. Expressing the power and virtue of being, *posse* acquires its fullest and most proper significance as referring to God who is the full power of Being.

Aquinas indeed finds the phrase 'the power of being' in Aristotle's theory of the celestial bodies: these have the power always to be.[134]

---

[130] *ST*, I-II, 55, 2: Dicendum quod virtus ex ipsa ratione nominis importat quamdam perfectionem potentiae. Unde cum duplex sit potentia, scilicet potentia ad esse, et potentia ad agere, utriusque potentiae perfectio virtus vocatur. Sed potentia ad esse se tenet ex parte materiae, quae est ens in potentia; potentia autem ad agere se tenet ex parte formae, quae est principium agendi, eo quod unumquodque agit, inquantum est actu.

[131] *Contra Gentiles* 1, 20, 174: Etsi detur quod in corpore caelesti non sit potentia quasi passiva ad esse, quae est potentia materiae, est tamen in eo potentia quasi activa, quae est virtus essendi: cum expresse Aristoteles dicat, in I Caeli et Mundi, quod caelum habet virtutem ut sit semper. See also *De Potentia* 5, 4 ad 1: Potentia ad esse non solum accipitur secundum modum potentiae passivae, quae est ex parte materiae, sed etiam secundum modum potentiae activae, quae est ex parte formae, quae in rebus incorruptibilibus deesse non potest. Nam quantum unicuique inest de forma, tantum inest ei de virtute essendi; unde et in I Caeli et Mundi Philosophus vult quod quaedam habeant virtutem et potentiam ut semper sint.

[132] *De Caelo et Mundo* I, vi, 62: (Averroes) fuit autem deceptus per hoc quod existimavit virtutem essendi pertinere solum ad potentiam passivam, quae est potentia materiae; cum magis pertineat ad potentiam formae, quia unumquodque est per suam formam. Unde tantum et tamdiu habet unaquaeque res de esse, quanta est virtus formae eius. Et sic non solum in corporibus caelestibus, sed etiam in substantiis separatis est virtus essendi semper.

[133] *Contra Gentiles* 1, 28, 262: Illa vero quae tantum sunt, non sunt imperfecta propter imperfectionem ipsius esse absoluti: non enim ipsa habent esse secundum suum totum posse, sed participant esse per quendam particularem modum et imperfectissimum.

[134] *Contra Gentiles* 1, 20, 174. See note 129 above. On the infinite power of being to endure infinitely in Proclus and the *Liber de Causis*, see *In de Causis* IV: Omne enim

What Aristotle's concept expresses is the vehemence of reality, its basic undeniable presence or force. All things, in so far as they exist, have an irrefutable character; most, however, are subject to generation and corruption and their power of being is transitory. Heavenly bodies endure eternally in existence. Aquinas' notion of virtual, intensive being, which admits of varying degrees of inner perfection, however, goes beyond this fundamental rigour of being. In this step he is inspired by Dionysius. Aquinas finds the vocabulary of *virtus essendi* in Dionysius: αὐτοῦ τοῦ εἶναι δύναμιν (*ipsius quod est esse virtutem*),[135] τὸ εἶναι δύναμιν εἰς τὸ εἶναι (*ipsum etiam esse virtutem ad hoc quod sit*).[136] But it is not so much this phraseology which inspires his appreciation of being as intensive, virtual perfection, (he does not give any special consideration to the passage in his Commentary), as the teaching of Dionysius on the central role of being which suggests to Aquinas the nature of being as perfective, dynamic actuality and intensive plenitude: the power of being which is the comprehensive, energising principle of all perfection.

In light of our earlier exposition of being as the fullness of finite perfection and its central role in the causality of creation, it is understandable that the phrase 'power of being' should attain its fullest significance for both Dionysius and Aquinas when referring to the infinite pre-eminence of divine being. The motifs of intensive being and of *virtus essendi* attain their full significance in divine being. Existence is at its highest intensity, and *virtus essendi* is complete, in the being of God: *Dei magnitudo est esse eius.*[137] (This could be affirmed of all beings; the greatness of each thing is its being. What Aquinas intends here is that God's greatness is unlimited, because his being is boundless.) God is infinite in power, possessing in advance and by excess (προέχων καὶ ὑπερέχων) all strength and energy, causing both individually and universally the power of being itself. While Being is for Dionysius the very energy, dynamism and power of all things, it is itself empowered by the divine supra-ontological power. The relation is thus expressed: 'Being itself, if it is proper to say so, has the power to be (δύναμιν εἰς

---

immobiliter ens infinitum est secundum potentiam essendi; si enim quod potest magis durare in esse est maioris potentiae, quod potest in infinitum durare in esse est quantum ad hoc infinitae potentiae. Ibid. XVI: Ea quae plus durare possunt, habent maiorem virtutem essendi; unde illa quae in infinitum durare possunt, habent quantum ad hoc infinitam potentiam.

[135] 8, 3, 332.

[136] 8, 3, 334. The phrase τοῦ εἶναι δύναμιν occurs three times in Proclus' *Commentary on the Timaeus* (Ed. Diehl, I, 267, 15; I, 268, 3; II, 131, 1-2: ἄπειρον τοῦ εἶναι δύναμιν). Is it possible that this is the source of Dionysius' phrase?

[137] IX, i, 808.

τὸ εἶναι) from the power which is beyond being (παρὰ τῆς ὑπερουσίου δυνάμεως).'[138] God is infinite in power because he is transcendent being. This is the understanding, moreover, which Dionysius brings to *Exodus* 3, 4: 'By a power beyond being, 'He who is' (ὁ ὤν) is substantial cause of all being (εἶναι) and creator of that which is.'[139] Commenting on another important Neoplatonic text, the *Liber de Causis*, Aquinas declares: 'If anything had the infinite power of being (*infinitam virtutem essendi*), such that it did not participate in being from another, then it alone would be infinite, and this is God.'[140]

Under the inspiration of Dionysius, Aquinas affirms the intensity of presence and perfection within the intimacy both of finite and infinite being. Such presence occurs at the finite level in the concentration of the entire perfection of each being within the primary actuality and fullness of its act of being; and universally, in the exemplary and causal presence of all existing things in absolute subsistent Being. At the finite level, all secondary aspects of things partake of the primary perfection of being; within the universal horizon, the ensemble of realities is in turn embraced in a pre-eminent and exemplary manner in divine Being.

Everything is real through the actuality of *esse*: *Necesse est participare ipsum esse. Esse* is the primary and ultimate act, the *actus ultimus, qui participabilis est ab omnibus; ipsum autem nihil participat.*[141] It can itself partake of none, since it is the universal act and plenary form of all. There is nothing more original in which it may share. Within creation, therefore, *esse* is the similitude par excellence of God. It is infinite in relation to the things which exist, their endless plenitude which can be shared in an infinity of ways. The paradox, however, is that it does not subsist in itself, but abides only in existing things. It is in turn itself contained in subsistent divine Being. 'The first act [God] is the universal principle of all acts, since it is infinite, pre-containing all things within itself, as Dionysius says.'[142]

Dionysius' inspiration for both aspects of the universally similar and analogous intensive presence of existence is evident in a passage from Aquinas' Commentary, which we have already had occasion to examine:

---

[138] 8, 3, 334.

[139] 5, 4, 262: ὁ ὢν ὅλου τοῦ εἶναι κατὰ δύναμιν ὑπερούσιός ἐστι ὑπόστατις αἴτια καὶ δημιουργὸς ὄντος.

[140] *In de Causis* IV, 109: Si autem aliquid sic haberet infinitam virtutem essendi quod non participaret esse ab alio, tunc esset solum infinitum et tale est Deus.

[141] *De Anima*, 6 ad 2. Cf. *In Hebd.* 2, 24: Ipsum esse est communissimum ... unde relinquitur quod id quod est, aliquid possit participare; ipsum autem esse non possit aliquid participare.

[142] *ST*, I, 75, 5, ad 1: Primus actus est universale principium omnium actuum quia est infinitum, virtualiter in se omnia praehabens, ut dicit Dionysius.

All existing things are contained under common *esse* itself, but not God; rather is *esse commune* contained under his power, since divine power extends farther than created being itself; and this is what he says, that *esse commune* is in God himself as that which is contained in that which contains, not that God himself is in that which is *esse*.[143]

All things are stored up in the fullness of *esse commune* and *esse commune* abides within the fullness of subsistent divine Being.

Esse Intensivum: *Primary Act and Perfection*

In his unique and original vision of being, Aquinas brings together the Aristotelian primacy of actuality—carrying this doctrine to a profound level not glimpsed by Aristotle—and the Platonist principle of perfect plenitude. For St Thomas, *esse* is the actualising and emergent plenitude of perfection to which all entitative determinations stand as potency towards act, as participant to perfect and pre-eminent fullness. Being is both primary actuality and universal formal perfection. Participation must be understood not as an act whereby a being 'has' something as its possession, i.e. as a having, but as a manner of existing or of being. In its metaphysical context, to participate is precisely to *be*. To participate in existence is to exercise the act of being even though this act has been received. Things abide *in se*, but not *per se*. As a value which is participated, being is the very act of being. Aquinas penetrates more profoundly, therefore, to the significance of both actuality and participation, discovering their profound meaning precisely in their unique identity as *esse*, the primary act and fullness of perfection in every thing.

This is made explicit by Aquinas in another context, where he gives it its radical foundation in infinite act: unlimited self-subsistent Being, the pure and perfect fullness in which all things (causally) participate:

> Everything which is participated is related to the participant as its act. Now whatever is proposed as a created form subsisting *per se* must participate in being; even life itself, or whatever is called thus, participates in being itself (*participat ipsum esse*), as Dionysius says in Chapter 5 of *Divine Names*. But participated being is limited to the capacity of the participant. Thus God alone, who is his own existence, is pure and infinite act.[144]

---

[143] V, ii, 660.

[144] *ST*, I, 75, 5 ad 4: Omne participatum comparatur ad participans ut actus eius. Quaecumque autem forma creata per se subsistens ponatur, oportet quod participet esse: quia etiam ipsa vita, vel quidquid sic diceretur, participat ipsum esse, ut dicit Dionysius, 5 cap. de Div. Nom. Esse autem participatum finitur ad capacitatem participantis. Unde solus Deus, qui est ipsum suum esse, est actus purus et infinitus.

Being as participated in is the act of the participant. This is expressed elsewhere as follows: 'Everything which participates is related to what is participated as potency to act; thus the substance of any created thing is related to its existence as potency to act.'[145]

The intimacy of being throughout its ontic determinations may be understood by considering that in living things their being is very life itself. In the animal, life is not a principle distinct from its *esse*, but rather an increased and enriched manner of existing, a power or virtue of being more noble than the simple fact of existence or manner of being of the inanimate. It is by the same principle of actuality that I exist and by virtue of which I am alive. To be alive is the 'to be' of what is living. Here Aquinas rejoins Aristotle: *Vivere enim viventibus est esse, Vivere enim viventis est ipsum esse ipsius.*[146] There is no separation or cleft between the life of the animal and its existence. To be, for the living thing, is to be alive; to live is precisely to be, but according to a more intense mode of being.

Aquinas remarks: 'It is clear that a living body is more noble than a nonliving body.'[147] This is the evidence of immediate observation and not yet the fruit of reflection and metaphysical insight. The difference between the phenomenological and the metaphysical viewpoints may be expressed in an apparent paradox: even though the living being is more perfect and noble than the nonliving, i.e. a body which simply is, being is more noble a perfection than life. Being is more intimate within the living body than life itself. In Aquinas' striking phrase: 'being inheres more vehemently than life' (*Esse vehementius inhaeret quam vivere*).[148]

Life does not add a restriction to being but draws rather all the more deeply from its inexhaustible wealth. It is thus that we must interpret the assertion: *Vita nihil addat supra esse nisi determinatum modum essendi seu determinatam naturam entis.*[149] Life is thus understood as a higher nobility of being: *Ea quae sunt et vivunt perfectiora (sunt) quam ea quae tantum sunt.*[150] This is but a realistic evaluation of an objective hierarchy in the order of things. There are indeed distinct degrees of value and perfection within the universe. Whereas matter is regarded as *esse debile*,[151] life and wisdom are praised by Aquinas as *nobilitates.*

---

[145] *Quodl.* 3, 8, 1: Omne autem participans se habet ad participatum, sicut potentia ad actum; unde substantia cuiuslibet rei creatae se habet ad suum esse, sicut potentia ad actum.

[146] *In de Causis* XII, 278.

[147] *ST*, I, 3, 1: Corpus vivum manifestum est quod est nobilius corpore non vivo.

[148] *In III Sent.,* 30, 2.

[149] *In de Causis* XII, 281.

[150] *Contra Gentiles* 1, 28, 259.

[151] *De Veritate* 2, 5, obj. 12: Materia prima habet minimum de esse. *Corpus*: Materia

Already central to Dionysius' vision was the fundamental appraisal of the pattern whereby some things are more perfect in their existence than others according to their proximity and likeness to the Good. This is wholly espoused by Aquinas who attributes their excellence to the fecundity and abundance of *esse* which is their embodied similitude to God. *Esse* is the plenitude of perfection; susceptible of variant measures of strength or intensity it is for Aquinas the ultimate foundation of metaphysical participation: 'Whether a thing has a vigorous or a feeble share in the act of being, it has this from God alone; and because each thing participates in an act of existence given by God, the likeness of each is found in him.'[152] The participation of *esse* either *forte sive debile* is but confirmation of the intensive proportioning of existence.

Crucial in the formation of Aquinas' notion of *intensive esse* is Dionysius' manner of attributing all perfections to the simplicity and superiority of Being. All qualities and modes of reality are contained within the superabundance of existence (*praehabens et superhabens*). In particular, Dionysius' understanding of rational, living, intelligent things as a pre-excellence of being was of singular importance in shaping Aquinas' appreciation of being as fullness. Thus, it is through Being that the perfection of life is actualised; it first participates in being and draws upon the perfection of life which is stored within the thesaurus of existence. Only then does the virtue of life imbue the inanimate. *Esse* first pervades that-which-is, raising it from the utter absence which is nothingness; life then infuses it with an increased perfection, a more intense degree of being. We may say, therefore, that living things exist more intensely; they have a higher pitch of being: they *are more*. The flower growing unobserved and hidden in a crevice upon the highest mountain has a greater interiority and intensity of being; it is *more* than the mountain, greater in its inner perfection than the giant and majestic beauty of the physical universe: it *is* more. In this light we may read Aquinas' remark: *nobilitas cuiusque rei est secundum suum esse*.[153]

All the perfections of a being are perfections of *esse*; this must not be understood as a tautology, but as expressing the depth of being as the intensity and fullness, the source and well-spring, of all that is present as positive in reality. *Esse* is the first and final perfection of

---

autem, propter debilitatem sui esse, quia est ens in potentia tantum, non potest esse principium agendi. Ad 12: Illa quae habent deficiens esse . . .

[152] *De Veritate* 2, 5: Res autem, sive forte sive debile esse participet, hoc non habet nisi a Deo; et secundum hoc similitudo omnis rei in Deo existit quod res illa a Deo esse participat. Translation, Robert W. Mulligan, SJ, *Truth*, Vol. I, p. 88.

[153] *Contra Gentiles* 1, 28, 260.

things. Being penetrates with its presence to the intimate core of each thing and fills out its every aspect. It is *esse* which originally grants reality, which makes things present to themselves and inserts them into the universal order. This is the ontological difference between being as primary actuality and that which is in potency towards its participated actuality.

Intelligent beings, likewise, have a greater excellence of being; they are yet more elevated on the *scala entis* and are closer to infinite goodness, since they embody a greater measure of the power or efficacy of being; they have a greater *virtus essendi*. They harbour a more profound and inner depth of existential wealth. The same complete identity cannot, however, be affirmed between the rational character of man and his act of existence because he is not exclusively or exhaustively rational but embraces many non-rational activities. (Moreover, to identify the activity of knowing with the very act of being would be to identify the substance with its accident and would entail the identity of the knowing subject with its object). We can affirm nevertheless the inherence of cognition within existence as a richness which is born out of the heart of being as the actuality of the knower. To know is a more excellent mode of existing (*modus existendi*) but is included in being and proceeds from *esse*.[154] In the simplicity and perfect unity of God, there is sheer identity between the endless perfections of Being, Life and Intelligence: *Ipsum intelligere primi Intelligentis est vita eius et esse ipsius*.[155] (Remarkable is the ease with which Aquinas, in referring this doctrine to Aristotle, perceives the harmony of the two approaches.)

What we are here calling to mind is that in all beings, *esse* is not a dimension alongside all other aspects of things but is their fullness and foundation. It is identical with them in so far as they are perfections— it is their very perfection—and transcends them in so far as they pose a limit to its infinity. Essence is thus a *modus essendi*, determining the nature of that which is. *Esse*, however, is not identical with its determinations, although it subsists alone in and through them. Being is the originative perfection which emerges to adopt the particular forms and determinations which constitute the individual. *Esse* infuses into all finite forms of the real a presence which actualises them from within at their most profound and intimate depth, fulfilling them but surpassing also their grasp so that it is never consumed or exhausted even by their ensemble. It resembles the source which feeds the stream and impels its flow, but which as distinct is never exhausted in its outpouring. *Esse* is

---

[154] *In de Causis* XII, 281: Haec duo (vivere et intelligere), prout sunt in ipso esse non sunt aliud quam esse.
[155] *In de Causis* XII, 278.

as the very illumination through which things first emerge and become manifest that they may appear and stand out in their own dimension and relief but which remains itself concealed; the universal and ubiquitous light which illumines all beings but cannot itself be seen. It is the silent and unceasing energy which nourishes and maintains the endless ferment of the universe. *Esse* is the quiet leaven (*aliquid fixum et quietum*) within the world of beings which, unobserved, perfects and harmonises each and every one within the ensemble and which lies at the origin of the whole. It is the unseen interior of things which reaches outward towards their utmost bounds, but is never enveloped by them.

Being is not simply one other among the endless forms or perfections of the created universe but is the most fundamental of all, embracing all others as secondary and implicit. In its generality it forms the foundation of the pyramid, comprehending all things universally within its power. In its simplicity it is the apex, containing all in a virtual manner according to a higher, pre-eminent presence. Being, however, is not merely the sum of all perfections and forms, but is their total simplicity and plenitude. All other qualities which the earlier Platonists would have established as independent, individual forms in themselves, Dionysius united in the simplicity of the single and universal form of Being. In characterising *esse* as intensive we view all perfections as contained eminently within the primary and plenary perfection of being. These are active only as emerging from the actuality and ontological fullness of being. In turn *esse* emerges and shines through the medium of beings. *Esse* is the pre-eminence of all wealth; it constitutes in anticipation all the qualities which are diffracted and dispersed according to its manifold wealth throughout the entitative dimensions of each thing. *Esse* is the *thesaurus* of all riches and resources, of whatever order, found within any being.[156] In an analogous but superior manner, St Thomas discovers the unity of wealth of all finite being which is diffused and dispersed throughout the multiplicity and hierarchy of creation as present and anticipated in Infinite Subsisting Being.

In the individual existent, *esse* is genetically, so to speak, the abundance of existential perfection from which all subsequent characters and determinations emerge, from which they blossom and spring forth. They are its manifestations or modes of presence. The act of being is not an empty, functional or efficient energy which in an instrumental manner simply effects into existence the modes of essence and accident of an individual, but is the wellspring which continually nurtures what-

---

[156] See Albert Keller, *Sein oder Existenz? Die Auslegung des Seins bei Thomas von Aquin*, p. 246.

is in all its diverse activity. It is not merely *initium* but also *fons et origo*, and more importantly it is their *plenitudo essendi*. This is the significance of the distinction made between existence as the mere fact of being, and *esse* as the fullness of perfection and enduring source which constantly renews within each being the ever-present creative power of God who is Absolute Being. To assert being as existential plenitude is to recognise that the perfections within beings over and above their simple existence are themselves perfections of being itself and that in origin being constitutes their excellence and their abundance. The principle of intensity allows us to conceive the existential richness and diversity of all things, individually and universally, as preserved virtually and causally, according to a higher mode of presence within the primary perfection of *esse*.

Essence and accidents participate in *esse* and draw from it their constant energy. *Esse* is thus the plenitude both of actuality and form, the *actus actuum* and the *forma formarum*. As primary act and plenary perfection, Being is the treasure store of value, a resevoir of richness and energy. *Esse* is thus at once both intensive and emergent act; it constitutes within an anterior simplicity and unity all the actuality and perfection of a being and diffuses it throughout its each and every aspect. *Esse* is the profound and inner pulsation which confers upon each thing its radical irruption and insurge, letting it stand out of and over against the void of nothingness. It is what is most intimate and fundamental within each thing,[157] what is most formal, since it includes every other determination. *Esse* is the exhaustive actuality, the inexhaustible source and fullness of the entire wealth which conjoins to establish and constitute each entity as a unique being and inserts it according to its due rank within the hierarchic order of the universe. Being is in each thing its first and final goodness, primary and supreme, fundamental and comprehensive, embracing all its entitative wealth and resources.

The Neoplatonic triad of Being, Life and Intelligence, taken from Proclus, Dionysius and the author of the *Liber de Causis*, is the frequent focus of Aquinas' reflection on the universal distribution and hierarchy of perfections. This is prominent in his Commentary on the *Liber de Causis*: *Considerandum est quod omnes gradus rerum ad tria videtur reducere, quae sunt: esse, vivere et intelligere.*[158] Aquinas' exposition of this is indeed ingenious. Each thing may be considered, he says, in three ways: firstly, in itself, in which respect *esse* is proper to it;

---

[157] *In Ev. Johannis*, I, 5, 183: Cum ergo esse sit intimum cuilibet rei.
[158] *In de Causis* XVIII, 338-9. See *In III Sent.*, Prol.

secondly, in so far as it tends towards another: this is characteristic of life; and thirdly, in so far as it has within itself what is other. Now, to possess something according to its form, immaterially, is the most noble mode of possession and this is the characteristic of knowledge. To be the origin of one's own movement is the most noble of motions and this is the nature of life. Common to all of these, however, and primary among perfections is being: *esse igitur, quod est primum, commune est omnibus.* Not all things have the perfection of self-movement or of knowledge, but only the more perfect among beings (*perfectiora in entibus*). Aquinas summarises the order of priority: *Intelligere praesupponit vivere et vivere praesupponit esse, esse autem non praesupponit aliquid aliud.* Being, therefore, is given through creation alone.

Dionysius, Source of Aquinas' Intensive Notion of Being

Aquinas' close reliance upon Dionysius and the inspiration of *DN* V, 1 is especially evident in the celebrated passage of *De Potentia* 7, 2, ad 9.[159] This is not always recognised, however. Albert Keller, for example, concluding his excellent study of the relation between the terms *esse* and *existentia*, makes no mention of Dionysius as the source of the final phrase of this passage, which he then proceeds to interpret as the primary enunciation of *esse* as plenitude.[160] More perceptive is the explicit statement of A. Solignac:

> Une analyse philologique rigoureuse démontrerait sûrement que la source de la doctrine thomasienne de l'*esse* n'est autre que le De Divinis Nominibus ch. V, 1-7, c'est-à-dire le chapitre qui traite de l'être comme nom divin par excellence. Le texte célèbre et fondamental sur l'*esse*—nous voulons parler de

---

[159] Hoc quod dico esse est inter omnia perfectissimum: quod ex hoc patet quia actus est semper perfectior potentia. Quaelibet autem forma signata non intelligitur in actu nisi per hoc quod esse ponitur. Nam humanitas vel igneitas potest considerari ut in potentia materiae existens, vel ut in virtute agentis, aut etiam ut in intellectu: sed hoc quod habet esse, efficitur actu existens. Unde patet quod hoc quod dico esse est actualitas omnium actuum, et propter hoc est perfectio omnium perfectionum. Nec intelligendum est, quod ei quod dico esse, aliquid addatur quod sit eo formalius, ipsum determinans, sicut actus potentiam: esse enim quod huiusmodi est, est aliud secundum essentiam ab eo cui additur determinandum. Nihil autem potest addi ad esse quod sit extraneum ab ipso, cum ab eo nihil sit extraneum nisi non-ens, quod non potest esse nec forma nec materia. Unde non sic determinatur esse per aliud sicut potentia per actum, sed magis sicut actus per potentiam. Nam et in definitione formarum ponuntur propriae materiae loco differentiae, sicut cum dicitur quod anima est actus corporis physici organici. Et per hunc modum, hoc esse ab illo esse distinguitur, in quantum est talis vel talis naturae. Et per hoc dicit Dionysius quod licet viventia sint nobiliora quam existentia, tamen esse est nobilius quam vivere: viventia enim non tantum habent vitam, sed cum vita simul habent et esse.

[160] Albert Keller, *Sein oder Existenz*, p. 246.

De Pot. VII. 2 ad 9um—suffit d'ailleurs à mettre sur la voie un lecteur attentif. Si saint Thomas designe Dieu comme l'*Ipsum esse per se subsistens*— et c'est de l'idée de Dieu que dérive toute la doctrine de l'*esse*—c'est parce qu'il avait lu dans le Pseudo-Denys que l'*esse* est la participation première, fondement de toutes les autres.[161]

The passage begins with the declaration by Aquinas: *Hoc quod dico esse est inter omnia perfectissimum: quod ex hoc patet quia actus est semper perfectior potentia.*[162] It is *esse* which first and alone makes the forms of perfection to be actually real. These may abide latently within the potency of matter, virtually within the power of their efficient cause or intentionally within the intellect. But it is only by having *esse* that they actually exist in reality (*sed hoc quod habet esse, efficitur actu existens*). 'Wherefore it is clear that what I call *esse* is the actuality of all acts and therefore the perfection of all perfections.' Not only does *esse* actualise all things, constituting in its universal extension the actuality of all acts, but it comprehends also intensively within its own fullness the many-graded perfections of all. This is, as Aquinas goes on to explain, because nothing can be added to *esse* as more formal, determining it as act determines potency. Being (*esse*) is essentially (*secundum essentiam*) different from that to which it is added and whereby it is determined. *Esse* belongs to an utterly different order from that of essence; there is an intransgressible distance between the orders of *esse* and *essentia*. Nothing can be added to *esse* as extraneous to it, since outside it lies only non-being, which can be neither form or matter. Hence being (*esse*) is not determined by something distinct, as potency by act, but rather as act by potency, in the same way as form is determined by the matter proper to itself, and soul is defined as the act of an organic physical body.

Here Aquinas touches on two aspects which are significant for the relation of being to those perfections signified as form (*forma signata*).

---

[161] A. Solignac, 'La doctrine de l'*esse* chez saint Thomas est-elle d'origine néo-platonicienne?', *Archives de Philosophie* 30 (1967), p. 448. See Pierre Faucon, *Aspects néoplatoniciens de la doctrine de Saint Thomas d'Aquin*, p. 448. Cornelio Fabro concludes his analysis of Chapter 5 of Aquinas' Commentary on *De Divinis Nominibus* with the following verdict: 'La source principale de la notion thomiste d'*esse* intensif est donc avant tout le mystérieux Auteur des *Areopagitica*' (*Participation et Causalité*, p. 229.), thus confirming his earlier view: 'L'Angelico ama riferire all'Areopagita alcuni degli aspetti più profondi del suo sistema quali la nozione "intensiva" dell'*esse*.' (*La nozione metafisica di partecipazione*, 2nd ed., pp. 89-90). Fabro estimates that this notion, which Aquinas received from Dionysius came to constitute more and more profoundly the central axis of thomist metaphysics (*Participation et Causalité*, p. 220). Again: 'Toute la métaphysique thomiste de la participation est basée sur cette notion simple et inépuisable de l'*esse*: l'*esse* est l'acte premier intensif qui embrasse et contient tout' (*Participation et Causalité*, p. 508).

[162] The Marietti edition incorrectly reads *perfectio*.

Being is, firstly, wholly and radically distinct from all its determinations. It constitutes an order unto itself. It may not be identified with matter, form, essence, substance or accident. As universal actuality, *esse* is determined, however, within every individual, and participated according to the capacity or potency of the principles of each. Moreover, the determinations of being, (i.e. the additions to the meaning of being whereby a thing is defined as a particular kind of being) emerge from the plenitude of being itself as concrete individual ways in which the universal actuality of being comes to presence. These determinations such as substance, genus, species, etc., through which beings are distinguished, are but so many *modi essendi*. The following passage from *De Veritate* is relevant:

> All the other conceptions of the intellect are had by additions to being. But nothing can be added to being as though it were something not included in being—in the way that a difference is added to a genus or an accident to a subject—for every reality is essentially a being . . . There are different modes of being according to which we speak when we speak of different levels of existence, and according to these grades different things are classified. Consequently, substance does not add a difference to being by signifying some reality added to it, but substance simply expresses a special manner of existing, namely, as a being in itself. The same is true of the other classes.[163]

Being is distinct from all of its determinations, it transcends them, is nevertheless their source. It is their plenitude and actuality anterior to being received in a unique mode within an individual which it thereby raises, not merely out of utter nothingness into existence but enthrones in its unique status of individual privilege and perfection according to the kind of being which it is determined to be. This is what Aquinas means when he states in the text of *De Potentia* which we are considering: 'Accordingly, this act of being (*esse*) is distinct from that *esse* inasmuch as it is the *esse* of this or that nature.' Here he is suggesting that there are degrees of perfection among the concrete acts of being which endow different individuals with perfection and actuality. Whereas prime matter is for Aquinas *esse debile*, living reality is more noble than what merely exists. And it is precisely to Dionysius that he here refers in favour of *esse* as the source and plenitude of perfection:

---

[163] *De Veritate* 1, 1: Omnes aliae conceptiones intellectus accipiuntur ex additione ad ens. Sed enti non potest addi aliquid quasi extranea natura, per modum quo differentia additur generi, vel accidens subiecto, quia quaelibet natura essentialiter est ens . . . Sunt enim diversi gradus entitatis, secundum quos accipiuntur diversi modi essendi, et iuxta hos modos accipiuntur diversa rerum genera. Substantia enim non addit supra ens aliquam differentiam, quae significet aliquam naturam superadditam enti, sed nomine substantiae exprimitur quidam specialis modus essendi, scilicet per se ens; et ita est in aliis generibus.

Et per hoc dicit Dionysius quod licet viventia sunt nobiliora quam existentia, tamen esse est nobilius quam vivere: viventia enim non tantum habent vitam, sed cum vita simul habent et esse. Being is more excellent than life since life is itself a mode of being; life is precisely the mode of being within a living thing. Whatever has life has also as such within its virtue the perfection of existence. Being, however, is of wider extension than life; there are, therefore, beings which partake of existence but not of life. As Keller puts it, *esse* is more perfect than *vivere*, but *ens* does not excel *vivens*.[164] Another author explains it: 'The transition from *vivens perfectius ente* to *esse praeeminet vitae* is the transition from a principally logical to a strictly metaphysical understanding of being.'[165]

This doctrine of the intensive and comprehensive value of being Aquinas appropriates completely as his own, as is evident from the originality and invention with which he finds it verified in the most unlikely contexts. To the question, for example, whether human happiness consists in bodily goodness,[166] Aquinas proposes as a hypothetical objection the view of Dionysius referred to, that to be (*esse*) is better than to be alive, and that life is better than the other things which are consequent upon it. But to the being and life of man, and therefore to his beatitude, concludes the objection, belongs most of all the health of the body. To this Aquinas brings the following distinction in the meaning of *esse*. Considered simply or absolutely in itself, as including all the perfection of existing, *esse* surpasses life and all subsequent perfections; in this sense being contains in itself all such secondary perfections which it transcends while embracing them.[167] This, says Aquinas, is the meaning intended by Dionysius. The objection posed presumes the alternative understanding of being, namely *esse* as participated in this or that thing which does not receive the full perfection of being, but which has *esse* in an imperfect manner, as is the minimum measure of being in any creature; in this case it is clear that being itself (*ipsum esse*) together with an additional perfection is more excellent. Because of this Dionysius can also say that living things are better than existing things and intelligent beings than living things.[168]

---

[164] *Sein oder Existenz?*, p. 246. See Fabro, *La nozione metafisica di partecipazione*, p. 202.

[165] Bernard Kelly, *The Metaphysical Background of Analogy*, p. 5.

[166] *ST*, I-II, 2, 5.

[167] *ST*, I-II, 2, 5 ad 2: Esse simpliciter acceptum, secundum quod includit in se omnem perfectionem essendi, praeeminet vitae et omnibus subsequentibus: sic enim ipsum esse praehabet in se omnia subsequentia.

[168] *ST*, I-II, 2, 5 ad 2: Sed si consideretur ipsum esse prout participatur in hac re vel in illa, quae non capiunt totam perfectionem essendi, sed habent esse imperfectum, sicut

Being, understood *secundum quod includit in se omnem perfectionem essendi*, is none other than the rich meaning of *esse* which Aquinas made the foundation and crowning of his metaphysics and natural theology. Dionysius and Aquinas here disclose a significant ambivalence in the notions 'living', 'wise' and 'being'. If 'wise' is taken as abstracting from the perfections of life and being, then it is less perfect than that which really is and lives. Referring to what is really wise, living and existent, the wise being is more perfect than the merely living or the simply existent. To be wise, however, is but a more perfect way of being. In both senses, therefore, being is more radical and fundamental.

Another interesting verification of the primacy of *esse* is found in his Commentary on the *Sentences*,[169] where Aquinas responds to the objection that charity (*caritas*) cannot be an accidental character of the soul, since it is through charity itself that the soul is perfect, and an accident cannot be more noble than its subject. Here too the radical significance of being is brought into clear focus, as well as the Dionysian provenance of this doctrine. Absolutely speaking, says Aquinas, the soul is more perfect than charity as any subject is superior to its accident; but *secundum quid* the reverse is the case. The reason for this is that *esse*, as Dionysius states, is more noble than everything else which follows upon *esse*; thus *esse* absolutely speaking is more noble, for example, than understanding (*intelligere*) if it is possible to understand *intelligere* without *esse*. That which excels in *esse*, therefore, is more noble absolutely than all those which excel in any of the perfections which follow upon *esse*, although it may be less noble in another respect. And because the soul and every substance has a more noble existence (*nobilius esse*) than its accident, it is more noble absolutely. But regarding a specific *esse*, or in a certain respect, an accident may be more noble since it is related to substance as act to potency; this secondary goodness substance receives from accidents, but not the primary goodness of being, the *bonitas prima essendi*.[170] Being

---

est esse cuiuslibet creaturae; sic manifestum est quod ipsum esse cum perfectione superaddita est eminentius. Unde et Dionysius ibidem dicit quod viventia sunt meliora existentibus, et intelligentia viventibus.

[169] *In I Sent.*, 17, 1, 2, ad 3. The reference given by Durantel, p. 179, is incorrect.

[170] *In I Sent.*, 17, 1, 2, ad 3: Esse secundum Dionysium, V cap. De div. nominibus, est nobilius omnibus aliis quae consequuntur esse: unde esse simpliciter est nobilius quam intelligere, si posset intelligi intelligere sine esse. Unde illud quod excedit in esse, simpliciter nobilius est omni eo quod excedit in aliquo de consequentibus esse; quamvis secundum aliud possit esse minus nobile. Et quia anima et quaelibet substantia habet nobilius esse quam accidens, ideo simpliciter nobilior est. Sed quantum ad aliquod esse, secundum aliquod, accidens potest esse nobilius, quia se habet ad substantiam sicut actus ad potentiam; et hanc bonitatem consequentem habet substantia ab accidentibus, sed non bonitatem primam essendi.

is the primary goodness of each thing, the substantial act of being, even though it may be further perfected in certain respects by its accidents to which it is related as potency in respect of these determinations. But these aspects of being are also themselves perfections of being. The priority and excellence of *esse* is thus reflected in the order of the principles which constitute being. All perfections 'follow upon' (*consequuntur*) *esse*; they are consequent to *esse* because they are implicit within it; they are stored up in advance within the treasury of being which is the universal fecundity of all.[171] Being is the fundamental power which each individual exercises according to its own unique and proper intensity, *forte sive debile*.

* * *

We may conclude our investigation into this aspect of Aquinas' theory of being by stating that it is legitimate and illuminating to employ the language of intensity to express the varying grades of the inner richness of things; for Aquinas, the 'intensity of being' is identical with *virtus essendi*. In the development of both themes—fundamentally one—Dionysius exerted profound influence and inspiration upon St Thomas. The 'principle of intensity' and the pre-eminence of *virtus* are operative at the heart of finite being, where existence is seen as primary and comprehensive perfection and, more originally, at the source of all reality in the plenitude of divine power which anticipates within its simplicity the existential wealth of all creatures.

Virtus essendi may be understood in a fundamental sense, literally as the basic force, strength or power 'exerted' by anything which exists: its *vehementia essendi*,[172] the resolute and irresistible manner with which something imposes itself within the order of reality. If something exists, it imposes itself with an absolute character. Try as we may, we cannot refute or flee from that which is. Each thing shares in the absolute

---

[171] In the following *Quaestio* (*In I Sent.*, 17, 2, 2, *Contra*) we find yet a further affirmation by Aquinas of the primacy of being which is inspired by Dionysius: Secundum Dionysium, V cap. De div. Nom., tantum distat inter ipsas Dei participationes et participantes, quod participatio quanto simplicior est tanto nobilior, participans vero quanto majorem habet compositionem donorum participatorum, tanto nobilius est; sicut esse est nobilius quam vivere, et vivere quam intelligere, si unum sine altero intelligatur: omnibus enim esse praeeligeretur.

[172] The term used by the Latin translator of Avicenna to denote a necessary being, which exists of itself. See Timothy McDermott, *Existence and Nature of God*, Volume 2, *Summa Theologiae* (London, 1964), p. 202. On p. 175 above, I have noted how Aquinas, on at least one occasion, uses the word to express the intensive sense of being.

character of existence; it exerts a sovereign and inescapable *puissance*.[173]
This is the sense of *virtus essendi* which Aquinas finds in Aristotle; from
Dionysius he acquires the enriching motif of intensity. It is indeed the
same word *virtus* which is used by Moerbeke to translate ἀρετή in
Aristotle and by Sarracenus to render δύναμις in Dionysius' text. This
is most significant as revealing the richness in meaning of the concept
of *virtus essendi* which Aquinas derived from his historical sources. *Esse*
is nobility and excellence, power and dynamic actuality. It is the virtue
of being which determines the intensity or degree of perfection endowed
upon an individual within the universal scale of beings. *Esse* determines,
as it were, the ontological density of each individual along the great
chain of Being. Rising in the universal scale, beings are filled more and
more with the richness and nobility of the universal perfection of
existence: *gradus in ipso esse inveniuntur*.[174] Different genera have
different modes of being; a more noble substance has a more noble
being: *nobilioris substantiae nobilius esse*.[175]

The meaning of intensity is borne out moreover in everyday usage.
We commonly speak of intense heat or cold; we use the language of
intensity to convey depths and degrees of light or colour. (It is of
course possible to measure such degrees of intensity instrumentally, but
such quantification is not required or presumed in such transferred
usage of the term.) It is not by chance that the examples chosen by
Aquinas to clarify the Neoplatonic motif of separate perfections are
precisely those of *albedo separata* and *calor separata*. We speak of the
intensity of pain; it also makes sense conversely to speak of pleasure as
more or less intense. Inner states, spiritual or emotional, while not
susceptible to numerical quantification, lend themselves to such
description: joy, love, amazement, sadness, grief, despair—such feelings
vary in intensity according to their ardour or lassitude. Running
through such usage is the connotation of an increase or decrease in

---

[173] With a reference to Aquinas' Commentary on *De Divinis Nominibus*, De Raeymaeker
writes: 'In al wat is, in elk zijnde, hoe broos het anderzijds ook weze, schuilt bijgevolg
een onwrikbaar taaie kracht, een onoverwinbaar weerstandsvermogen, kortom een kracht
die tegen alles is opgewassen, de absoluutsterke zijnskracht, *virtus essendi*, 'Zijn en
Absoluutheid', p. 199. See the same author's *Philosophy of Being*, p. 24: 'It is this reality
which possesses an unshakable solidity, an absolutely definitive consistency, an absolute
validity. This also holds good for all existence; whatever be its nature and its duration,
it etches into reality its indelible traits and it forces itself for ever and ever on the mind.
Being exists; and by its own peculiar power, its *virtus essendi*, it excludes radically and
without condition or any restriction all that would be opposed to it, and would tend to
justify a different affirmation. Outside of being there is only nothing, and so there is
nothing which could make it conditional. Being rests upon its own unshakable and
irresistible force; it is complete in itself, sufficient for itself, absolute.'
[174] *ST*, I, 48, 2.
[175] *Contra Gentiles* 2, 68, 1451.

quantity, distinct from the dimensive aspect of a physical kind. The language of intensity here signifies an escalation of inner attainment, as distinct from that of outward extension or expansion. It indicates a heightening or gathering of concentration rather than a loss of external dissipation or dispersion. An individual increases in respect of a particular perfection or determination not by extending outwards but through an increase of inner achievement; not by expanding its power to more or other objects, but through an enrichment of its own actuality: it *is* more.[176]

Such everyday use of the notion of intensity, in particular referring to spiritual realities or qualities, suggests the aptness and legitimacy of referring to existence as an actuality, perfection or power embodying varying measures of intensity. Being is a value; all value is grounded in and springs from existence. Being is the original power and perfection; conversely the value and power of being may be understood as a variable intensity enjoyed in its own measure by each individual.

---

[176] See Cornelio Fabro, *Participation et Causalité*, p. 260: 'On pourrait presque dire, en termes hégéliens, que tandis que la *quantitas extensiva* se manifeste comme "rapport à l'autre", la *quantitas virtualis* s'actualise comme "rapport à soi" en un complet retour sur soi comme le nouvel infini positif.' Fabro remarks: 'Pour Hegel aussi, comme pour saint Thomas, cet infini est simplement l'*esse*', and cites the following passage with Hegel's emphasis: '. . . Die *einfache Beziehung auf sich*, welche *Sein* ist. Aber es ist nun auch *erfülltes Sein*, der sich begreifende Begriff, das Sein als die konkrete, ebenso schlechthin *intensive* Totalität.' (*Wissenschaft der Logik*, ed. Lasson, II, p. 504).

CHAPTER SEVEN

GOODNESS OF GOD AS SUBSISTENT BEING

As we saw at the beginning of our enquiry, Aquinas greatly relied upon Dionysius in establishing his method of knowing and of naming God. We now turn to the influence of Dionysius on Aquinas' understanding of God's nature. Even though he interprets it according to his own priority of Being, Aquinas agrees with Dionysius that it is God's nature to be the very essence and plentitude of goodness itself. God alone is good exclusively and exhaustively; Aquinas repeats with approval the phrase from St Luke cited by Dionysius: *Nemo bonus nisi solus Deus.*[1] God is distinguished from all else by his goodness. It is his very nature: there is in God nothing more profound or proper. Goodness reveals and defines the whole divine essence. There is a consummate identity and reciprocity between God's goodness and his nature. All that God is, belongs to him through his goodness.[2] In his Commentary on the *Divine Names*, Aquinas advances two reasons for this identity of God's being and goodness. Firstly, the divine essence, unlike that of other beings, is goodness itself: God is good according to his essence, while other beings are good by participation. Aquinas explains this in the light of his own view of goodness as actuality and of being as fundamentally actual, not indeed to support the primacy of the good but to illustrate that God is goodness itself. Without pronouncing on the notional priority of either being or goodness, but because goodness and being are for Aquinas really convertible, he can establish the identity of God with his own goodness from the self-subsistence of his existence. He reasons: each thing is good in so far as it is in act; but as it is unique to God alone to be his own being, he alone is his own goodness.[3]

---

[1] *ST*, I, 6, 3, from Luke 18:19, although Aquinas attributes it both here and in *Contra Gentiles* 1, 38 to Matthew. In *In DN*, II, i, 112 and IV, i, 269 he cites the source correctly.

[2] II, i, 112: Per se bonitas laudatur ... sicut determinans, idest distinguens ab aliis et manifestans totam diviam essentiam, quodcumque est, quia cuicumque convenit divina essentia, convenit ei per se bonitatem esse et e converso.

[3] IV, i, 269: Et hoc, propter duo: primo, quidem quia ipsa divina Essentia est ipsa bonitas, quod in aliis rebus non contingit: Deus enim est bonus per suam essentiam,

The first argument bears upon the actuality of goodness and its foundation; Aquinas adduces secondly what could be called a reflection upon the order of the good and its finality. 'Other things, even though they are good in so far as they exist, nevertheless attain their perfect goodness only through something more which is added above and beyond their being; but God has in his own act of being the fullness of his goodness.' Moreover, other beings are good because they are ordered towards something else which is their final end. God is not directed towards any end other than himself. Aquinas thus concludes: 'The first characteristic of divine goodness is that goodness itself is the divine essence.' The second characteristic, he notes, following the order adopted by Dionysius, is that the divine goodness 'extends goodness to all things, which are said to derive through participation from him who is said (to exist) essentially.'[4]

God is affirmed as essentially good because he embraces within his existence in an infinite and unlimited power all the perfections manifest in finite beings. In creatures the perfection of being is limited and diverse, in God it is absolute and simple. The principles of intensity, participation and pre-eminent presence, determine the thought of both Dionysius and Aquinas. Aquinas emphasises the determination of perfection as act, universally grounded in the actuality of existence. God is known to be all-perfect because he is affirmed as cause of all things in their existence. It will be fruitful in this regard to have a closer look at these notions of causality and exemplarity in Aquinas' Commentary on the *Divine Names* and in other passages inspired by Dionysius.

Especially revealing of Dionysius' inspiration is Question 4 of *Summa Theologiae* I, where Aquinas considers the perfection of God; particularly article 2, where he reasons that God is universally perfect since in him are present the perfections of all things. Dionysius' influence is clear, firstly, from the appeal made to his authority in response to the objections which Aquinas advances against his own view. And considering in turn each of these objections, he again refers to Dionysius. God is perfect because, in Dionysius' words, he embraces all existing

---

omnia vero alia per participationem; unumquodque enim bonum est, secundum quod est res actu; Deo autem proprium est quod sit suum esse, unde ipse solus est sua bonitas.

[4] IV, i, 269: Item, res aliae, etsi inquantum sunt, bonae sint, tamen perfectam bonitatem consequuntur per aliquod superadditum supra eorum esse; sed Deus in ipso suo esse, habet complementum suae bonitatis. Item, res aliae sunt bonae per ordinem ad aliquid aliud, quod est ultimus finis; Deus autem non ordinatur ad aliquem finem extra se. Sic igitur, primum quod est proprium divinae bonitatis est quod ipsa bonitas est essentia divina; secundum proprium eius est quod extendit bonitatem ad omnia, quae per participationem dicuntur derivari ab Eo quod per essentiam dicitur.

things in a primordial unity: *Deus in uno existentia omnia praehabet.*[5] Aquinas, in the corpus of the article summarily repeats that the perfections of all things exist in God; he is said, therefore, to be totally or universally perfect, since he lacks none of the nobility of any nature.

St Thomas puts forward two lines of reflection to establish this view, suggesting that Dionysius has followed a similar reasoning. The first argument recalls a principle which is commonplace in Dionysius, echoed throughout Aquinas' metaphysics and repeated with frequency in the Commentary on the *Divine Names*: 'Whatever perfection there is in an effect must be found in its efficient cause.'[6] As Aquinas explains, this can occur in two ways: firstly an effect may be present potentially in its cause, in a manner identical with its own nature: as when one man, for example, generates another. The cause is in this case 'univocal' with its effect; it anticipates the effect by its own natural form. An effect may also be pre-contained in an eminent or more perfect manner when the cause is of a different and superior nature (*agens aequivocum*), as when the sun's power produces objects bearing a certain derived likeness to the sun. It is evident, Aquinas states, that such an effect pre-exists virtually, i.e. potentially, or within the power of its efficient cause and is present, moreover, in a pre-eminent and more perfect manner (*eminentiori modo*). He distinguishes between the superior, virtual presence of an effect in an agent cause, and potential presence in a material cause which is inferior. This entire article is pervaded by the notion of *virtus*: intensive, virtual or pre-eminent presence.[7] (In the following article Aquinas, in continuation of a passage from Dionysius, explains the deficiency of an effect in relation to its cause in terms of intensity or slackness—*secundum intensionem et remissionem*—and illustrates their difference with the example of things which are more or less white.[8] We find thus the juxtaposition of both *virtus* and *intensio* and the Neoplatonist theme of *albedo separata*).

Besides the example of the sun, which Dionysius had already adduced to illustrate the pre-eminent presence of effects within a superior cause,

---

[5] *ST*, I, 4, 2. See *DN* 5, 10, 284: ἐν ἑνὶ γὰρ τὰ ὄντα πάντα καὶ προέχει καὶ ὑπέστηκε. Sarracenus translates: 'In uno enim . . . existentia omnia et praehabet et subsistere facit.' The Marietti and Blackfriars editors give 5, 9 as the source of Aquinas' quotation. Durantel (p. 183) also cites 5, 10.

[6] *ST*, I, 4, 2: Quidquid perfectionis est in effectu oportet inveniri in causa effectiva. IV, iv, 33l: Causa superior praehabet in se quod in effectibus inferioribus invenitur; V, i, 631: Causa praeeminet effectibus . . . sicut effectus virtute praeexistunt in causa; IX, iv, 846: Omnes enim effectus praeexistunt virtualiter in sua causa.

[7] *ST*, I, 4, 2: Manifestum est enim quod effectus praeexistit virtute in causa agente: praeexistere autem in virtute causae agentis, non est praeexistere imperfectiori modo, sed perfectiori.

[8] *ST*, I, 4, 3 ad 1.

Aquinas in his Commentary cites the artistic causality of the architect or craftsman in whom the effect is anticipated and unified intentionally. Here, however, the cause bears only an extrinsic relation of similarity to its effect. Now, the most perfect and profound presence is that of all beings within the fullness of their creative cause. However, Aquinas notes that there is a certain analogy not only between each cause and effect, but between the relation of different causes to their respective effects. There is a parallel between the relation which a particular cause has to its individual effect and the relation of the supreme cause towards its universal effects.[9] By this he means that each effect is imbued with greater or lesser perfection according to the existential wealth and resources of its cause. The more perfect and supreme a cause, the more universal will be its causative power and efficacy; the more intimate its immanence in its effects and the presence of its effects within itself. 'The more elevated a nature, the more intimate is that which proceeds from it.' Since existence or being is what is most universal and profound in all things, their common and primary source can be only Being Itself: *Ipsum esse per se subsistens.* As universal and supreme cause, God is most intimately and powerfully present within creatures. (Such presence must be correctly understood: Aquinas remarks that 'beings are more properly in God than God in things.'[10]) And concluding his first argument for God's infinite perfection, Aquinas states: 'Since God is the first efficient cause of things, the perfections of all things must pre-exist in God in a pre-eminent manner.'[11] And St Thomas believes that this is the significance of Dionysius' statement: 'He is not this and not that, but he is all as cause of all.'[12]

The causality of beings derives in its totality through existence itself from the infinite plentitude of God's Being. All the goodness within beings thus flows from the singular perfection of their divine origin. Because he produces the perfection of all things, all perfection must pre-exist in God's own Being.[13] And not only must he possess perfection, but that he may originally cause perfection in the radical manner of creation, God must himself *be* the endless and subsistent perfection

---

[9] V, iii, 662: Eadem autem est proportio causae particularis ad suos particulares effectus et causae universalis ad suos.

[10] *ST*, I, 8, 3, 3.

[11] *ST*, I, 4, 2: Cum ergo Deus sit prima causa effectiva rerum oportet omnium rerum perfectiones praeexistere in Deo secundum eminentiorem modum. Et hanc rationem tangit Dionysius dicens de Deo quod non hoc quidem est hoc autem non est, sed omnia est ut omnium causa.

[12] 5, 8, 280: οὐ τόδε μέν ἐστι τόδε δὲ οὐκ ἐστιν·... ἀλλὰ πάντα ἐστὶν ὡς πάντων αἴτιος.

[13] V, ii, 662: Sic enim omnia praeexistunt in Deo, sicut Ipse omnium est productivus.

from which all created goodness flows. God is 'complete' (in his Being and Goodness) because he embraces universally all things within himself.[14] He is 'all in all' since he *is* causally the perfection of all things.[15]

The first argument proposed by Aquinas in *ST*, I, 4, 2 to illustrate God's universal perfection, proceeds from the diversity of perfections throughout beings to their unique and pre-eminent presence in the creative cause. God is the fontal abundance from which all things receive their individual wealth of existence. The second way outlined by Aquinas reflects upon the nature of God whose existence has been established, and whose essence is affirmed as self-subsisting Being, *Ipsum Esse Subsistens*. God does not *have* being or share in it according to any measure of its richness; he *is* Being Itself and embraces within his simple existence all the plenitude of the richness of Being: *Deus est ipsum esse per se subsistens: ex quo oportet quod totam perfectionem essendi in se contineat.*[16] God is infinitely perfect in himself and not merely as the cause of all finite perfection. He is not only the *Summum Bonum* of all things but is exhaustively and absolutely all-perfect in himself. He is infinitely and independently perfect. Existence is the perfection of all perfections and there is nothing more perfect than subsistent Being itself. God is indeed that than which no greater is possible or may be conceived.

To illustrate the infinite and universal perfection of God as subsistent being, Aquinas makes use of the Neoplatonic motif of separated perfection. He considers the hypothesis of subsistent heat: a warm body does not possess the full perfection of heat because it does not partake of heat according to its full nature. But if there existed a heat which subsisted in itself, it would lack nothing of the power or perfection proper to heat as such. Transferring the analogy to being, St Thomas states that since God is subsistent being itself, nothing of the perfection of being can be lacking in him. 'Now the perfections of all things belong to the perfection of being,' he continues, 'since beings are perfect according to the manner in which they have existence. It follows, therefore, that God does not lack any perfection.' And Aquinas again credits Dionysius with this reasoning when he writes in Chapter 5 of the *Divine Names* that God 'does not exist in a particular manner, but embraces primordially all being within himself simply and without limit', adding that 'he is the being of all that subsists.'[17]

---

[14] II, i, 113: Ipsa Deitas . . . dicatur tota, quasi praehabens in se universa.
[15] I, iii, 99: 'Omnia in omnibus', inquantum omnis perfectio est ipse Deus causaliter.
[16] *ST*, I, 4, 2.
[17] *ST*, I, 4, 2: Manifestum est enim quod, si aliquod calidum non habeat totam

Elaborating upon this same passage[18] in his Commentary on the *Divine Names*, Aquinas likewise traces the absolute goodness and complete perfection of God to the subsistent identity of his Being. Here he illustrates it with the hypothesis not of heat but of subsistent whiteness. A perfection which has its own self-subsistent presence is infinite and unique; received into another it is multiplied and limited. Participation is thus the root of finitude. Aquinas writes:

> Dionysius shows that all things are in some manner unified in God. This is evident when we consider that every form when received into anything is limited and measured according to the capacity of the recipient; thus an individual white body does not possess the complete whiteness proper to the full power of whiteness. But were there to exist a separate whiteness, it would lack in nothing which belongs to the power of whiteness. Now, all other things have being (*esse*) as received or participated and do not, therefore, have being according to the full power of being; God alone, who is subsisting being itself, has being according to the full power of being (*secundum totam virtutem essendi, esse habet*).[19]

This, states Aquinas, is what Dionysius means when he says that God can be the cause of being to all things, since he 'does not exist in a particular way' (οὐ πώς ἐστι, *non est existens quodam modo*), that is, according to some limited and finite mode, but embraces the fullness of existence, anticipating Being universally and infinitely within himself, since it pre-exists in him as cause and proceeds from him to others.[20] The ultimate ground of divine unity, perfection and creativity, therefore, is the self-subsistence of God's Being, his identity in his own act of

---

perfectionem calidi, hoc ideo est, quia calor non participatur secundum perfectam rationem: sed si calor esset per se subsistens, non posset ei aliquid deesse de virtute caloris. Unde, cum Deus sit ipsum esse subsistens, nihil de perfectione essendi potest ei deesse. Omnium autem perfectiones pertinent ad perfectionem essendi: secundum hoc enim aliqua perfecta sunt, quod aliquo modo esse habent. Unde sequitur quod nullius rei perfectio Dei desit. Et hanc etiam rationem tangit Dionysius, cap. 5 de Div. Nom., dicens quod Deus non quodammodo est existens, sed simpliciter et incircumscripte totum in seipso uniformiter esse praeaccipit: et postea subdit quod ipse est esse subsistentibus.

[18] 5, 4, 263-264: καὶ γὰρ ὁ θεὸς οὐ πώς ἐστιν ὢν ἀλλ᾽ ἁπλῶς καὶ ἀπεριορίστως ὅλον ἐν ἑαυτῷ τὸ εἶναι συνειληφὼς καὶ προειληφώς· διὸ καὶ βασιλεὺς λέγεται τῶν αἰώνων ὡς ἐν αὐτῷ καὶ περὶ αὐτὸν παντὸς τοῦ εἶναι καὶ ὄντος καὶ ὑφεστηκότος· καὶ οὔτε ἦν οὔτε ἔσται οὔτε ἐγένετο οὔτε γίνεται οὔτε γενήσεται, μᾶλλον δὲ οὔτε ἐστίν, ἀλλ᾽ αὐτός ἐστι τὸ εἶναι τοῖς οὖσι· καὶ οὐ τὰ ὄντα μόνον, ἀλλὰ καὶ αὐτὸ τὸ εἶναι τῶν ὄντων ἐκ τοῦ προαιωνίως ὄντος.

[19] V, i, 629: Ostendit quod omnia conveniunt Deo, quodammodo. Ad cuius evidentiam considerandum est quod omnis forma, recepta in aliquo, limitatur et finitur secundum capacitatem recipientis; unde, hoc corpus album non habet totam albedinem secundum totum posse albedinis. Sed si esset albedo separata, nihil deesset ei quod ad virtutem albedinis pertineret. Omnia autem alia, sicut superius dictum est, habent esse receptum et participatum et ideo non habent esse secundum totam virtutem essendi, sed solus Deus, qui est ipsum esse subsistens, secundum totam virtutem essendi, esse habet.

[20] V, i, 629.

esse. As Aquinas points out, God can be cause of existence for all beings only because he is himself the inexhaustible plenitude of existence, lacking in none of the perfection of Being. God exists, not according to one particular manner or mode but simply is, absolutely and infinitely, without condition or measure.[21] And he is unique through the self-subsistence of his Being: subsistent being can be one only; existence is limited when diffracted through a multiplicity of beings, as whiteness is likewise limited and multiplied when diversified amongst a variety of bodies. But if whiteness were subsistent and autonomous in itself, with an independent and separate existence apart from all white objects, it would also of necessity be one.[22]

The subsistent identity of God in his Being is again affirmed as the source of God's universal perfection in a remarkable passage of *Contra Gentiles*, 1, 28, where Aquinas once more invokes *Divine Names* 5, 4. He writes: 'God who is not other than his being, is a universally perfect being. And I call "universally perfect" that which is not lacking in the nobility of any genus.'[23] Aquinas declares that the nobility of anything accrues to it by virtue of its being. A man does not have any nobility from his wisdom, for example, unless through it he really is wise, i.e. unless his wisdom actually exists. The measure of nobility of anything is in accordance with its mode of being, for each thing is said to have a greater or lesser degree of excellence in so far as its act of existence is proportioned to some special nobility, of a greater or lesser degree. In other words, the excellence or nobility of each thing depends upon the measure in which it possesses the perfection of being; the perfection of every being is bestowed and determined in measure by its act of existence. If there is something, therefore, to which the whole power of being belongs (*tota virtus essendi*), it can lack none of the excellence of any being. Now anything which is its own act of being (*esse*) possesses being according to the total power of existence (*secundum totam essendi potestatem*). God, who *is* his own existence, has being, therefore, according to the complete power of being itself. Thus he cannot be lacking in any of the nobility which belongs to any thing. Aquinas

---

[21] *ST*, I, 7, 1: Cum igitur esse divinum non sit esse receptum in aliquo, sed ipse sit suum esse subsistens; manifestum est quod ipse Deus est infinitus et perfectus.

[22] *ST*, I, 44, 1: Deus est ipsum esse per se subsistens . . . esse subsistens non potest esse nisi unum: sicut si albedo esset subsistens, non potest esse nisi una, cum albedines multiplicuntur secundum recipientia.

[23] *Contra Gentiles* 1, 28, 259; This statement is preceded by a reference to Dionysius' own explanation that being is more perfect than life: Licet autem ea quae sunt et vivunt, perfectiora sint quam ea quae tantum sunt, Deus tamen qui non est aliud quam suum esse, est universaliter ens perfectum. Et dico universaliter perfectum, cui non deest alicuius generis nobilitas.

again employs the model of subsistent whiteness, which, were it to exist in separation from all objects and unlimited in its reception by the defect of any particular thing, would possess the full power of whiteness.[24] And once more he immediately aligns this manner of conceiving the infinite excellence of God as the subsistent identity and plenitude of Being with Dionysius' avowal: 'God does not exist in a certain way; he possesses and embraces primordially all being within himself absolutely and without limit.'[25]

The intensive participation and pre-eminent presence both of all perfections at the finite level within the perfection of being and, universally, of the perfections of all beings within divine subsistent being is brought out clearly by Aquinas in his reply to one of the objections in *ST*, I, 4, 2. The objection is that which Dionysius had already raised, hypothetically, to illustrate his own view of being as fundamental and all-embracing perfection. The objection states that a living thing is more perfect than one which simply exists, and a wise being more perfect than one which is merely alive, since to live is more perfect than merely to exist and to be wise more perfect than to live. But, Aquinas develops the argument, if God's essence is existence itself, he does not have such perfections as life and wisdom. In reply, Aquinas refers to Chapter 4 of *Divine Names*, where Dionysius states that even though being itself is more perfect than life, and life as such is more perfect than wisdom—when these are considered abstractly in themselves as distinguished by reason—nevertheless a living being, which both exists and is alive, is more perfect than one which simply exists; similarly, a wise being both exists and is alive.

> So, although to be existing does not include within it to be alive or to be wise (since it is not necessary that what participates in being should partake of it according to every mode of being), nevertheless the very being of God (*ipsum esse Dei*) embraces life and wisdom; since none of the perfections of being can be absent from him who is subsisting being itself.[26]

---

[24] *Contra Gentiles* 1, 28, 260: Omnis enim nobilitas cuiuscumque rei est sibi secundum suum esse: nulla enim nobilitas esset homini ex sua sapientia nisi per eam sapiens esset, et sic de aliis. Sic ergo secundum modum quo res habet esse, est suus modus in nobilitate: nam res secundum quod suum esse contrahitur ad aliquem specialem modum nobilitatis maiorem vel minorem, dicitur esse secundum hoc nobilior vel minus nobilis. Igitur si aliquid est cui competit tota virtus essendi, ei nulla nobilitatum deesse potest quae alicui rei conveniat. Sed rei quae est suum esse, competit esse secundum totam essendi potestatem: sicut si esset aliqua albedo separata, nihil ei de virtute albedinis deesse posset ... Deus igitur, qui est suum esse, habet esse secundum totam virtutem ipsius esse. Non potest ergo carere aliqua nobilitate quae alicui rei conveniat. See also, 1, 28, 261-2.

[25] *Contra Gentiles* 1, 28, 267: Dionysius etiam, in V cap. de Div. Nom. dicit: Deus non quodam modo est existens, sed simpliciter et incircumscriptive totum esse in seipso accepit et praeaccepit. Cf. *In I Sent.*, 8, 2, 3: Divinum esse, ut dicit Dionysius, De Divinis nominibus, V, 4, praeaccipit sicut causa in se omne quantum ad id quod est perfectionis in omnibus.

[26] *ST*, I, 4, 2 ad 3: Ad tertium dicendum quod, sicut in eodem capite idem Dionysius

Aquinas, in reliance upon Dionysius, here understands being in the intensive sense of primary and universal value: both the finite act of *esse* of the individual existent in which all particular perfections are rooted and in which they partake, and infinite subsistent Being in which the perfection of universal being is pre-eminently present in a unique superplenitude and intensity. As the essential plenitude of Being, divine being includes all life and wisdom, since these are themselves participant modes of being. There is an analogy between the participation of all finite value in the primary perfection of created existence and the universal embrace at the heart of divine Being of all created goodness. This kinship rests upon the principle that the perfection of an effect is present virtually and to an eminent degree in its cause; *esse* is the principle at the interior of each individual which actualises all its resources, as in the universal sphere God is the creative cause of all.[27]

The objection and the reply of Dionysius and Aquinas focus upon two distinct aspects of the concept of being: on the one hand existence as intensive universal value embracing all other perfections such as life and wisdom, which are but degrees of excellence within reality (thus one might say that to be wise is to *be* more, i.e., to exist in a more perfect manner), and on the other the most general concept of being which abstracts universally from all perfections. The concept of being is thus at once the most abstract and impoverished, yet the richest and most significant. Explicitly it expresses the minimum possible regarding any being, merely that it exists; latently, however, it embraces notionally in an absolute way the universal perfection of all that exists. It is this latter intelligibility, transposed to the transcendent level and intensified towards infinity, which provides the best conception within human grasp for the reality and goodness of God. The self-subsistent plenitude of the absolute Good may be expressed in a plurality of ways; although on first encounter the least expressive name is that of Being, it is ultimately the most significant denomination, allowing God to be understood as the pre-eminence and plenitude of perfection present in reality.

---

dicit, licet ipsum esse sit perfectius quam vita, et ipsa vita quam ipsa sapientia, si considerentur secundum quod distinguuntur ratione: tamen vivens est perfectius quam ens tantum, quia vivens est etiam ens; et sapiens est ens et vivens. Licet igitur ens non includat in se vivens et sapiens, quia non oportet quod illud quod participat esse, participet ipsum secundum omnem modum essendi: tamen ipsum esse Dei includit in se vitam et sapientiam; quia nulla de perfectionibus essendi potest deesse ei quod est ipsum esse subsistens.

[27] Cf. Cornelio Fabro, *Participation et Causalité*, pp. 428-9.

DIVINE IDENTITY, SIMPLICITY AND IMMUTABILITY

It is from God's nature as self-subsistent Being, furthermore, that are derived in turn, according to Aquinas, the qualities of identity, uniqueness, simplicity and immutability. These are suggested by Dionysius and admirably expounded by St Thomas in his Commentary. God is wholly immutable, he remarks, since in no way can he depart or decline from Being.[28] He is firmly grounded within himself according to his infinite power, excluding and transcending all diversity in his perfect identity.[29] He allows neither change nor transformation; as the plenitude of Being, he can become neither 'more' nor 'less'; in need of nothing, he seeks no alteration.[30] As Aquinas declares: 'God has a super-eminent and unalterable, that is, an intransmutable identity.'[31] He elaborates upon this in his commentary on the attributes of 'standing' and 'sitting', given by Dionysius to God. Here again he brings to bear his powers of profound insight and clear analysis, suggesting that God's standing or abiding in himself may be seen in three regards. Firstly, in respect of his Being, God is perfectly self-subsistent and stands exclusively within his own existence (*Ipse in se existit*). Unlike all else which rests or relies on some other reality, God remains within himself in simple and unalterable selfhood.[32] God receives the attributes of 'standing' and 'seating', secondly, in respect of his operations or activity. God works unceasingly with constant wisdom, power and goodness. He is in his being at once the subject and object of all his action. His operations and activity are directed towards himself as their only end, and object of all his action; it is in knowing and loving himself that God exercises his activity in relation to all things. His activity is self-rooted, abides in his own Being and is directed through self-love towards himself as its final end.[33] Thirdly, God is given the qualities of 'standing' and 'sitting', according to Aquinas, because he is free of all passion and change; he can undergo no affect and can be moved by nothing beyond himself, but is wholly immutable.[34]

---

[28] VIII, iii, 769: Deus, qui est omnino immutabilis, secundum nihil potest excidere ab esse.

[29] IX, ii, 816: Firmatus est enim in Seipso, secundum infinitatem suae virtutis ... in Deo est perfectissima identitas, omnem diversitatem excludens.

[30] IX, ii, 817.

[31] IX, ii, 827.

[32] IX, iv, 837: Secundum immobilem identitatem ... singulariter est simplex in Seipso.

[33] IX, iv, 837: Et circa idem, quantum ad objectum suae operationis: quia semper Eius operatio est circa seipsum, inquantum intelligendo et amando se, omnia operatur. (On God as end of all divine activity, see *Contra Gentiles* 1, 74; 3, 17).

[34] IX, iv, 837.

We have seen how Aquinas, with constant reference to Dionysius, explains the goodness and all-perfection of God as identical with his subsistent Being. However, on the specific meaning of the word 'perfect', Aquinas also provides some interesting remarks in his Commentary. The term 'perfect' (παντελῶς), he notes in Chapter 2, may not be referred to God in its literal meaning of what is 'completely made'. According to such a meaning, that which has not been made could not be called perfect. But because things, which are made, acquire perfection when they attain to the nature and virtue proper to their species, the word 'perfect' is also taken to signify everything which attains its proper nature and virtue. In this way, God is said to be perfect, since he is supreme in his nature and power.[35] And in *Summa Contra Gentiles* 1, 28, Aquinas states that something is 'completely made' when it has been fully brought forth from potency to act, and has no non-being but only being which is totally complete; 'perfect' can by extension, therefore, refer to that which is itself completely in act although it has not in any way been made.

DIVINE PERFECTION

Of special relevance are St Thomas' comments on the meaning of perfection in Chapter 13, *lectio* 1. In the opening lines of this chapter, Dionysius notes that Scripture not only predicates all things of their universal cause, but attributes them moreover in a unified manner (καὶ πάντα καὶ ἅμα πάντα), praising him as *perfect* and as *one* (ὡς τέλειον αὐτὸ καὶ ὡς ἕν ἀνυμνεῖ).[36] This is indeed, declares Dionysius, the 'strongest' or most valid nomination of God. Despite Sarracenus' mistranslation of καρτερώτατον as *brevissimum*, Aquinas recognises the importance of the terms and provides them with one of his most thoroughgoing analyses. From Dionysius' single paragraph he enumerates eleven points regarding God's perfection. His analysis of the passage goes beyond the scope of Dionysius himself. It is an example of Aquinas' ability to provide a detailed and enlightening exposé of the dense and obscure text of Dionysius. We can speak of the contribution made by Aquinas to the understanding of Dionysius.

---

[35] II, i, 114: Hoc nomen perfectum assumptum est ad significandum omnem rem quae attingit propriam virtutem et naturam. Et hoc modo Divinitas dicitur perfecta, inquantum maxime est in sua natura et virtute.
[36] XIII, i, 435.

According to Aquinas' analysis, Dionysius first shows (a), in what way God is said to be perfect (*quomodo Deo attribuatur perfectum*), and here he perceives four ways.[37] Secondly (b), Dionysius considers three ways, characteristic of created perfection, in which God is not said to be perfect.[38] Finally, (c), he shows what perfection signifies when attributed to God.[39]

Concerning (a), the way in which God is said to be perfect, Dionysius distinguishes, according to Aquinas, four ways in which divine perfection differs from that of creatures. This is expressed in the following text, as translated by Sarracenus: *Igitur perfectum quidem est, non solum sicut per se perfectum et secundum seipsum a seipso uniformiter segregatur et totum per totum perfectissimum, sed et sicut super perfectum secundum omnium excessum.* God is, firstly, perfect in and through himself, whereas creatures are perfect through something extrinsic added to them, as air through the light of the sun.[40] Secondly, not only is God perfect in himself but is totally perfect, i.e. according to the fullness of his essence. A creature may be perfect in itself by virtue of its natural form but not in its fullness, since its form is not identical with its being. Such a being is not totally perfect through itself but only in part. Aquinas notes that this is the case with material things which are composed of matter and form. In contrast, God is *perfectus secundum se totus.*[41] He enjoys total and formal perfection in the identity and fullness of his Being. Thirdly, not only is God fully and formally perfect, due to the simplicity of his nature; but in contrast to any immaterial substance which, although it subsists in its form, does not have its *esse* and its perfection from itself (*non habet esse a se*) but from another, God is *per se perfectum et secundum seipsum a seipso.*[42] God is perfect in virtue of himself alone and fully grounded in himself. Noteworthy is Aquinas' emphasis in attributing God's perfection to the selfhood of his existence, the aseity of divine Being. Finally, God is totally and wholly most perfect (*totum perfectissimum*), in contrast to creatures, which are in some manner composite, such that one part is more perfect than another. No creature is wholly and exhaustively perfect but only with respect to a particular part, as for example the soul is what is most perfect in man, and the intellect in the soul. Aquinas concludes that God is said by Dionysius to be perfect not only in the preceding modes but even to be 'supra-perfect in so far as he exceeds the perfection of all things.'[43]

---

[37] XIII, i, 436.
[38] XIII, i, 437.
[39] XIII, i, 438.
[40] XIII, i, 962: Deus dicitur perfectus, sicut per se perfectus.
[41] XIII, i, 962.
[42] XIII, i, 962.
[43] XIII, i, 962; In *Contra Gentiles* 3, 20, Aquinas gives a detailed account of the grades

Aquinas continues his reading of *Divine Names* 13, 1, by discerning
(b), three aspects of created perfection which are to be excluded from
our understanding of God. These he takes from the following lines with
their recognisable threefold division: *Et omnem quidem infinitatem
terminans, super omnem autem terminum extentum et a nullo captum aut
comprehensum.*[44] Firstly, notes Aquinas, God in his perfection bounds
all infinitude, since any (creaturely) infinity whatsoever, compared to
divine perfection, is finite and limited. In the second instance, a creature
is said to be perfect when and because it reaches the end proper to its
nature; God, however, is perfect not as attaining any limit or end but
as surpassing all limitation, since all limited things are derived from
him. Indeed, and this is the third distinction, a creature may be said to
be perfect because it is contained within certain limits; God, however,
is perfect because he is comprehended by no such limit.[45]

Having excluded the notion of creaturely perfection from our
understanding of God's excellence, Dionysius proceeds to show,
according to Aquinas, (c), the meaning of perfection as attributed to
God. From Dionysius' brief lines St Thomas discerns four characteristics.
The text which he interprets (Sarracenus' translation) is as follows:

> Sed extendens se ad omnia simul et super omnia indeficientibus immissionibus
> et interminabilibus operationibus. Perfectum autem rursus dicitur et sicut
> inaugmentabile et semper perfectum et sicut non minorabile, sicut omnia in
> seipso praehabens et supermanans secundum unam impausabilem et eamdem
> et superplenam et imminorabilem largitionem, secundum quam perfecta
> omnia perficit et propria adimplet perfectione.[46]

In its power God's perfection contrasts, firstly, with the imperfection of
a creature whose power does not extend far enough as to fulfil all the
operations which are proper to it, as a king whose power does not
extend to all those under his dominion. In contrast God extends in
power *to all things*, not gradually or in succession so that being present
to one he abandons another, but *to all at once*. Nor is his power simply
adequate to these objects as is the case with man's power; he exists,
rather, beyond all things.

---

of perfection in composite beings in virtue of their degrees of actuality and the
composition of act and potency. He conceives goodness and perfection as act, ultimately
identified with the act of existing.

[44] 13, 1, 437.

[45] XIII, i, 964.

[46] 13, 1, 438; Luibheid's translation: 'He reaches out to everything and beyond
everything and does so with unfailing generosity and unstinted activity. To speak of
perfection is to proclaim that it cannot be increased or diminished, for it is eternally
perfect, that it contains all things beforehand in itself, that it overflows in one unceasing,
identical, overflowing, and undiminished supply, thereby perfecting the perfect and filling
all things with its own perfection.'

Secondly, a finite being is imperfect either because it tends towards perfection (e.g. a boy during growth) or because it recedes from perfection (e.g. an ageing person in decline). A being is imperfect because it does not always possess its perfection immanently within itself; all changeable things are, therefore, said to be imperfect. In contrast, God is perfect because he *is* without increase, and is *always* perfect, without decrease.

Thirdly, a being is said to be imperfect when it lacks something it ought to possess, as a man who lacks a hand or foot, knowledge or virtue; however that which has all that is proper to itself is not absolutely perfect but only according to its nature. God, on the other hand, is said to be perfect absolutely or without qualification (*simpliciter*), because he pre-contains all things in unison within himself, as effects pre-exist within their cause.[47]

Fourthly, something is said to be perfect when it is able to make something similar to itself. God is, therefore, infinitely perfect since he pours his perfection out to all creatures, and does so, moreover, not according to different measures of his divine generosity but in a unique act of bestowal. God's giving does not falter but is unceasing and remains ever constant. It does not decrease; rather in giving affluently to all things its generosity remains superabundant, and is undiminished by its copious effusion. Through his generosity God 'makes all things perfect', filling them with the likeness of his own perfection.[48]

AQUINAS AND THE GOOD BEYOND BEING

Having reviewed earlier Aquinas' interpretation of the passages where Dionysius expounds the priority of goodness beyond Being, it will be of interest to evaluate this treatment in the light of Aquinas' own philosophy of being. A difficulty in our exposition of Dionysius from the outset has been the task of expressing in concepts and terms appropriate to beings that which is supposedly non-existent, i.e. prime matter, or which is beyond existence, namely, the divine Good. Is it not a matter of simple and elementary evidence that if something does not exist it cannot be in any way efficacious and cannot be uttered in the language proper to existent reality. The judgment 'It is', of itself, is in no way restricted in its power of reference but embraces necessarily

---

[47] XIII, i, 967: Deus autem dicitur simpliciter perfectus, quia simpliciter omnia in seipso praehabet, sicut effectus praeexistunt in causa, ut supra multoties dictum est.

[48] XIII, i, 968.

whatever exercises in any way the fundamental character of reality. It is the foundation of all coherent and intelligent discourse. Only of that which does not exist is it not possible to pronounce the affirmation of existence. Is it not contradictory, therefore, to speak of what is non-existent as desiring the Good, or of 'that which is not' as giving rise to being? Is not an *au-delà de l'être* inconceivable?

Expressing the ontological transcendence of the Thearchy with such phrases as ὄντως προών or ὤν ἐστιν ὑπερουσίως, Dionysius is relying upon entitative words and concepts to express the immeasurable distance between the finite and infinite. He is seeking to express a transcendence beyond Being through terms which rely for their emphasis on the very strength and evidence of Being itself. According to a simple and universal logic of being, there is, needless to say, a contradiction implicit in all such phrases; ὄντως is used to convey the supra-existential excellence of the Good but is itself proper to existence, which, according to Dionysius, is necessarily finite. Dionysius thus appeals to an evidence to which, on his own terms, he is not entitled.

Dionysius likewise speaks on two occasions of the Good as cause 'by its very being' of all things (αὐτῷ τῷ εἶναι).[49] This inherent difficulty whereby Dionysius is obliged to resort to the concept of Being in order to emphasise the transcendence of the Thearchy confirms indeed the need to affirm the universal and transcendent primacy of Being. Dionysius himself in one passage explicitly grounds the omnipotence and veracity of God in his very Being. In response to the magician Elymas who denies the omnipotence of God, because St Paul has declared that he cannot deny himself, Dionysius claims such an argument to be childish folly. In negating himself, he explains, God would be falling away from the truth; 'Truth, however, is being', states Dionysius, 'and a lapse from truth is a lapse from being. If, therefore, truth is being and the denial of truth is a fall from being, God cannot fall from Being since it is not possible for him not to be.'[50] This passage, however, is an exception. For Dionysius, Being is consistently portrayed as in itself limited, and restricted to the finite level of creation; even prime matter, which is not yet formed, is considered non-existent.

Does Aquinas' interpretation of Dionysius help solve this aporia? The reading of Dionysius' phrase τὰ οὐκ ὄντα as *non existens actu, quod est ens in potentia*, and of divine non-being as superabundant plenitude, is indeed plausible and allows him to provide a coherent appreciation of the doctrine, in harmony with his own metaphysics.

---

[49] 1, 5, 24. See 4, 1, 96.
[50] 8, 6, 341: εἰ τοίνυν ἡ ἀλήθεια ὄν ἐστιν ἡ δὲ ἄρνησις τῆς ἀληθείας τοῦ ὄντος ἔκπτωσις, ἐκ τοῦ ὄντος ἐκπεσεῖν ὁ θεὸς οὐ δύναται καὶ τὸ μὴ εἶναι οὐκ ἔστιν.

However, if St Thomas' interpretation of prime matter is correct, i.e. if prime matter can be simply designated as non-being, this does not express fully the doctrine of Dionysius regarding the transcendence of the Good. For Dionysius, the excellence of the primary Goodness as Non-Being does not merely consist in its transcendence beyond prime matter which is deprived of form. Dionysius intends something more; the Good is absolutely transcendent in itself. It exceeds all that is related in any manner whatever to being, and transcends every mode of negation which bears upon the limitation of finite beings. Our manner of negation is bound to that which it negates, namely beings, so that even our very negation is itself inadequate. God is to be praised by more than merely the negation of that which is. Dionysius goes so far as to say that God even transcends both affirmation and negation.

The reason Dionysius holds the Good to be transcendent is not simply because it 'extends both to beings and to non-being', i.e. because matter is conceived as non-being, and falls outside the scope of being but under the power of goodness. The Good transcends Being because goodness is essentially the very nature of God, who transcends all beings and is radically beyond all reality. For Dionysius, being has of necessity the status of a creature. 'Being is the first gift of absolute and substantial Goodness, which is praised by its primary participation.'[51] Being is not in itself the fullness of perfection, but a received perfection, albeit the first among the gifts of creation. Even as the most proper name drawn from creatures, it is nevertheless unworthy to denote the nature of God in himself. Being does not have the character of transcendence or of absoluteness which Dionysius attributes to God. That is to say, Dionysius did not have a fully developed appreciation of the absolute and transcendental nature of Being. Greek philosophy as a whole had not yet discovered the transcendent or universal and analogical value of Being, i.e. that as a concept unrestricted in itself, 'being' adequately expresses the reality both of creatures and of God while yet allowing their radical distinction. It failed, therefore, to harmonise faithfully within a unified order both the finite and infinite character of reality. Greek thought thus fell into the tendency of explaining either the absolute character of Being or its finite, changing features as a sort of non-being. As G. B. Phelan puts it, 'The efforts of Greek thinkers after Parmenides to render both being itself and the multiplicity and mutability of things, of beings, intelligible to mortals gave rise to the various devices adopted by the Atomists, Plato,

---

[51] 5, 6, 267.

Aristotle, right down to Plotinus, to give to some form of non-being *droit de cité* in the metropolis of philosophy.'[52]

A further difficulty of Dionysius is that he too, like Parmenides, had a restricted view of Being: Being is equated with existence as actual, without room for the concept of potency; he fails to penetrate to the absolute and universal nature of being, in itself transcendental and transcendent. To escape this restriction, the transcendence of the Good appeared as inevitable. The Aristotelian distinctions of act and potency which transcend the fixity of limited being, and the notion of final cause here come to the assistance of Aquinas in distinguishing between the varied features of the real as a condition of drawing them together in a unified vision of the whole.

In order to give a plausible interpretation of the primacy of the Good before Being in Dionysius' system, Aquinas merely takes *Bonum* as signifying both actual and potential being, while *Ens* refers only to actual being. *Potentia ad esse* is at once *ordo ad bonum* and signifies *ratio boni*. However, as Van Steenberghen remarks, Aquinas makes a questionable concession to Dionysius in agreeing that non-beings participate in the Good while they are only potentially in existence: 'C'est sacrifier indûment l'équivalence des notions transcendentales (*ens et bonum convertuntur*), indûment, car il est clair que les non-existants participent tout autant à l'être qu'au bien en tant qu'ils existent en puissance.'[53] Moreover, in the domain of causality, considered metaphysically or ontologically, the potentially existing can be actualised, brought into the completeness of its being, only by something which is already in existence. And universally, at the fundamental level, only that which is itself the very essence and subsistence of Being can cause what does not of itself exist. That which in no manner exists has no relation either towards being or goodness, and must be caused originally in its very being by plenary Being. We may not in any sense speak of a priority of goodness before being; we may indeed affirm the absolute priority of the Good as one and identical with Being. The transcendent concept of Being involves, therefore, more than the unity of act and potency. It signifies the absolute and actual fullness of all possible perfection. The central theme for Aquinas is that of perfection, both as primary goodness conferring actuality to things in their origin, and as goal or end of all.

Dionysius names God primarily as the Good because through his goodness he causes everything which is. That which he causes is itself

---

[52] G. B. Phelan, 'The Being of Creatures', *Selected Papers*, p. 83.
[53] F. Van Steenberghen, 'Prolegomènes à la *Quarta Via*', p. 104.

incapable of naming him. This is reminiscent of Plotinus' theory that a cause must be not only superior but also ontologically other than its effect. It may not be, or possess in the same manner, that which it bestows. As cause of Being, the Good is, therefore, ἐπέκεινα τῆς οὐσίας. For Aquinas also, the transcendent cause cannot be any of the things which it causes; the difference, however, is that for St Thomas, God is not Non-being but infinitely more than beings and radically distinct; he may be called 'Non-Being' only as distinct from, and more than, beings, i.e. as Being itself. 'God is none of the things he causes— not because of any lack of what they are, but because the perfections in them are proper to God in a way that ineffably exceeds any way in which the perfections can be represented in creatures.'[54]

Aquinas quotes Dionysius with approval in stressing the divine transcendence. God exists beyond all substance and is even said to be devoid of substance: *Deus est absque substantia, quasi super omnem substantiam existens.*[55] He exceeds all things supra-substantially (*secundum supersubstantialem Deitatis excessum*)[56] and, transcending as infinite all finite substances, embraces in advance the limitations of all.[57] He continually endeavours, nevertheless, to diminish the excesses in the doctrine of Dionysius regarding the transcendence of the Good beyond Being, by understanding it as expressing simply a transcendence beyond finite beings, rather than as exceeding the fullness of Being itself: *bonum est multo altius collocatum et super substantialiter existens et supra non-existens secundum quod invenitur in rebus.*[58] God is supra-substantial goodness, substance, life and wisdom, *secundum quod in seipsa supersubstantialiter existit super omnia quae in creaturis inveniuntur.*[59] Complete non-being is predicated only of the supreme Good in so far as he transcends all substance.[60] God is called non-being, not because he is lacking in existence, but because he is beyond all existing things.[61] Even imperfection is attributed to God, in so far as he is perfect as prior and superior to all things.[62] Replying in the *Summa* to an objection

---

[54] Joseph Owens, *Elements of Christian Philosophy*, p. 357.

[55] IV, xvi, 506.

[56] I, i, 32.

[57] I, ii, 75: Deus ergo, cum sit infinitus, excedit omnem substantiam finitam, praehabens in se fines omnium.

[58] IV, xiv, 478.

[59] V, i, 611.

[60] V, i, 611: Nihil est totaliter non-existens nisi secundum quod non-existens dicitur de summo bono, secundum suam supersubstantialitatem.

[61] IV, xiii, 463: Deus enim dicitur non-existens, non quia deficiat ab existendo, sed quia est super omnia existentia.

[62] VIII, iii, 721: . . . attribuimus Ei imperfectionem, inquantum est perfectus super omnia et ante omnia.

drawn from Dionysius, Aquinas repeats: *Deus non sic dicitur non existens, quasi nullo modo existens, sed quia est supra omne existens, inquantum est suum esse.*[63] God has a wholly other kind of Being from that of finite things and from the point of view of their existence, may be truly said not to exist.

Aquinas, as much as Dionysius, was concerned to emphasise the absolute transcendence of God beyond beings, but perceived this as a transcendence identical with, rather than beyond Being itself. God transcends all things, is beyond *ens*, not because he is separated goodness or unity but because he is infinite *esse*. In his Commentary on the *Liber de Causis*, Aquinas clearly contrasts his own theory of the infinity of divine Being with that of the *Platonici*: 'The first cause is indeed according to the Platonists beyond being, inasmuch as the essence of goodness and unity—which is the first cause—surpasses separated being itself. But in reality and truth, the first cause is beyond being (*ens*), inasmuch as it is infinite being itself (*ipsum esse infinitum*).' As Being itself, God is infinite and transcends all which is. For this reason also, God transcends human cognition whose proper object is not existence itself as such but that which shares it in a limited measure.[64]

For Dionysius, God is Good because as Non-Being he transcends Being; for Aquinas, he is Good because he is transcendent Being itself. According to Dionysius, God enjoys the fullness of perfection—that perfection which is mirrored or shared by creatures—because he is beyond reality. For Aquinas, he does so only because he is in an intensive manner *esse realissimum*. God's transcendence is precisely one of Being, of identity with Being in its fullness rather than a transcendence beyond Being.

It was indeed a merit of Platonism to seek a principle beyond beings, distinct and unique in itself. There must be 'something beyond beings', for the simple reason that beings as such are radically insufficient in themselves. However, it does not follow that being is bestowed only by a principle which itself 'is not'. Beings receive rather their reality from the unlimited fullness of existence itself. The original ground of reality,

---

[63] *ST*, I, 12, 1 ad 3.

[64] *In de Caus.*, VI, 175: Causa autem prima secundum Platonicos quidem est supra ens, in quantum essentia bonitatis et unitatis, quae est Causa prima, excedit etiam ipsum ens separatum . . . sed, secundum rei veritatem, Causa prima est supra ens, inquantum est ipsum esse infinitum. Ens autem dicitur id quod finite participat esse et hoc est proportionatum intellectui nostro, cuius obiectum est 'quod quid est' ut dicitur in III de Anima. Unde illud solum est capibile ab intellectu nostro quod habet quidditatem participantem esse; sed Dei quidditas est ipsum esse, unde est supra intellectum.

likewise its ultimate end and goal, must be found within reality and not outside or beyond it: it is beyond beings but not beyond existence.

In Aquinas' view, the key to God's transcendence lies in the distinction which he makes between God who is *Ens per essentiam*, and creatures which are *entia per participationem*. Both of these notions are shaped largely under the inspiration of Dionysius. God is unqualified ESSE; *entia* do not exhaust the perfection of *esse* but, as *habentia esse*, possess a restricted share of its richness. It is the subsistence of divine Being which radically distinguishes God from finite beings. His simple subsistence and selfhood are the ground of God's infinite perfection and goodness, and of his transcendence beyond all things. God's being is not received from any other but subsists in and of itself: *Cum igitur esse divinum non sit esse receptum in aliquo, sed ipse sit suum esse subsistens . . . manifestum est quod ipse Deus sit infinitus et perfectus.*[65] And because God is infinite, he embraces within himself all the plenitude of the perfection of total being: *Deus autem cum sit infinitus comprehendens in se omnem plenitudinem perfectionis totius esse.*[66] It is subsistent Being which radically constitutes the nature of God; it is the source and summation of all divine perfection and only as subsistent Being can God be the creative cause of being.

In the vision of Aquinas, therefore, the goodness of God is the intensity and unity of all perfections within his Being. Being is his perfection; as Aquinas remarks in his Commentary on the *Divine Names*: *Dei magnitudo est esse Eius.*[67] In the *Summa*, Aquinas graphically expresses the greatness of divine Being in an image borrowed from Damascene: God, who is most properly named as *Qui est*, is as the infinite ocean of substance (*pelagus substantiae infinitum*).[68] This is reminiscent of Gregory: πέλαγος οὐσίας ἄπειρον καὶ ἀόριστον[69] and is close to Dionysius' phrase in the *Celestial Hierarchy*: θεαρχικοῦ φωτὸς ἄπειρόν τε καὶ ἄφθονον πέλαγος.[70] Pera suggests that these writers are perhaps inspired by a common source.[71]

It is only as the subsistent essence of actual Being that God can cause the things which are. That which *has* being cannot be the self-

---

[65] *ST*, I, 7, 1. See I, 7, 1, ad 3: Esse Dei est per se subsistens non receptum in aliquo, prout dicitur infinitum, distinguitur ab omnibus aliis, et alia removentur ab eo. Sicut si esset albedo subsistens, ex hoc ipso, quod non esset in alio, differret ab omni albedine existente in subjecto. *In de Caus.* IV, 109: Si autem aliquid sic haberet infinitam virtutem essendi quod non participaret esse ab alio, tunc esset solum infinitum et tale est Deus.

[66] *ST*, I, 9, 1.

[67] IX, i, 808.

[68] *ST*, I, 13, 11.

[69] *Oratio 2a de Pascha*, cited by Pera, p. 239.

[70] *CH* IX, 3; ed. Heil, p. 135.

[71] See Plato, *Symposium*, 210D: τὸ πολὺ πέλαγος . . . τοῦ καλοῦ.

sufficient principle or source of its own reality, but can receive it only from what is in itself the essence and fullness of Being. The *manner* of God's causation is for Aquinas the clearest index of his transcendent power and nature. In this context there is a profound truth in the Neoplatonist tenet that the cause cannot be of the same nature as its effect: it is not what is caused which reveals the transcendence of its source but rather the mode of causation. In Question 65 of the *Summa*, St Thomas clarifies this fundamental distinction:

> The quantity of power (*quantitas virtutis*) of a cause is measured not only according to the thing produced but also according to the mode of production, since one and the same thing is effected differently by a greater and lesser power. But to produce something finite in such a way that nothing is presupposed belongs to an infinite power and is therefore impossible for any creature.[72]

Finite being of itself, considered simply as *what* it is, does not reveal the absolute power and greatness of God. The infinity of God's power and his transcendence as absolute subsistent Being is thus most forcefully expressed by Aquinas with respect to creation, the radical causation of things in their existence without the presupposition of any prior material cause.

While existence is what is most fundamental in each thing, it is beyond the power of the existing thing itself and can therefore only be received: *Nulla res habet potestatem supra suum esse.*[73] There obtains a total incommensurability between the power which lies within the range of finite beings and the *virtus essendi* which is their origin and source. The resources over which the individual being has dominion are themselves merely potential *vis-à-vis* existence. This is all the more evident, Aquinas points out, in the case of contingent or corruptible beings, i.e. those which can be and not be; they are related equally to two contraries, namely to being and non-being. It must be through a superior cause, therefore, that being accrues to them.[74] Now Aquinas declares that absolute non-being is infinitely distant from being. Non-being is more removed from an existing being than any two particular

---

[72] *ST*, I, 65, 3 ad 3: Quantitas virtutis agentis non solum mensuratur secundum rem factam, sed etiam secundum modum faciendi: quia unum et idem aliter fit et a maiori, et a minori virtute. Producere autem aliquid finitum hoc modo ut nihil praesupponatur, est virtutis infinitae. Unde nulli creaturae competere potest.

[73] *De Potentia* 6, 7, ad 4.

[74] *Contra Gentiles* 1, 15, 124: Videmus in mundo quaedam quae sunt possibilia esse et non esse, scilicet generabilia et corruptibilia. Omne autem quod est possibile esse, causam habet: quia, cum de se aequaliter se habet ad duo, scilicet esse et non esse, oportet, si ei approprietur esse, quod hoc sit ex aliqua causa.

beings from each other, however distant these may be,[75] so that only an infinite power can cause something to come into existence out of complete non-being,[76] since an infinite power is required to cause something at an infinite distance.[77] Whereas a finite cause may educe a thing from potentiality to act, only an infinite cause can make something radically come to be. Aquinas declares that of themselves created things are indeed closer to non-existence than to being.[78] Creation, therefore, which is precisely the causing and sustaining of beings outside of non-being, requires an infinite power; there is no greater power than that of creation since there is no greater distance than between being and non-being: 'Finite being is infinitely removed from absolute non-being and requires an infinite active power.'[79]

We find in Question 65 of the *Prima Pars*[80] an outline of Aquinas' view on the existential and created status of prime matter which is significant for an evaluation of Dionysius' position which, he believes, refers to non-being. Being, according to Aquinas, is primary in creatures and immediate in the process of creation. Matter is, therefore, radically dependent in its existence and falls, thus, within the immediate and universal reign of creative Being. Aquinas again rejects the view that things are caused by proceeding only gradually (*gradatim*) from God through the intermediate agency of a descending series of secondary

---

[75] In terms of the positive source of being, this distance expresses the divine transcendence: Deus plus distat a creaturis, quam quaecumque creaturae ab invicem.

[76] *De Potentia* 3, 4: Non esse autem simpliciter, in infinitum ab esse distat, quod ex hoc patet, quia a quolibet ente determinato plus distat non esse quam quodlibet ens, quantumcumque ab alio ente distans invenitur; et ideo ex omnino non ente aliquid facere non potest esse nisi potentiae infinitae.

[77] *De Potentia* 3, 4, *Sed Contra*: Ens et non ens in infinitum distant. Sed operari aliquid ex distantia infinita est infinitae virtutis. Ergo creare est infinitae virtutis.

[78] *In II Sent.* 1, 1, 2: In re quae creari dicitur, prius sit non esse quam esse: non quidem prioritate temporis vel durationis, ut prius non fuerit et postmodum sit; sed prioritate naturae, ita quod res creata si sibi relinquatur, consequatur non esse, cum esse non habeat nisi ex influentia causae superioris . . . res creata naturaliter prius habet non esse quam esse.

[79] *De Potentia* 3, 4 ad 2: Distantia autem entis finiti a non esse simpliciter est infinita . . . et requirit . . . potentiam infinitam agentem.

[80] *ST*, I, 65, 3: Respondeo dicendum quod quidam posuerunt gradatim res a Deo processisse: ita scilicet quod ab eo immediate processit prima creatura, et illa produxit aliam; et sic inde usque ad creaturam corpoream. Sed haec positio est impossibilis. Quia prima corporalis creaturae productio est per creationem per quam etiam ipsa materia producitur: imperfectum enim est prius quam perfectum in fieri. Impossibile est autem aliquid creari nisi a solo Deo. Ad cuius evidentiam, considerandum est quod quanto aliqua causa est superior, tanto ad plura se extendit in causando. Semper autem id quod substernitur in rebus, invenitur communius quam id quod informat et restringit ipsum: sicut esse quam vivere, et vivere quam intelligere, et materia quam forma. Quanto ergo aliquid est magis substratum, tanto a superiori causa directe procedit. Id ergo quod est primo substratum in omnibus, proprie pertinet ad causalitatem supremae causae.

causes. According to this view, God immediately causes only the first creature, which in turn produces a second, and so on until matter is finally produced.[81] According to St Thomas, this is impossible. In the process of generation or becoming (taken here from the viewpoint of the acquisition of determination in the effect as caused), the less perfect must precede what is more perfect. Rather than proceeding or deriving from what is above it on the scale of beings, it is presupposed as a requisite in the very constitution of what is superior. And since it underlies and is required by all determinations in the material world, matter must be caused immediately by God. Aquinas could not accept, therefore, the view that matter should lie outside the scope and power of transcendent Being.

From the point of view of causation this primacy can be expressed alternatively as follows: the more universal an effect the more comprehensive and supreme must be its cause (*quanto aliqua causa est superior, tanto ad plura se extendit in causando*).[82] But what is laid down as substrate, so to speak, is more universal than what informs and restricts it; thus *esse* is more universal than life, life more universal than intellect and matter more universal than form. The more something acts as a foundation or substrate, the more directly it proceeds from its superior cause. And that which is the first and fundamental substrate of all things belongs properly to the causality of the primary universal cause. Matter, therefore, must be created immediately by God because it is the foundation needed for all subsequent material determination.[83] Much more so, must *esse* be seen as proceeding immediately and universally from God since, although fully indeterminate, it transcends and precedes each division and determination of reality while yet embracing them all.

There is a parallel between the universality of being—regarded in its extensive sense as receptive of further determination through superior perfections such as life or intelligence—and matter, which, as pure potency in need of form, is most general and indeterminate in the corporeal world. Each (if one may allow their separation for the sake

---

[81] See *ST*, I, 47, 1 and *De Potentia* 3, 4. Aquinas has Avicenna, Algazel, his Averroist opponent Siger of Brabant, and the writer of *De Causis* in mind.

[82] See also *ST*, I, 45, 5: Oportet enim universaliores effectus in universaliores et priores causas reducere. Inter omnes autem effectus universalissimum est ipsum esse. Unde oportet quod sit proprius effectus primae et universalissimae causae, quae est Deus.

[83] See *In II Sent.*, 1, 1, 1: Quamvis deus nullo modo sit materia, nihilominus tamen ipsum esse, quod materia habet imperfectum, prout dicitur ens in potentia, habet a deo, et reducitur in ipsum sicut in principium. *Contra Gentiles* 2, 22, 986: Cum ipse sit causa materiae, quae non possibilis est causari nisi per creationem. Ipse etiam in agendo non requirit materiam: cum, nullo praeexistente, rem in esse producat.

of reflection) depends directly on the transcendent and creative cause of Being. The difference is that all determinations of being emerge from within—since none is extraneous—while every enrichment and determination is superadded to matter from without. 'Being' is understood by Aquinas' in *ST*, I, 65, 3, not according to its intensive meaning as the pregnant plenitude or superabundance of all existential richness, but as *existentia*, the basic presence of reality to which all further perfection is added—although these are already implicit within its signification.[84]

In the universal causation of reality, and in the material world firstly of prime matter, God's transcendence is one of Being. Recasting Dionysius' formulation of the transcendence of the Good, namely its dominion over being and non-being, we can say that for Aquinas divine Being is absolutely supreme since it reigns over the infinite divide between total non-being and the actuality of existence. God causes creatures radically to emerge out of absolute nothingness, to traverse the abyss which separates reality from non-being, a distance which for finite beings themselves is incommensurable and intransgressible. God causes things to be, summoning them into existence out of pure non-being, *de puro non-esse*,[85] but cannot himself be made by anyone.[86] He subsists supreme in an absolute reign over the absence and presence of being, willing things into existence through his goodness which as origin and end is identical with his Being. God is absolutely transcendent because he is subsistent and creative Being; he conquers non-being, commands being at its very origin and constitutes in himself the end of all existence.

It is only from the perspective of creation that the proper meaning of non-being may be clearly appraised. It is the void to which the power of creation does not extend. It is God's creative power alone which ceaselessly and continuously overcomes the endless distance from absolute nothingness to existence. As subsistent Being he may confer being, and as essential Goodness he wills to do so. Early in the *Summa*, Aquinas portrays admirably how the divine will reigns over the fathomless chasm between non-being and being:

> Before creatures existed their existence was possible not because of any created potentiality . . . but simply because God had the power to bring them into existence. Now just as bringing things into existence depends on God's will, so also preserving them in existence. For he preserves them in existence only by perpetually giving existence to them, and were he therefore to

---

[84] See the note to Q. 65 in *adnotationes ad primam partem*, Marietti ed., p. 579.

[85] *De Potentia* 3, 4, ad 14.

[86] *De Potentia* 3, 4, ad 15.

withdraw his activity from them, all things ... would fall back into
nothingness. So just as before things existed on their own it was in the
creator's power for them to exist, so now that they do exist on their own it
is in the creator's power for them not to exist ... God was able to bring
them into existence out of nothing, and is able to reduce them again from
existence to nothingness.[87]

To the ultimate reason for creation, namely the diffusion of being
through divine goodness, we now turn.

---

[87] *ST*, I, 9, 2; trans. Blackfriars edition.

PART FOUR

CREATIVE DIFFUSION OF THE GOOD

CHAPTER EIGHT

PSEUDO-DIONYSIUS: THE CYCLE OF CREATION

Dionysius employs the classic Neoplatonic triadic scheme μονή, πρόοδος, ἐπιστροφή to express God as the origin of all things; their procession forth and their return to him. God is the ἀρχή or origin of all beings, embracing them prior to their existence in a transcendent unity and fullness. Through his goodness he causes creatures to proceed forth by way of emanation and establishes them in being. He remains their abiding support, and calls all things to reunion with himself. This universal panorama and cyclic scheme becomes in turn the organic and architectonic structure of Aquinas' vision of God and the world. In what remains, I wish to consider briefly this order of emanation and return as espoused by Dionysius and appropriated by Aquinas. A complete treatment of the many related themes would require a much lengthier investigation and is beyond our present scope. Our intention is to indicate some of the remaining themes in Dionysius' integral metaphysics which form part of the Neoplatonist heritage of St Thomas.

Dionysius repeatedly affirms God's causality of every aspect of the world. As efficient cause, he freely causes all things through his superabundant goodness while remaining himself transcendent to his effects. As exemplary source he contains in a unified manner all of the diverse perfections manifest in creation. And as final cause he imbues all things with a latent native desire to return to him as their ultimate goal. As universal and comprehensive cause, God is praised with the names both of Goodness and Beauty.

> The Beautiful is origin (ἀρχή) of all things as their productive cause (ὡς ποιητικὸν αἴτιον) which moves the whole, embracing it through a love for its own beauty. It is the goal of all things and is loved as final cause (τελικὸν αἴτιον) since all things come to be for the sake of the beautiful; and it is the exemplary cause (παραδειγματικόν) according to which all things are determined . . . Therefore the Beautiful is the same as the Good because all things seek the Beautiful and the Good with respect to every cause, and there is no being which does not participate in the Beautiful and the Good.[1]

---

[1] 4, 7, 140-1; see 1, 7, 26; 4, 4, 121.

Dionysius expressly states: 'Because of him and through him and in him are all exemplary, final, efficient, formal and material (elemental) causes (καὶ ἐν αὐτῷ πᾶσα ἀρχὴ παραδειγματικὴ τελικὴ ποιητικὴ εἰδικὴ στοιχειώδης).' God is the origin (ἀρχή), coherence (συνοχή) and end (πέρας) of all.[2]

In accordance with the method which he has adopted, already in Chapter 2 of the *Divine Names*, Dionysius cites Scripture in support of God's universal and creative causality.[3] However, he formulates his philosophic exposition of divine causality in the categories of the Neoplatonist tradition. Indeed there is concurrence in the Christian and Platonist traditions on the most profound reason for creation; things exist because God is good: *Quia bonus est*. God is wholly and entirely perfect; he enjoys in an infinite manner all the riches which are in any way possible. As exhaustively and exclusively good in himself, he is the proper and adequate goal of his own love. God loves himself: this is the highest act of divine goodness. Fully sufficient in himself he is in need of nothing, but loving his own goodness he wishes it to be enjoyed also by others. Out of love, therefore, for himself and for others, God calls creatures into a communion of love with himself. For God, to love something is to cause it to exist.[4] Thus we find again the Platonist doctrine of God's unenvious but zealous goodness as foundation of creation. God's goodness overflows in a superabundant gift of his own perfection which causes things radically to come into being. Not enclosed within his own transcendence, God communicates with creatures in a total act of liberality and creative largesse, with a generosity which is generative of all things. Dionysius expresses this in the following passage which summarises the total causality of God as origin, cause, support and end of all:

> The cause of all things through an excess of goodness loves all things, produces all things, perfects all things, contains and turns all things toward himself; divine love is good through the goodness of the Good. Indeed love itself which produces the goodness of beings, pre-subsisting super-abundantly

---

[2] 4, 10, 154-5; see no. 153. Cf. Aquinas, *ST*, I, 44, 4 ad 4: Cum Deus sit causa efficiens, exemplaris et finalis omnium rerum, et materia prima sit ab ipso, sequitur quod primum principium omnium rerum sit unum tantum secundum rem. As Sheldon-Williams points out, the triad μονή, πρόοδος and ἐπιστροφή (triad of motion or rest) was also formulated: οὐσία, δύναμις, ἐνέργεια (triad of action or inaction). The latter was preferred by Christians after Dionysius, since it more clearly favoured creation (God acting freely) rather than an automatic process of emanation. (I. P. Sheldon-Williams, *The Cambridge History of Later Greek and Early Medieval Philosophy*, pp. 430-1).

[3] 2, 1, 32: τὰ πάντα ἐκ τοῦ θεοῦ.

[4] See *CH*, 4, 1, 177C; *Ep.* 8, 1085C.

in the Good, did not allow itself to remain unproductive but moved itself to produce in the super-abundant generation of all.[5]

Dionysius summarises this again when he declares: 'Divine love is ecstatic' (ἔστι δὲ καὶ ἐκστατικὸς ὁ θεῖος ἔρως).[6] God's love as creative is an 'outgoing' love, which Dionysius describes in the following manner:

> The cause itself of all beings, because of his beautiful and good love for all, in an excess of loving goodness goes out of himself (ἔξω ἑαυτοῦ γίνεται) in his providence for all beings; charmed, as it were, by goodness, affection and love he is drawn from his transcendence and separation above all into all beings by an ecstatic power beyond being, without departing from himself.[7]

The Good alone can cause what is good and can only cause that which is good.[8] 'It is the nature of the Good to produce and preserve',[9] just as it is the nature of fire to warm rather than chill. Moreover what is deprived of the Good cannot exist.[10] Existence is the first gift which pours forth from the abundance of transcendent Goodness.[11] God himself is perfect since he can be neither increased or diminished but pre-contains all things in advance within himself and overflows in a unique, unceasing, inexhaustible plenitude, filling all things with his own perfection.[12] God causes beings because he is entirely free of envy (ἄφθονος); and pre-containing all things according to a transcendent power he gives existence to all in a generous outpouring through an exceeding abundance of power.[13]

Divine causation is most frequently portrayed by Neoplatonism as a process of emanation. The being and perfection of creatures is an outpouring of God's superabundant goodness: an effusion (χύσις),[14] overflowing (ὑπερβλύζειν) or 'bubbling over',[15] outflowing or gushing

---

[5] 4, 10, 159.
[6] 4, 13, 168.
[7] 4, 13, 171. In a detailed study, C. J. De Vogel has pointed out the significance of Dionysius' innovation in attributing Love to God himself, the Cause of all things and giving to divine Love a central place in his theology. Cornelia J de Vogel. 'Amor quo caelum regitur', p. 31. Also 'Greek Cosmic Love and the Christian Love of God', p. 71.
[8] 4, 23, 214: τὸ γὰρ ἀγαθὸν ἀγαθὰ παράγει καὶ ὑφίστησι.
[9] 4, 19, 188: φύσις γὰρ τῷ ἀγαθῷ τὸ παράγειν καὶ σώζειν.
[10] 4, 23, 214: τὸ γὰρ πάντῃ ἄμοιρον τοῦ ἀγαθοῦ, οὔτε ἐν τοῖς οὖσι ἔσται. See 4, 20, 201-4; 4, 30, 237; 4, 30, 241; 4, 31, 242-3.
[11] 5, 8, 267; 6, 2, 289.
[12] 13, 1, 438.
[13] 8, 6, 343: ὑπερέχοντα καὶ προέχοντα πάντα τὰ ὄντα κατὰ δύναμιν ὑπερούσιον καὶ πᾶσι τοῖς οὖσι τὸ δύνασθαι εἶναι καὶ τόδε εἶναι κατὰ περιουσίαν ὑπερβαλλούσης δυνάμεως ἀφθόνῳ χύσει δεδωρημένον.
[14] 9, 2, 361.
[15] 9, 2, 361; 11, 2, 413.

forth (ἐκβλύζειν).[16] Creatures have their origin in the divine as a stream in its source. The image of a source (πηγή), fountain or stream serves to emphasise the autonomy and transcendence of God. He is the origin of the gifts in which all participate in an infinite bounty but which remain nevertheless unchanged, retaining the same abundance; they are undiminished by participation but overflow all the more.[17] God is as the transcendent source of beauty which through excess embraces all beauty within itself (ὡς παντὸς καλοῦ τὴν πηγαίαν καλλονὴν ὑπεροχικῶς ἐν ἑαυτῷ προέχον),[18] emitting things into their existence and calling them to complete fulfilment through final return to their source.

Other metaphors of diffusion refer to the expansive and emissive character of light, heat and smell. Sensible odours are for Dionysius the images of an intelligible transmission and diffusion.[19] Creatures radiate from God also as from an inexhaustible fire which remains 'undiminished in all its happy giving of itself'.[20] Divine causation is most suitably compared with the donation of light (φωτοδοσία)[21] or water; Dionysius even combines the diffusion of light and the abundant effusion from a source in the impressive image of God as a boundless ocean of light which generously bestows its gifts on all.[22]

The diffusive character of the Good is succinctly stated by Dionysius in the opening lines of Chapter 4: 'The Good, as the substantial essence of Good, through its very being extends its goodness to all beings.'[23] Dionysius uses the traditional image of the sun's radiation of light to illustrate the natural diffusion of the absolute Good. 'For as our sun neither through choice nor deliberation but by its own very being (ἀλλ' αὐτῷ τῷ εἶναι) illumines all things which are able to receive its light according to their own power of participation, so also the Good ... by its own subsistence sends forth to all beings in their own measure the rays of its total goodness.'[24] The diffusion of the sun has the attendant

---

[16] CH, 4, 1, 177C.

[17] 9, 2, 361; see EH, I, 3, 373C.

[18] 4, 7, 138.

[19] CH, 1, 3, 121D; see 332A.

[20] CH, 15, 2, 329C: ἀμείωτον ἐν πάσαις ταῖς πανολβίαις ἑαυτοῦ μεταδόσεσι.

[21] CH, 1, 2, 121B.

[22] CH, 9, 3, 261: μετάδοσιν ἀναπεπταμένον τοῦ θεαρχικοῦ φωτὸς ἄπειρόν τε καὶ ἄφθονον πέλαγος.

[23] 4, 1, 95: τῷ εἶναι ἀγαθὸν ὡς οὐσιῶδες ἀγαθὸν εἰς πάντα τὰ ὄντα διατείνει τὴν ἀγαθότητα.

[24] 4, 1, 96: καὶ γὰρ ὥσπερ ὁ καθ' ἡμᾶς ἥλιος, οὐ λογιζόμενος ἢ προαιρούμενος, ἀλλ' αὐτῷ τῷ εἶναι φωτίζει πάντα τὰ μετέχειν τοῦ φωτὸς αὐτοῦ κατὰ τὸν οἰκεῖον δυνάμενα λόγον, οὕτω δὴ καὶ τἀγαθόν, ὑπὲρ ἥλιον, ὡς ὑπὲρ ἀμυδρὰν εἰκόνα τὸ ἐξηρημένως ἀρχέτυπον, αὐτῇ τῇ ὑπάρξει, πᾶσι τοῖς οὖσιν ἀναλόγως ἐφίησι τὰς τῆς ὅλης ἀγαθότητος ἀκτῖνας. The source for the image of the sun is Proclus, Elements, 122.

limitations of an analogy which nevertheless succeeds in conveying a certain truth regarding the reality of the Good. The opening lines of Chapter 4 have been interpreted in the pantheistic sense that God does not will creation but is of his very nature required by necessity to bestow his goodness and communicate himself to creatures. The question whether divine diffusion is necessary or freely chosen is critical for the meaning of pagan Neoplatonism as received by Christian writers. One of the most disputed questions in Dionysius' thought concerns the relation of God to creatures. Is divine causation necessary or free? Is divine being in some manner identical with that of his effects? Is Dionysius a pantheist? A determinist interpretation may indeed be given to this passage but this may reflect a lack of precision in Dionysius' language rather than his real intentions. He wishes to show that as it is natural for the sun, as the very essence of light and luminosity, to diffuse itself and illumine the natural world, so it is natural and proper to God as subsistent goodness to diffuse and share his perfection.

Stiglmayr argues that the terminology employed by Dionysius clearly rejects any suggestion of pantheism or emanationism.[25] It is true that Dionysius uses the technical term for creation (κτίσις) only in his citation of Scripture.[26] However, he safeguards the transcendence and freedom of God's diffusion by declaring that God, who is beyond being, bestows existence on all things as a gift (ὄν ἐστιν ὁ θεὸς ὑπερουσίως δωρεῖται δὲ τὸ εἶναι τοῖς οὖσι καὶ παράγει τὰς ὅλας

---

[25] Josef Stiglmayr, *Des heiligen Dionysius Areopagita angebliche Schriften uber 'Göttliche Namen'*, p. 23, n. 1; Pantheism and emanationism are attributed to Dionysius by E. Falip, who praises Aquinas for escaping from such errors. *Influence de Denys l'aréopagite dans saint Thomas d'Aquin*, Thèse de doctorat presenté en 1904 à l'Institut Catholique de Toulouse, pp. 57-61. I am grateful to Professor Godefroid Geenen of the Angelicum, Rome, for granting me access to the manuscript copy of this thesis.

[26] 4, 4, 124: τὰ ἀόρατα τοῦ θεοῦ ἀπὸ κτίσεως κόσμου τοῖς ποιήμασι νοούμενα καθορᾶται ἥ τε ἀΐδιος αὐτοῦ δύναμις καὶ θειότης (Rom. I, 20). Faucon would seem to be incorrect on this point when he writes: 'La réduction de la synthèse thomiste aux systèmes qui l'ont préparée serait d'autant plus injustifiée qu'elle confère une importance capitale à la notion de création dont on ne trouve nulle trace ni chez Aristote, ni chez Denys... Le *Livre des Noms divins* ne fait pas état de la notion biblique de création.' More relevant is the remark: 'Faute de connaître la révélation biblique, Aristote ignore purement et simplement la question de l'origine radicale du monde.' There is no hesitation in the mind of Aquinas that Dionysius holds a theory of creation. Faucon himself remarks: 'Mais il est remarquable qu'au moment où Denys fait allusion à la fonction démiurgique du Bien divin dans son rapport à l'être Thomas d'Aquin introduise la notion de création: "... Deus, secundum suam super-eminentem virtutem, est causa substantificatrix omnium substantiarum, et creatrix omnium existentium, quia scilicet non producit substantias ex aliquo prae-existente, sed simpliciter omne existens ex virtute Ipsius provenit"' (*In DN*, V, i, 624). Faucon is correct in so far as Dionysius, as we have seen, has no profound appreciation of the radical signification of nothingness, which he identifies with matter. See Pierre Faucon, *Aspects néoplatoniciens de la doctrine de saint Thomas d'Aquin*, p. 475.

οὐσίας),²⁷ 'leading them into being' (εἰς οὐσίαν ἄγων,²⁸ πρὸς τὸ εἶναι παραγαγών).²⁹ As their single cause he 'imparts' existence to things,³⁰ 'radiating' being to them in an undefiled manner as unique and transcendent cause.³¹ He produces beings in a 'going-out' of existence: καὶ οὐσίας παράγει, κατὰ τὴν ἀπὸ οὐσίας ἔκβασιν.³²

Are not emanation and return both terms which signify movement? Dionysius himself asks how the unmoved one can 'proceed forth to all things and move.'³³ Earlier in our study we observed how Dionysius compares the distinct modes of cognition with the various kinds of motion—direct, spiral and circular. Now, according to Dionysius, these can also symbolise the different aspects of divine causality. Strictly speaking we must of course affirm that God neither moves nor is changed in any way: 'Unchanged and unmoved with respect to every movement he abides within himself in his eternal motion.'³⁴ Nevertheless, he brings all things into existence, supporting and wholly providing for them; he is present to all, extending to all his providential emanations and energies. Motion must, therefore, be predicated of God in a manner appropriate to divine nature. Direct or straight movement is taken, therefore, by Dionysius to signify the unchanging nature of God, the unswerving emanation of his energies and the generation of all things from himself.³⁵ ('Extension' also, when referred to God—πλάτος θεῖον— symbolises the divine emanation to all things.)³⁶ Spiral movement symbolises the steadfast procession of creatures from God and God's fruitful stability. Circular motion symbolises his identity, the union of middle and end and the return to God of what has proceeded from him.³⁷

Elsewhere Dionysius likens God's ecstatic love to an eternal circle which continually revolves because of the Good, from the Good, in the Good and to the Good in an unchanging circulation, forever proceeding from and abiding in and returning to itself.³⁸ God's love is a 'shining forth (ἔκφανσις) of himself through himself and a good emanation of his transcendent unity, a loving movement, simple, self-moved, self-

²⁷ 2, 11, 73.
²⁸ 7, 2, 315.
²⁹ CH, 13, 4, 308A; Also 4, 117B.
³⁰ 7, 2, 317: κατὰ μίαν αἰτίαν ὁ θεὸς πᾶσι τοῖς οὖσι τοῦ εἶναι μεταδίδωσι.
³¹ V, 8, 280: πᾶσι τὸ εἶναι κατὰ μίαν καὶ ὑπερηνωμένην αἰτίαν ἀχράντως ἐπιλάμπων.
³² V, 8, 281.
³³ 9, 9, 379.
³⁴ 10, 2, 389: . . . ἐν τῷ ἀεὶ κινεῖσθαι μένοντα ἐφ' ἑαυτοῦ.
³⁵ 9, 9, 379.
³⁶ 9, 5, 371.
³⁷ 9, 9, 380.
³⁸ 4, 14, 178.

active, pre-subsisting in the Good, flowing forth from the Good to beings and again returning to the Good.'[39] God causes all things through love, leading them into being, stirring within them a zealous and loving desire for himself, and moves them to return to him.[40] Every being proceeds from God as its fundamental origin and turns back to him for final fulfilment. In the words of Ecclesiastes, which Albert the Great borrows to express the universal movement of issue and return in all creation: *Ad locum, unde exeunt, flumina revertentur, ut iterum fluant.*[41]

The very mystery of creation—which may be concluded but remains uncomprehended—is that God, who is supremely transcendent to all things, is nevertheless intimately and universally present within each. Transcendence and immanence of the unique divine cause are the fundamental hallmarks of all Neoplatonist philosophy. God's intimacy is depicted by Dionysius as follows: leading all things into being through his creative emanation he pervades all and fills them with his own being (διὰ πάντων φοιτῶσα καὶ πάντα ἐξ ἑαυτῆς τοῦ εἶναι πληροῦσα), rejoicing in all beings.[42] Dionysius sums up the intense presence yet ontological transcendence of the divine Good: 'The being of all things is the divinity beyond being' (τὸ γὰρ εἶναι πάντων ἐστὶν ἡ ὑπὲρ τὸ εἶναι θεότης).[43] This formulation is not beyond the peril of a pantheist interpretation; out of his plenitude God leads beings into existence, filling them with his being. He is the Being of all things: how can determinism and pantheism possibly be avoided? Dionysius is attempting in fact to combine both poles of the creative relation, a relation which constitutes totally the reality of the creature but which enters in no way into the divine which transcends all relations whatsoever. God is not divine because he creates; he creates because he is divine; he is known to be divine through his creation but his nature remains undisclosed.

This is not simply a paradox but is the profound mystery of creation; it is its very meaning. Unaffected in himself, God gives reality to creatures through a relation which in no way influences his own nature but which causes creatures radically and totally, exclusively and exhaustively. Without creation God remains infinitely divine; without God beings do not exist. From the perspective of creatures God is 'all things in all', from that of his divine nature he is 'nothing in any of

---

[39] 4, 14, 178.
[40] 4, 13, 172.
[41] Eccl. I, 7; See Albertus Magnus, *Opera*, Vol. XIV, p. 1.
[42] 5, 9, 284.
[43] *CH*, 4, 1, 177D.

them' (καὶ ἐν πᾶσι πάντα ἐστὶ καὶ ἐν οὐδενὶ οὐδέν).[44] 'Pervading all things, God is undefiled but supra-ontologically transcendent to all.'[45] Beings flow forth from God but abide and return within his power; God goes forth into all things, while remaining within himself (καὶ ἐπὶ πάντα προϊὼν καὶ μένων ἐφ᾽ ἑαυτοῦ).[46] God's supreme unity and simplicity, Dionysius emphasises, are unaffected by the emanation of creatures. Indeed only as the One can God impart existence to creatures.[47] All beings are attributed to him in a unique all-transcendent unity.[48] God is the transcendent One; his unity precedes all multiplicity proceeding from him as source.

Dionysius' theory of the issue of the created multiplicity from the divine unity is contained in his notion of 'Distinctions'. God reveals himself in what Dionysius terms 'Divine Distinctions'; the term is synonymous with 'procession' or 'manifestation'.[49] They are the 'beneficent processions of the divine union which in a transcendent unity abounds and multiplies through its goodness.'[50] Distinction, however, is not division. The gifts which flow from God through this creative distinction are undivided in their outpouring. Being, Life, Wisdom and the others remain identical in God. Their distinction through creatures does not entail division at their source, no less than it does a diminution of their transcendent and absolute plenitude.

> We called the beneficent emanation of the divinity 'Divine Distinction' (διάκρισιν θείαν); for bestowing itself upon all beings and pouring forth to them a participation of all its goods, it is distinguished in a unified manner (is unified even in its distinction), increases while remaining single and multiplies without proceeding from the One. Moreover, since God is Being in a supra-ontological manner (ἐπειδὴ ὤν ἐστι ὁ θεὸς ὑπερουσίως) and gives being to all beings, producing all substances, his unique Being is said to be multiplied through the production of many beings out of himself. He remains nonetheless One in his multiplication, unified in his procession and full in his distinction through his supra-ontological transcendence beyond all beings, through the unitive production of all and the unreduced profusion (χύσει) of his undiminished gifts.[51]

---

[44] 7, 3, 322.

[45] 2, 10, 65.

[46] 5, 10, 284.

[47] 7, 2, 317: κατὰ μίαν αἰτίαν ὁ θεὸς πᾶσι τοῖς οὖσι τοῦ εἶναι μεταδίδωσι.

[48] 5, 9, 284: πάντα οὖν αὐτῇ τὰ ὄντα κατὰ μίαν τὴν πάντων ἐξηρημένην ἕνωσιν ἀναθετέον.

[49] 2, 4, 40: τὰς διακρίσεις δὲ τὰς ἀγαθοπρεπεῖς τῆς θεαρχίας προόδους τε καὶ ἐκφάνσεις.

[50] 2, 5, 49.

[51] 2, 11, 72-3.

These διακρίσεις, also called δύναμεις, are the different perfections which proceed from God, as his primary participations in which all things partake—in the first place Being, Life and Wisdom. They are 'expresssions of divine providence' (προνοίαι ἐκφαντόρικαι),[52] affirmed of God by positive theology. Distinctions, emanations or powers which proceed into creatures are contained in advance according to a unified manner in God. They are the exemplars, paradigms or model ideas. God is the universal exemplar of all things. He is their transcendent archetype (τὸ ἐξῃρημένως ἀρχέτυπον),[53] embracing by anticipation according to a union beyond being the models of all substances (τῶν ὄντων παραδείγματα κατὰ μίαν ὑπερούσιον ἕνωσιν).[54] As absolute or transcendent Good and Beauty, God is the universal model according to which all things are determined and defined (παραδειγματικὸν αἴτιον ὅτι κατ' αὐτὸ πάντα ἀφορίζεται).[55] Dionysius presents a clear and succinct statement of divine exemplarity, explaining the nature of the divine ideas:

What we call paradigms are those reasons (λόγοι), which, pre-existing in God as a unity, produce the substance of beings (οὐσιοποιούς); theology calls them predeterminations: the divine and good volitions defining and producing beings, according to which the transcendent (cause) beyond being (ὁ ὑπερούσιος) predetermined and produced all being.[56]

For Dionysius, creatures are, therefore, images or likenesses of the original divine models: εἰκόνας καὶ ὁμοιώματα τῶν θείων ... παραδειγμάτων.[57] The 'paradeigmata' reside within creatures as their immanent λόγοι, leading the sensible and intelligible worlds back to their creator as the principles of their ἐπιστροφή. The forms proceed from the eternal first principle; they reside within their effects and lead them to be absorbed again in final union within their source. We have seen how Dionysius, in an advance beyond Platonism and Neoplatonism, unites all creative forms in the simplicity of the divine One. Within the unique divine simplicity resides a diversity of Forms which does not jeopardise its unity. God is the single and simple creator of all and contains in anticipation the creative perfections of all beings. It is through causation that a diversity proceeds from God, without, however, affecting his transcendent simplicity.

---

[52] 3, 1, 78.
[53] 4, 1, 96.
[54] 5, 8, 281.
[55] 4, 7, 140.
[56] 5, 8, 282.
[57] 7, 3, 321.

Dionysius employs a number of metaphors to illustrate the relation of the created multiplicity to the transcendent simplicity and unity of God. God is shared by all things equally, as the point of a circle by all its radii or a seal by each impression. Here is expressed likewise the unity present in the various distinctions or perfections proceeding from God. The seal, moreover, is participated as archetype by all impressions in full and not merely in part; any differences are due to the nature of the material which receives it and not to the seal which gives itself fully and equally to all. Thus, though all participate in the divine perfection, this is according to the measure of each.

These illustrations safeguard, moreover, the imparticipability (ἀμεθε-ξία) of the divinity who is cause of all, since it neither has contact nor mingles with its participants in its communion with them.[58] He is participated wholly by all participants but in such a manner that none has any part of him.[59] All that they are, is a share in his infinite richness, but he is in no manner received within creatures. Beings are fully participations in God but do not participate in his fullness. The being and essence of the creature is to be a participation in God; without this sharing they would cease to be. They share the perfection created by him in a manner which in no way diminishes his transcendence or enters as a real relation into his nature. God's essence and Being are not participated. This is the mystery of creation: creatures participate exclusively and exhaustively in the infinite causal perfection of God who is in no wise participated according to his essence. We have thus, in summary, the following triadic scheme: 1, God as he is in himself, in whom nothing participates and who participates in nothing (ἀμέθεκτος); 2, God as efficient cause who is participated by the effects into which he proceeds (μεθεκτός); 3, Creatures which through participation proceed from God, abide within themselves and return to God as final cause (μετέχων).[60]

---

[58] 2, 5, 52.

[59] 2, 5, 49.

[60] See Sheldon-Williams, *The Cambridge History of Later Greek and Early Medieval Philosophy*, p. 459. In the order of participation, Kern discerns the following schema: 1. God, 2. the paradigms reposing in him, 3, the λόγοι residing in the world, and 4, the world itself. (C. Kern. 'La structure du monde d'après le ps.-Denys', p. 209).

CHAPTER NINE

CREATIVE DIFFUSION IN AQUINAS

DIVINE GOOD AS ORIGIN OF CREATION

Cornelio Fabro remarks that while St Augustine presents Aquinas with a metaphysics *del Vero e del Verbo*, the Pseudo-Dionysius inspires him with a metaphysics *dell'Amore e del Bene*.[1] Despite the danger of the contrast, overstated for the sake of expression, this view points to a notable emphasis in Dionysius and a profoundly significant influence in Aquinas.[2] Under the inspiration of Dionysius, Aquinas presents within his philosophy a parallel to the sublime revelation '*Deus caritas est.*' According to both Dionysius and Aquinas, the ultimate key to the wonder of the world is the very mystery of the abounding love of God. The most fundamental and universal love of all is that with which God loves his own goodness.[3] Of necessity God loves his goodness[4] but communicates it freely to beings through creation. Divine love is the principle of the universe in its origin, its internal order and immanent dynamism, and its ultimate finality. In God alone is there fully perfect love; given, as it were, on loan by God and reflected throughout creation in the love which beings have for each other, it is returned through the native desire which all things have for total fulfilment.

The will, as Aquinas notes, tends naturally towards goodness. Now, in God alone are will and essence identical, since the good which is loved is wholly contained within the essence of him who wills. God wills nothing beyond himself except because of his goodness. God is himself the only proper object of his own love. To him, in its paramount

---

[1] Cornelio Fabro, *La nozione metafisica della partecipazione*, p. 88.

[2] Fabro declares indeed that the influence of Dionysius complements that of Augustine. (Ibid.) See also *Breve introduzione al tomismo*, p. 18. De Gandillac remarks on Aquinas: 'Or c'est Denys, tout autant qu'Augustin, qui lui sert d'autorité lorsqu'il corrige l'aristotélisme en substituant au Moteur impassible le Bien qui se diffuse par amour.' (*Oeuvres complètes du Pseudo-Denys l'aréopagite*, Introduction, p. 54).

[3] See X, i, 858; *Contra Gentiles* 4, 19, 3563.

[4] *ST*, I, 19, 3.

sense, can be applied Aquinas' principle: *ex hoc quod aliquid est unum secum, sequitur quod amat ipsum.*[5] Selfhood and identity are the universal roots of love. In the case of God, as plenary and subsistent being, there is no distinction between his powers and his essence. Divine will and intellect are identical with God's existence.[6] This does not signify that his nature is devoid of inner life or movement; his Being is the fullness of all actuality. There is within it an infinite and intimate exchange of love. His will has no limits and his infinite goodness alone is its adequate object. Now to will, explains Aquinas, is a kind of motion and it is by his own goodness that God's will is moved. God loves, therefore, through an immanent movement of his own which leads from himself to himself. It is God's own goodness which moves his will. God is himself, therefore, his own love, since the will with which he desires his own good is identical with his very being and substance. He is the essence of Love itself. There is in him identity between lover and beloved. The good he loves is none other than his own Being and the love with which he loves this good is the movement of his own will.[7] Whereas human will is moved by a good distinct from itself, the object of God's will is his own goodness, his very essence.[8]

The question which we wish to consider is why God, who is fully perfect in himself, calls into existence a universe of finite beings which cannot reciprocate the love which is their origin. Let us follow Aquinas' explanation of the origin of creation and its diversity. Although he is one in essence, in knowing his unity and power God knows all that exists virtually within himself, and knows that diverse things may proceed from him. He is capable of being imitated in an endless variety of ways. He knows himself as the infinite and universal exemplar of

---

[5] IV, xi, 449. See *ST*, I, 60, 4: Unumquodque diligit id quod est unum sibi.

[6] *ST*, I, 19, 1: . . . sicut suum intelligere est suum esse, ita et suum velle; *De Potentia* 3, 15, ad 20: Voluntas Dei est eius essentia.

[7] IV, xi, 444: Deus dicitur amor et amabilis quia Ipse amat motu sui ipsius . . . Deus est suus amor. See Etienne Gilson, *Spirit of Medieval Philosophy*, p. 275.

[8] *ST*, I, 19, 1 ad 3: Voluntas cuius obiectum principale est bonum quod est extra volentem oportet quod sit mota ab alio, sed obiectum divinae voluntatis est bonitas sua, quae est eius essentia; unde cum voluntas Dei sit eius essentia, non movetur ab alio a se, sed a se tantum, eo modo loquendi quo intelligere et velle dicitur motus. Et secundum hoc Plato dixit quod primum movens movet se ipsum. *Contra Gentiles* 4, 19, 3563: Quia proprium obiectum divinae voluntatis est eius bonitas, necesse est quod Deus primo et principaliter suam bonitatem et seipsum amet. Cum autem ostensum sit quod amatum necesse est aliqualiter esse in voluntate amantis; ipse autem Deus seipsum amat: necesse est quod ipse Deus sit in sua voluntate ut amatum in amante. Est autem amatum in amante secundum quod amatur; amare autem quoddam velle est: velle autem Dei est eius esse, sicut et voluntas eius est eius esse; esse igitur Dei in voluntate sua per modum amoris, non est esse accidentale, sicut in nobis, sed essentiale. Unde oportet quod Deus, secundum quod consideratur ut in sua voluntate existens, sit vere et substantialiter Deus.

endless participation, and loving and willing his own goodness loves the perfections which are pre-contained within himself. God does not wish, however, to produce in the natural world of existence all the things which he knows can proceed from him.[9] God does not necessarily will that all the things he loves within himself as possible participations should exist in reality. Only those which he wills to be, receive existence: *Si Deus aliquid vult, illud erit.*[10] Indeed Aquinas argues in the *Contra Gentiles* from the finite number of creatures which are in existence, to the freedom of the divine will in creation. God is infinitely participable, yet there is in existence a finite number of beings. If, however, God had willed by necessity all the participations which he loves within himself, there would exist an infinite number of beings, sharing his goodness in an infinity of ways, and in ways, moreover, different to those enjoyed by creatures now existing. God, therefore, must have freely willed the limited number of beings and modes of participation now in actual existence.[11] He cannot have been obliged to cause all or any of his possible participations. It is through a free choice of his will, therefore, that God desires through love to call into existence the universe of beings. The ultimate reason why God is free in creating is that he is himself the absolute perfection of Being. He can exist without other beings since they bring about no increase in his perfection. It is not absolutely necessary, therefore, for him to will them.[12] Furthermore, since he is not determined according to any limited mode of being, but contains within himself the total perfection of being (*totam perfectionem essendi*), he does not act by a necessity of his nature to cause any particular effect. In this he differs from beings which have a determinate being and a specific nature.[13]

---

[9] The things he knows can proceed from him are *rationes intellectae*; only those in whose imitation he wishes to create beings are exemplars proper. Cf. V, iii, 665: Deus enim, etsi sit in essentia sua unus, tamen intelligendo suam unitatem et virtutem, cognoscit quidquid in Eo virtualiter existit. Sic igitur cognoscit ex Ipso posse procedere res diversas; huiusmodi igitur quae cognoscit ex Se posse prodire rationes intellectae dicuntur. Non autem omnes huiusmodi rationes exemplaria dici possunt: exemplar enim est ad cuius imitationem fit aliud; non autem omnia quae scit Deus ex Ipso posse prodire, vult in rerum natura producere; illae igitur solae rationes intellectae a Deo exemplaria dici possunt, ad quarum imitationem vult res in esse producere, sicut producit artifex artificata ad imitationem formarum artis quas mente concepit, quae etiam artificialium exemplaria dici possunt.

[10] *Contra Gentiles* 1, 85, 716.

[11] *Contra Gentiles* 1, 81, 685: Cum autem divina bonitas sit infinita, est infinitis modis participabilis, et aliis modis quam ab his creaturis quae nunc sunt participetur. Si igitur, ex hoc quod vult bonitatem suam, vellet de necessitate ea quae ipsam participant, sequeretur quod vellet esse infinitas creaturas, infinitis modis participantes suam bonitatem. Quod patet esse falsum: quia si vellet, essent; cum sua voluntas sit principium essendi rebus. Non igitur ex necessitate vult etiam ea quae nunc sunt.

[12] *ST*, I, 19, 3: Unde cum bonitas Dei sit perfecta, et esse possit sine aliis, cum nihil ei perfectionis ex aliis accrescat; sequitur quod alia a se eum velle, non sit necessarium absolute.

[13] *ST*, I, 19, 4: Omne enim agens per naturam habet esse determinatum. Cum igitur

Given the freedom of the divine will, we have not as yet, however, asked why in fact God created the world. He is in no way required to call beings into existence since he is absolute in himself and in need of nothing. Can there indeed be any reason for creation? If the universe adds nothing to God's perfection is it not thus superfluous? Is it not absurd that God, who is himself total perfection and plenitude should act for an end from which, it seems, he has no gain? Aquinas would of course reject such a conclusion. It does not follow, he declares, that since God is fully content with his own goodness he may not will anything else. What indeed imposes itself as a conclusion is that whatever God wills, he can will only for the sake of his own goodness.[14] Nevertheless, while God necessarily loves his own goodness, he does not will by necessity the things which he desires on account of his goodness.[15] While it is for his own sake that he creates the universe, he is not necessitated to do so. That God loves his goodness is necessary, but it is not necessary that this love be communicated to creatures. Divine goodness is perfect without them. Aquinas therefore remarks thatalthough the production of beings in *esse* has its origin in the rational character of divine goodness, it depends entirely on the will of God.[16]

Because he wills himself to be, God likewise wills other things, which are ordered to him as to end.[17] That is not to say that God is obliged to will other things, but that the reason he wills them is for his own end. There is indeed a reason for creation, since God's action cannot be futile, but there is neither need nor cause[18] and the only sufficient reason for creation can be God's love for his own goodness.[19] 'Divine goodness precedes creation both as its end and primary motive.'[20]

---

esse divinum non sit determinatum, sed contineat in se totam perfectionem essendi, non potest esse quod agat per necessitatem naturae.

[14] *ST*, I, 19, 2 ad 3: Ex hoc quod voluntati divinae sufficit sua bonitas, non sequitur quod nihil aliud velit: sed quod nihil aliud vult nisi ratione suae bonitatis. *ST*, I, 19, 2 ad 2: Cum Deus alia a se non velit nisi propter finem qui est sua bonitas, non sequitur quod aliquid aliud moveat voluntatem eius nisi bonitas sua. Et sic, sicut alia a se intelligit intelligendo essentiam suam, ita alia a se vult, volendo bonitatem suam.

[15] *ST*, I, 19, 3 ad 2: Licet Deus ex necessitate velit bonitatem suam, non tamen ex necessitate vult ea quae vult propter bonitatem suam: quia bonitas eius potest esse sine aliis. *ST*, I, 19, 3: Voluntas enim divina necessarium habitudinem habet ad suam bonitatem, quae est proprium eius obiectum. Unde bonitatem suam esse Deus ex necessitate vult. *ST*, I, 19, 10: Deus suam bonitatem velit ex necessitate, alia vero non ex necessitate.

[16] *Contra Gentiles* 3, 97, 2735: Sic igitur quod Deus suam bonitatem amet, hoc necessarium est: sed hoc non necessario sequitur, quod per creaturas repraesentetur, cum sine hoc divina bonitas sit perfecta. Unde quod creaturae in esse producantur, etsi ex ratione divinae bonitatis originem habeat, tamen ex simplici Dei voluntate dependet.

[17] Cf. *Contra Gentiles* 7, 75.

[18] *ST*, I, 79 ad 5: Voluntas Dei rationabilis est, non quod aliquid sit Deo causa volendi, sed inquantum vult unum esse propter aliud.

[19] *Contra Gentiles* 2, 46, 1234: Ad productionem creaturarum nihil aliud movet Deum

Now, while God is not obliged in any way, as it were, through justice even towards his own goodness, nevertheless it is befitting of his goodness, Aquinas suggests, to give existence to the universe. God creates, he states, 'through a certain appropriateness'.[21] But since he acquires no gain from creation his motive is sheer generosity. It is, he says, appropriate for God as infinitely Good to share his goodness. Through the love which he has for himself, God freely calls into existence creatures which may reflect and share that love. Originating in and returning to himself, it is, however, a totally unselfish act of love. Rejoicing in his own perfection, God freely chooses to share with creatures the love which he has for his own perfect Being, Beauty and Goodness. (Aquinas indeed declares that of all affections, only joy and love can properly exist in God, though not as passions as they are in us.[22] God properly delights in himself, but he takes joy both in himself and in other things.[23] 'Love and joy, which are properly in God, are the principles of the other affections, love in the manner of a moving principle and joy in the manner of an end.')[24] As Gilson puts it, 'Because God loves his own perfection, he wants to have, so to speak, co-lovers of it; hence his will to create.'[25] Through an utter and total act of love, from which he himself merits no gain, God bestows the ultimate and fundamental endowment of existence itself. In a gratuitous celebration of the love which he has for his own goodness, God departs from the transcendence of his eternal and endless unity and draws into the intimacy of his infinite self-love creatures receiving a share of his goodness. Although he gains nothing through creation, it is nonetheless for his own sake that he creates.[26]

---

nisi sua bonitas, quam rebus aliis communicare voluit secundum modum assimilationis ad ipsum.

[20] *Contra Gentiles* 2, 28, 1053: Ipsa enim divina bonitas praecedit ut finis et primum motivum ad creandum. IV, x, 439: Sua bonitas movet seipsum in seipso.

[21] *Contra Gentiles* 2, 28, 7056: . . . per modum cuiusdam condecentiae. Ibid.: 1, 86, 721: Vult autem bonum universi quia decet bonitatem ipsius. *ST*, I, 21, 3: Considerandum est quod elargiri perfectiones rebus, pertinet et ad bonitatem divinam.

[22] See *Contra Gentiles* 1, 91, 763.

[23] *Contra Gentiles* 1, 90, 754.

[24] *Contra Gentiles* 1, 91, 766.

[25] Etienne Gilson, *The Elements of Christian Philosophy*, p. 187.

[26] See A. D. Sertillanges, *Somme Théologique*, Éditions de la revue des jeunes, Vol. 3, p. 276, n. 13: 'Il faut conclure qu'en toute rigueur de termes, Dieu n'a pas d'autre objet de volonté que lui-même, comme on a dit plus haut que Dieu n'a pas d'autre objet de connaissance que lui-même. Les vouloirs de Dieu relatifs aux creatures sont noyés dans l'éternelle complaisance de Dieu en sa propre bonté. Ses vouloirs particuliers et ce vouloir essentiel ne font pas addition, comme ne font pas addition ses connaissances particulières et son éternelle intuition de lui-même, comme ne font pas addition l'être qu'il communique aux creatures et l'être qui lui est propre. Mystère! . . .'

The greatest mystery of all and in which we are ourselves involved is that God, who is infinite and in need of nothing, should have created the universe. Creation is an outpouring of God's excessive goodness. In its most proper and positive sense, the created universe is indeed *superfluous* to God's being. Without God, the world would indeed be *de trop*: the most extreme absurdity imaginable; it is unconceivable. For Sartre, reality is 'superfluous', because it does not fall under the domination of human freedom. According to Dionysius and Aquinas, creation is radically superfluous, an outpouring of the goodness of God; without need for it he freely causes it to overflow from the superabundance of his infinite bounty. It is divinely superfluous in its origin and this is infinite mystery rather than abject absurdity.

The universe of finite beings flows as a total gift from the sheer generosity of divine goodness. Creation is the 'gift outright'; beings add nothing to the perfection of God, just as God would be none the lesser had he not created.[27] I can add no more to God's being than the very nothingness from which I have come. I am entirely a gift to myself bestowed by God. I add nothing to his perfection, yet I must be of eternal value to him; otherwise he would not have freely created me. Ultimately, God is his own gift to man; man is in a sense the reason for creation and his purpose is, for his own sake, to enjoy the gift of divine goodness.

Aquinas points out that perfection can be bestowed by God for many reasons: goodness, justice, generosity or mercy. Absolutely speaking, the communication of perfection pertains to goodness. If given in proportion to merit it derives from justice. In so far as God gives perfections to beings, not for his utility but for the sake of his goodness, it pertains to his generosity (*liberalitas*).[28] Aquinas endorses with total and emphatic agreement Dionysius' view that it is 'through an excess of goodness' (*propter bonitatis excessum*)[29] that God gives

---

[27] *De Potentia* 3, 15 ad 12: Suae enim bonitati nihil deperiret, si communicata non esset.

[28] *ST*, I, 21, 3: Prima autem origo bonitatis Deus est, ut supra dictum est. Sed considerandum est, quod elargiri perfectiones rebus pertinet quidem et ad bonitatem divinam, et ad justitiam, et ad liberalitatem, et misericordiam, tamen secundum aliam, et aliam rationem. Communicatio enim perfectionum absolute considerata pertinet ad bonitatem. Sed inquantum perfectiones rebus a Deo dantur secundum earum proportionem, pertinet ad justitiam. Inquantum vero non attribuit rebus perfectiones propter utilitatem suam, sed solum propter suam bonitatem, pertinet ad liberalitatem. Inquantum vero perfectiones datae rebus a Deo omnem defectum expellunt, pertinet ad misericordiam. *ST*, II-II, 117: Secundum Philosophum, in IV Ethic. ad liberalem pertinet *emissivum* esse. Unde et alio nomine liberalitas largitas nominetur: quia quod largum est, non est retentivum, sed est emissivum.

[29] IV, 10, 159: δι᾽ ἀγαθότητος ὑπερβολήν.

existence to all things, fills them with their individual perfections, conserves them in *esse* and ordains them towards himself as their end. Love is the universal root of all desire[30] and Aquinas agrees with Dionysius that divine Love is both good itself and is directed towards the good: God is the origin of love and his love is for the sake of his goodness. *Deus enim nihil amat nisi propter suam bonitatem.*[31] Since God's love is for the good, Aquinas, emphasising Dionysius' words (*inquam*), states that divine love did not allow itself to remain without seed, i.e. without the production of creatures; love moved it to be active in the most excellent manner of operation whereby it produced all things into *esse*. Thus the love with which God loves beings causes the goodness in them. 'He went forth out of love for his goodness in such a manner that he wished to diffuse his goodness and communicate it to others, in so far as possible, namely by way of similitude, so that his goodness would not remain in him alone but would flow forth to others.'[32]

God loves and wills his own goodness infinitely and since this is complete and absolute it cannot be increased in itself or multiplied according to its essence. It can be multiplied only according to its likeness, which can be infinitely shared.[33] Because he wills and loves his own essence, God therefore wills the multitude of beings in order that the likeness of his goodness be imprinted on them. Thus Aquinas notes that while it is necessary that God should love his goodness, it is not necessary that his goodness be represented in creatures; but God, moved only by his own goodness, wills to communicate it to other things.[34] Loving his goodness, he wishes it to be multiplied in the only mode possible, namely according to his similitude; this is the source of goodness and perfection in creatures: *per similitudinem, non participabiliter, inquantum essentia manet imparticipata.*[35]

---

[30] IV, ix, 408: Amor est communis radix appetitus.

[31] IV, ix, 409.

[32] IV, ix, 409; IV, ix, 424: (Deus) amat et se et alia propter suam pulchritudinem et bonitatem; *Contra Gentiles* 1, 96, 806: Voluntas Dei in alia a se fertur, inquantum, volendo et amando suum esse et suam bonitatem vult eam diffundi, secundum quod possibile est, per similitudinis communicationem. Hoc igitur est quod Deus in rebus aliis a se vult, ut in eis sit suae bonitatis similitudo. Hoc autem est bonum uniuscuiusque rei, ut similitudinem divinam participat: nam quaelibet bonitas alia non est nisi quaedam similitudo primae bonitatis. Igitur Deus unicuique rei vult bonum. Nihil igitur odit.

[33] *Contra Gentiles* 1, 75, 641.

[34] *Contra Gentiles* 3, 97, 2724. *Contra Gentiles* 2, 46, 1234: Ad productionem creaturarum nihil aliud movet Deum nisi sua bonitas, quam rebus aliis communicare voluit secundum modum assimilationis ad ipsum.

[35] II, iii, 160. *In II Sent.*, 1, 2, 1: Deo competit agere propter amorem finis, cuius bonitati nihil addi potest. Ipse enim bonitatem suam perfecte amat, et ex hoc vult quod

Thus, whereas similarity in being is the cause of love among creatures,[36] divine love is the very foundation raising beings radically out of nothing and drawing them into union with God. And since every being is caused totally and exhaustively by God, it bears within itself a pervasive likeness of its transcendent origin. Its *esse* IS its similitude to God: *Esse est similitudo Dei.* Creation is thus the ground of all love between creatures, since being itself is a likeness of divine goodness.[37] Whatever God produces in creatures—being, life and all other perfections—proceeds totally from divine goodness and belongs totally to the goodness of the creature.[38]

Aquinas exploits Dionysius' definition of love as a unitive power, (*virtus unitiva*, δύναμις ἑνοποιός),[39] but more radically, God's love is also an originative and creative power; it is the cause of all. In contrast to the human will, which loves something because it is beautiful and good, a being is in itself beautiful because it is first loved by God. Our will is not the cause of things but is only moved by them. Man is exterior to things; God, despite the abyss which separates him, is intimately interior. Through a 'movement' of his will, however, God is himself the cause of things; his love thus causes them to be and to be good, not vice versa; since his goodness moves himself within himself, which is not the case with our will.[40] God loves both himself and others because of his beauty and goodness.[41]

It is God's love of himself, for his own beauty and goodness which moves him to lead beings out of nothingness and to raise creatures into union with himself, a union in which each one is transformed by the likeness of its all-powerful creator.[42] Divine love, therefore, is distinct from human love: for God to love is to cause the beloved to be. Divine love operates in the profound manner of a production: *habet efficaciam ad producendum.*[43] Beings are wrought from nothingness, the vast, unimagined void of total and overwhelming absence, and elevated into

---

bonitas sua multiplicetur per modum qui possibilis est, ex sui scilicet similitudine, ex quo provenit utilitas creaturae, inquantum similitudinem divinae bonitatis recipit.

[36] *ST*, I-II, 27, 3: Similitudo, proprie loquendo, est causa amoris.

[37] *De Veritate* 22, 2, ad 2: Ipsum esse est similitudo divinae bonitatis.

[38] III, 228: Quidquid Deus facit creaturis, sive esse sive vivere et quodcumque aliud totum ex bonitate divina procedit et totum ad bonitatem pertinet creaturae.

[39] IV, 12, 167; see *ST*, I-II, 26, 2 ad 2.

[40] IV, x, 439. *ST*, I, 20, 4: Voluntas Dei est causa bonitatis in rebus; *ST*, I, 20, 4 ad 5: Cum voluntas Dei sit causa bonitatis in rebus.

[41] IV, ix, 424: Amat et se et alia propter suam pulchritudinem et bonitatem.

[42] *Contra Gentiles* 1, 91, 760: Amoris est ad unionem movere, ut Dionysius dicit . . . Deus autem movet omnia alia ad unionem: inquantum enim dat eis esse et alias perfectiones, unit ea sibi per modum quo possibile est. Deus igitur et se et alia amat.

[43] IX, xii, 455.

union with eternal and transcendent love. God's love infuses and creates goodness within beings;[44] God's goodness is his reason for willing that other things be. It is by his will that he produces things in being. Thus the love by which he loves his own goodness is the cause of the creation of things. Aquinas takes this doctrine from Dionysius but finds it already anticipated in the poetry of Hesiod and Parmenides for whom the love of the gods is the cause of all things.[45]

Aquinas also exploits Dionysius' view of love as an ecstatic virtue and inserts it into his own vision of God's universal causality. In creating the world, God 'goes out' from himself in an ecstatic profusion of power: 'He who is the cause of all through his beautiful and good love with which he loves all, according to the abundance of his goodness whereby he loves things, goes out of himself, inasmuch as he provides for all existing things through his goodness and love and affection.'[46] God in a sense emerges from his transcendence and enters with his presence into all things 'through the effects of his goodness, according to a certain manner of ecstasy which allows him to be in all inferior things in such a way that his suprasubstantial power does not leave him. He fills all things in such a manner that his power is deficient in none.'[47] Without affecting his transcendence, God's diffusion guarantees his providential presence in the universe. Dionysius' doctrine is also incorporated into the teaching of the *Summa* regarding God's universal love for all things:

> The lover is transported outside himself into the loved one inasmuch as he wills the good of the beloved and acts for its providence. Dionysius therefore says: 'We dare to affirm and declare in truth that he who is cause of all through the abundance of his loving goodness goes beyond himself in his providence for all existing things.'[48]

---

[44] *ST*, I, 20, 2: Amor Dei est infundens et creans bonitatem in rebus; *ST*, I, 20, 3: Amor Dei causa bonitatis rerum.

[45] *Contra Gentiles* 4, 20, 3570: Bonitas Dei est eius ratio volendi quod alia sint, et per suam voluntatem res in esse producit. Amor igitur quo suam bonitatem amat, est causa creationis rerum; unde et quidam antiqui philosophi amorem deorum causam omnium esse posuerunt, ut patet in I Metaph.; et Dionysius dicit, IV cap de Div. Nom., quod divinus amor non permissit ipsum sine germine esse. Aquinas alters the meaning of Hesiod and Parmenides somewhat, since in both passages referred to, 'Love' is said to be the first among the gods to be made. Cf. Aristotle, *Metaphysics* I, iv, 948b 23-29 and Plato, *Symposium*, 17 which is probably Aristotle's source. Cf. *Contra Gentiles* 1, 91, 765: Philosophi etiam quidam posuerunt rerum principium Dei amorem. Cui consonat Dionysii verbum, IV cap. de Div. Nom.; dicentis quod divinus amor non permisit ipsum sine germine esse.

[46] IV, x, 437.

[47] IV, x, 437.

[48] *ST*, I, 20, 2 ad 1.

God, who has no need for creatures but is in himself fully perfect, goes beyond his self-sufficiency to things which are in need of him. This does not contradict the truth that it is primarily in virtue of his love for himself that God is ecstatic and creative. 'God wills the created universe for its own sake, although he wills its existence for his own sake: for these two are not incompatible with each other.'[49]

EMANATION AND RETURN OF CREATURES

Because God is himself the purpose for the sake of which beings are created, he directs them to return to him. He not only creates beings, but invests them with an intrinsic and dynamic order by which they return to their source. Not only is he the origin of all things but is also their ultimate goal. There is thus within creation a circular movement which leads it forth from the original fullness of the source and returns it to God as its final fulfilment. There are within creatures two 'strains' or tendencies of being: being from God and being towards God.[50] Placed within existence by God, who establishes them from within as totally distinct from himself, they bear within themselves a profound need of their origin.[51]

Aquinas himself is thus explicit in espousing the Neoplatonist principle of the cyclic movement of emanation and return within creation, i.e. *exitus* and *reditus*: 'In the issue of creatures from the first principle there is observed a certain circulation or gyration, in that all things are returned as to an end to that from which they proceed as from their origin.'[52]

---

[49] *De Potentia*, 5, 4: Deus autem creaturarum universitatem vult propter se ipsam, licet et propter se ipsum eam vult esse; haec enim duo non repugnant. Vult enim Deus ut creaturae sint propter eius bonitatem, ut eam scilicet suo modo imitentur et repraesentent; quod quidem faciunt in quantum ab ea esse habent, et in suis naturis subsistunt. Unde idem est dictu, quod Deus omnia propter se ipsum fecit (quod dicitur Proverb. xvi, 4: Universa propter semetipsum operatus est Dominus), et quod creaturas fecerit propter earum esse, quod dicitur Sap. i, 14: Creavit enim (Deus) ut essent omnia.
[50] *De Veritate* 20, 4: Cum Deus sit principium omnium rerum et finis; duplex habitudo ipsius ad creaturas invenitur: una secundum quam omnia a Deo procedunt in esse; alia secundum quam ad eum ordinantur ut in finem.
[51] VI, ii, 688: ... per superemanationem suae bonitatis ... convertit et revocat ad seipsam.
[52] *In I Sent.*, 14, 2, 2: Respondeo dicendum, quod in exitu creaturarum a primo principio attenditur quaedam circulatio vel regiratio, eo quod omnia revertuntur sicut in finem in id a quo sicut principio prodierunt. Et ideo oportet ut per eadem quibus est exitus a principio, et reditus in finem attendatur. See *In IV Sent.* 49, 1, 3, ad 1: Omnia creata secundum impressionem a creatore receptam inclinantur in bonum appetendum secundum suum modum; ut sic in rebus quaedam circulatio inveniatur; dum, a bono

The movement whereby something proceeds from God bears within it as the directing impulse of its own fulfilment an inverse tendency of assimilation and conversion to its origin. It is saturated with a desire to return to its fontal source. The dynamic diffusion of divine goodness into beings through efficient causation endowing creatures with divine similitude finds its ultimate significance in the conversion of all things and their perfect re-assimilation into their absolute exemplary source. *Exitus* and *reditus*, going out and return, are obverse sides of an identical relation; inverse movements of the unique and universal causality of God who is causally all as origin and end. He is their source for the sake of himself as their goal, and he can be their goal only because he is their source. Outside of God nothing has origin or end. The impulse towards reunion is ingrained within the movement through which God causes beings to proceed from him; they are caused to proceed forth only to return again. Aquinas accepts from Neoplatonism the principle that every effect is converted to the cause from which it proceeds; the reason is that each thing desires its good, and the good of an effect derives from its cause. It seeks its cause, therefore, as its own good. Because all things are derived from God, they turn to him through desire.[53] This is expressed for Aquinas in the words of Dionysius: πάντα πρὸς ἑαυτὴν ἡ ἀγαθότης ἐπιστρέφει: *Bonitas omnia convertit ad seipsum*.[54]

Creation represents, in other words, an outward movement within the transcendent cycle of divine love, leading from itself to itself in perfect union. In an ecstatic and loving gesture, God departs from his transcendence and establishes in autonomous, nevertheless dependent,

---

egredientia, in bonum tendunt. Haec autem circulatio in quibusdam perficitur creaturis, in quibusdam autem remanet imperfecta. Illae enim creaturae quae non ordinantur ut pertingant ad illud primum bonum a quo processerunt, sed solummodo ad consequendam eius similitudinem qualemcumque; non perfecte habent hanc circulationem; sed solum illae creaturae quae ad ipsum primum principium aliquo modo pertingere possunt; quod solum est rationabilium creaturarum, quae deum ipsum assequi possunt per cognitionem et amorem: in qua assecutione beatitudo eorum consistit. Et ideo sicut quaelibet res alia naturaliter appetit suum bonum, ita quaelibet creatura rationalis naturaliter suam beatitudinem appetit.

[53] I, iii, 94; Cf. 99, also IV, iii, 314-19.

[54] 4, 4, 120. Speaking of Plotinus, Elmer O'Brien writes: 'The One is term because it is principle, at the origin of the return because it is the source of participation. Effect is drawn towards cause. Image tends towards prototype. There is at the core of every existing thing an ontic desire for what is lacking to its perfectness, and this perfectness it can find in its fullness solely within that which initially engendered it. Indigence is at the root of this ontic desire. But not merely indigence. There is as well the drive to make up for this indigence. It is a commonplace in Plato that Desire is the child of Penury and Plenitude, and ... Plotinus agrees with him. It is what centuries later Pascal has God say to the Christian soul: "You would not seek Me if you had not already found Me."' *The Essential Plotinus*, p. 21.

existence a universe which reflects in an outward way his own intimate dialogue of love. Through the love which God has for himself he causes all things and generates within them a love for himself. Creation is at once both an act of love and an act creative of love—analogous to the eternal act by which he loves himself.[55] Eternally pre-existing in the sovereign Good, and flowing to things by an act of free generosity, God emits love to other things and generates within them a love resembling his own.[56]

The profound reason for the existence of things is the mysterious desire of God, who is the unbounded fullness of perfection and goodness, to freely share his love with beings other than himself. Commenting on a passage where Dionysius speaks of God as Love, 'pre-subsisting in the Good, gushing forth from the Good to beings and returning to the Good',[57] Aquinas gives his personal appreciation and approval in the following paragraph which shows how much he has appropriated the cyclic vision of the Good:

> This love, in the first place, is in that very Good which is God and has emanated from this Good into existing things; participated in turn by beings it turns towards its own source which is the Good. He shows the unending character of divine love and its absence of origin as proper to a circle; for in love there is a kind of circulation, as it proceeds from the Good and returns towards the good, an eternal circulation of divine love ... Thus he says that love is an eternal circle because it has the Good as its object, it derives from the Good as its source, it endures in the Good and tends towards the attainment of the Good, thus moving around the Good in an unerring cycle by its uniformity.[58]

The single universal love from which all others derive is the divine love which moves out of itself down to the last among existing things, and ascending again from there returns by a kind of circulation to the primary good.[59]

Concretely, Aquinas makes his own Dionysius' triadic scheme of God's universal causality as origin, support and end.[60] God is the source of existence of all things (Aquinas modifies Dionysius' phrase praising God as *principalis substantia omnium* to read: *principium*

---

[55] See Gilson, *Spirit of Medieval Philosophy*, p. 275.

[56] IV, xi, 444: Deus dicitur amor et dilectio causaliter, quia scilicet est causa amoris, inquantum immittit amorem aliis et quodammodo in eis amorem generat secundum quamdam similitudinem; ... ad Deum autem pertinet quod moveat et causet motum in aliis et ideo ad eum pertinere videtur quod sit amabilis, in aliis amorem creans.

[57] 4, 17, 178.

[58] IV, xi, 450.

[59] IV, xii,460.

[60] 1, 7, 26: πάντων ὑποστάτις ἀρχηγικὴ καὶ τελειωτικὴ καὶ συνεκτικὴ φρουρὰ καὶ ἑστία καὶ πρὸς ἑαυτὴν ἐπιστρεπτική.

existendi omnibus, thus avoiding any lure of pantheism). He perfects beings, conserving them in *esse* and turns them towards himself, making them desire him as their end.[61] Everything which is, is 'from the Beautiful and the Good' which is God, as from an efficient principle; and it is 'in the Beautiful and the Good', as in a principle which sustains and preserves them; and it is 'turned towards the Beautiful and the Good', desiring him, as towards an end; he is end not only because he is desired, but because he orders all substances and actions towards himself. He moves things, not for the sake of any extraneous end, but for his own sake, that he may himself be attained by creatures.[62]

Completing his commentary on Chapter 4 with the remark that what has been expounded *secundum veritatem in praecedentibus, sunt vera*,[63] Aquinas emphatically endorses Dionysius' manner of conceiving God as origin and end of all things (*sicut principium et finis omnium*; ὡς ἀρχὴ καὶ πέρας πάντων)[64] and of goodness as a circle-like movement which occurs in beings (*manifestatur quasi quidam circulus in existentibus*). Aquinas discovers the full spectrum of causality in the following phrase of Dionysius which he recasts, however, in the mould of Aristotle: *Omnis quocumque modo existentis, praeexistens est principium et causa et omnia Ipso participant et a nullo existentium recedit et Ipse est ante omnia, et omnia in Ipso constitunt.*[65] In contrast to the builder of a house who is cause of its coming to be (*quantum ad fieri*) what it is, but not of its existence, if God were to recede from his effect, it would cease to be, since he is the cause of its very being.

Aquinas adopted from Dionysius and Neoplatonism the universal cycle of love with its rhythm of procession and reversion as the architectonic principle of his own magnificent vision. Even in his early reading of Peter Lombard, following the example of Alexander of Hales,[66] Aquinas suggests that whereas the first two books of the

---

[61] I, iii, 100.

[62] See IV, viii, 390; Aquinas is referring here to 4, 10, 154-54; IV, iii, 317 (Dionysius, 4, 4, 121: πάντα αὐτῆς ὡς ἀρχῆς ὡς συνοχῆς ὡς τέλους ἐφίεται) and XIII, iii, 986 on 13, 3, 448.

[63] IV, xxiii, 605.

[64] 4, 35, 256.

[65] 5, 1, 265: παντὸς ὁπωσοῦν ὄντος, ὁ προὼν ἀρχὴ καὶ αἰτία· καὶ πάντα αὐτοῦ μετέχει καὶ οὐδενὸς τῶν ὄντων ἀποστατεῖ καὶ αὐτός ἐστι πρὸ πάντων καὶ τὰ πάντα ἐν αὐτῷ συνέστηκε. He interprets ἀρχή as efficient principle (*principium effectivum*) and αἰτία as final cause (*causa finalis*); all things partake of it, moreover, *sicut prima forma exemplari*: the entire universe of beings pre-exists virtually, i.e. within the power of God as cause. God is cause not only of the coming to be of things but is the support of their continued existence: *non solum quantum ad fieri rerum, sed et quantum ad totum esse et durationem.* This is contained in the words καὶ οὐδενὸς τῶν ὄντων ἀποστατεῖ.

[66] *Glossa in Quattor Libros Sententiarum Petri Lombardi*, I, Quarrachi, 1951, p. 4, n.8: Sed quaeri potest quare ordine praepostero in praedicta auctoritate librorum fit distinctio.

Sentences deal with the *exitus* of all things from God, the latter two
deal with their *reditus*. Divine nature is revealed through the production
of creatures and their restoration and perfection.[67] Weisheipl remarks:
'This dual aspect of the flow of all things from God and the return of
all things to God was to remain a basic framework for Thomas. His
Summa Theologiae would also be organised in the same way; it is the
great Dionysian and Plotinian cycle of emanation and return.'[68] But
whereas in the case of his Commentary on the *Sentences* this division
was imposed upon Lombard's work, it provided the seminal project of
Aquinas' *Summa*, which seeks a knowledge of God 'not only as he is
in himself, but as the beginning and end of all things and especially of
rational creatures.'[69] The *prima pars*, Aquinas states, deals with the one
and triune God and 'the procession of all creatures from him'; the
secunda pars discusses 'the journey to God of rational creatures' and
the *tertia pars* considers Christ, 'who as man is our way of tending
toward God.'[70] This vast vision provides a magnificent source of
intelligibility for all things: everything is viewed in the light of its
ultimate origin and end—*sub specie aeternitatis*.[71]

As to the source of this doctrine, M.-D. Chenu has written as follows:
'*Exitus et reditus*: c'est évidemment chez les néoplatoniciens chrétiens
que saint Thomas peut trouver expression et aliment pour ce grand
thème, et en fait, dans la tradition dionysienne alors si vivace, où il
conserve une valeur ontologique et cosmique.'[72] The significance of this
inspiration for the structure of the *Summa* has been questioned due to
the lack of express reference.[73] The use of *exitus : reditus* is not explicit
in the *Summa Theologiae* but its meaning is nevertheless present as a
latent and organic principle of order. Apart from the question of its
architectonic role in the *Summa*, there is no doubt that it profoundly
orders Aquinas' vision of creation. Even his use of the Dionysian
doctrine, *Bonum diffusivum sui*, which he recasts as a principle of

---

Respondeo: duplex est ordo. Est ordo rerum prout exeunt a Creatore vel Reparatore, et
sic proceditur in hoc opere. Et est ordo rerum prout reducuntur ad Creatorem, et hoc
via agitur in exemplo auctoritatis praedictae, in parte.

[67] *In I Sent.*, Prol.: Per sapientiam enim Dei manifestantur divinorum abscondita,
producuntur creaturarum opera, nec tantum producuntur, sed restaurantur et perficiuntur.

[68] James A. Weisheipl, *Friar Thomas d'Aquino*, p. 71.

[69] *ST*, I, 2, Prol.: Principalis intentio huius doctrinae est, Dei cognitionem tradere, et
non solum secundum quod in se est, sed etiam secundum quod est principium rerum, et
finis earum, et specialiter rationalis creaturae.

[70] Cf. *ST*, I, 1, 7: Omnia autem pertractantur in sacra doctrina sub ratione Dei, vel
quia sunt ipse Deus vel quia habent ordinem ad Deum ut ad principium et finem.

[71] See M.-D. Chenu, *Introduction à l'Étude de Saint Thomas d'Aquin*, p. 261.

[72] Ibid., p. 262.

[73] See G. Lafont, *Structures et méthode dans la Somme Théologique de Saint Thomas
d'Aquin*, pp. 28-30, and A. Hayen, *Saint Thomas d'Aquin et la vie de l'Eglise*, pp. 80-2.

finality, confirms how profoundly the principles of emanation and return are unified.[74]

Aquinas enthusiastically adopts from Dionysius the Neoplatonist language of emanation and diffusion to describe the free and total causation of the universe of beings by God. This is evidenced not only in his Commentary but in his systematic works. *Emanatio, diffusio* and *effusio*, all characteristically Neoplatonist terms, are fully adopted and become part of the linguistic fabric of Aquinas' thought. God's Being is the 'universal and fontal source of all being.'[75] Through his goodness God *diffuses* perfections to all creatures.[76] All existence 'flows' from the first and supreme Being.[77] Creation is defined explicitly as the emanation of entire being from the primary principle: *emanatio totius entis universalis a primo principio.*[78] The treatment of creation is most Dionysian in tenor. It is the exodus of universal being from God: *exitus universi esse a Deo.*[79] Creatures 'proceed' from God; divine goodness and wisdom 'proceed' into creatures; beings proceed from non-being into being.[80]

In the Commentary on the *Divine Names*, in particular, Aquinas makes his own Dionysius' concepts and language of emanation and diffusion. God is the 'fountain of all goodness';[81] from him flow all perfections to creatures through emanation.[82] Creatures are made to subsist in being through a diffusion of the rays of divine goodness.[83] As

---

[74] Chenu's interpretation was enthusiastically praised by Gilson, who placed him 'parmi les plus profonds interprètes de saint Thomas'. *Bulletin Thomiste*, 8 (1951), p. 9; More recently, it has been espoused by Weisheipl. See also Wayne Hankey, 'Aquinas' First Principle: Being or Unity?', p. 169: 'The *exitus-reditus* form is found at all levels of his *Summa*.' See also the excellent article by Th.-André Audet, 'Approches historiques de la *Summa Theologiae*'.

[75] *De Substantiis Separatis*, ed. Lescoe n. 76: Ipsius esse est universale et fontale principium omnium esse.

[76] *In I Sent.*, 34, 3, 1 ad 2: Deus per suam bonitatem perfectionis in omnes creaturas diffundit.

[77] *De Potentia* 3, 16: Omne esse a primo ente effluere.

[78] *ST*, I, 45, 1; Cf. Q. 44, 2, ad 1: . . . loquimur de rebus secundum emanationem earum ab universali principio essendi. A qua quidem emanatione nec materia excluditur. Question 45 is entitled 'De modo emanationis rerum a primo principio, qui dicitur creatio.' I, 45, 1: Oportet considerare . . . emanationem totius entis a causa universali, quae Deus est: et hanc quidem emanationem designamus nomine creationis . . . ita creatio, quae est emanatio totius esse, est ex non ente quod est nihil..

[79] *De Potentia* 3, 17.

[80] *De Potentia* 10, 1: Dicimus quod corpus procedit de non esse in esse . . . dicimus divinam sapientiam aut bonitatem in creaturas procedere, ut Dionysius dicit, ix cap. de divin. Nomin.: et etiam quod creaturae procedunt a Deo.

[81] IV, i, 286.

[82] II, i, 126; II, ii, 135; IV, ii, 307: . . . processus rerum in esse a divina Bonitate; XII, 939: . . . emanatio perfectionum a Deo in creaturas.

[83] IV, i, 276.

the sun gives being through generation, divine goodness gives being (*esse*) through creation.[84] Aquinas also readily takes over and develops Dionysius' image of God as an all-powerful root, producing and sending forth many fruits; God's omnipotence is seen also in its great power of attraction, converting all things to itself as an all-supporting foundation.[85]

The multitude of creatures proceeds from divine unity as through an effusion, in an outpouring as when many rivers arise from a single source or water from a spring spills out (*diffundit*) into many streams. In the division and multiplicity of gifts from divine goodness there is no lessening of the original; the divine goodness remains undivided in its essence, unspent and simple.[86] (For an evocative reversal of this image, we read in *Contra Gentiles* 2, 2 that, meditating on the works of God, the mind is kindled into a love for God's goodness. All the perfections scattered throughout the universe flow together in him who is the spring of all goodness: 'If, therefore, the goodness, beauty, and sweetness of creatures so capture the minds of men, the fountainhead of the goodness of God himself, in comparison with the rivulets of goodness which we find in creatures, will draw the inflamed minds of men wholly to itself.')[87] Now, as Aquinas points out, effects can overflow only from a cause which is the plenitude of a perfection; what is not fully hot cannot diffuse warmth; a vessel which is not itself full cannot overflow. Moreover, the greater the plenitude, the greater the effusion and the more primary and fundamental what is received through the outpouring. Thus, since God is the superabundant plenitude of goodness, it follows that he causes the fullness of every gift. And as fontal or primordial cause, his gifts are primal and universal; whatever else is received in beings, from any cause whatever, presupposes what they receive from God.[88]

God's greatness is his Being (*Dei magnitudo est esse eius*) and he diffuses his infinite greatness in a universal superabundance. It is received by creatures not in its infinity but according to their finite measure.[89] The outpouring of the divine gift is infinite in its source; it is not diminished, however much it is shared. Rather, the more it is

---

[84] IV, iii, 312.

[85] X, i, 852: πυθμήν: plantatio, i.e. stock, stem.

[86] II, vi, 214-15., VIII, iii, 770: . . . dat omnibus bonitates copiose effundendo. Dat enim omnibus abundanter. 'Effusion' is in fact the word used to convey the outpouring of God's wisdom in all his works; See Eccl. 1, 10.

[87] *Contra Gentiles* 2, 2, 861. Cf. Dionysius, 4, 2, 103: ἐκ τῆς παναιτίου καὶ πηγαίας ἐστὶν ἀγαθότητος (ex omnium causa et fontana sunt bonitate).

[88] IX, i, 807.

[89] VIII, iii, 770: Et hoc convenit Ei ex abundantia suae excedentis virtutis quae dat omnibus copiose effundendo. Dat enim omnibus abundanter, ut dicitur Jacob. I.

participated, the more it flows from above; this is because the more a creature acquires of divine gifts, the greater its capacity to receive. However, God's plenitude is infinite and never decreases in itself.[90] Nor is God's power divided in causing different and distinct things; he causes all by a single power and the diffusion of his goods is not diminished.[91]

Regarding the language of emanation and diffusion, R. Roques remarks: 'C'est précisément l'autorité de Denys qui suggère à saint Thomas ces formulations de type platonicien. Même remarque pour la métaphore de la diffusion solaire et pour l'axiome qu'illustre cette métaphore: *Bonum est diffusivum sui.*'[92] We wish to turn our attention now to the meaning and importance of this very principle, which captures the dynamic optimism of both Neoplatonist and Christian metaphysics. It expresses the inherent and underlying impulse and purpose of the universal movement of πρόοδος and ἐπιστροφή, *exitus* and *reditus*, the cycle of enrichment which proceeds from the good as its origin and attains full and final fruition within the good as end. For Dionysius it expresses the divine procession into creatures and for Aquinas it emphasises the final purpose of creation.

DIFFUSION OF THE GOOD: EFFICIENT OR FINAL CAUSATION?

Although the phrase is nowhere to be found in such lapidary form in his works, medieval authors without exception attribute it to the Pseudo-Areopagite.[93] As Durantel aptly puts it, 'Nous sommes là encore en présence d'une formule frappée, d'une sorte de monnaie d'école, dont le métal a été extrait de Denis.'[94] The maxim could well have been

---

[90] IX, i, 808.

[91] II, vi, 216. Cf. I, ii, 45; Dionysius, 2, 11, 73.

[92] *L'Univers dionysien*, p. 102; Cf. Gilson, *Le Thomisme*, 202, n. 35: 'C'est intentionellement que nous maintenons le terme *exode* contre un de nos critiques qui lui trouve une saveur panthéiste inquiétante, car il est authentiquement thomiste: "Aliter dicendum est de productione unius creaturae, et aliter de exitu totius universi a Deo." (*De Potentia*, 3, 17, ad Resp.) Saint Thomas a librement usé des termes *deductio, exitus, emanatio*, pour décrire la procession des créatures à partir de Dieu. User du même langage est sans inconvénient, pourvu qu'on lui donne le même sens.'

[93] Julien Péghaire, 'L'axiome *Bonum est diffusivum sui* dans le néoplatonisme et le thomisme', p. 6: 'Tous les éditeurs de saint Thomas, ceux d'Albert le Grand, et récemment encore les Franciscains de Quaracchi, pour Alexandre de Hales, renvoient à propos de cet axiome au chapitre IV du *De Divinis Nominibus* du Pseudo-Denys. Et Albert le Grand lui-même, dans sa *Somme*, après avoir cité quelques lignes de ce même chapitre, écrit: *Idem* (c'est-à-dire, que le Bien est cause efficiente) *videtur, per id quod IBIDEM dicit Dionysius, quod Bonum est diffusivum esse et sui.*'

[94] *Saint Thomas et le Pseudo-Denis*, p. 154.

distilled from the opening lines of Chapter 4, already cited: ἀγαθὸν ὡς οὐσιῶδες ἀγαθὸν εἰς πάντα τὰ ὄντα διατείνει τὴν ἀγαθότητα—in the Latin translation used by Albertus Magnus and Aquinas: *Ea quae est bonum, ut substantiale bonum, ad omnia existentia extendit bonitatem.*[95] There is more or less exact verbal correspondence between the two phrases. The reduplicative '*sui*' replaces the repetition of the word 'goodness' and διατείνειν is faithfully rendered by *diffundere*. Formulating the principle in the context of an objection,[96] Aquinas writes as follows: *Bonum est diffusivum sui esse, ut ex verbis Dionysii accipitur*, giving as his reference 4, 4, [121]: *bonum est ex quo omnia subsistunt et sunt* (τἀγαθόν ἐστιν ἐξ οὗ τὰ πάντα ὑπέστε καὶ ἔστιν). Thus Aquinas himself recognises that the axiom is derived from Dionysius rather than taken directly from his works.

Predictably, the Good is for Dionysius at once efficient, exemplary and final cause alike: πάντα αὐτῆς (ἀγαθότης) ὡς ἀρχῆς ὡς συνοχῆς ὡς τέλους ἐφίεται· καὶ τἀγαθόν.[97] However, we may take it from Péghaire's analysis that Dionysius understands the causation of the Good to be primarily that of efficiency rather of finality.[98] This would appear evident from the use of the word διατείνει: *ad omnia existentia extendit bonitatem*. This is confirmed, as Péghaire points out, by the manner in which the diffusion of the Good is illustrated by the illumination of the sun. It 'sends forth' (ἐφίησι) to all beings the rays of its total goodness.[99] The manner in which Dionysius conveys the dependence of all things on the Good, and their preservation in being, also suggests efficient causation: the use of the preposition ἐκ with the genitive, Péghaire notes, 'nous oblige à exclure l'idée de fin pour ne garder que celle d'agent.'[100]

It may appear paradoxical that Aquinas, who attributes universal primacy and transcendence to existence, should regard the finality of goodness as primary within causality, rather than the efficiency whereby things become actual (since actuality is the hallmark of existence); in contrast to Dionysius, for whom it is the Good—beyond Being—which first confers existence upon all creatures. The paradox, however, is resolved in the ultimate perspective of Being which is the horizon of Aquinas' reflection. For Aquinas goodness is an aspect of being rather

---

[95] 4, 1, 95.
[96] *ST*, I, 5, 4, 2.
[97] 4, 4, 121.
[98] 'L'axiome *Bonum est diffusivum sui*', p. 16. Cf. J. de Finance, *Être et agir dans la philosophie de Saint Thomas*, p. 70; Gilson, *Le Thomisme*, p. 151, n. 58.
[99] 4, 1, 96.
[100] Ibid., p. 17; Cf. 4, 1, 100: τὴν μόνην ἐκ τῆς ἀγαθότητος ἔχουσι ... 4, 2, 103: ἐκ τῆς παναιτίου καὶ πηγαίας ... ἀγαθότητος.

than a dimension which exceeds it. We have already seen in detail that for Aquinas finality holds priority over efficiency in the order of causality. This does not in any way imply a precedence of goodness over being but rather the priority of act over potency and the very identity of being and goodness. He succeeds in outlining the primacy of finality even with respect to diffusion. Although the proper use of the word diffusion, i.e., 'to pour out', implies the operation of an efficient cause, in a broad sense it can refer to any kind of cause, such as 'influence', 'make' etc.

> Now when it is said that the good is of its nature diffusive, this is not to be understood as implying an efficient cause—an effusion—but rather final causality... Good expresses the diffusion of a final cause and not of an agent cause: both because the latter is not as such the measure and perfection of an effect but rather its beginning, and because the effect participates in the efficient cause only in an assimilation of its form, whereas a thing pursues its end according to its total being. And it is in this that the nature of goodness consists.[101]

As we saw, finality is prior even within the sphere of finite beings, where the end does not yet already exist in reality but is grasped intentionally as yet to be attained.[102] Here, the end, *intended as real*, exercises the power of causation by diffusing the attraction through which the agent tends to act. To be fully intelligible, however, the primacy of finality must be brought beyond the domain of finite causes which act in view of ends which are not actually real but merely intended. It is impossible that, universally, everything should strive for a goal which does not exist but has yet to be realised. The ultimate end must be prior to all things in existence (*in essendo*) and not merely in intention.[103] God is not an end waiting to be realised or constituted by beings which merely intend him as their goal; rather he pre-exists as

---

[101] *De Veritate* 21, 1, ad 4: Dicendum, quod diffundere, licet secundum proprietatem vocabuli videatur importare operationem causae efficientis, tamen largo modo potest importare habitudinem cuiuscumque causae sicut influere et facere, et alia huiusmodi. Cum autem dicitur quod bonum est diffusivum secundum sui rationem, non est intelligenda effusio secundum quod importat operationem causae efficientis, sed secundum quod importat habitudinem causae finalis; et talis diffusio non est mediante aliqua virtute superaddita. Dicit autem bonum diffusionem causae finalis, et non causae agentis: tum quia efficiens, in quantum huiusmodi, non est rei mensura et perfectio, sed magis initium; tum quia effectus participat causam efficientem secundum assimilationem formae tantum, sed finem consequitur res secundum totum esse suum, et in hoc consistebat ratio boni.

[102] IV, xiv, 477.

[103] *Contra Gentiles* 3, 18, 2000: Sic enim est ultimus finis omnium rerum quod tamen est prius omnibus in essendo. Finis autem aliquis invenitur qui, etiam si primatum obtinet in causando secundum quod est in intentione, est tamen in essendo posterius... Aliquis autem finis invenitur qui, sicut est praecedens in causando, ita etiam in essendo praecedit... Deus igitur sic est finis rerum sicut aliquid ab unaquaque re suo modo obtinendum.

the plenitude of perfection which each one must in its own manner acquire. In the term *praeexistens*, Aquinas reflects in an adequate manner a proper and profound parallel to the primacy attributed by Dionysius to the Good as preceding and transcending being: προών. Whereas for Aquinas, it is subsistent Being which diffuses causality in the first place through its finality or attraction, for Dionysius it is the transcendent Good preceding Being which as efficient source brings creatures into existence.

Whereas for creatures there is a difference between being as actually possessed and their goodness which is to be attained, there pre-exists in God a perfect identity in God between his goodness and being. The distance within beings between the measure of their actual existence and their final goodness is ultimately resolved in the simplicity of their all-perfect source of existence. Aquinas uses the term *praeexistens* to denote the absolute and unqualified perfection of God which precedes the striving of all creatures for their final goodness. For creatures, simple and unqualified goodness is an ideal yet to be attained from the resources of their potency. As *praeexistens*, in Aquinas' sense, God exists prior to all beings and is himself the fullness of Being.[104]

Moreover, whereas beings exist only for some purpose, Being, universally, can have no goal beyond itself; nor is there anything outside itself which might be its cause. The cause and goal of finite beings (*entia per participationem*) is Absolute and subsistent Being (*ens per essentiam, Ipsum Esse Subsistens*). God is himself the reason for his Being and is without cause. He cannot act in view of anything less than himself but is the end of all his actions. Since he creates the world for his own sake, it is through final causality that he creates. It is in terms of diffusion that Aquinas describes the universal finality of divine causation: the more perfect the power of a being, the more universal and intimate is its causality. Now the causality of an end consists in this, that it is desired in itself while other things are desired for its sake. The more perfect an end, therefore, the more it is willed. But the divine essence is most perfect because of its nature as goodness and end. It diffuses its causality, therefore, supremely to all things.[105]

---

[104] *Contra Gentiles* 3, 18, 2001: Non potest igitur Deus sic esse finis rerum quasi aliquid constitutum, sed solum quasi aliquid praeexistens obtinendum.

[105] *Contra Gentiles* 1, 75, 644: Quanto aliquid est perfectioris virtutis, tanto sua causalitas ad plura se extendit et in magis remotum, causalitas autem finis in hoc consistit quod propter ipsum alia desiderantur. Quanto igitur finis est perfectior et magis volitus, tanto voluntas volentis finem ad plura extenditur ratione finis illius. Divina autem essentia est perfectissima in ratione bonitatis et finis. Igitur diffundet suam causalitatem maxime ad multa, ut propter ipsam multa sint volita; et praecipue a Deo, qui eam secundum totam suam virtutem perfecte vult.

The notional division between Being and Goodness, efficiency and finality, is ultimately resolved in the unity and simplicity of God who as fullness of Being is as once efficient and final cause.[106] In his concept of God as *Ipsum Esse Subsistens*, efficient and final cause, Aquinas can incorporate the Neoplatonist primacy of the Good into his own priority of Being by attributing causal priority to God as universal end of all things. Indeed, by giving priority precisely to finality, he emphasises even more strongly Dionysius' own view of the primacy of the Good. For Aquinas, it is as final cause, i.e. as the supreme instance of Goodness (because identical with the fullness of Being) that God creates and loves all things. Indeed, Aquinas thus goes further than Dionysius in giving precedence universally to goodness by interpreting the diffusion of the Good as the principle of finality itself—the first and final reason why beings are created. With due reserve for the inadequacy of the formulation, we could say, for the sake of contrast, that the concept of God, considered as the *Summum Bonum* drawing all things towards full and final fruition, is more ultimate than the concept of God as efficient creative cause which inaugurates things initially into existence. It is for the purpose of finally assimilating things to himself that God indeed creates beings. The reason for creation is the union of creatures with God as their final end.

Now whereas 'diffusion' is the term used by Aquinas to denote the primacy of finality, he also emphasises in creation the aspect of divine efficiency which is expressed in the word *communicatio*. Now, by causal efficiency is understood an activity whereby one thing enriches another by pouring out its perfection into it, thus sharing its actuality. The agent proceeds outward and gives something of itself. In other words, it pertains to the nature of the good to communicate itself to others.[107] And if the things of nature, in so far as they are perfect, communicate their good to others, it pertains all the more to divine will to communicate its good to others through similitude.[108] Divine goodness proceeds into things in so far as it communicates itself to them.[109]

---

[106] *Contra Gentiles* 3, 18, 2001: Deus est simul ultimus rerum finis, et primum agens.

[107] *Contra Gentiles* 3, 1, 1: Pertinet ad rationem boni, ut se aliis communicet.

[108] *ST*, I, 19, 2: Unde si res naturales inquantum perfectae sunt suum bonum aliis communicant, multo magis pertinet ad voluntatem divinam ut bonum suum aliis per similitudinem communicet, secundum quod possibile est.

[109] *ST*, I, 73, 2: Divina bonitas quodammodo movetur et procedit in res, secundum quod se eis communicat, ut Dionysius dicit, 2 cap. de Div. Nom.; III, 1, 1: Pertinet autem ad rationem boni ut se aliis communicet: ut patet per Dionysium, 4 cap. de Div. Nom. Unde ad rationem summi boni pertinet quod summo modo se creaturae communicet; IV, ix, 409: Ex amore enim bonitatis suae processit quod bonitatem suam voluit diffundere et communicare aliis, secundum quod fuit possibile, scilicet per modum similitudinis et quod eius bonitas non tantum in ipso maneret, sed ad alia efflueret.

Out of love for his own goodness God wishes to communicate it to others. Through love for himself as their ultimate end God wishes that all things should be. And while he is 'moved' by an end in order to cause, it is not so as to acquire any increase in goodness since this is impossible: God acts, not through desire for an end to be attained, but through love for an end which he wishes to communicate.[110] In his Commentary on the *Divine Names*, Aquinas notes that an agent which is not fully perfect in itself will act out of desire for that which it does not possess; an agent which is perfect acts, however, through love of what it possesses. 'Dionysius adds, therefore, that Beauty itself which is God, is the efficient, moving and supportive cause, "by love of its own beauty." Because he possesses his own beauty, he wishes to multiply it in so far as possible, through the communication of his likeness.'[111]

The activity of what is imperfect, besides perfecting its object, tends also towards the perfection of the being from which it emanates. The primary agent, the first cause of all, on the other hand, is fully actual and does not act to acquire any end but only to communicate its perfection and goodness: *Intendit solum communicare suam perfectionem, quae est eius bonitas.*[112]

---

[110] *Contra Gentiles* 3, 18, 2003: Deus autem qui est primum agens omnium rerum, non sic agit quasi sua actione aliquid acquirat, sed quasi sua actione aliquid largiatur: quia non est in potentia ut aliquid acquirere possit, sed solum in actu perfecto, ex quo potest elargiri. Res igitur non ordinantur in Deum sicut in finem cui aliquid acquiratur, sed ut ab ipso ipsummet suo modo consequantur, cum ipsemet sit finis.

[111] IV, v, 352: Causa agens, quaedam agit ex desiderio finis, quod est agentis imperfecti, nondum habentis quod desiderat; sed agentis perfecti est ut agat per amorem eius quod habet . . . et propter hoc subdit quod pulchrum, quod est Deus, est causa effectiva et motiva et continens, 'amore propriae pulchritudinis.' Quia enim propriam pulchritudinem habet, vult eam multiplicare, sicut possibile est, scilicet per communicationem suae similitudinis.

[112] *ST*, I, 44, 4: Omne agens agit propter finem: alioquin ex actione agentis non magis sequeretur hoc quam illud, nisi a casu. Est autem idem finis agentis et patientis, inquantum huiusmodi sed aliter et aliter: unum enim et idem est quod agens intendit imprimere, et quod patiens intendit recipere. Sunt autem quaedam quae simul agunt et patiuntur, quae sunt agentia imperfecta: et his convenit quod etiam in agendo intendant aliquid acquirere. Sed primo agenti, qui est agens tantum, non convenit agere propter acquisitionem alicuius finis; sed intendit solum communicare suam perfectionem, quae est eius bonitas. Et unaquaeque creatura intendit consequi suam perfectionem, quae est similitudo perfectionis et bonitatis divinae. See also *In IV Sent.*, 46, 1, 1b: Bonitas enim importat in Deo rationem finis, in quo est plenissima perfectio; finis autem movet efficientem ad agendum; unde et bonitas Dei movet quodam modo ipsum ad operandum, non quidem ut ipse bonitatem acquirat, sed ut bonitatem aliis communicet. Deus non agit propter appetitum finis, sed propter amorem finis, volens communicare bonitatem suam, quantum possibile est et decens secundum eius providentiam; et ideo sicut finis in omnibus operabilibus est primum principium, ita divina bonitas est primum principium communicationis totius, qua Deus perfectiones creaturis largitur.

Through love of his goodness, God desires to share his perfection and bestows it as a gift. Thus, whereas the principle *Bonum diffusivum sui* expresses the finality or purposiveness of divine causality, it should be completed: *Bonum est diffusivum sui et communicativum.*[113] Efficiency and finality both belong to the causality of goodness.[114] The final causality with which God loves himself moves him through the manner of efficiency to cause others whose purpose is likewise to love him. God's love, therefore, is also radically efficient; communication, however, is not itself the ultimate purpose of creation, rather a manner of reflecting and rendering honour to his own goodness which is the end of creation.

According to Aquinas, therefore, God is both efficient and final cause. Whereas Aristotle's God moves as the object of desire (κινεῖ ὡς ἐρώμενον),[115] since any other causality would imply change, this presents no difficulty to Aquinas, since any 'relation' which holds between God and creatures is not really in God but in creatures.[116]

Now the communicative character of goodness, i.e. its efficient causality, is rooted fundamentally in its nature as act, i.e. in perfection as actuality. To be perfect or good is to be in some measure actual. And it is in the nature of what is actual to be self-expansive: every agent acts in so far as it is in act.[117] Of itself, act tends to realise itself according to its fullness; it is limited only by potency.[118] Act is, therefore, of itself essentially generous: its nature is to communicate itself in so far as possible. This is signified in the very notion of act: *communicatio enim sequitur rationem actus.*[119]

The things of nature, therefore, tend towards their own good, says Aquinas, not only to acquire it, but also to diffuse it to others in so far as possible. It belongs to the nature of will to share with others the

---

[113] *De Reg. Princip.*, 4, 1040: Cum bonum sit diffusivum et sui communicativum, quanto res communior est, tanto plus de bonitate habere videtur. Ergo omnia communicare plus habet de ratione virtutis et bonitatis;.

[114] *In Metaph.*, I, 8: Bonum autem potest intelligi dupliciter. Uno modo sicut causa finalis, inquantum aliquid fit gratia alicuius boni. Alio modo per modum causae efficientis, sicut dicimus quod bonus homo facit bonum.

[115] *Met.* 1072b 3.

[116] *ST*, I, 6, 3 ad 1: Relatio autem qua aliquid dicitur relative ad creaturas non est realiter in Deo sed in creaturis, in Deo vero secundum rationem.

[117] *Contra Gentiles* 3, 3, 1883: Omne agens agit secundum quod est actu. Aristotle, *Physics*, 3, iii, 202a: ἔστιν ἐνεργητικὸν τοῦ κινητοῦ.

[118] *De Potentia* 2, 1: Natura cuiuslibet actus est, quod seipsum communicet quantum possibile est. Unde unumquodque agens agit secundum quod in actu est. Agere vero nihil aliud est quam communicare illud per quod agens est actu, secundum quod est possibile. Natura autem divina maxime et purissime actus est. Unde et ipsa seipsam communicat quantum possibile est.

[119] *In I Sent.*, 4, 1 ad 1.

good it possesses. And in diffusing its goodness, each agent causes
something similar to itself: *Omne agens agit sibi simile*; this is the
greatest sign of its perfection.[120] All active beings, in so far as they are
perfect, i.e. in act, reproduce their like.[121] Thus in the measure that
things are actual they tend to diffuse their perfection; but in the measure
that they are potential they seek—as actual—to acquire the enrichment
in actuality of the good which they lack and towards which they are
by nature oriented. Act is oriented towards finality, i.e. to perfection,
which is synonymous with fulfilment or complete actuality. Goodness,
therefore, is identical with actuality—both as the source of its diffusion
or efficacy and its measure of perfection at any point, and as the goal
for which beings strive in seeking complete fulfilment.

Now something is desired as good only in so far as it is in actual
existence: existence is thus the measure of its perfection; likewise it can
cause only in the measure that it is actual. It is desired in so far as it
is perfective of another and this is in turn possible according as it
exercises in act the existential resources from which it can impart the
richness to which the other is receptive. Only a being which itself exists
in act can cause an effect: *Agere autem aliquem effectum per se convenit
enti in actu.*[122] *Esse* is both the actualising source of all activity and the
goal desired by all. Thus, it is not fully adequate to say with de
Finance: 'La notion aristotélicienne de génération, la participation
platonicienne, l'émanation des néoplatoniciens, convergent, dans le
thomisme, en une notion plus fondamentale encore, celle de la diffusion
de l'acte.'[123] Act, participation and emanation are all rooted more
profoundly in, and flow from, intensive and emergent *esse*, *actus actuum*
and *perfectio perfectionum*: the inner and profound act of all beings,
the existential source in which they share; which they aspire to
participate in ever more richly, and which in its fullness is their universal
origin and final good. The perspectives of Plato and Aristotle
complement each other: communication of act and diffusion of
goodness; goodness gives of itself and act is expansive. Aquinas is able
to synthesise the Aristotelian and Platonist theories of causality.
Moreover, in *esse*, the duality of Aristotle's principles is overcome: it

---

[120] *Contra Gentiles* 2, 6, 882.

[121] *ST*, I, 19, 2: Res enim naturalis non solum habet naturalem inclinationem respectu
proprii boni, ut acquirat ipsum cum non habet, vel ut quiescat in illo cum habet, sed
etiam ut proprium bonum in alia diffundat secundum quod possibile est. Unde videmus
quod omne agens, inquantum est actu et perfectum, facit sibi simile. Unde et hoc pertinet
ad rationem voluntatis ut bonum quod quis habet aliis communicet, secundum quod
possibile est.

[122] *Contra Gentiles* 2, 6, 881.

[123] Joseph de Finance, *Être et agir dans la philosophie de Saint Thomas*, p. 67.

belongs to act to fulfil itself by actualising others, and the good is what all things desire: act as expansive or communicative and act as desirable are identical in the act of existing.

Now, as the pure actuality of Being, God is pre-eminently capable of causing others in his own likeness.[124] As subsistent Act, he alone can cause things in their very existence.[125] But whereas imperfect causes, which are both active and passive, seek even in acting to acquire something, the first cause, who is agent only since he is fully actual, acts not for the acquisition of any end but solely to communicate his perfection, his own goodness.[126] Because God's will is perfect, he has the power to communicate his being by way of likeness.[127] And because he has no gain, it is from his goodness that God bestows being on other things: *Ex bonitate autem Dei est quod aliis esse largitur: unumquodque enim agit inquantum est actu perfectum.*[128]

As pure actuality, God is not only the cause through his goodness of all beings, but as the plenitude of goodness he is desired universally by all as their final good. Each creature intends to acquire its own perfection which is the likeness of divine perfection and goodness.[129] In the act of *esse*, Aquinas thus unifies the Dionysian motif of goodness (diffusive and desirable) with actuality as both efficient and final—both within the realm of finite goals or causes, and ultimately in the divine ground of subsistent Being. All of these principles and perspectives are synthesised in the following paragraph from *Contra Gentiles*:

> The communication of being and goodness arises from goodness. This is evident from the very nature and definition of the good. By nature, the good of each thing is its act and perfection. Now, each thing acts in so far as it is in act, and in acting it diffuses being and goodness to other things. Hence it is a sign of a being's perfection that 'it can produce its like,' as may be seen from the Philosopher in *Meteorologica* iv. Now, the nature of the good comes from its being something appetible. This is the end, which also moves the agent to act. That is why it is said that the good is diffusive of itself and of

---

[124] *Contra Gentiles* 2, 6.

[125] *ST*, I-II, 79, 2: Omne enim ens, quocumque modo sit, oportet quod derivetur a primo ente; ut patet per Dionysium, 5 cap. de Div. Nom. Omnis autem actio causatur ab aliquo existente in actu, quia nihil agit nisi secundum quod est actu: omne autem ens actu reducitur in primum actum, scilicet Deum, sicut in causam, qui est per suam essentiam actus. Facere autem aliquid actu consequitur ad hoc quod est esse actu, ut patet in Deo; ipse enim est actus purus et est prima causa essendi omnibus.

[126] *ST*, I, 44, 4.

[127] *Contra Gentiles* 2, 6, 883: Cum igitur divina voluntas sit perfecta, non deerit ei virtus communicandi esse suum alicui per modum similitudinis. Et sic erit ei causa essendi.

[128] *Contra Gentiles* 3, 21, 2019.

[129] *ST*, I, 44, 4: Et unaquaeque creatura intendit consequi suam perfectionem, quae est similitudo perfectionis et bonitatis divinae.

being. But this diffusion befits God because, as we have shown above, being through himself the necessary being, God is the cause of being for other things. God is, therefore, truly good.[130]

GOD'S CREATIVE FREEDOM

With the identification of Being and Goodness, and of final and efficient causality in God, we come closest to an understanding of the ultimate origin and reason for the 'why' and the 'how' of the existence of all things. A significant question, arises: is God, by virtue of the communicative character of act, and the diffusive nature of goodness, governed by an impulse to create? It would seem from Aquinas' view as we have just outlined it, that according to his nature God is compelled to communicate his goodness. We must, however, distinguish here between creation as willed by God and as known by us. Thus, we read in Aquinas' Commentary on Dionysius that the primary characteristic of divine goodness is that goodness itself constitutes the divine essence and that its second characteristic is to extend its goodness to all things.[131] And in *Contra Gentiles*[132] we read: *In Deo autem est bonitas et diffusio bonitatis in alia.* While God is the very essence of goodness itself, it is a sign of even greater perfection in that which is good to be a cause also of goodness in others.[133] The teacher is better if he teaches his students not only to be learned but also to become teachers of others; and that which both shines in itself and lights up others is more like the sun than that which only shines in itself.[134]

Since God is the most perfect Being possible, is he not therefore required as a consequence of his goodness to cause beings in the likeness of his perfection? Every agent, in so far as it is perfect, causes something similar to itself. It is the nature of the will that whatever good a person has he shares with others. But if natural beings share their goodness, must not the divine will communicate his goodness according to his likeness? In willing himself, must he not also will the existence of things which share his similitude?

---

[130] *Contra Gentiles* 1, 37, 307; See Aristotle, *Meteorologica*, IV, 3 380a 13-15.
[131] IV, i, 269.
[132] *Contra Gentiles* 2, 45, 1222.
[133] *ST*, I, 103, 6: Maior autem perfectio est quod aliquid in se sit bonum, et etiam sit aliis causa bonitatis, quam si esset solummodo in se bonum.
[134] *Contra Gentiles* 2, 45, 1222. *Contra Gentiles* 3, 21, 2022: Tunc maxime perfectum est unumquodque quando potest alterum sibi simile facere: illud enim perfecte lucet quod alia illuminare potest.

This is, needless to say, according to Aquinas not the case! It is a *sign* of perfection in a being that it can cause its resemblance.[135] It is a sign of excellence that it *can* produce its like, but that it must necessarily do so would be indeed a sign of imperfection. A sign of greater perfection is to do *freely* that of which one is capable. Whereas plants and animals already manifest the perfection of reproducing their kind, it is only with human life and the appearance of will that there emerges to some degree the power of being able freely to fulfil one's possibilities. We may, within the limits of the human condition, choose whether or not to seek certain goals or ends. We may choose either to act or not to act, and how to act. To an infinitely greater extent, it follows that God is not required—even by his goodness—to will creation. It does not follow from the fact that because God *can* do something he will choose to do so; he acts not by necessity of his nature, but according to his will.[136]

The principle *Bonum diffusivum sui et communicativum* must not be seen as a law governing the self-communication of God's goodness but is itself an expression of the fathomless freedom pertaining to the ultimate ground of Being, which gratuitously calls everything finite to being and goodness.[137] It is God's free decision to radiate his goodness which inscribes the diffusive tendency as a universal character of the created world. The diffusive and dynamic tendency of finite goodness is a reflection of divine generosity, and experiencing its limited instances within the universe we can, through reflection, understand how fitting or appropriate it is that God should have created.

Bonum diffusivum is not itself a universal and necessary principle flowing from the nature of existence, as are, for example, the laws of non-contradiction and sufficient reason. It is through reflection on the world, disclosed as a gift of God's generosity, that we can conclude that it is consonant with God's goodness to communicate his love. God's goodness is necessarily diffusive only in the love which he inspires within himself. Otherwise the principle of diffusion is but a created impulse or tendency resulting from a free desire of love.

We can, reflecting *a posteriori* upon creatures, observe many examples of the diffusive and expansive character of goodness in act: the sun sheds its illumination, life propagates itself, chemical substances irradiate

---

[135] *Contra Gentiles* 2, 6, 882: Signum perfectionis in rebus inferioribus est quod possunt sibi similia facere. *In DN*, XIII, i, 968: Perfectum autem est unumquodque cum potest facere sibi simile.

[136] *De Potentia* 3, 14 ad 5: Non sequitur, si Deus aliquid potuit facere, quod illud fecerit, eo quod est agens secundum voluntatem, non secundum necessitatem naturae. Cf. *Contra Gentiles* 2, 26, 1038; *Contra Gentiles* 1, 66, 550; *Contra Gentiles* 3, 97, 2735.

[137] See John A. Peters, *Metaphysics, A Systematic Survey*, p. 476.

a determinate influence in mutual interaction. The fecundity of goodness is reflected also at the human level: the learned person shares his knowledge, the lover seeks the good of the beloved, joy is infective—when we are sad we withdraw, when happy we feel the urge to spread our gladness. These are examples of a creaturely tendency, but creation itself is not governed by this principle. We must, therefore, qualify Aquinas' statement that it is characteristic of divine goodness to be self-diffusive, since otherwise this would suggest that it is automatic for God to create. We must add that the diffusion of divine goodness is the second characteristic which we can discover *quoad nos*. It does not necessarily belong to God's nature that he must create, only that he can create; it belongs to him 'accidentally' that he has created. Creation adds nothing to his perfection.

God creates neither out of need, i.e. to acquire any perfection which he is lacking, nor because of any intrinsic necessity to bestow his goodness. He alone is *maxime liberalis*.[138] Aquinas defends Dionysius from any determinist interpretation which might attend the illustration of creation by its parallel with the sun which 'without reflection or choice, but by its very being,'[139] illuminates all things. With the words *non ratiocinans aut praeeligens*, Dionysius does not intend to exclude all choice from God but only choice of a certain kind, namely that of giving his goodness only to some beings and not to all.[140] The nerve of the parallel is found in the words *per ipsum suum esse illuminat*. By his very Being, through his essence, God irradiates his goodness to all things. Any danger of determinism is removed when Aquinas points out that, in contrast to the sun, God has intellect and will which are identical with God's Being. Thus what God does according to his being, he does also according to his will and intellect.[141] Though they may be distinguished by reason, God's Being and essence are one with his

---

[138] *ST*, I, 44, 4, ad 1.

[139] 4, 1, 96.

[140] *ST*, I, 19, 4 ad 1: Dionysius per verba illa non intendit excludere electionem a Deo simpliciter, sed secundum quid: inquantum scilicet, non quibusdam solum bonitatem suam communicat, sed omnibus: prout scilicet electio discretionem quamdam importat. Klaus Kremer believes that this passage means that 'the Good cannot be good if it does not communicate its goodness.' See 'Das "Warum" der Schopfung: *'quia bonus' vel/et 'quia voluit'*? Ein Beitrag zum Verhältnis von Neuplatonismus und Christentum an Hand des Prinzips *bonum est diffusivum sui*', p. 256. See also p. 262: 'Plotins Anschauung uber das Gute gipfelte in dem Satz: Das Gute (Gott) kann nicht gut sein..., wenn es nicht von seinem Eigensein einem Anderen mitteilt. Ähnlich Proklos und Dionysius!'

[141] IV, i, 271: Sed sicut de sole dixerat quod per ipsum suum esse illuminat, ita de Deo subdit quod per suam essentiam omnibus bonitatem tradit. Esse enim solis non est eius intelligere aut velle, etiam si intellectum et voluntatem haberet et ideo quod facit per suum esse, non facit per intellectum et voluntatem. Sed divinum esse est eius intelligere et velle et ideo quod per suum esse facit, facit per intellectum et voluntatem.

wisdom and will.[142] If creation, therefore, is the work of his essence, it is *eo ipso* the work of his knowledge and will. God creates *ex libertate voluntatis, et non ex naturae necessitate.*[143] The analogy with the sun refers not to the absence of will or the necessity of action but to the universality of diffusion.[144] The sun sends forth its rays of light to all material bodies, down to the very last, without differentiating one from another; so it is also with divine goodness.[145] Against an objection which appeals to Dionysius, that God does not love some creatures as his specially chosen, Aquinas explains that, taken universally, the communication of divine goodness is without discernment, in so far as there is nothing which does not have a share in his goodness. God does choose, however, to love some creatures more than others. This is the reason for the hierarchy among beings.[146]

This is clarified, according to Aquinas, in another phrase of Dionysius: ὡς ἀγαθότητος ὕπαρξις αὐτῷ τῷ εἶναι πάντων ἐστὶ τῶν ὄντων αἰτία.[147] It is not according to any created circumstance or condition that God is cause of things, but as the essence of goodness in his own being. His creative power is not restricted in any way to what he creates.[148] God's wisdom, power and goodness are not limited to this particular course and order of things but are infinitely super-abundant.[149] He creates *non ex necessitate sed ex gratia.*[150] Possessing the full perfection of complete being (*totius esse perfectionem plenam possidens*), God bestows *esse* on

---

[142] I, iii, 88: per ipsum esse suum est causa omnium existentium; nec per hoc excluditur quin agat per intellectum et voluntatem, quia intelligere Eius et velle est ipsum esse Eius.

[143] *In I Sent.*, 43, 2, 2, ad 2: Sicut voluntas et essentia et sapientia in Deo idem sunt re, sed ratione distinguuntur; ita etiam distinguuntur et operationes secundum rationes diversorum attributorum, quamvis sit una tantum ipsius operatio, quae est sua essentia. Et ideo, quia creatio rerum quamvis sit operatio essentiae eius, non tamen inquantum solum est essentia, sed etiam inquantum est sapientia et voluntas; ideo sequitur conditionem scientiae et voluntatis; et quia voluntas libera est, ideo dicitur Deus ex libertate voluntatis res facere, et non ex naturae necessitate. Cf. *De Potentia* 3, 15 ad 6.

[144] *In I Sent.* 43, 2, 2, ad 1: Dionysius non intendit assignare convenientiam bonitatis divinae ad solem visibilem quantum ad necessitatem agendi, sed quantum ad universalitatem causandi: quod patet ex hoc quod continuo ostendit radios divinae bonitatis usque ad ultima entium diffundi.

[145] *De Potentia* 3, 15, ad 1: Similitudo Dionysii est intelligenda quantum ad universitatem diffusionis; sol enim in omnia corpora radios effundit, non discernendo unum ab alio, et similiter divina bonitas. Non autem intelligitur quantum ad privationem voluntatis. Cf. *De Veritate* 21, 6 ad 11.

[146] *ST*, I, 23, 4, ad 1.

[147] 1, 5, 24; in Sarracenus' translation: Bonitatis essentia, per ipsum esse, omnium est existentium causa.

[148] I, iii, 88.

[149] XII, 948.

[150] I, i, 37; (Dionysius, 1, 1, 10: ἀγαθοπρεπῶς); I ii, 58: Omnia sunt deducta ad esse ex bonitate Eius, substantificante res, non autem ex necessitate naturae. Cf. *De Potentia*, 3, 17 ad 4.

all existing things from the abundance of his perfection: *ex sui perfectionis abundantia.* He confers *esse* upon creatures not through a necessity of nature but by a free decision of his will.[151]

If God, in creating, acts according to his nature, this does not imply that he acts through necessity. Is it not precisely in free activity that we act in a manner most properly human and in harmony with our own nature? Is the parent or lover deprived of freedom because it is profoundly natural for them to love? Compulsion against the freedom of activity occurs, rather, if one is required to act in a manner contrary to one's nature. It is exactly because we are not obliged to perform an action, that we may do so, out of sheer generosity. To the expression of gratitude for a generous gift or deed 'It was not necessary', one has perhaps heard the revealing response 'That is why I did it.'

God is the fontal cause of all life and being, not by any process of necessary emanation—*non quidem propter suam necessitatem, sed propter bonitatem Ipsius.*[152] As Aquinas clearly points out, divine will transcends the categories of necessity and contingency, 'natural' and 'unnatural'. As a cause it lies outside the order of beings and pours forth all of being and all its differences, including those of possibility and necessity. The very origin of necessity and contingency is the divine will itself, which as primary cause transcends the order of necessity and contingency (*transcendit ordinem necessitatis et contingentiae*).[153] What we are here considering is not the contrast between contingency and necessity but that between freedom and necessity. Aquinas' point is nevertheless highly significant within the present context. God is beyond all distinctions within being, and surpasses every category whereby we comprehend creaturely being. As subsistent Being, there is nothing to constrain him; since he is perfectly simple there is in him no distinction which could occasion inherent or internal opposition. Even the distinction 'natural: unnatural' is inappropriate: 'God's willing of any of the things he is not bound to will is not natural, nor is it unnatural or against nature; it is voluntary.'[154]

---

[151] *Contra Gentiles* 3, 1, 1862: Ex sui perfectionis abundantia omnibus existentibus esse largitur . . . Esse autem aliis tribuit non necessitate naturae, sed secundum suae arbitrium voluntatis.

[152] I, ii, 52. See I, ii, 53-54.

[153] *In Peri Herm.*, I, xiv, 197: Nam voluntas divina est intelligenda ut extra ordinem entium existens, velut causa quaedam profundens totum ens et omnes eius differentias. Sunt autem differentiae entis possibile et necessarium; et ideo ex ipsa voluntate divina originantur necessitas et contingentia in rebus . . . omnes dependeant a voluntate divina, sicut a prima causa, quae transcendit ordinem necessitatis et contingentiae.

[154] *ST*, I, 19, 3 ad 3: Non est naturale Deo velle aliquid aliorum quae non ex necessitate vult, neque tamen innaturale, aut contra naturam, sed est voluntarium.

PRESENCE AND TRANSCENDENCE OF GOD

Emphasising the liberality of creation, Aquinas is also concerned to clarify the manner of creation and God's relation to creatures. The freedom of creation implies also the transcendence of God: emanationism would imply pantheism! God's freedom in creating implies his transcendence beyond creatures. Certain phrases favoured by Dionysius to emphasise the presence of God through his power within beings might invite a pantheist interpretation. He writes, for example, that God is 'the life of living things and the substance of beings.'[155] Dionysius, moreover, follows Corinthians[156] in speaking of God as 'all in all', (omnia in omnibus);[157] he is 'the substance of all substances',[158] and 'the Being of existing things':[159] Esse omnium est superesse divinitatis.[160]

It has been noted that in his Commentary on the Divine Names, Aquinas more than 70 times warns against a pantheistic interpretation of Dionysius.[161] Théry also remarks that Eriugena's translation of Dionysius tends to reinforce the apparently pantheistic tone of some passages.[162] Aquinas, however, strongly criticises such a false understanding. It must not be understood that God is the substance, existence or essence which enters formally or essentially into the constitution of creatures (formaliter, essentialiter).[163] He is present to all creatures causally and effectively, in the manner of exemplarity (causaliter, exemplariter). Only as their cause and origin is God the life of living beings and the essence of existing things.[164]

---

[155] I, 3, 12: ἡ τῶν ζώντων ζωὴ καὶ τῶν ὄντων οὐσία: viventium vita, existentium substantia.

[156] 1, 15, 28.

[157] 1, 7, 25: ᾗ τὰ πάντα ἐν πᾶσι. 7, 3, 322: καὶ ἐν πᾶσι πάντα ἐστί.

[158] 2, 10, 65: οὐσία ταῖς ὅλαις οὐσίαις.

[159] V, 4, 264: τὸ εἶναι τοῖς οὖσι.

[160] CH 4, 1, 177D: τὸ γὰρ εἶναι πάντων ἐστιν ἡ ὑπὲρ τὸ εἶναι θεότης. See La Hiérarchie Céleste, ed. Heil, p. 94, n. 1. Cf. Eriugena, De Divisione Naturae, I, 72; III, 4.

[161] Gabriel Théry, 'Scot Erigène, introducteur de Denys', p. 106-7, n. 30.

[162] See M. Dominic Twohill, The Background and St Thomas Aquinas' Reading of the De Divinis Nominibus of the Pseudo-Dionysius, p. 136-7.

[163] I, ii, 52: Et quia dixerat quod Deus est substantia et vita omnium, ne aliquis intelligeret quod Deus esset essentia aut vita formalis veniens in compositionem rerum, hunc perversum intellectum excludit, cum subdit: et, ut simpliciter dicatur, idest universaliter dicatur, vita viventium et substantia, idest essentia existentium, qui est principium agens et causa fontalis omnis vitae et substantiae, non quidem propter suam necesssitatem, sed propter bonitatem Ipsius, quae existentia et deducit ad esse et continet, idest conservat ea in esse. See also V, i, 630.

[164] I, iii, 99; VII, iv, 731: Deus est omnia in omnibus causaliter, cum tamen nihil sit eorum quae sunt in rebus essentialiter. In I Sent., 8, 1, 2, p. 198: Patet quod divinum

Aquinas censures the *intellectus PERVERSUS* of those who take the words of Dionysius *'esse omnium est superessentialis Divinitas'* to mean that God is the formal being itself of all things; this interpretation even contradicts the writer's words: 'For if divinity is the formal being of all things, it will not be beyond all things but amidst all, indeed a part of all.' As Aquinas explains, in saying that God is beyond all things, Dionysius indicates that he is according to his nature distinct from all things and established above all things. And in saying that the divinity is the 'Being of all things', he shows that there is in all beings a certain similitude of divine being coming from God.[165]

Aquinas, like Dionysius, wishes to emphasise both God's infinite transcendence beyond creatures, yet his intimate actuality and immanence. And in harmonising these aspects, the influence of Dionysius is clearly evident.[166] Since *esse* is what is most intimate and profound within each thing as its first perfection, and since creation is properly the giving of being, that which is its cause cannot cease to operate without the thing itself ceasing to exist. God is intimately present within each thing, just as its own *esse* is proper to every being. It can neither commence nor endure without the activity of God. God is immediately active in all things; wherefore he must be within them all.[167] *Deus est supra omnia per excellentiam suae naturae, et tamen est in omnibus rebus ut causans omnium esse.*[168] God is in a sense more intimate to each creature than it is to itself. As de Finance remarks,[169] each creature remains in some way exterior to itself; it does not coincide with what is most profound and central to it: its being. God, however, through

---

esse producit esse creaturae in similitudine sui imperfecta: et ideo esse divinum dicitur esse omnium rerum, a quo omne esse creatum effective et exemplariter manat. Ibid., 17, 1, 5, p. 408: Dionysius dicit quod esse divinum est esse omnium, quia ab eo omne esse traducitur et exemplatur.

[165] *Contra Gentiles* 1, 26, 246: Primum est quarundam auctoritatum intellectus perversus. Invenitur enim a Dionysio dictum, IV cap. Cael. Hier.: esse omnium est superessentialis Divinitas. Ex quo intelligere voluerunt ipsum esse formale omnium rerum Deum esse, non considerantes hunc intellectum ipsis verbis consonum esse non posse. Nam si divinitas est omnium esse formale, non erit super omnia, sed inter omnia, immo aliquid omnium. Cum ergo divinitatem super omnia dixit, ostendit secundum suam naturam ab omnibus distinctum et super omnia collocatum. Ex hoc vero quod dixit quod divinitas est esse omnium, ostendit quod a Deo in omnibus quaedam divini esse similitudo reperitur. Cf. *In I Sent.*, 8, 1, 2 ad 1: Et per hoc patet solutio ad dictum Dionysii, quod ita intelligendum est, ut patet ex hoc quod dicit 'superesse'. Si enim Deus esset essentialiter esse creaturae, non esset superesse. See *In DN*, I, ii, 52.

[166] See de Finance, *Être et Agir*, p. 151, n. 1.

[167] *In I Sent.*, 8, 1: Esse autem est illud quod est magis intimum cuilibet et quod profundius omnibus inest . . . Unde oportet quod Deus sit in omnibus rebus et intime. Cf. Ibid., 37, 1, 1; also ad 2.

[168] *In I Sent.*, 8, 1, ad 1.

[169] Ibid., p. 150.

his causality is present at this very centre. He is more interior to things than they are to themselves: not as an intrinsic principle entering into their constitution but as the abiding source of their *esse*.[170] Aquinas himself indeed relies on this Dionysian mode of expression in his claim that God is universally perfect, containing within himself the perfections of all things.[171] In saying that God 'is the being of all that subsists', Dionysius is emphasising that he does not exist in a limited or determined way, but precontains in himself all being in an unlimited manner. God is causally 'all in all' inasmuch as he is causally the total perfection of all things.[172]

God is cause not only of beings in their origin but in their continuing existence. Aquinas develops Dionysius' image of the sun to illustrate both God's pervasive and abiding presence, yet his eminent transcendence. Just as the air is lighted only so long as it is illuminated by the sun, and recedes into darkness when the rays of the sun's light are withdrawn, creatures are likewise preserved in being by the diffusion of God's goodness; if he withdraws his presence, they fall back into the void of non-being.[173] As the sun is naturally luminous, while air is lighted by sharing in the light of the sun although it does not partake of its nature, so also God alone is by his essence Being, while every creature is being through participation since its essence is not identical with its *esse*.[174] Beings do not share in divine essence but in the illuminative effusion of divine Being which emanates from him.

---

[170] Cf. *In I Sent.*, 37, 1, 1 ad 1: Quamvis essentia divina non sit intrinseca rei quasi pars veniens in constitutionem eius; tamen est intra rem quasi operans et agens esse uniuscuiusque rei; *Contra Gentiles* 3, 68; *In DN*, III, 234-5.

[171] *ST*, I, 4, 2: Utrum Deus sit universaliter perfectus, omnium in se perfectiones habens.

[172] *ST*, I, 4, 2: Cum ergo Deus sit prima causa effectiva rerum oportet omnium rerum perfectiones praeexistere in Deo secundum eminentiorem modum. Et hanc rationem tangit Dionysius dicens de Deo quod non hoc quidem est hoc autem non est, sed omnia est ut omnium causa ... Omnium autem perfectiones pertinet ad perfectionem essendi, secundum hoc enim aliqualiter perfecta sunt quod aliquo modo esse habent. Unde sequitur quod nullius rei perfectio Deo desit. Et hanc rationem tangit Dionysius dicens quod Deus non quodammodo est existens sed simpliciter et incircumscripte totum in seipso esse praeaccipit, et postea subdit quod ipse est esse subsistens.

[173] *ST*, I, 8, 1: Hunc autem effectum causat Deus in rebus non solum quando primo esse incipiunt sed quamdiu in esse conservantur, sicut lumen causatur in aere a sole quamdiu aer illuminatus manet.

[174] *ST*, I, 104, 1: Sic autem se habet omnis creatura ad Deum sicut aer ad solem illuminantem. Sicut enim sol est lucens per suam naturam, aer autem fit luminosus participando lumen a sole, non tamen participando naturam solis, ita solus Deus est ens per essentiam suam, quia eius essentia est suum esse; omnis autem creatura est ens participative, non quod sua essentia sit eius esse. In the Blackfriars' edition, Vol. 14, there is a crucial omission of text in the English translation which makes the passage and the analogy meaningless.

Aquinas' position may be summarised: God is present in all things not according to his essence but through a participation of his created likeness. Through creation, God 'transfuses' into beings a likeness to himself.[175] Creation is in Dionysius' word a theophany, a manifestation of God's mystery and goodness. Creation is caused through God's diffusion of his similitude throughout beings. Divine similitude is not just a gift bestowed upon beings, but is their very being itself. Diffusion, similitude, participation—these notions are integral to a proper understanding of creation and the relation of creatures to God: their total presence within God, God's infinite intimacy within them; their utter separation and his infinite transcendence. Diffusion leaves God untouched in his nature; it safeguards the divine presence within beings without entering into relation with creatures. Creatures participate in God's presence but God is not participated. Beings share in the similitude of God while God in no manner resembles them.

Aquinas introduces in his Commentary the important concept of similitude to explain the 'relation' between God and creatures. The notion of similitude allows us to conceive of creation without endangering God's unity beyond the multiplicity of creatures, or confusing the infinity of his Being with the finite being of his creation. In contrast to the procession within the divine Trinity, where the divine essence itself is communicated, in the procession of creatures it remains beyond communication and sharing.[176] It is his similitude which is generated and multiplied and thus the divinity somehow, according to his likeness and not his essence, proceeds into creatures, and is somehow multiplied in them. Creation may be called a 'divine distinction' with respect to divine likeness, but not with respect to the divine essence.[177]

God's presence through similitude safeguards his unity and his transcendence. Aquinas himself inserts the word *similitudo*, which does not appear in Dionysius' text, to preserve the unparticipated transcendence of God and at the same time his mysterious presence within creatures. The divine essence goes out of itself *ex sua bonitate* and is multiplied *secundum suam similitudinem*.[178] Through the gifts of being, life and wisdom, God is participated by his effects in the manner of his likeness: *per similitudinem, non participabiliter, inquantum essentia*

---

[175] I, i, 30: Transfundens in omnia aliqualiter suam similitudinem.

[176] See Pierre Faucon, *Aspects néoplatoniciens de la doctrine de Saint Thomas d'Aquin*, p. 229.

[177] II, iii, 158. II, iv, 178: Deus ita participatur a creaturis per similitudinem, quod tamen remanet imparticipatus super omnia per proprietatem suae substantiae; *De Potentia* 9, 7: Ex illa perfectione divina descendunt perfectiones creatae, secundum quamdam similitudinem imperfectam.

[178] II, iii, 159.

manet imparticipata.[179] Because this occurs *per similitudinem*, God can be participated totally and not partially: that would imply a mingling or mixture of his substance.[180] God, who is pure act and contains all things virtually, is not participated partially, but totally by a diffusion of similitude, according as beings, each in its fullness, proceed from him; he is neither shared partially—it is not from 'part' of God that beings derive—nor is he fully acquired and possessed by creatures.[181]

Aquinas approves of and comments in detail upon the images which Dionysius uses to illustrate the participation of creatures in God, e.g. the lines which radiate from the central point of a circle: it is participated by all but does not depart from itself; the seal which impresses its character upon the wax but is not confused with the wax itself.[182] The seal is present according to its likeness (*secundum similitudinem*) but not through a mingling of substance (*per substantiae commixtionem*). Between God and creatures there is even less possibility of substantial contact.[183]

Although Aquinas introduces the notion of similitude, he finds it suggested in Dionysius' use of the word 'image' *(ἐικών)*. In 2, 8, 58, we find the following significant phrase where Dionysius summarises the teaching on exemplarity and participated presence: 'There is no exact comparison between cause and effect but effects possess according to their capacity the images of the causes . . . The natures of effects pre-subsist abundantly and essentially in their causes.' The term *'imagines'* expresses for Aquinas this relation of similitude: *Omnis enim causa producit suum effectum per aliquem modum similitudinis, non tamen causata consequuntur perfectum similitudinem causae.*[184]

The multiplicity of creation proceeds through a diffusion or effusion of the divine likeness; divine goodness abides according to its essence, undivided, unified and established in itself.[185] 'The divinity itself in some manner proceeds into effects, while it transmits its likeness to things, according to their proportion, but in such a manner that its excellence

---

[179] II, iii, 160; Cf. II, vi, 220: Nihil egreditur de divina Essentia.

[180] II, iii, 161: Dicit autem 'totam' eam 'participari', non tamen totaliter vel perfecte, qui omnibus incomprehensibilis est.

[181] *ST*, I, 75, 5, ad 1.

[182] II, iii, 163-4; cf. *Contra Gentiles* 1, 26, 246; *In DN*, XIII, ii, 971: effects are in their cause, not as a multiplicity, but 'secundum unam virtutem', just as all radii are present within the centre of the circle from which they proceed.

[183] II, iii, 164-5; cf. II, v, 201; on similitude, II, iv, 185.

[184] II, iv, 185; cf. *De Potentia* 7, art 5, ad 7: Sicut omnia participant Dei bonitatem,— non eamdem numero, sed per similitudinem—ita participant per similitudinem esse Dei. Cf. *In DN* IX, ii, 823; IX, iii, 832.

[185] II, vi, 215.

and singularity remain within itself, not communicated to things and hidden to us.'[186]

In diffusing his likeness, God establishes the being of creatures in themselves while losing none of his fullness, nor departing from his unity but remaining fully transcendent. We can perhaps illustrate this by analogy with the diffusion of spiritual goods. Whereas material goods, when shared, lose their unity and wholeness, spiritual beings may be simultaneously possessed by many without diminution or division.[187] Consider, for example, the diffusion and participation of knowledge. Sharing his learning, the wise person does not lose his identity nor his fullness and depth of wisdom; it may even encourage an increase. His disciples acquire according to their capacity the gift of knowledge which he bestows. The same is evident in the case of love, virtue, joy etc. Spirit is a principle of unity rather than division. And at an even superior level of freedom and independence is the gift of existence, unlimited in itself, which is bestowed and participated without diminishing the richness of its source. The infinite and intensive fullness of Being Itself, who is knowledge, wisdom and love itself, since his essence is *to be*, can cause his likeness in creatures, without departing from his unity and transcendence.

HIERARCHY AND ORDER OF BEINGS

I wish to conclude our overview of the integral metaphysics born out of the encounter of Aquinas and Dionysius with some remarks concerning the dynamic order and unity of beings, and especially on the place of man within the universal hierarchy.

One of the most striking features of the world is its richness of variety and diversity; it is, however, not a sheer multiplicity: an utter, unrelated, diversity would not provide promise or orientation in our search for a fruitful reflection on the ultimate origin, value or purpose of beings. This diversity, however, is encompassed within the original community of being, since all things agree with respect to their existence.[188] But neither can we remain at the horizontal level of common plurality, devoid of depth and density. Thus a source of even greater wonder and grateful admiration is the manner in which some

---

[186] II, ii, 136; cf. V, iii, 672.

[187] *ST*, III, 23, 1, ad 3: Bona spiritualia possunt simul a pluribus possideri, non autem bona corporalia. Cf. Garrigou-Lagrange, 'Fecundity of Goodness', p. 235.

[188] *Contra Gentiles* 2, 52: Esse autem, inquantum est esse, non potest esse diversum.

beings excel others in the manner in which they exercise their existence. God not only gives being to creatures but infuses them with an order and dynamic élan. All creatures are pre-ordered and pre-oriented within the whole. The gradation of things within the universe thus illuminates the profound depths and dimensions of existence itself.

The multiplicity of beings, together with the distinct measures in which the richness of reality is possessed, discloses a fundamental distinction within the deepest centre of every entity, i.e. the ontological difference between that which it is, the nature which it constitutes, and the existence which actualises it, the first perfection of *to be* which it circumscribes. Here the most intimate indigence of each being becomes apparent to metaphysical reflection. Whatever the resources of any existing thing, no matter how sublime and profound, these do not include the very first power of being itself—the radical presence which separates them from the complete void of nothingness. It does not belong to it of right, but lies beyond and is anterior to its resources.

We thus observe at each stage in the hierarchy of beings an increasing intensity and concentration of existence; an accumulation of entitative perfection, limited at each level and insufficient in its very foundation. The ascending scale of values throughout reality points both in its richness and indigence, its poverty and plenitude, towards the summit and fullness of perfection which embraces not only the wealth of everything that exists, but has radically the creative power to bestow the free gift of being. In reflecting on the mystery of existence, we discern the most profound depth that dwells within each thing, a depth on which all else is grounded. Existence itself demands that it be infinite, since there is nothing which can limit it. Considered on its own, finite being would seem a contradiction, and is intelligible only in light of the affirmation of infinite creative Being.

Creation proceeds from God as a descending flow of perfection. For Aquinas and Dionysius, this does not occur, as for Plotinus and Proclus, by the lessening of God's causality within creatures, since he is immediately and directly actual within all. But while God loves all things in a constant and single act of will, some are better because he wills more good to them, i.e. he loves them more.[189] The manifold variety of creation is clear proof of the inexhaustible wealth of God's Being. The reason why there is profuse diversity in creation, according to Aquinas, is that a solitary creature would not suffice to communicate

---

[189] *ST*, I, 20, 3: Necesse est dicere, quod Deus quaedam aliis magis amat. Cum enim amor Dei sit causa bonitatis rerum, non esset aliquid alio melius, si Deus non vellet uni maius bonum quam alteri. *ST*, I, 20, 4: Ex hoc sunt aliqua meliora, quod Deus eius maius bonum vult; unde sequitur, quod meliora plus amet.

and show forth the splendour of divine goodness. Aquinas even uses the word 'necessary' in this regard:

> In order that the likeness of divine goodness might be more perfectly communicated to things, it was necessary for there to be a diversity of things, so that what could not be perfectly represented by one thing might be, in more perfect fashion, represented by a variety of things in different ways . . . the perfect goodness which is present in God in a unified and simple manner cannot be in creatures except in a diversified manner and through a plurality of things.[190]

Thus God makes many and diverse creatures so that what is lacking in one may be supplied by another. According to Aquinas, commenting on Dionysius, the universe would not be complete if there were but one grade of goodness in beings, i.e. if they were all equal. Diversity and gradation among beings belong to the perfection of the universe: *diversitas graduum in entibus, magis et minus bonum*.[191] Although there can never be an adequate likeness of God in the universe, this would be even more restricted if all things were of one degree. For this reason, therefore, there is distinction in created things, in order that they may receive God's likeness more perfectly by multiplicity than by unity.[192]

Causality, for example, would be impossible unless there were plurality and inequality among creatures. The agent is distinct from, and more noble (*honorabilius*) than, the effect. Since causality is a reflection of God's own outpouring of goodness, a creature resembles God all the more perfectly if it is not only good but also causes goodness in others; for there to be a more perfect imitation of God in creatures, it is necessary, therefore, that there be different degrees in things.[193]

A further argument of Aquinas is based on the infinity of God's intellect. He knows himself to be imitable in an infinity of ways. 'But an intellect that understands many things is not reproduced sufficiently in one. Since, then, the divine intellect understands many things, it reproduces itself more perfectly if it produces many creatures of all degrees than if it had produced one only.'[194] Moreover, order itself is a certain good, a sign of perfection, i.e. order among diverse things. But order could not be if there were no diversity and inequality of creatures.[195]

---

[190] *Contra Gentiles* 3, 97, 2724.
[191] IV, xvi, 501-9.
[192] *Contra Gentiles* 2, 45, 1221.
[193] *Contra Gentiles* 2, 45, 1222.
[194] *Contra Gentiles* 2, 45, 1225.
[195] *Contra Gentiles* 2, 45, 1225: . . . diversitas et inaequalitas creaturarum.

Diversity and inequality of beings require diverse grades of perfection. The created universe is, therefore, a diversity which is ordered according to different grades of perfection.[196] This is indeed evident in the natures of things: diversity is achieved by a gradation which ranges from inanimate bodies to plants and irrational animals, attaining its peak in man and intellectual substances. Moreover, there is diversity within each level; some species are more perfect, some individuals surpass others and embody more excellence.[197] We note again in this context that the comparative perfection of creatures is determined by their excellence or nobility of being: different natures have different modes of being and more noble substances a more noble *esse*.[198]

The gradation of perfection among creatures is rooted in their degrees of participation in and proximity to transcendent and absolute perfection.[199] 'The nearer a thing approaches the divine likeness, the more perfect it is.'[200] This doctrine Aquinas receives from Dionysius: God is the measure and order of all beings, the *mensura essendi*:[201] μέτρον ἐστὶ τῶν ὄντων.[202] Beings possess their measure of being, their *nobilitas essendi* according as they are nearer to or more distant from God.[203] The universe comprises, thefore, a scale of perfection; a vertical order or hierarchy, corresponding to the scheme portrayed by Neoplatonism in the gradual outflow of emanation.

From Dionysius, Aquinas receives not only a theory of the grades of being but also of their metaphysical continuity; at their highest point, beings of a lower nature resemble and are joined to that which is lowest in the order immediately superior to it. This is found in Dionysius' words: ἀεὶ τὰ τέλη τῶν προτέρων συνάπτουσα ταῖς ἀρχαῖς τῶν δευτέρων.[204] Aquinas encapsulates this principle in the lapidary

---

[196] *Contra Gentiles* 4, 97, 2725: Formarum diversitas diversum gradum perfectionis requirit . . . gradatim rerum diversitatem compleri.

[197] This is so also among angels, Aquinas notes, following Dionysius: Sicut in tota angelorum multitudine est hierarchia suprema, media et infima; ita in qualibet hierarchia est ordo supremus, medius et infimus; et in quolibet ordine supremi, medii et infimi. See *Contra Gentiles* 2, 95, 1809.

[198] *Contra Gentiles* 2, 68, 1451: Diversorum enim generum est diversus modus essendi; et nobilioris substantiae nobilius esse.

[199] *In de Causis*, XXII, 385: Propter abundantem participationem divinae Bonitatis ex propinquitate ad Deum.

[200] *Contra Gentiles* 3, 97, 2725: Quanto autem aliquid propinquius ad divinam similitudinem accedit, perfectius est. Cf. *De Spirit. Creat.*, art. 1.

[201] II, c, 203.

[202] 4, 4, 116.

[203] IV, iii, 310: . . . ex hoc potest sciri quantum unumquodque existentium habeat de nobilitate essendi, quod appropinquat Ei vel distat ab Eo. Aquinas again applies the analogy of whiteness; II, v, 203: . . . unumquodque intantum habet esse, inquantum appropinquat Ei.

[204] 7, 3, 324. For Dionysius' source see Proclus, *Elements*, Prop. 147.

expression: *Supremum infimi ordinis attingit infimum supremi.*[205] This is one of the most important laws governing the hierarchy of beings. Not only is there a continuity or succession which links and unifies all beings within a scale, from the most inferior to the supreme; there is also a bond or assimilation of nature. Each level of being, at its highest peak, participates after a manner in its superior, possessing in rudimentary form and incipient mode the perfection of the level which surpasses it. Conversely, it transmits to its immediate inferior something of its own perfection and excellence.

According to Aquinas, this 'wondrous connection of things' (*mirabilis rerum connexio*),[206] is to be found to a most intimate degree at all levels of the scale of being. Thus we find that some plants, by virtue of their mode of propagation reflect in some way the distinction of gender proper to animals.[207] Moreover, the generative power of the plant, which causes something outside itself, in some way approximates to the dignity of the sensible soul whose activity—in a more universal and excellent manner—is oriented to external things.[208] Conversely, the lowest in the animal kingdom, being immobile, scarcely surpasses the level of plant life.[209] Thus oysters, for example, which have only the

---

[205] *De Spirit. Creat.*, art. 2. cf. *Contra Gentiles* 2, 91, 1775: Natura superior in suo infimo contingit naturam inferiorem in eius supremo; *Contra Gentiles* 1, 57, 480; *Contra Gentiles* 3, 49, 2271; *ST*, I, 78, 2: Supremum enim inferioris naturae attingit id quod est infimum superioris, ut patet per Dionysium, in 7 cap. de Div. Nom. *De Veritate* 15, 1:... inferior natura in suo summo attingit ad aliquid infimum superioris naturae. *De Veritate* 16, 1: Sicut Dionysius, VII cap. de divin. Nomin., divina sapientia coniungit fines primorum principiis secundorum; naturae enim ordinatae ad invicem sic se habent sicut corpora contiguata, quorum inferius in sui supremo tangit superius in sui infimo: unde et inferior natura attingit in sui supremo ad aliquid quod est proprium superioris naturae, imperfecte illud participans. *In III Sent.*, 25, 1, 2: Omnis natura inferior in sui supremo attingit ad infinitum naturae superioris, secundum quod participat aliquid de natura superioris, quamvis deficienter. For other references, see Durantel, p. 189; Cf. Fabro, *Breve introduzione al tomismo*, p. 20, where this principle is praised as 'una chiave preziosa per sfuggire al trabocchetto dell'averroismo.' For a comprehensive treatment of this principle, see B. Montagnes, 'L'axiome de continuité chez Saint Thomas'.

[206] *Contra Gentiles* 2, 68, 1453.

[207] *In de Causis* XIX, 352: Ubicumque autem diversi ordines sub invicem coniunguntur, oportet quod id quod est supremum inferioris ordinis propter propinquitatem ad superiorem ordinem aliquid participet de superioris ordinis perfectione. Et hoc manifeste videmus in rebus naturalibus: nam quaedam animalia participant aliquam rationis similitudinem et quaedam plantae participant aliquid de distinctione sexus, quae est propria generi animalium. Unde et Dionysius dicit VII cap. de Divinis Nominibus quod per divinam sapientiam 'fines primorum' coniunguntur 'principiis secundorum'.

[208] *ST*, I, 78, 2: Vis generativa habet effectum suum, non in eodem corpore, sed in alio: quia nihil est generativum sui ipsius. Et ideo vis generativa quodammodo appropinquat ad dignitatem animae sensitivae, quae habet operationem in res exteriores, licet excellentiori modo et universaliori: supremum enim inferioris naturae attingit id quod est infimum superioris, ut patet per Dionysium.

[209] *Contra Gentiles* 3, 97, 2725.

sense of touch, Aquinas suggests, are fixed to the earth like plants.[210] At the next level, the sensation of animals resembles and participates in that which is lowest in human knowledge, namely discursive knowledge. Their estimative sense, which is instinctive, is a form of concrete or practical reason.[211] Moreover, through its concupiscence and irascibility, the animal reflects in some way the faculty of will. It participates thus in both the powers of apprehension and appetite.[212]

The continuity and harmony of distinct levels of power and perfection are observed in a most wonderful manner in the unity and simplicity of man. His body is what is most perfect in the material realm and receives the soul which occupies the lowest level among intellectual substances.[213] More exactly, the human soul, which is the lowest in the order of spiritual substances, can communicate its *esse* to the human body, which is what is most dignified in the material world.[214] Within this union, sense knowledge is itself an incipient intellection. And although it is characterised by discursive reason, there is at the highest point of human intellection a certain participation in the simple knowledge of higher, intellectual substances.[215] Human intelligence is

---

[210] *Contra Gentiles* 2, 68, 1453.

[211] *De Veritate* 14, 1 ad 9: Potentia cogitativa est quod est altissimum in parte sensitiva, ubi attingit quodammodo ad partem intellectivam ut aliquid participet eius quod est in intellectiva parte infimum, scilicet rationis discursum, secundum regulam Dionysii, II cap. de divin. Nomin., quod principia secundorum coniunguntur finibus primorum. Unde ipsa vis cogitativa vocatur particularis ratio, ut patet a Commentatore in III de Anima: nec est nisi in homine, loco cuius in aliis brutis est aestimatio naturalis. Et ideo ipsa etiam universalis ratio, quae est in parte intellectiva, propter similitudinem operationis, a cogitatione nominatur.

[212] *De Veritate* 25, 2: Tam ex parte apprehensivarum virium quam ex parte appetitivarum sensitivae partis, aliquid est quod competit sensibili animae secundum propriam naturam; aliquid vero, secundum quod habet aliquam participationem modicam rationis, attingens ad ultimum eius in sui supremo; sicut dicit Dionysius, in VII cap. de divinis Nominibus, quod divina sapientia coniungit fines primorum principiis secundorum. Cf. *In III Sent.*, 26, 1, 2.

[213] *Contra Gentiles* 2, 68, 1453.

[214] VII, iv, 733: Modum autem huius ordinis subiungit, quia semper fines primorum, idest infima supremorum, coniungit principiis secundorum, idest supremis inferiorum, ad modum quo supremum corporalis creaturae scilicet corpus humanum, infimo intellectualis naturae, scilicet animae rationali unit; Cf. *De Spirit. Creat.*, art. 2. This communication of the single act of being is the source of the unity of the human person. Cf. Etienne Gilson, *The Elements of Christian Philosophy*, Chapter 9, "The Human Soul".

[215] *De Veritate* 15, 1: Quamvis cognitio humanae animae proprie sit per viam rationis, est tamen in ea aliqua participatio illius simplicis cognitionis quae in substantiis superioris invenitur, ex quo vim intellectivam habere dicuntur; et hoc secundum illum modum quem Dionysius, VII cap. de divin. Nomin. assignat dicens, quod divina sapientia semper fines priorum coniungit principiis secundorum; hoc est dictu: quod inferior natura in suo summo attingit ad aliquid infimum superioris naturae . . . illud quod est superioris naturae, non potest esse in inferiori natura perfecte, sed per quamdam tenuem participationem; sicut in natura sensitiva non est ratio , sed aliqua participatio rationis, in quantum bruta habent quamdam prudentiam naturalem, ut patet in principio Metaphysic.

endowed with a kind of intuition, a mode of cognition which is entirely proper to angels. Even among these higher substances there is, moreover, also a hierarchy; the highest stand, as it were, at the threshold of divine nature.[216]

The highest form of human knowledge, namely that of first principles, is by simple intuition; it is non-discursive and thus resembles the natural knowledge proper to an angel. At the highest point of our nature we reach somehow the lowest degree in that of an angel.[217] The manner of knowing proper to angelic nature is free from inquiry and the movement of reason; that proper to human nature is by investigation, which moves from one object to another. In knowing some truths immediately and without inquiry, however, the human soul approximates to something of what is proper to angels but remains inferior, since his knowledge begins with the senses.[218]

Globally, the hierarchy of the universe consists in its graded participation in those fundamental and universal perfections which proceed from God: Being, Life and Knowledge. Bodies possess existence alone (*esse tantum*); more noble bodies possess soul and participate in the perfection of life (*vivere*). The most noble souls have the power of knowledge and share the perfection of *intelligere*.[219] All proceed from the unique first principle according to a certain mutual continuity and reciprocal relation: the order of material bodies touches that of souls; this joins the realm of intellects, and at its most sublime the latter is

---

[216] *In de Causis*, XIX, 353: Dionysius dicit quod supremi Angeli sunt quasi 'in vestibulis' Deitatis collocati.

[217] *De Veritate*, 8, 15: Unde, sicut intellectus noster se habet ad ista principia, sic se habet angelus ad omnia quae naturaliter cognoscit. Et cum cognitio principiorum in nobis sit altissimum nostrae scientiae, patet quod in supremo nostrae naturae attingimus quodammodo infimum naturae angelicae. Ut enim dicit Dionysius, VII de Divin. Nomin., divina sapientia fines primorum coniungit principiis secundorum. Unde sicut nos sine discursu principia cognoscimus simplici intuitu, ita et angeli omnia quae cognoscunt; unde et intellectuales dicuntur; et habitus principiorum in nobis dicitur intellectus.

[218] *De Veritate* 16, 1: Sicut dicit Dionysius VII cap de divin. Nomin., divina sapientia coniungit fines primorum principiis secundorum; naturae enim ordinatae ad invicem sic se habent sicut corpora contiguata, quorum inferius in sui supremo tangit superius in sui infimo: unde et inferior natura attingit in sui supremo ad aliquid quod est proprium superioris naturae, imperfecte illud participans. Natura autem animae humanae est infra angelicam, si consideremus naturalem modum cognoscendi utriusque. Naturalis enim modus cogn oscendi et proprius naturae angelicae est,ut veritatem cognoscat sine inquisitione et discursu; humanae vero proprium est ut ad veritatem cognoscendam perveniat inquirendo, et ab uno in aliud discurrendo. Unde anima humana, quantum ad id quod in ipsa supremum est, aliquid attingit de eo quod proprium est naturae angelicae; ut scilicet aliquorum cognitionem subito et sine inquisitione habeat, quamvis quantum ad hoc inveniatur angelo inferior, quod in his veritatem cognoscere non potest nisi a sensu accipiendo.

[219] *In de Causis*, XIX, 351.

united to the divine.[220] As we have seen, *esse* exhibits many degrees of perfection: *gradus invenitur in esse*; this is manifest within our own experience. Even in the mineral world we recognise levels of beauty and value. That which is living exercises greater powers than inanimate existence; in the vegetable realm there are objective grounds on which we judge some individuals to be more beautiful or more perfect than others. A greater degree of individuation is observed in the animal world, where self-movement and self-preservation are characteristics of the individual. Most marvellous of all, however, is the *saltum qualitatis* from beast to man: incorporating within himself the properties of the inorganic, vegetal, and the animate, man rises beyond these and assumes a relationship towards all of reality. With the emergence of spirit there blossoms forth the vast world of human culture which opens upon the infinite and the eternal, the absolute and the universal. Man is given the responsibility for his own life and being within the universal spectrum of existence.

The universal emanation and return of all creatures is symbolised for Aquinas in Ecclesiastes 1, 7: *Ad locum unde exeunt, flumina revertuntur, ut iterum fluant*. These *flumina*, he states, are the streams of natural goodness which God pours into creatures: *esse, vivere, intelligere*.[221] All the graded perfections of beings may be reduced to these three: being, life and knowledge.[222] But, whereas in other creatures these streams of perfection are distinct, in man they are somehow joined together.[223] There is thus in man a certain similitude of the entire order of the universe: he is said to be a microcosm (*minor mundus*), since all natures, as it were, flow together in man.[224] Man constitutes thus, Aquinas notes, a horizon, inhabiting the frontier between spiritual and bodily reality: he is the medium between the two worlds, partaking both of spiritual and bodily goodness.[225]

The human soul resides on the boundary of the temporal and the eternal, the material and spiritual, beneath eternity and beyond time.[226]

---

[220] *In de Causis*, XIX, 352.

[221] *In III Sent., Prol.*: Flumina ista sunt naturales bonitates quas Deus creaturis influit, ut esse, vivere, intelligere et huiusmodi.

[222] *In de Causis*, XVIII, Pera 338: Omnes gradus rerum ad tria videtur reducere, quae sunt: esse, vivere et intelligere.

[223] *In III Sent., Prol.*: Ista flumina in aliis creaturis inveniuntur distincta; sed in homine quodammodo omnia congregantur.

[224] *In II Sent.*, 1, 2, 3, Sed Contra.

[225] *In III Sent.*, Prol.: Homo enim est quasi horizon et confinium spiritualis et corporalis naturae, ut quasi medium inter utrasque, utrasque bonitates participet et corporales et spirituales. See G. Verbeke, 'Man as "Frontier" according to Aquinas', p. 197-9.

[226] *In de Causis* IX, 220: Anima est in horizonte aeternitatis et temporis existens infra aeternitatem et supra tempus.

A spiritual substance, it is the form of the human body.[227] This is the most wonderful instance of the *mirabilis rerum connexio*, whereby, according to the principle received from Dionysius, divine wisdom joins the lowest of the superior grade to what is highest within the inferior. Man is a part of nature and yet a nature apart; inserted within the physical world he also stands beyond it.

As spiritual, man has a relation to all of reality. Because the soul is in some manner all things,[228] since its nature is to know all, 'it is possible for the perfection of the entire universe to exist in one thing.' Thus according to Avicenna, the ultimate perfection which the soul can attain is to have delineated in it the entire order and causes of the universe; Aquinas relates this to man's ultimate end which is the vision of God.[229] On the horizon of the material and spiritual, man receives all things, sensible and spiritual. 'The senses receive the species of all sensible things, the intellect those of intelligible things; thus through sense and intellect the soul of man is in some way all things. In this manner those endowed with knowledge have a likeness to God, in whom, according to Dionysius, all things pre-exist.'[230] The intellect has an endless capacity which cannot be satisfied by any finite thing. Nothing limited can satisfy its desire,[231] since it extends in its intellection to the infinite.[232] Man has an infinite capacity for truth and goodness; this need for infinity is shown both by the intellect and also by the will. Man has need for total happiness: to know and enjoy infinite goodness itself: it is only in discovering his infinite origin and goal that man ultimately discovers himself—in knowing him who knows all things. Only in complete union of mind and will with divine goodness and truth can the mind of man be filled and his heart be stilled. Only in union with divine Good and Being will man, according to Dionysius and Aquinas, find peace and harmony of will. In God he finds the

---

[227] *Contra Gentiles* 2, 68, 1453: Anima intellectualis dicitur esse quidam horizon et confinium corporeorum et incorporeorum, inquantum est substantia incorporea, corporis tamen forma.

[228] *De Anima* III, 8, 431b, 21: ἡ ψυχὴ τὰ ὄντα πώς ἐστι πάντα. Also III, 5, 430a 14: καὶ ἔστιν ὁ μὲν τοιοῦτος νοῦς τῷ πάντα γίνεσθαι.

[229] *De Veritate* 2, 2: Dicitur animam esse quodammodo omnia, quia nata est omnia cognoscere. Et secundum hunc modum possibile est ut in una re totius universi perfectio existat. Unde haec est ultima perfectio ad quam anima potest pervenire, secundum philosophos, ut in ea describatur totus ordo universi, et causarum eius; in quo etiam finem ultimum hominis posuerunt, qui secundum nos erit in visione Dei.

[230] *ST*, I, 80: Sensus recipit species omnium sensibilium, et intellectus omnium intelligibilium, ut sic anima hominis sit omnia quodammodo secundum sensum et intellectum: in quo quodammodo cognitionem habentia ad Dei similitudinem appropinquant, in quo omnia praeexistunt, sicut dicit Dionysius.

[231] *Contra Gentiles* 3, 50, 2279: Nihil finitum desiderium intellectus quietare potest.

[232] *Contra Gentiles* 1, 43: 365: Intellectus noster ad infinitum in intelligendo extenditur.

fullness of all desires: 'the loveliness of Spring, the brightness of Summer, the abundance of Autumn and the repose of Winter.'[233]

Through the openness of consciousness towards all of reality there is an isomorphism in the intentional order between the interiority of man and the external universe of created being. Yet man's perfection is not merely cognitive but, more intrinsically, ontological in origin. The perfections of all things are reflected in him not merely intentionally, but are existentially present within his nature. Within himself man discovers the scale and diversity of being. All the distinct levels of reality are unified within the complex simplicity of human being: material, biological, animal, spiritual. Not only through the outward relatedness of knowledge, but within himself also, man can sound the distinct depths of being and the differences of density pertaining to the real. All streams of created perfection flow together in the simple unity of man. They are intensified and joined in the experience of personal existence. Within the self are harmonised the many levels of reality— from material to spiritual, from individual to universal. Within himself man experiences at its highest pitch and intensity the richness and mystery of being.[234] Immersed within the material world, he feels the weight of his sensible nature, but through his spiritual activity assumes a personal freedom within the universe. Man was created, notes Aquinas, that the universe might be complete;[235] all of nature tends towards the perfection of man.[236] It is not man, needless to say, but God who gives the world its meaning. Man's presence, however, gives an intelligible visibility to the world which it would not otherwise have. He is, so to speak, the eye of the universe, which gives the world a meaning it would not have except in his sight. The person is the place where we best read the likeness of the creator. For his part, man discerns his nature by discovering his unique status; it is his identity and destiny to be elevated within a scale which infinitely transcends him.

The ascending order and affinity of creatures constitutes the beauty of the universe, infusing it with due order and proportion. God causes a twofold harmony or *consonantia* in things. There is, firstly, their universal and final ordinance towards him and, secondly, the mutual

---

[233] *Opuscula Theologica* II, p. 288: Ubi est amoenitas vernalis, luciditas aestivalis, ubertas autumnalis, et requies hiemalis.

[234] To modify a phrase from Hopkins, I 'savour' existence best at the tankard of the self: 'I find myself both as a man and as myself something more determined and distinctive, at pitch more distinctive and higher pitched than anything else I see.' Gerard Manley Hopkins, *Poems and Prose*, Penguin Books, 1953, p. 145.

[235] *Contra Gentiles* 2, 45.

[236] *Contra Gentiles* 3, 22.

harmony of creatures towards each other.[237] The co-operation of
creatures is itself directed towards their common final end.[238] While the
ultimate end of God's will is his own goodness (since it is through love
for himself that he brings things into existence), all creation is ordered
towards God; thus the most perfect aspect of the created universe is
this very order itself. While the ultimate end of God's will is his own
goodness, the nearest to this among created things is the good of the
order of the whole universe; every particular good of this or that thing
is directed to it as end, as the less perfect to what is more perfect. Each
part is for the sake of the whole. The universal solidarity among things
is in view of their orientation towards God.[239] Here Aquinas sees a
verification of the Platonist principle that higher things are in lower
natures by participation; inferior natures are contained in a more
excellent manner in their superiors: thus 'all things are in all' (*omnia in
omnibus*) according to a certain order.[240] The beauty of the universe is
more than that of individuals: it is their community. To form such a
community they must be adapted and suited to each other; one part is
aided by another; finally, there must be due harmony amongst the
parts. As the harmony of music is caused by due numerical proportion,
so also the order of things in the universe.[241]

In Aquinas' Commentary on Dionysius there is an admirable
portrayal of the fundamental harmony of creatures within the universe
and their universal solidarity in being. The order and harmony of
creatures is that they 'exist from God' and 'exist towards God.'
Differing in nature and according to perfection, all beings are united in
the unique source of their existence, and even more significantly in the
dynamic finality which draws them towards a common ultimate end.

---

[237] IV, v, 340: Deus sit causa consonantiae in rebus; est autem duplex consonantia in
rebus: prima quidem, secundum ordinem creaturarum ad Deum et hanc tangit cum dicit
quod Deus est causa consonantiae, sicut vocans omnia ad seipsum, inquantum convertit
omnia ad seipsum sicut ad finem . . . secunda autem consonantia est in rebus, secundum
ordinationem earum ad invicem.

[238] VII, iv, 733: . . . res invicem se coadunant in ordinem ad ultimum finem.

[239] *Contra Gentiles* 3, 64, 2393: Unumquodque intendens aliquem finem, magis curat
de eo quod est propinquius fini ultimo: quia hoc etiam est finis aliorum. Ultimus autem
finis divinae voluntatis est bonitas ipsius, cui propinquissimum in rebus creatis est bonum
ordinis totius universi: cum ad ipsum ordinetur, sicut ad finem, omne particulare bonum
huius vel illius rei, sicut minus perfectum ordinatur ad id quod est perfectius; unde et
quaelibet pars invenitur esse propter suum totum. Id igitur quod maxime curat Deus in
rebus creatis, est ordo universi.

[240] IV, v, 340: Superiora sunt in inferioribus, secundum participationem; inferiora vero
sunt in superioribus, per excellentiam quamdam et sic omnia sunt in omnibus; Also IV,
vi, 364; Cf. Dionysius, 4, 7, 145: αἱ πάντων ἐν πᾶσιν οἰκείως ἑκάστῳ κοινωνίαι. On this
principle, see Werner Beierwaltes, *Proklos*, pp. 94-6, and 130-2.

[241] Cf. IV, vi, 364.

Forming a myriadic universe, containing uncounted worlds; extending outward in time and space and inwardly according to manifold depths of essence and nobility of being, the multiplicity of creation seeks to return along the path by which it emanated from God and rejoin the plenitude of its origin. The ultimate source of unity among creatures is their common orientation towards the final Good. The order of the universe is, therefore, not of a static nature, rather a living order which breathes with a single aspiration. This intrinsic and dynamic unity is the highest good of the universe itself and it is within this order that each individual attains its perfection, not in isolation but in loving and promoting the good of the whole: advancing the good of its inferiors and sharing in the excellence which surpasses itself. But the source and goal of this unity is God himself who alone is 'tota ratio existendi et bonitatis'.[242]

All love is naturally grounded in some unity which causes one thing to be inclined towards another in so far as it bears some relation or likeness to itself.[243] Now, the ultimate affinity and source of unity among beings is their existence: Omnes partes universi conveniunt in ratione existendi.[244] The natural love which each thing has for itself and its native impulse towards preservation of being transports it beyond itself into union with the whole; only in the universal context of all things, in unity with the absolute Good, will it encounter its total good. Each being, therefore, is incomplete within itself and has a native affinity with and need for universal being. The part is perfect only within the whole; thus the part naturally loves the whole and spontaneously seeks the good of the whole.[245] 'That which is the greatest good in caused things is the good of the order of the universe.'[246] This is reflected at every level in the desire which each thing has towards all else. Thus a universal and native zeal for Being moves higher beings to providence for their inferiors; it inspires beings which are equal to share what they have in common, and converts lesser things towards their superiors, turning to them in submission as to their causes, seeking them as the source of their universal good. When the desired good is

---

[242] ST, I, 60, 5 ad 1.

[243] See IV, xii, 456.

[244] IV, vi, 364.

[245] IV, ix, 406.

[246] Contra Gentiles 3, 64, 2392: Id autem quod est maxime bonum in rebus causatis, est bonum ordinis universi . . . Bonum igitur ordinis rerum causatarum a Deo est id quod est praecipue volitum et causatum a Deo. Ibid., 2, 44, 1204: Optimum autem in rebus creatis est perfectio universi, quae consistit in ordine distinctarum rerum: in omnibus enim perfectio totius praeminet perfectioni singularium partium. Ibid., 2, 45, 1228: (ordo universi) est ultima et nobilissima perfectio in rebus.

more perfect, the one which loves is related to it as part to the whole, since whatever is partially in the imperfect is present completely in the perfect. That which desires belongs in some way to that which is loved. The virtue of love, thus, turns lesser things towards their superiors, as to the causes of the good which they desire. The inferior seeks the whole, through a participation in its superior. The cause is the source of the perfection which is communicated to it. It is the intermediary principle which channels a good which has its ultimate source in the universal and transcendent cause of Being and goodness.

When the being which loves is more perfect than that which is loved, the one which loves is borne towards the loved as towards something of its own. When a being loves a good which is equal to itself, it is united to it through a common perfection which each possesses according to the same measure; they are parts of a whole which transcends and embraces both and which binds them to each other. When the being which is loved is less perfect,[247] it becomes enriched by the perfection of the lover. It is part of a whole of which the lover as principle communicates a participation of its goodness. The love which it has for its object is a gratuitous love; what it loves in the other is itself, i.e., its own perfection in so far as it enriches others by communicating itself to them: love of itself in others, as the author of their good through pure generosity.[248]

---

[247] Here we are speaking of *amor amicitiae* as opposed to *amor concupiscentiae*. Cf. IV, x, 428.

[248] IV, ix, 406: Et quia unumquodque amamus inquantum est bonum nostrum, oportet tot modis variare amorem, quot modis contingit aliquid esse bonum alicuius. Quod quidem contingit quadrupliciter: uno modo, secundum quod aliquid est bonum suipsius et sic aliquid amat seipsum; alio modo, secundum quod aliquid per quamdam similitudinem est quasi unum alicui et sic aliquid amat id quod est sibi aequaliter coordinatum in aliquo ordine, sicut homo amat hominem alium eiusdem speciei et sicut civis amat concivem et sicut consanguineus, consanguineum; alio modo, aliquid est bonum alterius quia est aliquid eius, sicut manus est aliquid hominis et universaliter pars est aliquid totius; alio vero modo, secundum quod, e converso, totum est bonum partis: non enim est pars perfecta nisi in toto, unde naturaliter pars amat totum et exponitur pars sponte pro salute totius. Quod enim est superius in entibus, comparatur ad inferius sicut totum ad partem, inquantum superius, perfecte et totaliter, habet quod ab inferiori, imperfecte et particulariter habetur et inquantum supremum continet in se, inferiora multa. IV, x, 430f.: Sic igitur talis amor extasim facit, quia ponit amantem extra seipsum. Sed hoc contingit tripliciter; potest enim illud substantiale bonum, in quod affectus fertur, tripliciter se habere: uno modo sic, quod illud bonum sit perfectius quam ipse amans et per hoc amans comparetur ad ipsum ut pars ad totum, quia quae totaliter sunt in perfectis partialiter sunt in imperfectis; unde secundum hoc, amans est aliquid amati. Alio modo sic, quod bonum amatum sit eiusdem ordinis cum amante. Tertio modo, quod amans sit perfectius re amata et sic amor amantis fertur in amatum, sicut in aliquid suum. IV, xii, 456: Sed unitio et concretio in amore naturali est ex quadam convenientia naturali ex qua provenit ut aliquid inclinetur in alterum, sicut in sibi conveniens et talis inclinatio amor naturalis dicitur. Ad quid autem se extendat virtus amoris ostendit

The beauty of the universe consists in the harmony, proportion, order and mutual solidarity of beings which are infused with a single desire for their unique and universal end. All creatures 'conspire' together to produce this universal harmony.[249] To the question whether God could have made the world better than it is, Aquinas replies that, given the manner in which the present world actually exists, it could not be better, since the good of the universe consists in the order given to it by God as most fitting. To improve upon one element within this universe would destroy its universal design and global harmony of the whole, as a melody is distorted if one string of the lute is overstretched. God could indeed cause things to be better (referring to that which is made rather than to the manner of making) but this would result in a different universe. Indeed, God's power is infinite and infinitely transcends creation; he can make ever more perfect worlds without any of them exhausting his creative power. There is, therefore, no such thing as a 'best possible world'.[250]

For Dionysius and St Thomas, divine beauty is the cause and goal of creation. Out of love for his beauty God wishes to multiply it through the communication of his likeness.[251] He makes all things, that they may imitate divine beauty.[252] Aquinas is thus able to declare: 'The beauty of the creature is nothing other than the likeness of divine

---

subdens, quod movet superiora ad providentiam inferioribus; aequalia ad alternatim sibi convenientia communicandum invicem; et inferiora ut convertantur ad sua superiora, subiiciendo se eis et attendendo ad ea, sicut ad suas causas et desiderando ea, sicut ex quibus dependent eorum bona. See Joseph Legrand, *L'Univers et l'homme dans la philosophie de saint Thomas* pp. 49-53, 82-93 and 266-76.

[249] VII, iv, 733: Divina Sapientia est omnium causa effectiva, inquantum res producit in esse et non solum rebus dat esse, sed etiam esse cum ordine in rebus, inquantum res invicem se coadunant in ordinem ad ultimum finem; et ulterius, est causa indissolubilitatis huius concordiae et huius ordinis, quae semper manent, qualitercumque rebus immutatis. Modum autem huius ordinis subiungit, quia semper fines primorum, idest infima supremorum, coniungit principiis secundorum, idest supremis inferiorum, ad modum quo supremum corporalis creaturae scilicet corpus humanum, infimo intellectualis naturae, scilicet animae rationali unit; et simile est videre in aliis; et sic operatur pulchritudinem universi per unam omnium conspirationem, idest concordiam et harmoniam, idest debitum ordinem et proportionem.

[250] *ST*, I, 25, 6 ad 3: Universum non potest esse melius propter decentissimum ordinem his rebus attributum a Deo, in quo bonum universi consistit. Quoniam si unum aliquid esset melius, corrumperetur proportio ordinis. Sicut, si una chorda plus debito intenderetur, corrumperetur citharae melodia. Posset tamen Deus alias res facere, vel alias addere istis rebus factis: et sic esset illud universum melius.

[251] IV, v, 352: Pulchrum, quod est Deus, est causa effectiva et motiva et continens, amore propriae pulchritudinis (*DN*, 4, 7, 140: τῷ τῆς οἰκείας καλλονῆς ἔρωτι). Quia enim propriam pulchritudinem habet, vult eam multiplicare, sicut possibile est, scilicet per communicationem suae similitudinis.

[252] IV, v, 353: Omnia enim facta sunt ut divinam pulchritudinem qualitercumque imitentur.

beauty participated in things.'[253] And a little later: 'Created being itself (*ipse esse creatum*) is a certain participation and likeness of God.'[254] The beauty of the creature is its very being; divine beauty is the source of existence in all things: . . . *ex divina pulchritudine esse omnium derivatur.*[255] Each being is a participation in the divine beauty, an irradiation of the divine brilliance.[256] In his Commentary on the *Divine Names*, Aquinas suggests that no one seeks to make an image or a representation for any reason other than beauty.[257] As Maritain has remarked, the universe is the only truly gratuitous work of art.

---

[253] IV, v, 337: Pulchritudo enim creaturae nihil est aliud quam similitudo divinae pulchritudinis in rebus participata.

[254] V, ii, 660: Ipse esse creatum est quaedam participatio Dei et similitudo Ipsius.

[255] IV, v, 349: Dicit ergo primo quod ex pulchro isto provenit esse omnibus existentibus . . . unde patet quod ex divina pulchritudine esse omnium derivatur. (Dionysius, *DN* 4, 7, 139: ἐκ τοῦ καλοῦ τούτου πᾶσι τοῖς οὖσι τὸ εἶναι.)

[256] IV, v, 340: Quomodo autem Deus sit causa claritatis, ostendit subdens, quod Deus immittit omnibus creaturis, cum quodam fulgore, traditionem sui radii luminosi, qui est fons omnis luminis; quae quidem traditiones fulgidae divini radii, secundum participationem similitudinis sunt intelligendae et istae traditiones sunt pulchrificae, idest facientes pulchritudinem in rebus. See Armand A. Maurer, C.S.B., *About Beauty. A Thomistic Interpretation*, p. 116.

[257] IV, v, 354: Nullus curat effigiare vel repraesentare, nisi ad pulchrum.

EPILOGUE

In the course of the preceding chapters I have sought to chart, by way of concrete example and close reference, the considerable influence of Pseudo-Dionysius upon the metaphysics of Aquinas. In St Thomas' exposition and exegesis of Dionysius' writings, it is possible to discover an integral philosophy of reality. Our enquiry broadly focused on two themes which characterise their respective visions, and in the dialectic of which the development of metaphysics from Dionysius to Aquinas becomes most evident: Goodness and Being. The pervasive influence of Dionysius is especially evident in the fundamental themes which have been investigated: the discovery of the absolute, its transcendent nature, the themes of Being, creation, diffusion of goodness, hierarchy of creatures and the return of all to God as final end. In each of these areas the propensity of Dionysius and St Thomas, in turn, towards the primacy of goodness and existence is dominant.

In agreement with the Platonist tradition, Dionysius asserts the primacy of the Good. God is the absolute Good, 'surpassing Being in both dignity and power', and as infinite perfection and love the Good is the diffusive source of creation. Unlike his predecessors, however, Dionysius reduces all perfections of finite reality to the pervasive presence and power of being, eminent and immanent, which is the first effect of God's creative action. The unity of causation brings the primacy of Being into clear focus as the first created perfection, and restores universal and absolute transcendence to God as unique creative cause. Being, according to Dionysius, is thus the primary perfection of finite reality, its first and immediate participation in the absolute.

Aquinas fully adopts the priority of Being within finite reality but, deepening the notion of being as perfection, establishes its transcendental character so as to apply it in a pre-eminent sense to God. For Aquinas, therefore, Being is not simply the first participation of finite reality in a transcendent Good, but is itself perfection unlimited—the very essence of God and thus his proper name. Goodness is a co-extensive aspect of Being, identical with it in reality but notionally secondary in signification. We may say, therefore, that Aquinas makes his own Dionysius' notion of Being but deepens it in the light of Dionysius' notion of goodness, adopting the primacy of the Good asserted by Dionysius, while restoring it to the implicit meaning of Being which, on deeper reflection, is appreciated as primary.

Establishing the primacy of Being in an absolute sense, Aquinas in turn ascribes to it the excellence of the Neoplatonist Good, attributing to it the generative diffusion of perfection. He unites, therefore, within a more profound theory of Being, Dionysius' view both of the primacy of existence in the realm of the finite and of the transcendent character of the Good. Indeed the transformation effected by Aquinas can even be seen as a more profound and persistent application of an insight into the radical character of Being which Dionysius had restricted to finite reality.

Although we reflected primarily on Aquinas' debt to Pseudo-Dionysius as a tributary of the metaphysical tradition arising from Plato, tangentially we had frequent occasion to observe the inspiration also of Aristotle. It is a hazardous endeavour to chart the history of intellectual influence; and in attempting to clarify the role of a chosen author, there is an unconscious temptation to extol his importance beyond due measure. For Aquinas, Aristotle was—and remained—the *Philosophus*; he was the master whom he followed as a sure guide in elaborating his philosophy. He adopted from Aristotle the method of pursuing metaphysical truth, grounded always in empirical experience. In his own way Dionysius also looked to the sensible world in his first steps on an ascending path which led rapidly to a transcendent plane.

Pseudo-Dionysius, in life and work an intriguing embodiment of complementary and mutually enriching characteristics, will likely remain forever a historical mystery. Perhaps this is appropriate, since his works express the vision not of a single individual, but reflect the meditative quest of many across the ages. His importance for Aquinas, both in philosophy and theology, should not be underestimated; the phrases and themes of Dionysius appear almost at every turn and in the most unexpected contexts. From the perspective of the history of philosophy, Dionysius was for an unwitting Aquinas, not only a channel of Neoplatonism, but a source in which was distilled one of the most fruitful and profound encounters of Greek and Christian reflection and contemplation. For his part, Aquinas' facility to draw upon elements from every available source, in particular from the two great classic traditions of philosophy, entwining and fusing them continually so as to fashion a profound and novel synthesis, is arguably unparalleled in the history of thought.

BIBLIOGRAPHY

1. Texts and Translations of Pseudo-Dionysius' Writings

CORDERIUS, BALTHASAR, (ED.)
Omnia Opera. Patrologia Graeca III. Paris: Migne, 1857. Reprinted, Turnhout: Brepols, 1977.

CAMPBELL, THOMAS L.
Dionysius the Pseudo-Areopagite: The Ecclesiastical Hierarchy Lanham/New York: University Press of America, 1981. [First two chapters published, Washington: Catholic University of America, 1955.]

CHEVALLIER, PHILLIPE
Dionysiaca. Recueil donnant l'ensemble des traductions latines des ouvrages attribués au Denys de l'aréopage, 2 Vols. Bruges: Desclée de Brouwer, 1937-1950.

DARBOY, JUSTINE
Oeuvres de Saint Denys Paris: Maison de la bonne presse, n.d.

DE GANDILLAC, MAURICE
Oeuvres complètes du Pseudo-Denys l'aréopagite. Aubier Montaigne, 1980.

DULAC, J.
Oeuvres de Saint Denys. Paris, 1865.

HEIL, GUNTHER
La hiérarchie céleste. Introduction par René Roques, Étude et texte critiques par Gunther Heil, Traduction et notes par Maurice de Gandillac. Paris: Éditions de Cerf, 1970.

HENDRIX, P. (ED.)
Pseudo-Dionysii Areopagitae De Caelesti Hierarchia. Leiden: Brill, 1959.

JONES, JOHN D.
Pseudo-Dionysius Areopagite. The Divine Names and Mystical Theology. Milwaukee: Marquette University Press, 1980.

LUIBHEID, COLM
Pseudo-Dionysius. The Complete Works. London: SPCK, 1987.

PARKER, JOHN H.
The Works of Dionysius the Areopagite [Divine Names, Mystic Theology, Letters]. London: Parker, 1897.
The Celestial and Ecclesiastical Hierarchy. London: Skeffington, 1894.

PERA, CESLAUS
S. Thomae Aquinatis. In Librum Beati Dionysii de Divinis Nominibus Expositio. Turin: Marietti, 1950.

ROLT, C. E.
The Divine Names and The Mystical Theology. London: SPCK, 1972.

SCAZZOSO, PIERO
Dionigi Areopagita. Tutte le Opere. Introduzione, prefazioni, parafrasi, note e indici di Enzo Bellini. Milan: Rusconi, 1983.

SHRINE OF WISDOM, EDITORS OF THE
The Divine Names. Fintry: Shrine of Wisdom, 1957.
The Mystical Theology and the Celestial Hierarchy. Fintry: Shrine of Wisdom, 1965.

STIGLMAYR, JOSEPH
Des heiligen Dionysius Areopagita angebliche Schriften über 'Göttliche Namen'. Angeblicher Brief an den Mönch Demophilus. Munich: Kösel & Pustet, 1933.

278 BIBLIOGRAPHY

TRITSCH, W.
Dionysius Areopagita: Mystische Theologie und Andere Schriften, mit einer Probe aus der 'Theologie' des Proklus. Munich, 1956.
Die Hierarchien der Engel und der Kirche, Einführung von H. Ball. Munich, 1956.
TUROLLA, E.
Dionigi Areopagita, *Le Opere.* Versione e interpretazione. Padua: CEDAM, 1956.
VON IVÁNKA ENDRE
Dionysius Areopagita. *Von den Namen zum Unnennbaren.* Einsiedeln: Johannes Verlag, 1956.
WYTZES, J.
Pseudo-Dionysius Areopagita. *De kerkelijke rangorde.* Amsterdam: Uitgevers-maatschappij Holland, 1953.

2. Writings of St Thomas Aquinas

Scriptum Super Libros Sententiarum, Vols. 1 and 2, Ed. P. Mandonnet, Paris: Lethielleux, 1929.
Scriptum Super Sententiis, Vols. 3 and 4, Ed. M. F. Moos, Paris: Lethielleux, 1933-1947.
Summa Contra Gentiles, Ed. P. Marc, C. Pera et al., 3 Vols., Turin: Marietti, 1961-1967.
Summa Theologiae, Pars Prima et Prima Secundae, Ed. P. Caramelo. Turin: Marietti, 1952.
Summa Theologiae, Pars Secunda Secundae, Ed. P. Caramello. Turin: Marietti, 1952.
Summa Theologiae, Tertia Pars et Supplementum, Ed. P. Caramello. Turin: Marietti, 1956.
De Veritate, Ed. R. Spiazzi, in *Quaestiones Disputatae,* Vol. 1. Turin: Marietti, 1964.
De Potentia, Ed. P. Pession, in *Quaestiones Disputatae,* Vol. 2. Turin: Marietti, 1965.
De Anima, Ed. M. Calcaterra and T. Centi, in *Quaestiones Disputatae,* Vol. 2. Turin: Marietti, 1965.
De Spiritualibus Creaturis, Ed. M. Calcaterra and T. Centi, in *Quaestiones Disputatae,* Vol. 2. Turin: Marietti, 1965.
De Malo, Ed. P. Bazzi and M. Pession, in *Quaestiones Disputatae,* Vol. 2. Turin: Marietti, 1965.
Quaestiones Quodlibetales, Ed. R. Spiazzi. Turin: Marietti, 1956.
Opuscula Philosophica, Ed. R. Spiazzi. Turin: Marietti, 1973.
Opuscula Theologica, Vol. 1, Ed. R. Verardo. Turin: Marietti, 1954.
Opuscula Theologica, Vol. 2, Ed. R. Spiazzi and M. Calcaterra. Turin: Marietti, 1954.
Expositio super librum Boethii De Trinitate, Ed. Bruno Decker. Leiden: Brill, 1955.
In Librum Beati Dionysii De divinis nominibus expositio, Ed. C. Pera. Turin: Marietti, 1950.
In Duodecim Libros Metaphysicorum Aristotelis Expositio, Ed. M. R. Cathala and R. Spiazzi. Turin: Marietti, 1964.
Super Librum de Causis Expositio, Ed. H. D. Saffrey. Fribourg: Société Philosophique; Louvain: Nauwelaerts, 1954.
In Librum de Causis Expositio, Ed. C. Pera. Turin: Marietti, 1955.
In Aristotelis Libros Peri Hermeneias et Posteriorum Analyticorum Expositio, Ed. R. Spiazzi. Turin: Marietti, 1964.
In Aristotelis de Caelo et Mundo, Ed. R.M. Spiazzi, Turin: Marietti, 1952.

3. Translations of St Thomas Aquinas' Writings

ANDERSON, JAMES F.
An Introduction to the Metaphysics of St Thomas Aquinas. Chicago: Henry Regnery, 1953.
BOURKE, VERNON J.
(Ed.) *The Pocket Aquinas. Selections from the Writings of St. Thomas.* New York: Washington Square Press, 1962.

BRENNAN, SR. ROSE EMMANUELLA.
  The Trinity and *The Unicity of the Intellect* by St. Thomas Aquinas. St Louis:
  Herder, 1946.
CLARKE, MARY T. (Ed.)
  An Aquinas Reader. London: Hodder and Stoughton, 1974.
D'ARCY, M. C.
  Selected Writings (Everyman's Library) London: Dent, 1964.
ENGLISH DOMINICAN FATHERS.
  On the Power of God, 3 Vols. London: Burns Oates and Washbourne, 1932–1934.
GILBY, THOMAS.
  Philosophical Texts. New York: Oxford University Press, 1960.
GILBY, THOMAS, (Ed.)
  Summa Theologiae, Latin text and English translation, Ed. T. Gilby, 60 Vols.
  [Blackfriars Edition] London: Eyre & Spottiswoode, 1964–1974.
LESCOE, FRANCIS J.
  Treatise on Separate Substances. A Latin-English edition of a newly-established text
  based on 12 mediaeval manuscripts, with introduction and notes. West Hartford:
  St. Joseph College, 1963.
MAURER, ARMAND.
  *The Division and Methods of the Sciences: Questions V and VI of his Commentary
  on the De Trinitate of Boethius.* Translated with Introduction and Notes. Toronto:
  Pontifical Institute of Mediaeval Studies, 1953.
OESTERLE, JEAN T.
  Aristotle: *On Interpretation.* Commentary by St. Thomas and Cajetan (Peri
  Hermeneias). Milwaukee: Marquette University Press, 1962.
PEGIS, ANTON; ANDERSON, J.F.; BOURKE, V.J.; AND O'NEIL, C.J.
  On the Truth of the Catholic Faith. Summa Contra Gentiles. 5 Vols. New York:
  Doubleday, 1955–1957.
ROWAN, JOHN P.
  Commentary on the Metaphysics of Aristotle, 2 Vols. Chicago: Henry Regnery, 1961.
SERTILLANGES, A.-D. ET AL.
  Somme Théologique. Paris: Revue des Jeunes, 1925–1967.
VOLLERT, CYRIL.
  Compendium of Theology. St. Louis/London: Herder, 1955.

4. *Secondary Literature*

ALBERT, KARL. 'Exodusmetaphysik und metaphysische Erfahrung', *Thomas von Aquin.
  Interpretation und Rezeption*, Ed. Willehad Paul Eckert.
ALBERTUS MAGNUS. *Super Dionysium De Divinis Nominibus*, Ed. Paul Simon. Münster:
  Aschendorff, 1972.
ALLARD, G. H. 'The Primacy of Existence in the Thought of Eriugena', *Neoplatonism
  and Christian Thought*, Ed. Dominic J. O'Meara, 89–96, 249–50.
ALLEGRO, CALOGERO. *Il mètodo e il pensiero di S. Tommaso d'Aquino.* Rome: Città
  Nuova, 1978.
ANDERSON, JAMES F. 'Is God's Knowledge Scientific? A Study in Thomism', *An Etienne
  Gilson Tribute.* Milwaukee: Marquette University Press, 1959, 1–19.
——, *The Bond of Being. An Essay on Analogy and Existence.* New York: Greenwood,
  1969.
——, *The Cause of Being.* St. Louis: Herder, 1952.
ANNICE, M, C.S.C. 'Historical Sketch of the Theory of Participation', *The New
  Scholasticism* 26 (1952), 49–79.
ARISTOTLE. *Physics*, tr. Richard Hope. Lincoln and London: University of Nebraska
  Press, 1961.
——, *Physics*, tr. Philip H. Wicksteed and Francis M. Cornford. 2 Vols. (Loeb Ed.).
  London: Heinemann, 1929, 1935.
——, *Nicomachean Ethics*, tr. H. Rackham, London: Heinemann, 1962.

ARMSTRONG, ARTHUR HILARY. 'Negative Theology, Myth and Incarnation', *Neoplatonism and Christian Thought*, Ed. Dominic J. O'Meara, 213–22, 290–2.

——, 'Negative Theology', *The Downside Review*, 95 (1977), 176–89.

——, *Aristotle, Plotinus and St. Thomas*. Oxford: Blackfriars, 1946.

——, 'The Escape of the One', *Studia Patristica* 13 (1975), 77–89.

AUDET, TH.-ANDRÉ. 'Approches historiques de la *Summa Theologiae*', *Études d'histoire littéraire et doctrinale*. Montréal: Institut d'Études Médievales, (1962), 7–29.

BAEUMKER, CLEMENS. 'Der Platonismus im Mittelalter', *Platonismus in der Philosophie des Mittelalters*, Ed. Werner Beierwaltes, 1–55.

BARDY, G. 'Sur les sources patristiques grecques de saint Thomas dans la première partie de la somme théologique', *Revue des sciences philosophiques et théologiques* 12 (1923), 493–502.

BARNARD, CHARLES-ANDRÉ, S.J. 'Les formes de la Théologie chez Denys l'Aréopagite', *Gregorianum* 59 (1978), 36–69.

BASTABLE, PATRICK K. *Desire for God*. London/Dublin: Burns Oates and Washbourne, 1947.

BECK, EDMONDO, AND FABRO, CORNELIO. 'Dionigi l'Areopagita', *Enciclopedia Cattolica* IV, Vatican, 1950, 1662–8.

BECKER, KLAUS MARTIN. *Das Schöne und dessen Grund. Untersuchung der metaphysischen Gründe des Schönen nach der Lehre des Thomas von Aquin namentlich anhand seines Kommentars zu des Dionysius "De Divinis Nominibus"*. PhD Dissertation, Rome: Lateran University, 1961.

BEIERWALTES, WERNER. 'Der Begriff des "Unum in Nobis" bei Proklos', *Miscellanea Mediaevalia*, (Vol. 2, *Die Metaphysik im Mittelalter*) Walter de Gruyter, Berlin, (1962), 255–66.

——, 'Der Kommentar zum *Liber de Causis* als neuplatonisches Element in der Philosophie der Thomas von Aquin', *Philosophische Rundschau* 11 (1963), 192–215.

——, 'Review of Klaus Kremer, *Die Neuplatonische Seinsphilosophie und ihre Wirkung auf Thomas von Aquin*', *Philosophische Rundschau* 16 (1969), 141–52.

——, *Platonismus und Idealismus*. Frankfurt: Klostermann, 1972.

——, '*Negati Affirmatio*', *Dionysius* 1 (1977), 127–59.

——, *Proklos: Grundzüge seiner Metaphysik*. Frankfurt: Klostermann, 2nd. ed., 1979.

——, *Identität und Differenz*. Frankfurt: Klostermann, 1980.

——, *Das Denken des Einen*: Studien zur neuplatonischen Philosophie und ihrer Wirkungsgeschichte. Frankfurt: Klostermann, 1985.

——, *Platonismus in der Philosophie des Mittelalters*. (Ed.) Darmstadt: Wissenschaftliche Buchgesellschaft, 1969.

BORTOLASO, G. 'Originalità della teologia negativa secondo Tommaso d'Aquino', *Tommaso d'Aquino nel suo settimo centenario*, III, *Dio e l'economia della salvezza*. Naples: Edizioni Domenicane Italiane, 1975, 113–16.

BRANICK, VINCENT P. 'The Unity of the Divine Ideas', *The New Scholasticism* 42 (1968), 171–201.

BRETON, STANISLAS. 'L'Idée de transcendental et la genèse des transcendentaux chez saint Thomas d'Aquin', *Saint Thomas d'Aquin aujourd'hui*. *Recherches de Philosophie*, 3. Paris: Desclée de Brouwer (1963), 45–74.

BRONS, BERNHARD. *Gott und die Seienden. Untersuchungen zum Verhältnis von neuplatonischer Metaphysik und christlicher Tradition bei Dionysius Areopagita*. Göttingen: Vandenhoeck & Ruprecht, 1976.

——, 'Pronoia und das Verhältnis von Metaphysik und Geschichte bei Dionysius Areopagita', *Freiburger Zeitschrift fur Philosophie und Theologie* 24 (1977), 165–80.

BRONTESI, A. *L'incontro misterioso con Dio. Saggio sulla teologia affermativa e negativa nello Pseudo-Dionigi*. Brescia: Morcelliana, 1970.

BURRELL, DAVID R., C.S.C. *Aquinas, God and Action*. London: Routledge and Kegan Paul, 1979.

——, *Exercises in Religious Understanding*. Notre Dame/London: University of Notre Dame Press, 1974.

CARABINE, DEIRDRE. *Occulti Manifestatio: The Negative Theology of Latin Neo-Platonism and its Greek Origins.* MA Thesis, Queen's University of Belfast, 1983.

CARLO, WILLIAM E. 'Commentary on Gerald B. Phelan "The Being of Creatures" ', *Proceedings of the American Catholic Philosophical Association* 31 (1957), 126–8.

———, *The Ultimate Reducibility of Essence to Existence in Existential Metaphysics.* The Hague: Nijhoff, 1966.

CARMODY, MICHAEL F. *References to Plato and the Platonici in the Summa Theologiae of St. Thomas Aquinas.* PhD Dissertation, University of Pittsburgh, 1949.

CARROLL, WILLIAM JOSEPH. *Participation in Selected Texts of Pseudo-Dionysius the Areopagite's 'The Divine Names',* PhD Thesis, Catholic University of America, 1981. Ann Arbor: University Microfilms International.

———, 'Unity, Participation and Wholes in a Key Text of Pseudo-Dionysius the Areopagite's "The Divine Names" ', *The New Scholasticism* 57 (1983), 253–62.

CATAN, JOHN R. 'Aristotele e San Tommaso intorno all "actus essendi" ', *Rivista di filosofia Neo-Scolastica* 639–55.

CAVALLERA, FERDINAND. 'J. Durantel — S. Thomas et le Pseudo-Denis', *Revue d'ascétique et mystique* 1 (1920), 288–91.

CENTORE, FLORESTANO. 'Lovejoy and Aquinas on God's "need" to create', *Angelicum* 59 (1982), 23–36.

CHAPMAN, IMMANUEL. 'The Perennial Theme of Beauty and Art', *Essays in Thomism,* Ed. Robert E. Brennan, O.P., Sheed and Ward, New York, 1942, 335–46, 417–19.

CHENU, M.D., O.P. *Introduction à l'Étude de Saint Thomas d'Aquin.* Montréal: Institut d'Études Médiévales; Paris: Vrin, 1950.

———, *La Théologie comme science au xiiie siècle,* 3 ed. Paris: Vrin, 1969.

———, 'Création et Histoire', *St. Thomas Aquinas 1274–1974. Commemorative Studies.* Toronto: Pontifical Institute of Mediaeval Studies, 2 (1974), 391–9.

———, *Nature, Man and Society in the Twelfth Century.* The University of Chicago Press, Chicago and London, 1968.

———, 'Le plan de la Somme théologique de S. Thomas', *Revue Thomiste* 47 (1939), 93–107.

———, *La théologie au douzième siècle.* Paris: Vrin, 1957.

CLARKE, W. NORRIS, S.J. 'Commentary on Gerald B. Phelan "The Being of Creatures" ', *Proceedings of the American Catholic Philosophical Association* 31 (1957), 128–32.

———, 'The Problem of the Reality and Multiplicity of Divine Ideas in Christian Neoplatonism', *Neoplatonism and Christian Thought,* ed. Dominic J. O'Meara, 109–27, 256–8.

———, 'The Limitation of Act by Potency: Aristotelianism or Neoplatonism', *The New Scholasticism* 26 (1952), 167–94.

———, 'The Metaphysics of Religious Art: Reflections on a Text of St. Thomas Aquinas', *Graceful Reason,* ed. Lloyd P. Gerson, 301–14.

———, 'St. Thomas and Platonism', *Thought* 32 (1957), 437–44.

CLAVELL, LUIS. 'El Nombre mas proprio de Dios y el Acto de Ser', *Tommaso d'Aquino nel suo settimo centenario: Dio e l'economia della salvezza.* Naples: Edizioni Domenicane Italiane, 1975, 269–74.

———, 'La Belleza en el comentario tomista al *De Divinis Nominibus*', *Anuario filosófico* 17 (1984), 93–99.

COLERIDGE, S. T. *Aids to Reflection.* London: Ward, Lock, and Co., n.d.

COLISH, MARCIA L. *The Mirror of Language: A Study in the Mediaeval Theory of Knowledge.* New Haven and London: Yale University Press, 1968.

COOMARASWAMY, ANANDA K. 'Mediaeval Aesthetic I: Dionysius the Pseudo-Areopagite and Ulrich Engelberti of Strassburg', *Art Bulletin* 17 (1935), 31–47.

———, 'Mediaeval Aesthetic II: St Thomas Aquinas on Dionysius and a Note on the Relation of Beauty to Truth', *Art Bulletin* 20 (1938), 66–77.

COPLESTON, FREDERICK, S.J. *A History of Philosophy,* Vol. 2, Mediaeval Philosophy. New York: Image Books, 1962.

———, *Aquinas.* Penguin Books, 1977.

CORRIGAN, KEVIN. 'A Philosophical Precursor to the Theory of Essence and Existence in St. Thomas Aquinas', *The Thomist* 48 (1984), 219–40.

CORSINI, EUGENIO. *Il Trattato De Divinis Nominibus dello Pseudo-Dionigi e i commenti neoplatonici al Parmenide*. Turin: G. Giappichelli, 1962.

CORVEZ, MAURICE. 'Existence et Essence', *Revue Thomiste* 51 (1951), 305–30.

COULOUBARITSIS, L. 'Le sens de la notion "démonstration" chez le Pseudo-Denys', *Byzantinische Zeitschrift* 1982, 317–35.

——, 'Le statut de la critique dans les Lettres du Pseudo-Denys', *Byzantion* 51 (1981), 112–21.

COUSINEAU, ROBERT-HENRI. 'Creation and Freedom. An Augustinian Problem: "Quia Voluit"? and/or "Quia Bonus"?', *Recherches Augustiniennes* 2 (1962), 253–71.

CURTIN, MAURICE. 'God's Presence in the World. The Metaphysics of Aquinas and Some Recent Thinkers', *At the Heart of the Real*, ed. Fran O'Rourke, Dublin: Irish Academic Press, 1992, pp. 121–34.

CURTIS, S. J. *A Short History of Western Philosophy in the Middle Ages*. London: MacDonald and Co, 1950.

CZAPIEWSKI, WINFRED. *Das Schöne bei Thomas von Aquin*. Freiburg: Herder, 1964.

DALY, C. B. 'The Knowableness of God', *Philosophical Studies* 9 (1959), 90–137.

DANIÉLOU, JEAN. *God and the Ways of Knowing*. New York: Meridian Books, 1960.

D'ARCY, MARTIN C. *St. Thomas Aquinas*. Dublin: Clonmore and Reynolds, 1953.

——, *The Mind and Heart of Love*. London: Fontana, 1962.

——, *No Absent God. The Relations Between God and the Self*. London: Catholic Book Club, 1962.

DE BRUYNE, EDGAR. *Études d'Esthétique Médiévale* III, *Le XIIIe siècle*. Bruges: de Tempel, 1946.

DE FINANCE, JOSEPH. *Être et agir dans la philosophie de Saint Thomas*. Paris: Beauchesne, 1945.

——, 'Être et Subjectivité', *Doctor Communis* 2 (1948), 240–58.

——, *Existence et Liberté*. Paris-Lyon: Vitte, 1955.

——, *Connaissance de l'être. Traité d'Ontologie*. Paris: Desclée de Brouwer, 1966.

DE GANDILLAC, MAURICE. Traduction et notes, Denys l'Aréopagite, *La hiérarchie céleste*. Paris: Les Éditions du Cerf, 1970.

DE KONINCK, CHARLES. 'Du bien qui divise l'être', *Laval Théologique et Philosophique* 10 (1954), 99–103.

——, 'L'être principal de l'homme est de penser', *Die Metaphysik im Mittelalter* (Miscellanea Mediaevalia Band 2). Berlin: de Gruyter (1963), 325–27.

DELVIGNE, T. 'L'inspiration propre du traité de Dieu dans le Commentaire des Sentences de Saint Thomas', *Bulletin Thomiste* 9 (1932), 119–22.

DE MUNTER, J. 'Bij een studie over de Pseudo-Areopagitica', *Wetenschappelijke Tijdingen* 6 (1941), 201–06.

DE RAEYMAEKER, LOUIS. 'Zijn en absoluutheid', *Tijdschrift voor Philosophie* 20 (1958), 179–209.

——, 'L'idée inspiratrice de la métaphysique thomiste', *Aquinas* (1960), 61–81.

——, 'La profonde originalité de la métaphysique de Saint Thomas d'Aquin', *Die Metaphysik im Mittelalter* (Miscellanea Mediaevalia 2) Berlin: de Gruyter (1961), 14–29.

——, *The Philosophy of Being*, Tr. Edmund H. Ziegelmeyer. St. Louis: Herder, 1966.

DE STRYKER, EMILE. 'L'idée du Bien dans la République de Platon', *L'Antiquité Classique* 39 (1970), 450–67.

DE VOGEL, CORNELIA J. 'Antike Seinsphilosophie und Christentum im Wandel der Jahrhunderte', *Reformation, Schicksal und Auftrag*. Festgabe Joseph Lortz, Vol I, Baden-Baden: Grimm, 1958, 527–48.

——, ' "Ego sum qui sum" et sa signification pour une philosophie chrétienne', *Revue des Sciences Religieuses* 35 (1961), 337–55.

——, 'Amor quo caelum regitur', *Vivarium* I (1963), 2–34.

——, 'Reflexions on the *Liber de Causis*', *Vivarium* 4 (1966), 67–82.

———, 'Greek Cosmic Love and the Christian Love of God. Boethius, Dionysius the Areopagite and the author of the Fourth Gospel', *Vigiliae Christianae* 35 (1981), 57–81.

———, '*Deus Creator Omnium*. Plato and Aristotle in Aquinas' Doctrine of God', *Graceful Reason*, ed. Lloyd P. Gerson, 203–27.

DE VRIES, JOSEF. 'Existenz und Sein in der Metaphysik des heiligen Thomas', *Die Metaphysik im Mittelalter* (Miscellanea Mediaevalia 2). Berlin: de Gruyter (1963), 328–33.

———, 'Das "esse commune" bei Thomas von Aquin', *Scholastik* 39 (1964), 163–77.

DEWAN, LAWRENCE. 'St. Thomas and the Divine Names', *Science et Esprit* 32 (1980), 19–33.

DICTIONNAIRE DE SPIRITUALITÉ. 'Denys l'Aréopagite (Le Pseudo-)', Paris: Beauchesne, Vol. 3. 1975, 244–429.

DODDS, E. R. Proclus. *The Elements of Theology*. Oxford University Press, 1971.

DOHERTY, K. F. 'Toward a Bibliography of Pseudo-Dionysius the Areopagite: 1900–1955', *Modern Schoolman* 33 (1956), 257–68.

———, 'Peter Caramello's Introduction to C. Pera's Edition of the Divine Names of St. Thomas', *Thomist Reader* 1 (1958), 72–93.

———, 'Pseudo Dionysius the Areopagite: 1955–1960', *Modern Schoolman* 40 (1962/63), 55–9.

———, 'St. Thomas and the Pseudo-Dionysian Symbol of Light', *The New Scholasticism* 34 (1960), 170–89.

DONDAINE H. F., O.P. *Le Corpus Dionysien de l'Université de Paris au XIIIe siècle*. Rome: Edizioni di Storia e Letteratura, 1953.

DONNELLY, PHILIP J., S.J. 'St. Thomas and the Ultimate Purpose of Creation', *Theological Studies* 2 (1941), 53–83.

DOUGLASS, J.W. 'The Negative Theology of Dionysius the Areopagite', *Downside Review* 81 (1963), 115–24.

DUCLOW, DONALD F. 'Pseudo-Dionysius, John Scotus Eriugena, Nicholas of Cusa: an Approach to the Hermeneutic of the Divine Names', *International Philosophical Quarterly* 12 (1972), 260–78.

DUMÉRY, HENRI. 'L'Être et l'Un', *Miscellanea Albert Dondeyne*. Leuven: University Press (1974), 331–50.

DURANTEL, J. *Le retour à Dieu par l'intelligence et la volonté dans la philosophie de saint Thomas*. Paris: Alcan, 1918.

———, *Saint Thomas et le Pseudo-Denis*. Paris: Alcan, 1919.

ECKERT, WILLEHAD PAUL (Ed.). *Thomas von Aquin. Interpretation und Rezeption. Studien und Texte*. Mainz: Matthias Grünewald, 1974.

———, 'Der Glanz des Schönen und seine Unerfüllbarkeit im Bilde-Gedanken zu einer Theologie der Kunst des heiligen Thomas von Aquino', *Thomas von Aquin. Interpretation und Rezeption*. Ed. Willehad Paul Eckert, 229–44.

ECO, UMBERTO. *Il problema estetico in Tommaso d'Aquino*. Milan: Bompiani, 1970.

ELDERS, LEO J. 'Justification des "cinq voies"', *Revue Thomiste* 41 (1961), 207–25.

———, 'L'ordre des attributs divins dans la somme théologique', *Divus Thomas* (Piacenza) 82 (1979), 225–32.

———, 'St. Thomas Aquinas and the problems of speaking about God', *Doctor Communis* 35 (1982), 305–16.

ELORDUY, E. *Ammonia Sakkas. I. La doctrina de la creación y del mal en Proclo y el Pseudo-Areopagita*. Oña, 1959.

FABRO, CORNELIO. *La nozione metafisica di partecipazione secondo S. Tommaso d'Aquino*, 2 Ed. Turin: Società Editrice Internazionale, 1950.

———, 'Dionigi l'Areopagita', *Enciclopedia Cattolica* IV, Vatican, 1950, 1662–68.

———, *Breve Introduzione al Tomismo*. Rome: Desclée, 1960.

———, *Participation et Causalité selon S. Thomas d'Aquin*. Louvain: Publications Universitaires, 1961.

———, 'Notes pour la fondation métaphysique de l'être', *Revue Thomiste* 2 (1966), 214–37.

——, 'Elementi per una dottrina tomistica della partecipazione', *Divinitas* 2 (1967), 559–86.

——, *Esegesi Tomistica*. Rome: Libreria Editrice della Pontifica Università Lateranense, 1969.

——, *Tomismo e Pensiero Moderno*. Rome: Liberia Editrice della Pontifica Università Lateranense, 1969.

——, 'Platonismo, neoplatonismo e tomismo: convergenze e divergenze', *Aquinas* 12 (1969), 217–42.

——, 'Platonism, Neo-Platonism and Thomism: Convergencies and Divergencies', *The New Scholasticism* 44 (1970), 69–100.

——, 'The Intensive Hermeneutics of Thomistic Philosophy: The Notion of Participation', *Review of Metaphysics* 27 (1974), 449–91.

——, 'Die Wiederaufnahme des thomistischen *Esse* und der Grund der Metaphysik', *Tijdschrift voor Filosofie* 43 (1981), 90–116.

——, 'Intorno al fondamento dell'essere', *Graceful Reason*, ed. Lloyd P. Gerson, 229–37.

——, 'The Overcoming of the Neo-Platonic Triad of Being, Life and Intellect by Saint Thomas Aquinas', *Neoplatonism and Christian Thought*, ed. Dominic J. O'Meara, 97–108, 250–55.

FABRO, CORNELIO, AND BECK, EDMONDO. 'Dionigi l'Areopagita', *Enciclopedia Cattolica* IV, Vatican City, 1950, col. 1662–8.

FAES DE MOTTONI, BARBARA. *Il "Corpus Dionysianum" nel Medioevo. Rassegna di studi: 1900–1972.* Bologna: Il Mulino, 1977.

FALIP, ETIENNE H. *Influence de Denys l'Aréopagite dans saint Thomas d"Aquin*, Doctoral Thesis, Institut Catholique de Toulouse, 1904.

FARRE, LUIS. *Tomas de Aquino y el Neoplatonismo*. La Plata: Instituto de Filosofia, Universidad Nacional de La Plata, 1966.

FAUCON DE BOYLESVE, PIERRE. *Aspects néoplatoniciens de la doctrine de saint Thomas d'Aquin*. Lille: Université Lille 3, 1975.

——, *Être et Savoir. Étude du fondement de l'intelligibilité dans la pensée médiévale*. Paris: Vrin, 1985.

FAY, THOMAS A. 'Participation: The Transformation of Platonic and Neoplatonic Thought in the Metaphysics of Thomas Aquinas', *Divus Thomas* 76 (1973), 50–64.

FEDER, ALFRED S.J. 'Des Aquinaten Kommentar zu Pseudo-Dionysius "De Divinus Nominibus". Ein Beitrag zur Arbeitsmethode des heiligen Thomas', *Scholastik* 1 (1926), 321–51.

FLOOD, PATRICK F. *Thomas Aquinas and Denis the Areopagite on the Being of Creatures*. PhD Thesis, University of Ottawa, 1968.

FORTE, BRUNO. 'L'universo dionisiano nel prologo della *Mistica Teologica*', *Medioevo* 4 (1978), 1–57.

FREI, WALTER. 'Versuch einer Einführung in das areopagitische Denken', *Theologische Zeitschrift* 16 (1960), 91–109.

GARDNER, EDMUND G. *Dante and the Mystics*. London: Dent, 1913.

GARRIGOU-LAGRANGE, REGINALD. *Le sens du mystère et le clair-obscur intellectuel. Nature et surnaturel*. Paris: Desclée de Brouwer, 1934.

——, 'The Fecundity of Goodness', *The Thomist* 2 (1940), 226–36.

GAY, J. H. 'Four Medieval Views of Creation', *Harvard Theological Review* 56 (1963), 243–73.

GEENEN, GODEFROID. 'Une étude inédite sur le Ps. Denys et Saint Thomas', *Divus Thomas* 31 (1953), 169–84.

GEFRÉ, CLAUDE-J. 'Théologie naturelle et révélation dans la connaissance du Dieu un', *L'Existence de Dieu*, Cahiers de l'Actualité Religieuse, 16, Tournai-Paris: Castermann, 1961, 297–317.

GEIGER, LOUIS-BERTRAND. *Le problème de l'amour chez saint Thomas d'Aquin*. Montréal: Institut d'Études Médiévales, 1952.

——, *La participation dans la philosophie de saint Thomas d'Aquin*, 2nd ed. Paris: Vrin, 1953.

——, *Philosophie et Spiritualité*. Paris: Cerf, 1963.

——, 'Les idées divines dans l'oeuvre de S. Thomas', *St. Thomas Aquinas 1274–1974. Commemorative Studies*. Toronto: Pontifical Institute of Mediaeval Studies, 1974, 175–209.

GERSH, STEPHEN. *From Iamblichus to Eriugena. An Investigation of the Prehistory and Evolution of the Pseudo-Dionysian Tradition*. Leiden: Brill, 1978.

GERSON, LLOYD P. ed. *Graceful Reasons: Essays in Ancient and Medieval Philosophy Presented to Joseph Owens, CSSR*. Toronto: Pontifical Intitute of Mediaeval Studies, 1983.

GILSON, ÉTIENNE. *L'esprit de la philosophie médiévale*. Paris: Vrin, 1932. 2. rev. ed., 1968.

——, *The Spirit of Mediaeval Philosophy*. New York: Charles Scribner's Sons, 1936.

——, *Being and Some Philosophers*. Toronto: Pontifical Institute of Mediaeval Studies, 1952.

——, *History of Christian Philosophy in the Middle Ages*. New York: Random House, 1955.

——, *The Christian Philosophy of St. Thomas Aquinas*. New York: Random House, 1956.

——, 'La Paix de la Sagesse', *Aquinas* (1960), 28–46.

——, 'Notes sur l'être et le temps', *Recherches Augustiniennes* 2 (1962), 205–23.

——, *L'Être et l'essence*. Paris: Vrin, 2. ed., 1962.

——, *The Elements of Christian Philosophy*. New York: Mentor-Omega, 1963.

——, 'Virtus Essendi', *Mediaeval Studies* 26 (1964), 1–11.

——, 'De la notion d'être divin dans la philosophie de saint Thomas d'Aquin', *De Deo in philosophia S. Thomae et in hodierna philosophia* (Acta VI Congressus Thomistici Internationalis I) Rome: Catholic Book Agency, 1965.

——, *The Spirit of Thomism*. New York: Harper and Row, 1966.

——, *Le Thomisme. Introduction à la philosophie de saint Thomas d'Aquin*, 6. ed. Paris: Vrin, 1972.

——, *God and Philosophy*. New Haven/London: Yale University Press, 1974.

——, *La philosophie au moyen âge*, 2 vols., Paris: Payot, 1976.

——, *Constantes philosophiques de l'être*. Paris: Vrin, 1983.

——, 'Eléments d'une métaphysique thomiste de l'être', *Autour de Saint Thomas*. Paris: Vrin, 1983, 97–126.

GRAEF, HILDA. *The Light and the Rainbow. A Study in Christian Spirituality from its Roots in the Old Testament and its Development through the New Testament and the Fathers to Recent Times*. London: Longmans, 1959.

GREENSTOCK, DAVID L. 'Exemplar Causality and the Supernatural Order', *The Thomist* 16 (1953), 1–31.

GRUMEL, V. 'J. Durantel, Saint Thomas et le Pseudo-Denis', *Échos d'Orient* 23 (1924), 505–8.

GUSTAFSON, GUSTAF J. *The Theory of Natural Appetency in the Philosophy of St. Thomas*. Washington: Catholic University of America, 1944.

GUTHRIE, W. K. C. *A History of Greek Philosophy*. Vol. IV. Cambridge University Press.

HADOT, P. 'Dieu comme acte d'être dans la néoplatonisme, à propos des théories d'E. Gilson sur la métaphysique de l'Exode', *Dieu et l'être*. Paris: Centre d'études des religions du livre, 1978, 57–63.

HANKEY, W. J. 'Theology as System and as Science: Proclus and Thomas Aquinas', *Dionysius* 6 (1982), 83–93.

——, 'The Structure of Aristotle's Logic and the Knowledge of God in the *Pars Prima* of the *Summa Theologiae* of Thomas Aquinas', *Sprache und Erkenntnis im Mittelalter* (Miscellanea Mediaevalia 13, Vol. 2) Berlin: de Gruyter, 1981, 961–68.

——, 'Aquinas' First Principle: Being or Unity?', *Dionysius* 4 (1980), 133–72.

HARRIS, R. BAINE, Ed. *The Structure of Being. A Neoplatonic Approach*. State University of New York Press, 1982.

HART, CHARLES A. 'Participation and the Thomistic Five Ways', *The New Scholasticism* 26 (1952), 267–82.

HATHAWAY, RONALD F. *Hierarchy and the Definition of Order in the Letters of Pseudo-Dionysius*. The Hague: Martinus Nijhoff, 1969.

HAYEN, ANDRÉ, S.J. *L'Intentionnel dans la philosophie de Saint Thomas.* Paris: Desclée de Brouwer, 1942.

——, *Saint Thomas d'Aquin et la vie de l'Eglise.* Louvain: Publications Universitaires, 1952.

——, *La Communication de l'être d'après saint Thomas d'Aquin,* 2 Vols., Paris: Desclée de Brouwer, 1957, 1959.

HEIL, GUNTHER. Étude et texte critiques, Denys l'Aréopagite. *La Hiérarchie Céleste.* Paris: Les Editions du Cerf, 1970, 1–63.

HENLE, R. J. *Saint Thomas and Platonism.* The Hague: Nijhoff, 1956.

——, 'A Note on Certain Textual Evidence in Fabro's *La nozione metafisica di partecipazione*', *The Modern Schoolman* 34 (1957), 265–82.

HERIS, CH.-V., O.P. 'L'amour naturel de Dieu', *Mélanges thomistes* (Bibliothèque Thomiste III) 1923, 289–310.

HO, JOSEPH CHIU YUEN. 'La doctrine de la participation dans la commentaire de saint Thomas sur le *Liber de Causis*', *Revue Philosophique de Louvain* 70 (1972), 360–83.

HOCHSTAFFL, JOSEF. *Negative Theologie. Ein Versuch zur Vermittlung des patristischen Begriffs.* Munich: Kösel, 1976.

HODGSON, PHYLLIS. 'Dionysius the Areopagite and Christian Mystical Tradition', *The Contemporary Review* 176 (1949), 281–5.

HOPKINS, GERARD MANLEY. *Poems and Prose,* selected with an Introduction and Notes by W. H. Gardner. Penguin Books, 1953.

HORN, GABRIEL. 'Note sur l'unité, l'union dans les noms divins du Pseudo-Aréopagite', *Archives de Philosophie* 2 (1924), 422–32.

HORNUS, JEAN-MICHEL. 'Quelques réflexions à propos du Pseudo-Denys l'Aréopagite et de la mystique chrétienne en général', *Revue d'histoire et de philosophie religieuses* 27 (1947), 37–63.

——, 'Les recherches récentes sur le Pseudo-Denys l'Aréopagite', *Revue d'histoire et de la philosophie religieuses* 35 (1955), 404–48.

——, 'Les recherches dionysiennes de 1955 à 1960', *Revue d'histoire et de la philosophie religieuses* 41 (1961), 22–81.

HOUDE, R. 'A Note on *St. Thomas and Platonism*', *The New Scholasticism* 4 (1960), 270–71.

HOYE, WILLIAM J. *Actualitas Omnium Actuum. Man's Beatific Vision of God as Apprehended by Thomas Aquinas.* Meisenheim am Glan: Anton Hain, 1975.

HUIT, C. 'Les éléments platoniciens de la doctrine de saint Thomas', *Revue Thomiste* 19 (1911), 724–66.

INCIARTE, FERNANDO. *Forma formarum. Strukturmomente der Thomistischen Seinslehre im Rückgriff auf Aristoteles.* Freiburg-Munich: Karl Alber, 1970.

JOHANN, ROBERT O. *The Meaning of Love. An Essay towards a Metaphysics of Intersubjectivity.* London: Geoffrey Chapman, 1954.

JOHNSON, HAROLD JOSEPH. 'Via negationis and via analogia. Theological Agnosticism in Maimonides and Aquinas', *Actas del V Congreso internacional de filosofia medieval* II, Madrid: Nacional (1979), 843–55.

JONES, JOHN D. 'The Character of the Negative (Mystical) Theology for Pseudo-Dionysius Areopagite', *Proceedings of the American Catholic Philosophical Association* 51 (1977), 66–74.

——, 'The Ontological Difference for St. Thomas and Pseudo-Dionysius', *Dionysius* 4 (1980), 119–32.

——, 'A Non-Entitative Understanding of Being and Unity: Heidegger and Neoplatonism', *Dionysius* 6 (1982), 94–110.

JONES, RUFUS M. *Studies in Mystical Religion.* London: Macmillan, 1909.

JORDAN, MARK D. 'The Order of Lights: Aquinas on Immateriality as Hierarchy', *Proceedings of the American Catholic Philosophical Association* 52 (1978), 112–20.

——, 'The Grammar of *Esse*: Re-reading Thomas on the Transcendentals', *Thomist* 44 (1980), 1–26.

——, 'The Intelligibility of the World and the Divine Ideas in Aquinas', *The Review of Metaphysics* 38 (1984), 17–32.

JOSSUA, JEAN-PIERRE. 'L'Axiome *Bonum diffusivum sui* chez S. Thomas d'Aquin', *Revue des sciences religieuses* 40 (1966), 127–53.

JOURNET, CHARLES. *Connaissance et inconnaissance de Dieu*. Paris: Desclée de Brouwer, 1969.

KAINZ, HOWARD P. *'Active and Passive Potency' in Thomistic Angelology*. The Hague: Martinus Nijhoff, 1972.

KALINOWSKI, G. 'Discours de louange et discours métaphysique. Denys l'Aréopagite et Thomas d'Aquin', *Rivista di Filosofia Neoscolastica* 73, 399–404.

KEANE, KEVIN P. 'Why Creation? Bonaventure and Thomas Aquinas on God as Creative Good', *Downside Review* 93 (1975), 100–21.

KELLER, ALBERT. 'Arbeiten zur Sprachphilosophie Thomas von Aquins', *Theologie und Philosophie* 49 (1974), 464–76.

——, *Sein oder Existenz? Die Auslegung des Seins bei Thomas von Aquin*. Munich: Max Hueber, 1968.

KELLY, BERNARD. *The Metaphysical Background of Analogy*. London: Blackfriars, 1958.

KERN, CYPRIEN. 'La structure du Monde d'après le Pseudo-Denys', *Irénikon* 29 (1956), 205–9.

KLUBERTANZ, GEORGE P., S.J. *St. Thomas Aquinas on Analogy. A Textual Analysis and Systematic Synthesis*. Chicago: Loyola University Press, 1960.

——, 'The Problem of the Analogy of Being', *Review of Metaphysics* 10 (1957), 553–79.

——, 'St. Thomas' Treatment of the Axiom *Omne Agens Agit Propter Finem*', *An Etienne Gilson Tribute*, Ed. Charles J. O'Neil. Milwaukee: Marquette University Press, 1959, 101–17.

KOCH, HUGO. *Pseudo-Dionysius Areopagita in seinen Beziehungen zum Neuplatonismus und Mysterienwesen*. Mainz: Kirchheim, 1900.

KOCH, JOSEPH. 'Augustinischer und Dionysischer Neuplatonismus und das Mittelalter', *Platonismus in der Philosophie des Mittelalters*, Ed. Werner Beierwaltes 317–42.

KOVACH, FRANCIS J. 'Der Einfluss der Schrift des Pseudo-Dionysius *'De Divinus nominibus'* auf die Schönheitslehre des Thomas von Aquin', *Archiv fur Geschichte der Philosophie* 63 (1981), 150–66.

——, *Die Ästhetik des Thomas von Aquin. Eine genetische und systematische Analyse*. Berlin: Walter de Gruyter, 1961.

——, 'The Transcendentality of Beauty in Thomas Aquinas', *Die Metaphysik im Mittelalter*, (Miscellanea Mediaevalia 2) Berlin: Walter de Gruyter, 1963, 386–92.

KRAHE, MARIA-JUDITH. *Von der Wesensart negativer Theologie. Ein Beitrag zur Erhellung ihrer Struktur*. Dissertation, University of Munich, 1976.

KREMER, KLAUS. 'Die *Creatio* nach Thomas von Aquin und dem *Liber de Causis*', *Ekklesia*, Festschrift für Bischof Dr. Matthias Wehr, Trier: Paulus Verlag, 1962, 321–44.

——, 'Das "Warum" der Schöpfung: *"quia bonus" vel/et "quia voluit"*? Ein Beitrag zum Verhältnis von Neuplatonismus und Christentum an Hand des Prinzips *"bonum est diffusivum sui"'*, Festschrift für J. Hirschberger. Frankfurt, 1965, 241–64.

——, *Die Neoplatonische Seinsphilosophie und ihre Wirkung auf Thomas von Aquin*, 2. ed. Leiden: Brill, 1971.

LAFONT, GHISLAIN. *Structures et méthode dans la Somme Théologique*. Bruges: Desclée de Brouwer, 1961.

LAKEBRINK, BERNHARD. 'Die thomistische Lehre vom Sein des Seienden im Gegensatz zu ihrer existenzialen und dialektischen Umdeutung', *Thomas von Aquin. Interpretation und Rezeption*, ed. Willehad Paul Eckert, 48–79.

LANGEN, JOSEPHUS. 'Dionysius vom Areopag und die Scholastiker', *Revue internationale de théologie* 8 (1900), 201–8.

LANGER, HANS-DIETER. 'Zur Hermeneutik theozentrischer und christologischer Aussagen bei Thomas von Aquin', *Thomas von Aquin. Interpretation und Rezeption*, ed. Willehad Paul Eckert, 16–47.

LAPOINTE, E. 'Le problème de l'*esse* chez saint Thomas', *Archives de Philosophie* 26 (1963), 59–70.

LEE, PATRICK. 'Language about God and the Theory of Analogy', *The New Scholasticism* 58 (1984), 40–66.

LEGRAND, JOSEPH. *L'Univers et l'homme dans la philosophie de Saint Thomas*, 2 vols., Brussels: L'Edition Universelle, 1946.

LEHMANN, PAUL. 'Zur Kenntnis der Schriften des Dionysius Areopagita im Mittelalter', *Revue Benedictine* 35 (1923), 81–97.

LEONISSA, JOSEPHUS A. 'Des Areopagiten Lehre vom Übel beleuchtet vom Aquinaten', *Jahrbuch für Philosophie und spekulative Theologie* 15 (1901), 147–56.

——, 'Zur Frage der Areopagitica', *Jahrbuch für Philosophie und spekulative Theologie* 27 (1912), 437–51.

——, 'Des Areopagiten Buch von den göttlichen Namen nach St. Thomas', *Jahrbuch für Philosophie und spekulative Theologie* 14 (1900), 427–42.

LILLA, S. 'The Notion of Infinitude in Ps.-Dionysius Areopagita', *The Journal of Theological Studies* 31 (1980), 93–103.

LITTLE, A. G. *The Platonic Heritage of Thomism*. Dublin: Golden Eagle Books, 1950.

LIUZZI, TIZIANA. 'L'*esse* in quanto similitudine di Dio nel commento di Tommaso d'Aquino al *De Divinis Nominibus* di Dionigi Areopagita', *Vetera Novis Augere*. Studi in onore di Carlo Giacon. Rome: La goliardica editrice, 1982.

LOSSKY, VLADIMIR. 'La notion des "analogies" chez Denys le Pseudo-Aréopagite', *Archives d'histoire doctrinale et littéraire du moyen age* 5 (1930), 279–309.

——, *La théologie négative dans la doctrine de Denys l'Aréopagite*. Revue des sciences philosophiques et théologiques, 1939, 204–21.

——, *Théologie négative et connaissance de Dieu chez Maître Eckhart*. Paris: Vrin, 1973.

——, *The Mystical Theology of the Eastern Church*. Cambridge: James Clarke, 1973.

LOTZ, JOHANNES BAPTIST. 'Das Sein selbst und das subsistierende Sein nach Thomas von Aquin', *Martin Heidegger zum siebzigsten Geburtstag*, Ed. Günther Neske, Pfullingen: Neske, 1959, 180–94.

LOUTH, ANDREW. *The Origins of the Christian Mystical Tradition from Plato to Denys*. Oxford: Clarendon Press, 1981.

LYTTKENS, HAMPUS. *The Analogy between God and the World. An Investigation of its Background and Interpretation of its Use by Thomas of Aquino*. Wiesbaden: Otto Harrassowitz, 1953.

MCCALL, ROBERT E. AND JAMES P. REILLY, JR. 'The Metaphysical Analysis of the Beautiful and the Ugly', *Proceedings of the American Catholic Philosophical Association* 30 (1956), 137–54.

MCINERNY, RALPH M. '*Esse ut Actus Intensivus* in the Writings of Cornelio Fabro', *Proceedings of the American Catholic Philosophical Association* 38 (1964), 137–42.

——, *The Logic of Analogy. An Interpretation of St. Thomas*. The Hague: Nijhoff, 1971.

——, 'Can God be Named by us? Prolegomena to Thomistic Philosophy of Religion', *Review of Metaphysics* (1978), 53–73.

MACKINNON, D. M. *The Problem of Metaphysics*. Cambridge University Press, 1974.

MACNEILE DIXON, W. *The Human Situation*. Pelican Books, 1958.

MACQUARRIE, JOHN. *In Search of Deity. An Essay in Dialectical Theism*. London: SCM Press, 1984.

MAHONEY, EDWARD P. 'Neoplatonism, the Greek Commentators and Rennaissance Aristotelianism', *Neoplatonism and Christian Thought*, Ed. Dominic O'Meara, 169–77, 264–82.

MANARANCHE, ANDRÉ. *Des Noms pour Dieu*. Paris: Fayard, 1980.

MANNO, A. G. 'S. Tommaso e la Teologia Negativa', *Tommaso d'Aquino nel suo settimo centenario*, III, *Dio e l'economia della salvezza*. Naples: Edizioni Domenicane Italiane, 1975, 141–52.

MANSER, G.M. *Das Wesen des Thomismus*. Fribourg: Paulus Verlag, 1949.

MARIN, D. 'I nomi di Dio e la teologia negativa nel pensiero di Tommaso d'Aquino', *Tommaso d'Aquino nel suo settimo centenario*, III, *Dio e l'economia della salvezza*. Naples: Edizioni Domenicane Italiane, 1975, 337–48.

MARITAIN, JACQUES. *A Preface to Metaphysics*. New York: Sheed and Ward, 1946.

——, *Distinguer pour unir ou les degrés du savoir*, 4. ed., rev. and enl., Paris: Desclée, 1946.

——, *Approches de Dieu*. Paris: Alsatia, 1953.

——, *The Degrees of Knowledge* tr. G. B. Phelan. London: Geoffrey Bles, 1959.

——, *Existence and the Existent*. New York: Vintage Books, 1966.

MASCALL, ERIC L. *He Who Is*. London: Darton, Longman and Todd, 1966.

——, *Existence and Analogy*. London: Darton, Longman and Todd, 1966.

——, *Words and Images. A Study in the Possibility of Religious Discourse*. London: Darton, Longman and Todd, 1968.

MAURER, ARMAND A., C.S.B. *About Beauty. A Thomistic Interpretation*. Houston: Center for Thomistic Studies, University of St. Thomas, 1983.

MELENDO GRANADOS, TOMÁS. *Ontología de los opuestos*. Pamplona: Eunsa, 1982.

MEYENDORFF, JOHN. *Christ in Eastern Christian Thought*. Washington: Corpus Books, 1969.

MIEHTE, TERRY L., AND BOURKE, VERNON J. *Thomistic Bibliography, 1940–1978*. Westport, Connecticut; London: Greenwood Press, 1980.

MONDIN, BATTISTA. 'Il principio "omne agens agit simile sibi" e l'analogia dei nomi divini nel pensiero di san Tomasso d'Aquino', *Divus Thomas* (1960), 336–48.

——, *The Principle of Analogy in Protestant and Catholic Theology*. The Hague: Martinus Nijhoff, 1968.

——, *St. Thomas Aquinas' Philosophy in the Commentary to the Sentences*. The Hague: Nijhoff, 1975.

——, *Il problema del linguaggio teologico dalle origini ad oggi*, 2. ed. Brescia: Queriniana, 1975.

——, 'Il problema del linguaggio teologico nel "Commento alle Sentenze" ', *Tommaso d'Aquino nel suo settimo centenario*, III, *Dio e l'economia della salvazione*. Naples: Edizione Domenicane Italiane, 1975, 165–82.

MONTAGNES, BERNARD. *La doctrine de l'analogie de l'être d'après saint Thomas d'Aquin*. Louvain: Publications Universitaires, 1963.

——, Comte rendu sur *Participation et causalité* de C. Fabro, *Bulletin Thomiste* 11 (1960–62), 15–21.

——, 'L'axiome de continuité chez saint Thomas', *Revue des sciences philosophiques et théologiques* (1968), 201–21.

MOREAU, J. 'Le platonisme dans la Somme Théologique', *Tommaso d'Aquino nel suo settimo centenario*, I, *Le Fonti del Pensiero di S. Tommaso*. Naples: Edizioni Domenicane Italiane, 1975, 238–47.

MÜLLER, H.F. *Dionysios, Proklos und Plotinos*. Münster: Aschendorffsche Verlagsbuchhandlung, 1918.

MÜLLER, LUDGER. 'Das Schöne im Denken des Thomas von Aquin', *Theologie und Philosophie* 53 (1982), 413–24.

MUÑIZ RODRIGUEZ, VICENTE. *Significado de los nombres de Dios en el Corpus Dionysiacum*. Salamanca: Universidad Pontificia, 1975.

MURRAY, JOHN COURTNEY, S.J. *The Problem of God Yesterday and Today*. New Haven/London: Yale U.P., 1964.

NAGAKURA, HISAKO. 'Le problème du langage dans la théologie de l'image de Dieu chez saint Bonaventure et saint Thomas', *Sprache und Erkenntnis im Mittelalter* (Miscellanea Mediaevalia, XIII, 2) Berlin: de Gruyter, 952–60.

NEIDL, WALTER N. *Thearchia. Die Frage nach dem Sinn von Gott bei Pseudo-Dionysius Areopagita und Thomas von Aquin*. Regensburg: Josef Habbel, 1976.

NEUMANN, SIEGFRIED. *Gegenstand und Methode der theoretischen Wissenschaften nach Thomas von Aquin aufgrund der Expositio super Librum Boethii De Trinitate*. Münster: Aschendorffsche Verlagsbuchhandlung, 1965.

NICOLAS, JEAN-HERVÉ. *Dieu connu comme inconnu*. Paris: Desclée de Brouwer, 1966.

NICOLAS, MARIE-JOSEPH. 'Bonum diffusivum sui', *Revue Thomiste* 55 (1955), 363–76.

NINCI, MARCO. *L'Universo e il non-essere*. Vol. I: *Trascendenza di Dio e molteplicità del reale nel monismo dionisiano*. Rome: Edizioni di Storia e Letteratura, 1980.

NORMANN, FRIEDRICH. *Teilhabe—ein Schlüsselwort der Vätertheologie.* Münster: Aschendorff, 1978.

NYGREN, ANDERS. *Sinn und Methode. Prolegomena zu einer wissenschaftlichen Religionsphilosopie und einer wissenschaftlichen Theologie,* Translated from Swedish by Gerhard Klose, Vorwort Ulrich Aschendorff. Göttingen: Vandenhoeck & Ruprecht, 1979.

O'BRIEN, ELMER., S.J. *The Essential Plotinus,* Selected and Translated with Introduction and Commentary. New York: Mentor, 1964.

O'BRIEN, IGNATIUS., O.P. 'Analogy and our Knowledge of God', *Philosophical Studies* 6 (1956), 91–104.

O'BRIEN, T.C. 'The Dionysian Corpus', in St. Thomas Aquinas, *Summa Theologiae.* London: Blackfriars, 1975, Vol. 14, Appendix 3, 182–93.

O'CONNOR, WILLIAM. *The Natural Desire for God.* Milwaukee: Marquette U.P., 1948.

O'DALY, GERARD. 'Dionysius Areopagita', *Theologische Realenzyklopädie* Vol. 7 (1981), 772–80.

OEING-HANHOFF, LUDGER. *Ens et Unum Convertuntur. Stellung und Gehalt des Grundsatzes in der Philosophie des Hl. Thomas von Aquin.* Münster: Aschendorffsche Verlagsbuchhandlung, 1953.

O'MEARA, DOMINIC J., Ed. *Neoplatonism and Christian Thought* (Vol. 3, Studies in Neoplatonism: Ancient and Modern). Albany: State Univ. of New York Press, 1982.

O'ROURKE, FRAN. '*Virtus Essendi*: Intensive Being in Pseudo-Dionysius and Aquinas', *Dionysius* 15 (1991).

——, 'Being and Non-Being in the Pseudo-Dionysius', *The Relationship between Neoplatonism and Christianity.* Eds. Thomas Finan and Vincent Twomey. Dublin: Four Courts (1992), 55–78.

OWENS, JOSEPH. *The Doctrine of Being in the Aristotelian 'Metaphysics'.* Toronto: Pontifical Institute of Mediaeval Studies, 1963.

——, 'Analogy as a Thomistic Approach to Being', *Mediaeval Studies* 24 (1962), 303–22.

——, *An Interpretation of Existence.* Milwaukee: Bruce, 1968.

——, 'Aquinas—"Darkness of Ignorance" in the Most Refined Notion of God', *Southwestern Journal of Philosophy* 5 (1974), 93–110.

PADELLARO DE ANGELIS, ROSA. *L'Influenza di Dionigi l'Areopagita sul pensiero medioevale.* Rome: ELIA, 1975.

PATTIN, A., O.M.I. *De Verhouding tussen Zijn en Wesenheid en de Transcendentale Relatie in de 2e Helft der XIIIe Eeuw.* Brussels: Paleis der Academiën, 1955.

PÉGHAIRE, JULIEN., C.S.Sp. 'L'axiome *bonum est diffusivum sui* dans le néoplatonisme et le thomisme', *Revue de l'Université d'Ottawa* 1 (1932), Section Spéciale, 5–30.

PEGIS, ANTON C. 'The Dilemma of Being and Unity. A Platonic Incident in Christian Thought', *Essays in Thomism,* Ed. Robert E. Brennan, O.P. New York: Sheed and Ward (1942), 151–83, 379–82.

——, 'Necessity and Liberty: An Historical Note on St. Thomas Aquinas', *Proceedings of the American Catholic Philosophical Association* 16 (1940), 1–27.

——, '*Penitus manet ignotum*', *Mediaeval Studies* 27 (1965), 212–26.

PELIKAN, JAROSLAV. *The Christian Tradition. A History of the Development of Doctrine,* Vol. 1. *The Emergence of the Catholic Tradition.* Chicago: University of Chicago, 1971.

——, '*Imago Dei.* An Explication of *Summa Theologiae,* Part I, Question 93', *Calgary Aquinas Studies,* Ed. Anthony Parel. Toronto: Pontifical Institute of Mediaeval Studies (1978), 27–48.

PENIDO, M.T.-L. *Le rôle de l'analogie en théologie dogmatique.* Paris: Vrin, 1931.

PÉPIN, JEAN. 'Univers Dionysien et Univers Augustinien', *Recherches de Philosophie* II, *Aspects de la Dialectique.* Desclée de Brouwer (1956), 179–224.

PERA, CESLAO, O.P. 'Il Tomismo di fronte alle correnti Platoniche e neo-Platoniche', *Aquinas* 3 (1960), 279–90.

PERPEET, WILHELM. *Ästhetik im Mittelalter.* Freiburg: Karl Alber, 1977.

PETERS, JOHN A. *Metaphysics. A Systematic Survey.* Pittsburgh: Duquesne U.P., 1963.

PHELAN, GERALD B. 'The Being of Creatures', *Proceedings of the American Catholic Philosophical Association* 31 (1957), 118–25.
——, *Selected Papers*, Ed. Arthur G. Kirn. Toronto: Pontifical Institute of Mediaeval Studies, 1967.
PHILIPPE, MARIE-DOMINIQUE. 'Analyse de l'être chez saint Thomas', *Tommaso d'Aquino nel suo settimo centenario*. Atti del Congresso Internazionale, VI, Naples: Edizioni Domenicane Italiane, 1977, 9–28.
PIEPER, JOSEF. *Die Wirklichkeit und das Gute*. Leipzig: Jakob Hegner, 1935.
——, *Wahrheit der Dinge. Eine Untersuchung zur Anthropologie des Hochmittelalters*. Munich: Kösel, 1947.
——, *Was heißt Philosophieren?* Munich: Kösel, 1949.
——, *The Silence of Saint Thomas*. London: Faber and Faber, 1957.
——, *Happiness and Contemplation*. London: Faber and Faber, 1959.
——, 'The Meaning of "God Speaks" ', *The New Scholasticism* 43 (1969), 205–28.
——, 'The Concept of "Createdness" and its Implications', *Tommaso d'Aquino nel suo settimo centenario*. Atti del congresso internazionale, V, Naples: Edizioni Domenicane Italiane, 1975, 20–27.
PÖLTNER, GÜNTHER. 'Zum Gedanken des Schönen bei Thomas von Aquin', *Salzburger Jahrbuch für Philosophie* (1974), 239–81.
——, 'Die Stellung der transzendentalen Seinsbestimmungen im Gottesbeweis des Thomas von Aquin', *Theologie und Glaube* 71 (1981), 17–34.
PONTIFEX, DOM MARK. *The Existence of God. A Thomist Essay*. London: Longmans, Green and Co., 1949.
POUILLON, HENRI. 'La beauté, propriété transcendentale, chez les scolastiques (1220–1270)', *Archives d'histoire doctrinale et littéraire du Moyen Age* 15 (1946), 263–329.
PRELLER, VICTOR. *Divine Science and the Science of God*. Princeton, New Jersey: Princeton U.P., 1967.
PROCLUS. *In Platonis Timaeum*, ed. E. Diehl, 3 vols., Amsterdam: Hakkert, 1965.
——, *Elements of Theology*, tr. E.R. Dodds, Oxford, 1971.
PUECH, HENRI-CHARLES. 'La ténèbre mystique chez le Pseudo-Denys l'Aréopagite et dans la tradition patristique', *Études Carmélitaines* 23 (1938), 33–53.
PUNTEL, L. BRUNO. *Analogie und Geschichtlichkeit*. Freiburg: Herder, 1969.
PUTNAM, CAROLINE CANFIELD., R.S.C.J. *Beauty in the Pseudo-Denis*. Washington: Catholic University of America Press, 1960.
——, 'The Philosopher-Monk according to Denis the Pseudo-Areopagite', *Studies in Philosophy and the History of Philosophy*, Vol. 4. Washington: Catholic University of America Press, 1969, 3–17.
——, 'The Mode of Existence of Beauty: A Thomistic or a Kantian Interpretation?', *Studies in Philosophy and the History of Philosophy* Vol. 5, ed. John K. Ryan. Washington: Catholic University of America Press, 1970, 223–41.
RAHNER, KARL. 'Über die Unbegreiflichkeit Gottes bei Thomas von Aquin', *Tommaso d'Aquino nel suo settimo centenario*, III, *Dio e l'economia della salvezza*. Naples: Edizioni Domenicane Italiane, 1975, 9–18.
——, 'Thomas Aquinas on the Incomprehensibility of God'. *Celebrating the Medieval Heritage: A Colloquy on the Thought of Aquinas and Bonaventure. The Journal of Religion*, Ed. David Tracy, Supplement 58, 1978. The University of Chicago Press, S107–S125.
RASSAM, JOSEPH. *La métaphysique de S. Thomas*. Paris: Presses Universitaires, 1968.
REICHMANN, JAMES B. 'From Immanently Transcendent to Subsistent *Esse*: Aquinas and the God-Problem', *Proceedings of the American Catholic Philosophical Association* 48 (1974), 112–20.
——, 'Immanently Transcendent and Subsistent *Esse*: A Comparison', *The Thomist* 38 (1974), 332–69.
REITER, JOSEF. Critique of Walter M. Neidl, *Thearchia*, Salzburger Jahrbuch für Philosophie 23–4.
RICHSTÄTTER, KARL., S.J. 'Der "Vater der christlichen Mystik" und sein verhängnisvoller Einfluss', *Stimmen der Zeit* 114 (1928), 241–59.

RICOEUR, PAUL. ' "Response" to Karl Rahner's Lecture: On the Incomprehensibility of God', *Celebrating the Medieval Heritage. A Colloquy on the Thought of Aquinas and Bonaventure*, Ed. by David Tracy. *The Journal of Religion* 58 (1978), Supplement, 126–31.

RIEDL, JOHN O. 'The Nature of the Angels', *Essays in Thomism*, Ed. Robert E. Brennan, New York: Sheed and Ward (1942), 113–48, 374–78.

RIESENHUBER, KLAUS. 'Partizipation als Strukturprinzip der Namen Gottes bei Thomas von Aquin', *Sprache und Erkenntnis im Mittelalter* (Miscellanea Mediaevalia XIII, 2). Berlin: Walter de Gruyter (1981), 969–82.

RIO, MANUEL. *La Liberté. Choix-Amour-Création*. Paris: Alsatia, 1961.

RIOUX, BERTRAND. *L'Être et la vérité chez Heidegger et saint Thomas d'Aquin*. Paris: PUF, 1963.

RIST, JOHN M. 'A Note on Eros and Agape in Pseudo-Dionysius', *Vigiliae Christianae* 20 (1966), 235–43.

ROBERT, HENRI-DOMINIQUE. 'Connaissance et inconnaissance de Dieu, au plan de la raison', *L'Existence de Dieu*, Cahiers de l'Actualité Religieuse, 16 Tournai/Paris: Casterman (1961), 331–51.

ROBERT, JEAN-DOMINIQUE. 'A propos d'un texte capital d'Etienne Gilson', *Revue Thomiste* 80 (1980), 439–55.

ROBINSON, CHARLES K. 'Theological Predication in the Areopagite and Thomas Aquinas', *Anglican Theological Review* 66 (1964), 297–306.

ROQUES, RENÉ. 'Le primat du Transcendant dans la purification de l'intelligence selon le Pseudo-Denys', *Revue d'ascétique et de mystique* 23 (1947), 142–70.

——, 'Note sur la notion de *Théologia* chez le Pseudo-Denys L'Aréopagite', *Revue d'ascétique et de mystique* 25 (1949), 200–12.

——, 'De l'implication des méthodes théologiques chez le Pseudo-Denys', *Revue d'ascétique et de mystique* 30 (1954), 268–74.

——, *L'Univers dionysien. Structure hiérarchique du monde selon le Pseudo-Denys*. Paris: Aubier, 1954; Reprinted 1983, Les Éditions du Cerf.

——, 'Denys l'Aréopagite (Pseudo-)', *Dictionnaire de spiritualité*. III, Paris: Beauchesne, 1957, columns 245–86.

——, 'Symbolisme et théologie négative chez le Pseudo-Denys', *Bulletin de l'Association Guillaume Budé* 1 (1957), 97–112. Reprinted in *Structures théologiques de la gnose à Richard de Saint Victor*, 164–79.

——, 'Dionysius Areopagita', *Reallexikon für Antike und Christentum*, III, Stuttgart: Anton Hiersemann (1957), 1075–1121.

——, 'Connaissance de Dieu et théologie symbolique d'après l'*In Hierarchiam Coelestem Sancti Dionysii* de Hugues de Saint-Victor', *Recherches de Philosophie* III–IV, *De la Connaissance de Dieu*. Paris: Desclée de Brouwer (1958), 187–226.

——, 'A propos des sources du Pseudo-Denys', *Revue d'histoire ecclésiastique* 56 (1961), 449–64.

——, *Structures théologiques de la Gnose à Richard de Saint-Victor*. Paris: Presses Universitaires de France, 1962.

——, 'Libres sentiers vers l'ériginisme', Roma: Ed. dell'Ateneo, 1975.

——, Denys l'Aréopagite. *La Hiérarchie Céleste*. Introduction par R. Roques. Paris: Les Éditions du Cerf, 1970, v–xci.

——, 'Denys l'Aréopagite', *Encyclopaedia Universalis*, V, 435–6.

ROREM, PAUL. 'The Place of *The Mystical Theology* in the Pseudo-Dionysian Corpus', *Dionysius* 4 (1980), 87–98.

ROSS, ROBERT R.N. 'The Non-existence of God: Tillich, Aquinas and the Pseudo-Dionysius', *The Harvard Theological Review* 68 (1978), 141–66.

ROSSO, LUCIANO. 'Aspetti della problematica di Dionigi il Mistico in S. Tommaso nel pensiero di Ceslao Pera', *Aquinas* 18 (1974), 403–11.

ROY, LUCIEN., S.J. *Lumière et Sagesse. La grâce mystique dans la théologie de saint Thomas d'Aquin*. Montréal: L'Immaculée-Conception, 1948.

RUELLO, FRANCIS. *La notion de vérité chez Saint Albert le Grand et Saint Thomas d'Aquin de 1243-1254*. Louvain: Nauwelaerts, 1969.

——, 'Étude du terme ἀγαθοδότις, dans quelques commentaires médiévaux des Noms Divins', *Recherches de théologie ancienne et médiévale* 24 (1957), 225–66; 25 (1958), 5–25.

——, 'Le commentaire du *De Divinis nominibus* de Denys par Albert le Grund. Problèmes de méthode', *Archives de Philosophie* 43 (1980), 589–613.

RUTLEDGE, DOM DENYS. *Cosmic Theology. The Ecclesiastical Hierarchy of Pseudo-Denys: An Introduction*. London: Routledge and Kegan Paul, 1964.

SACCHI, MARIO ENRIQUE. 'La Restauración de la metafísica tomista', *Thomas von Aquin. Interpretation und Rezeption* ed. Willehad Eckert, 170–95.

SAFFREY, H.D. 'L'état actuel des recherches sur la *Liber de Causis* comme source de la métaphysique au moyen âge', *Die Metaphysik im Mittelalter*. Berlin: de Gruyter, 1968, 267–81.

——, 'New Objective Links between the Pseudo–Dionysius and Proclus', *Neoplatonism and Christian Thought*, Ed. Dominic J. O'Meara, 64–74, 246–48.

——, 'Un lien objectif entre le Pseudo-Denys et Proclus', *Studia Patristica* 9 (1966), 98–105.

SANTELER, J. *Der Platonismus in der Erkenntnislehre des heiligen Thomas von Aquin*. Innsbruck, 1939.

SARTORI, A. 'Il dogma della divinità nel "Corpus Dionysiacum" ', *Didaskaleion* 5 (1927), II, 35–125; III, 1–53.

SCAZZOSO, PIERO. 'Valore del superlativo nel linguaggio Pseudo-Dionisiano', *Aevum* 32 (1958), 434–46.

——, 'Elementi del linguaggio pseudo-dionisiano', *Studia Patristica* 7 (1960), 385–400.

——, *Ricerche sulla struttura del linguaggio dello Pseudo-Dionigi Areopagita. Introduzione alla lettura delle opere pseudo-dionisiane*. Milan: Società Editrice Vita e Pensiero, 1967.

——, 'La teologia antinomica dello Pseudo-Dionigi', *Aevum* 49 (1975), 1–35. *Aevum* 50 (1976), 195–234.

SCHÖNBERGER, ROLF. *Nomina Divina. Zur theologischen Semantik bei Thomas von Aquin*. Frankfurt am M.: Peter D. Lang, 1981.

SCIACCA, MICHELE FEDERICO. *Prospettiva sulla metafisica di San Tommaso*. Rome: Città Nuova Editrice, 1975.

SEMMELROTH, OTTO., S.J. 'Gottes überwesentliche Einheit. Zur Gotteslehre des Ps-Dionysius Areopagita', *Scholastik* 25 (1950), 209–34.

——, 'Gottes geeinte Vielheit. Zur Gotteslehre des Ps-Dionysius Areopagita', *Scholastik* 25 (1950), 389–403.

——, 'Die θεολογία συμβολική des Ps-Dionysius Areopagita', *Scholastik* 27 (1952), 1–52.

——, 'Die Lehre das Ps-Dionysius Areopagita vom Aufstieg der Kreatur zum göttlichen Licht', *Scholastik* 29 (1954), 24–52.

SHARPE, A. B. *Mysticism: Its True Nature and Value. With a Translation of the 'Mystical Theology' of Dionysius, and of the Letters to Caius and Dorotheus*. London: Sands and Co., 1910.

SHELDON-WILLIAMS, I. P. 'Introduction: Greek Christian Platonism' (Chapter 28, 425–31) and 'The Pseudo-Dionysius' (Chapter 30, 457–72), *The Cambridge History of Later Greek and Early Medieval Philosophy*, Ed. A. H. Armstrong, Cambridge University Press, 1970.

——, 'Eriugena's Interpretation of the Ps.-Dionysius', *Studia Patristica* 12 (1975), 151–4.

SILLEM, EDWARD. *Ways of Thinking about God*. London: Darton, Longman and Todd, 1961.

SIMONIN, H. D. 'Autour de la solution thomiste du problème de l'amour', *Archives d'histoire doctrinale et littéraire du moyen âge* 6 (1931), 174–276.

SMITH, SISTER ENID., O.S.B. *The Goodness of Being in Thomistic Philosophy and its Contemporary Significance*. Washington: Catholic University of America Press, 1947.

SMITH, GERARD. *Natural Theology. Metaphysics II*. New York: Macmillan, 1959.

SMITH, GERARD AND KENDZIERSKI, LOTTIE H. *The Philosophy of Being. Metaphysics I*. New York: Macmillan, 1961.

SOKOLOWSKI, ROBERT. *Presence and Absence. A Philosophical Investigation of Language and Being.* Bloomington and London: Indiana University Press, 1978.

SOLIGNAC, A. 'La doctrine de l'*esse* chez saint Thomas est-elle d'origine néoplatonicienne?', *Archives de Philosophie* 30 (1967), 439–52.

SPEARRIT PLACID. 'The Soul's Participation in God according to Pseudo-Dionysius', *The Downside Review* 83 (1970), 378–92.

——, 'Dionysius the Pseudo-Areopagite', *Dictionary of Christian Theology*. London: SCM Press Ltd., 1969.

——, *A Philosophical Enquiry into Dionysian Mysticism*. PhD Dissertation. University of Fribourg, Switzerland, 1968.

SPIAZZI, RAIMONDO. 'Il Silenzio di Dio e la "Nostalgia del totalmente Altro"', *Tommaso d'Aquino nel suo settimo centenario*, III, Naples: Edizioni Domenicane Italiane, 1975, 454–69.

SPIAZZI, RAYMOND. 'Toward a Theology of Beauty', *The Thomist* 17 (1954), 350–66.

STEEL, CARLOS. '*Omnis corporis potentia est finita.* L'interprétation d'un principe aristotélicien: de Proclus à S. Thomas', *Philosophie im Mittelalter*, Ed. Jan P. Beckman et al., Hamburg: Meiner, 1987, 213–24.

STEIN, EDITH (SR. THERESA BENEDICTA A CRUCE, O.C.D.). 'Ways to Know God. The "Symbolic Theology" of Dionysius the Areopagite ands its Factual Presuppositions', trans. Rudolph Allers, *Thomist* 9 (1946), 379–420.

——, *Wege der Gotteserkenntnis—Dionysius der Areopagit*. Munich: Kaffke, 1979.

STÉPHANOU, E. 'Les derniers essais d'identification du pseudo-Denys l'Aréopagite', *Echos d'Orient* 31 (1932), 446–69.

STIGLMAYR, JOSEF. 'Das Aufkommen der Pseudo-Dionysischen Schriften und ihr Eindringen in die christliche Literatur bis zum Lateranconcil 649', *Jahresbericht des öffentlichen Privatgymnasiums an der Stella Matutina zu Feldkirch*, 4, Feldkirch: 1895, 3–66.

STRASSER, MICHAEL WILLIAM. *Saint Thomas's Critique of Platonism in the Liber de Causis*. PhD Disseration. University of Toronto, 1963.

SWEENEY, LEO., S.J. 'Research Difficulties in the *Liber de Causis*', *The Modern Schoolman* 36 (1959), 109–16.

——, 'Doctrine of Creation in *Liber de Causis*', *An Etienne Gilson Tribute*, Ed. Charles J. O'Neil. Milwaukee: Marquette University Press (1959), 274–89.

——, 'Metaphysics and God: Plotinus and Aquinas', *Die Metaphysik im Mittelalter* (Miscellanea Mediaevalia 2) Berlin: de Gruyter (1963), 232–39.

——, 'Participation and the Structure of Being in Proclus' *Elements of Theology*', *The Structure of Being, A Neoplatonic Approach*, Ed. R. Baine Harris, (1982), 140–55, 177–81.

TAYLOR, RICHARD C. 'St. Thomas and the *Liber de Causis* on the hylomorphic composition of separate substances', *Mediaeval Studies* 41 (1979), 506–13.

THEILL-WUNDER, HELLA. *Die Archaische Verborgenheit. Die philosophischen Wurzeln der negativen Theologie.* Munich: Fink, 1970.

THÉRY, GABRIEL. 'Recherches pour une édition grecque historique du Pseudo-Denys', *New Scholasticism* 3 (1929), 353–442.

——, 'L'Entrée du Pseudo-Denys en occident', *Mélanges Mandonnet*, Vol. 2, Paris: Vrin (1930), 23–30.

——, 'Scot Erigène, Introducteur de Denys', *The New Scholasticism* 7 (1933), 91–108.

——, 'Recherche pour une édition grecque historique du Pseudo-Denys', *The New Scholasticism* 3 (1929), 353–443.

——, 'Le Manuscrit Vat. Grec 370 et Saint Thomas d'Aquin', *Archives d'histoire doctrinale et littéraire du moyen âge* 6 (1931), 5–23.

THIBAULT, HERVÉ J. *Creation and Metaphysics. A Genetic Approach to Existential Act.* The Hague: Martinus Nijhoff, 1970.

THUM, BEDA. 'Mystik und Negative Theologie', *Kairos* 24 (1982), 232–53.

TOMASIC, T. 'Negative Theology and Subjectivity. An Approach to the Tradition of the Pseudo-Dionysius', *International Philosophical Quarterly* 9 (1969), 406–30.

TURBESSI, JOSEPH. ['Influence du Pseudo-Denys en occident'] 'Saint Thomas d'Aquin', *Dictionnaire de Spiritualité*, III, Paris: Beauchesne (1957), 349–56.

TWOHILL, SISTER M. DOMINIC., O.P. *The Background and St. Thomas Aquinas' Reading of the De Divinis Nominibus of the Pseudo–Dionysius*. PhD Dissertation, New York: Fordham University, 1960.

VAN DEN DAELE, ALBERT. 'De oorzakelijkheidsleer bij Pseudo-Dionysius den Areopagiet', *Bijdragen van de Philosophische en Theologische Faculteiten der Nederlandsche Jezuieten* 3 (1940), 19–72, 331–94.

——, *Indices Pseudo-Dionysiani*. Louvain: Bibliothèque de l'Université, 1941.

VANIER, PAUL. *Théologie trinitaire chez saint Thomas d'Aquin. Evolution du concept d'action notionnelle*. Montréal: Institut d'études médiévales/Paris: Vrin, 1953.

VANNESTE, JEAN. *Le Mystère de Dieu. Essai sur la structure rationnelle de la doctrine mystique du Pseudo-Denys l'Aréopagite*. Desclée De Brouwer, 1959.

——, 'De Théologie van Pseudo-Dionysius de Areopagiet, Kritische Beschouwingen', *Bijdragen van de Philosophische en Theologische Faculteiten der Nederlandsche Jezuiten* 20 (1959), 39–56.

——, 'Endre von Ivánkas Studien über Pseudo-Dionysius', *Kairos* 2 (1960), 183–85.

——, 'La doctrine des trois voies dans la *Théologie Mystique* du Pseudo-Denys l'Aréopagite', *Studia Patristica* 8 (1966), 462–7.

——, 'Is the Mysticism of Pseudo-Dionysius Genuine?', *International Philosophical Quarterly* 3 (1963), 286–306.

——, 'La théologie mystique du Pseudo-Denys l'Aréopagite', *Studia Patristica* 5 (1962), 401–15.

——, 'Echte of onechte mystiek bij Pseudo-Dionysius?', *Bijdragen van de Philosophische en Theologische Faculteiten der Nederlandsche Jezuiten* 24 (1963), 154–70.

VAN STEENBERGHEN, FERNAND. 'Le problème de l'existence de Dieu dans le *Scriptum super Sententiis* de saint Thomas', *Studia mediaevalia in honorem Raymondi J. Martin*. Bruges: De Tempel, (1948), 331–49.

——, *Dieu Caché. Comment savons-nous que Dieu existe?* Louvain: Publications Universitaires de Louvain, 1961.

——, *La philosophie au XIIIe siècle*. Louvain: Publications Universitaires, 1966.

——, *Ontologie*. Louvain: Publications Universitaires, 1966.

——, *Le problème de l'existence de Dieu dans les écrits de S. Thomas d'Aquin*. Louvain-la-Neuve: Éditions de l'Institut Supérieur de Philosophie, 1980.

——, 'Prolégomènes à la *quarta via*', *Rivista di filosofia neo–scolastica* 70 (1978), 99–112.

VANSTEENKISTE, CLEMENS, O.P. 'Platone e S. Tommaso', *Angelicum* 34 (1957), 318–28.

——, 'Il *Liber de causis* negli scritti di San Tommaso', *Angelicum* 35 (1958), 325–74.

VERBEKE, GÉRARD. 'Man as "Frontier" according to Aquinas', *Aquinas and Problems of his Time*, Ed. G. Verbeke and D. Verhelst. Leuven: University Press, 1976, 195–223.

——, 'The Meaning of Potency in Aristotle', *Graceful Reason*, ed. Lloyd P. Gerson, 55–73.

VÖLKER, WALTHER. *Kontemplation und Ekstase bei Pseudo-Dionysius Areopagita*. Wiesbaden: Steiner, 1958.

——, 'Der Einfluss des Pseudo-Dionysius Areopagita auf Maximus Confessor', *Universitas*. Festschrift für Bischof Dr. Albert Stohr, Mainz: 1960, 243–54.

VON BALTHASAR, HANS URS. *Wahrheit*. Einsiedeln: Benziger, 1947.

VON IVÁNKA, ENDRE. 'Der Aufbau der Schrift De divinis Nominibus des Pseudo-Denys', *Scholastik* 15 (1940), 386–99.

——, 'Teilhaben, Hervorgang und Hierarchie bei Pseudo-Dionysios und bei Proklos. Der Neuplatonismus des Pseudo-Dionysios', *Actes du XI congrès international de philosophie*, Bruxelles, 1953, Vol. 12; Louvain, (1953), 153–8.

——, 'Zum Problem des christlichen Neuplatonismus I. Was heißt eigentlich "Christlicher Neuplatonismus"?' *Scholastik* 31 (1956), 31–40.

——, 'Zum Problem des christlichen Neuplatonismus II. Inwieweit ist Pseudo-Dionysius Areopagita Neuplatoniker?', *Scholastik* 31 (1956), 384–403.

——, *Plato Christianus*. Einsiedeln: Johannes Verlag, 1964.

——, 'Le problème des "Noms de Dieu" et de l'ineffabilité divine selon le Pseudo-Denys l'Aréopagite', *L'Analyse du langage théologique. Le nom de Dieu*, Ed. Enrico Castelli, Paris: Editions Montaigne, (1969), 201–5.

——, 'S. Thomas Platonisant', *Tommaso d'Aquino nel suo settimo centenario*, I, *Le Fonti del Pensiero di Tommaso* Naples: Edizioni Domenicane Italiane, 1975, 256–7.

Von Rintelen, Fritz-Joachim. 'Le fondement métaphysique de la notion du bien', *Revue des sciences philosophiques* 35 (1951), 235–48.

——, 'The Good and the Highest Good in the Thought of St. Thomas', *Proceedings of the American Catholic Philosophical Association* 48 (1974), 177–86.

——, 'Die Frage nach Sinn und Wert bei Thomas von Aquin', *Salzburger Jahrbuch für Philosophie* 19, 129–76.

Waldmann, Michael. 'Thomas von Aquin und die "Mystische Theologie" des Pseudo-Dionysius', *Geist und Leben* 22 (1949), 121–45.

Walgrave, Jan H. 'Spreken over God en Analogie bij Thomas van Aquino', *Miscellanea Albert Dondeyne*. Leuven University Press, 1974, 393–414.

——, 'Understanding of God according to Thomas Aquinas', *Selected Writings*. Leuven University Press, 1982, 38–43.

——, 'Word of God and Human Language', *Selected Writings*. Leuven University Press, 1982, 383–95.

Wallis, R. T. *Neoplatonism*. London: Duckworth, 1972.

——, 'Divine Omniscience in Plotinus, Proclus, and Aquinas', *Neoplatonism and Early Christian Thought. Essays in honour of A. H. Armstrong.* Ed. H. J. Blumenthal and R. A. Markus. London: Variorum Publications Ltd. 1981, 223–35.

Wéber, Edoard-Henri, O.P. *L'Homme en Discussion à l'Université de Paris en 1270. La controverse de 1270 à l'université de Paris et son retentissement sur la pensée de S. Thomas d'Aquin.* Paris: Vrin, 1970.

——, 'Langage et méthode négatifs chez Albert le Grand', *Revue des sciences philosophiques et théologiques* 65 (1981), 75–99.

——, 'Eckhart et l'ontothéologisme: histoire et conditions d'une rupture', *Maître Eckhart à Paris. Une critique médiévale de l'ontologie*. Paris: PUF, 1984, 13–83.

Weertz, Heinrich. 'Pseudo-Dionysius oder Dionysius Areopagita?', *Pastor Bonus* 17 (1904/05), 97–106.

——, 'Die Gotteslehre des sog. Dionysius Areopagita', *Theologie und Glaube* 4 (1912), 637–59,749–60.

——, *Die Gotteslehre des Ps. Dionysius Areopagita und ihre Einwirkung auf Thomas von Aquin.* Cologne: Theissing, 1909.

——, 'Die Gotteslehre des sog. Dionysius Areopagita; Gott als das Gute', *Theologie und Glaube* (1914), 812–31.

Weigel, Gustave, s.j., and Madden, Arthur G. *Religion and the Knowledge of God.* Englewood Cliffs, N.J.: Prentice-Hall, 1961.

Weischedel, W. 'Dionysios Areopagita als philosophischer Theologe', *Festschrift für Joseph Klein*. Göttingen: Vandenhoeck & Ruprecht, (1967), 104–13.

Weisheipl, James A. *Friar Thomas d'Aquino*. Oxford: Blackwell, 1975.

Welte, Bernhard. '*Ens per se subsistens*. Bemerkungen zum Seinsbegriff des Thomas von Aquin', *Philosophisches Jahrbuch* 71 (1964), 243–52.

——, *Auf der Spur des Ewigen*. Freiburg: Herder, 1965.

——, *Zeit und Geheimnis*. Freiburg: Herder, 1975.

Westra, Laura. 'The Soul's Noetic Ascent to the One in Plotinus and to God in Aquinas', *The New Scholasticism* 58 (1984), 98–126.

White, Victor. *God the Unknown and Other Essays*. London: Harvil Press, 1956.

Wilhelmsen, Frederick D. *The Metaphysics of Love*. New York: Sheed and Ward, 1962.

——, 'The *Triplex via* and the Transcendence of *Esse*', *The New Scholasticism* 44 (1970), 223–35.

——, 'Existence and Esse', *The New Scholasticism* 50 (1976), 20–45.

Wippel, John F. 'Quidditative Knowledge of God According to Thomas Aquinas', *Graceful Reason*, Ed. Lloyd P. Gerson, 273–99.

——, 'Quidditative Knowledge of God', *Metaphysical Themes in Thomas Aquinas*. Washington: Catholic University of America Press, (1984), 215–41.

WITTMANN, M. 'Neuplatonisches in der Tugendlehre des hl. Thomas von Aquin', *Philosophia Perennis*, Festgabe J. Geyser, Vol. I. Regensburg: 1930, 155–78.

WOLFSON, HARRY AUSTRYN. 'Albinus and Plotinus on Divine Attributes', *Harvard Theological Review* 45 (1952), 115–30.

——, 'Negative Attributes in the Church Fathers and the Gnostic Basilides', *The Harvard Theological Review* 50 (1957), 145–56.

——, 'St. Thomas on Divine Attributes', *Mélanges offerts à Etienne Gilson*. Toronto: Pontifical Institute of Medieval Studies, 1959, 673–700.

YANNARAS, CHRISTOS. *De l'absence et de l'inconnaissance de Dieu d'après les écrits aréopagitiques et Martin Heidegger*. Paris: Eds du Cerf, 1971.

ZUM BRUNN, ÉMILIE. 'La "métaphysique de l'Exode" selon Thomas d'Aquin', *Dieu et l'Être*. Paris: Études Augustiniennes, 1978, 245–69.

INDEX OF PROPER NAMES

STUDIEN UND TEXTE ZUR GEISTESGESCHICHTE DES MITTELALTERS

HERAUSGEGEBEN VON

DR. ALBERT ZIMMERMAN

3. Koch, J. (Hrsg.). *Humanismus, Mystik und Kunst in der Welt des Mittelalters*. 2nd. impr. 1959. *reprint under consideration*
4. Thomas Aquinas, *Expositio super Librum Boethii De trinitate*. Ad fidem codicis autographi nec non ceterorum codicum manu scriptorum recensuit B. Decker. Editio photomechanice iterata 1965. ISBN 90 04 02173 6
5. Koch, J. (Hrsg.). *Artes liberales*. Von der antiken Bildung zur Wissenschaft der Mittelalters. Repr. 1976. ISBN 90 04 04738 7
6. Meuthen. E. *Kirche und Heilsgeschichte bei Gerhoh von Reichersberg*. 1959. ISBN 90 04 02174 4
7. Nothdurft, K.-D. *Studien zum Einfluss Senecas auf die Philosophie und Theologie des Zwölften Jahrhunderts*. 1963. ISBN 90 04 02175 2
9. Zimmerman, A. (Hrsg.). *Verzeichnis ungedruckter Kommentare zur Metaphysik und Physik des Aristoteles aus der Zeit von etwa 1250-1350*. Band I. 1971. ISBN 90 04 02177 9
10. McCarthy, J.M. *Humanistic emphases in the educational thought of Vincent of Beauvais*. 1976. ISBN 90 04 04375 6
11. William of Doncaster. *Explicatio Aphorismatum Philosophicorum*. Edited with annotations by O. Weijers. 1976. ISBN 90 04 04403 5
12. Pseudo-Boèce. *De Disciplina Scolarium*. Édition critique, introduction et notes par O. Weijers. 1976. ISBN 90 04 04768 9
13. Jacobi, K. *Die Modalbegriffe in den logischen Schriften des Wilhelm von Shyreswood und in anderen Kompendien des 12. und 13. Jahrhunderts*. Funktionsbestimmung und Gebrauch in der logischen Analyse. 1980. ISBN 90 04 06048 0
14. Weijers, O. (éd.). *Les questions de Craton et leurs commentaires*. Édition critique. 1981. ISBN 90 04 06340 4
15. Hermann of Carinthia. *De Essentiis*. A critical edition with translation and commentary by Ch. Burnett. 1982. ISBN 90 04 06534 2
16. Goddu, A. *The physics of William of Ockham*. 1984. ISBN 90 04 06912 7
17. John of Salisbury. *Entheticus Maior and Minor*. Edited by J. van Laarhoven. 1987. 3 vols. 1 Introduction, texts, translations; 2. Commentaries and notes; 3. Bibliography, Dutch translations, indexes. ISBN 90 04 07811 8
18. Richard Brinkley. *Theory of sentential reference*. Edited and translated with introduction and notes by M.J. Fitzgerald. 1987. ISBN 90 04 08430 4
19. Alfred of Sareshel. *Commentary on the Metheora of Aristotle*. Critical edition, introduction and notes by J.K. Otte. 1988 ISBN 90 04 08453 3
20. Roger Bacon. *Compendium of the study of theology*. Edition and translation with introduction and notes by T.S. Maloney. 1988. ISBN 90 04 08510 6
21. Aertsen, J.A. *Nature and creature*. Thomas Aquinas's way of thought. 1988 ISBN 90 04 08451 7
22. Tachau, K.H. *Vision and certitude in the age of Ockham*. Optics, epistemology and the foundations of semantics 1250-1345. 1988. ISBN 90 04 08552 1
23. Frakes, J.C. *The fate of fortune in the Early Middle Ages*. The Boethian tradition. 1988. ISBN 90 04 08544 0

24. MURALT, A. DE. *L'enjeu de la philosophie médiévale*. Études thomistes, scotistes, occamiennes et grégoriennes. 1991. ISBN 90 04 09254 4

25. LIVESEY, S.J. *Theology and science in the fourteenth century*. Three questions on the unity and subalternation of the sciences from John of Reading's Commentary on the *Sentences*. Introduction and critical edition. 1989. ISBN 90 04 09023 1

26. ELDERS, L.J. *The philosophical theology of St. Thomas Aquinas*. 1990. ISBN 90 04 09156 4

27. WISSINK, J.B. (ed.). *The eternity of the world in the thought of Thomas Aquinas and his contemporaries*. 1990. ISBN 90 04 09183 1

28. SCHNEIDER, N. *Die Kosmologie des Franciscus de Marchia*. Texte, Quellen und Untersuchungen zur Naturphilosophie des 14. Jahrhunderts. 1991. ISBN 90 04 09280 3

29. LANGHOLM, O. *Economics in the Medieval Schools*. Wealth, Exchange, Value, Money and Usury according to the Paris Theological Tradition 1200-1350. 1992. ISBN 90 04 09422 9

30. RIJK, L.M. DE. *Peter of Spain (Petrus Hispanus Portugalensis): Syncategoreumata*. First Critical Edition with an Introduction and Indexes. With an English Translation by JOKE SPRUYT. 1992. ISBN 90 04 09434 2

31. RESNICK, I.M. *Divine Power and Possibility in St. Peter Damian's* De Divina Omnipotentia. 1992. ISBN 90 04 09572 1

32. O'ROURKE, F. *Pseudo-Dionysius and the Metaphysics of Aquinas*. 1992. ISBN 90 04 09466 0

33. HALL, D.C. *The Trinity*. An Analysis of St. Thomas Aquinas' *Expositio* of the *De Trinitate* of Boethius. 1992. ISBN 90 04 09631 0